The Galitzianers:

The Jews of Galicia, 1772-1918

Austria was a land of the free in the eyes of most Russian Jews, and their cousins just across the border—the Galitzianer, with their strange Yiddish accent and irksome quality of seeming coarseness combined with Germanic airs of cultural superiority—were inclined to agree.

—Ronald Sanders, *Shores of Refuge*

The Galitzianers: The Jews of Galicia, 1772–1918

Requests for permission to make copies of any part of this publication should be addressed to:

Suzan Wynne
3603 Littledale Road
Kensington, MD 20895

Printed in the United States of America

First Printing

Library of Congress Cataloging-in-Publication Data

Wynne, Suzan F.
The Galitzianers: The Jews of Galicia, 1772-1918/
by Suzan F. Wynne
p. cm.
Includes bibliographical references.
ISBN
1. Jews—Galicia (Poland and Ukraine)—Genealogy—Archival resources—Directories. 2. Galicia (Poland and Ukraine)—Genealogy—Archival resources—Directories. I. Title

International Standard Book Number: 1-58736-609-6
Library of Congress Control Number: 2006921369

To the Galitzianers who died in the Shoah

Contents

Preface

This book is a substantially revised version of *Finding Your Jewish Roots in Galicia: A Resource Guide*, published by Avotaynu, Inc. in 1998. In this book, I have sought to provide readers with more information about the geopolitics of the region, highlights of key events and the overall context for the way Jewish Galitzianers lived their lives. The rest of the book offers state-of-the art strategies and resources for conducting successful genealogical research about individual families.

My personal research began in 1977, when I read Alex Haley's *Roots*. Surely, if Haley could find information about his African ancestors, I could learn more about my Jewish roots in Europe. Many others were inspired by Haley's work and archives and libraries were flooded with people wanting to know more about their families. At the time, librarians in specialized Jewish libraries and archives were, generally, discouraging if not hostile to the Jews who asked for help in finding genealogical material, claiming that they had little that would be helpful. Now librarians and archivists in these same repositories are eager partners of genealogists.

My own quest started with a slight booklet of family trees that my uncle had prepared some years before. In it, he said that the family was "Austrian." Not being a keen student of world history at the time, I assumed that this meant the small country of Austria that we know today in Central Europe. But, my uncle had written the word, Przemyśl in the book's introduction and, when I looked up the word in an atlas, I found that this place, which I then found unpronouncable, was in eastern Poland, almost on the border with Ukraine. Thus, began my own education about the 18ᵗʰ century dismantling of Poland by Austria, Prussia and Russia.

When I began learning about the formation of Galicia, I consulted many written sources and visited the Library of Congress to acquire maps. I was under the impression that I was the only Jew interested in family history and this part of the world. I saw no reason to document sources for the information I was gathering. The exercise was purely my personal quest. Then, I found Dan Rottenberg's book in a bookstore. Rottenberg's book was the first "how to" in the Jewish genealogy movement. Titled, *Finding Our Fathers: A Guidebook to Jewish Genealogy,"* the book galvanized Jews all over the United States. But, in the late 1970s, almost nothing had been written, specifically, in English about the Jews of Galicia. There were a few intriguing photgraphic compilations depicting Jewish life in Eastern Europe, which provided some visual context. In the process of learning some basic historical information from these few sources, including my in-laws' collection of European history texts, I became hooked....my family would say, obsessed, with genealogy. It was like a great mystery story in puzzle form, only the story was mine and each piece of the puzzle brought a new sense of excitement and satisfaction. As it slowly evolved that my father's family was rooted in a rabbinic family that could be traced back to antiquity, I was filled with awe and so, the other aspect of my quest was that I began to feel more deeply connected, not only to my ancestors, but to the whole Jewish people.

It was in this context that I learned about a meeting of Jews interested in family history to be held in the early days of 1981in New York City. It is hard to recreate in words the sense of excitement that the relatively small number of attendees at that first conference felt in being in a room where everyone was interested in genealogy. For most of us, our passion was greeted with utter disinterest, if not disdain, from our families. We posted the names and towns of interest on a bulletin board and everyone eagerly studied the board to see if there were any matches. That's how I met Estelle Guzik. She and I shared some towns of interest and we began to share our family trees to see if we shared any surnames. Estelle later became a contributor to a family book compiled by a group of cousins and published by me in 1986 because we, indeed, were part of each others extended family.

Shortly after that meeting, Sallyann Sack from a suburb of Washington, DC, whom I had met at the New York meeting, organized the first meeting of the Jewish Genealogy Society of Greater Washington. I attended and soon became drawn into various leadership roles.

Estelle Guzik and I visited Poland in 1986 to search our over-lapping and separate ancestral communities for signs of vital records and a deeper understanding of Poland's local and national archival systems. Just before leaving, a cousin found a gold mine of Galician vital records among his mother's belongings. Among those records was a reference to my great grandfather as a *propinator*. While in Poland, our guide and translator taught us about the archaic *arenda* system, in which Jews leased land and the products of the land of Polish nobility and about the similarly archaic occupation of *propinator*, which was a person engaged in the production and sales of alcoholic drinks, generally, based on on an *arenda* contract for the grain, and, sometimes, the wood for the barrels to distill the liquor. Much later, Hillel Levin's book about these arrangements and occupations further enlightened me about the importance of them in the daily lives of many thousands of Jews.

Upon returning home from Poland, I completed writing and publishing the first edition of the Langsam-Spira family history, and then turned my attention to organizing a Special Interest Group of Jews who were interested in Galicia. By the time that Gesher Galicia finally came together in 1993, I had amassed a good deal of material, including maps, travel literature, new and old, books by Holocaust survivors and others who had grown up in Galicia, and various history books. Still, though I had acquired considerably more knowledge about Galicia, I still had only a vague understanding of the self-governing system around which the Jewish community was organized.

Finding Your Jewish Roots in Galicia: A Resource Guide in 1997–1998 was conceived as a means of drawing together material that had been published in the Gesher Galicia newsletter, The *Galitizianer*, including: indexes to various collections; lists of information and guidance for learning more from available written resources; and, the gazetteer of Galician towns and Jewish administrative districts that a colleague had found in an 1877 booklet published by the Austrian government. The book was to create a baseline of information that people new to the Jewish genealogy movement could share without starting their family history projects where I had started 21 years before. Strange as it seems, the Internet was very new at the time and there were relatively few people among the Jewish genealogy movement who had access to it. Indeed, a fair percentage did not even own computers! In the years since, the information revolution has taken off and we are now at ease with the notion that much of what took months, or even years, to gather, can be learned within minutes. So, it was time to do another book, this time with a great deal more about the geopolitical context, as well as about the daily lives of our ancestors, as well as acknowledgment of the valuable resources now available on the Internet.

However, my failure to systematically document sources at various points in my personal learning process, means that I have a difficult time pinpointing just how I learned something. I decided that it would be best to write what I know and create a bibliography that includes as many of my sources as possible. These materials, of course, will lead you to other sources used by those authors. When relevant, I have cited specific passages from specific authors.

The organized Jewish genealogical movement began in the late 1970s, first in New York City and eventually branching out to more than 60 functioning societies around the world. These societies, and affiliated groups, are part of the International Association for Jewish Genealogical Societies (IAJGS), which sponsors an annual conference and provides technical support to newly forming and long-established societies. Many Jewish genealogy societies publish newsletters, have websites and conduct regular meetings of their members. By the late 1980s, individual and groups of researchers had begun to organize Special Interest

Groups (SIGs) to address the particular characteristics and resources of geographical regions or countries. Gesher Galicia, which means bridge to Galicia, is one such Special Interest Group. It was formed from a group of about 100 people with whom I had been informally corresponding for several years. An organizing meeting was held at the 1993 IAJGS conference, which was that year, held in Toronto.

With no formal structure or governing body and prior to the widespread use of what was then called, The Worldwide Web, members exchanged information through a quarterly newsletter, of which I was the editor, and the publication of a directory listing the towns and surnames being researched. George Bodner suggested the SIG's name, Gesher Galicia; many members suggested *The Galitzianer* as an appropriate name for the newsletter. Bea Cohen agreed to maintain the member list and generate labels for mailings.

At the 1995 IAJGS annual conference in Washington, D.C., Gesher Galicia members met to select a governing body of eight members, thus launching the SIG into a new era of structure and formality. Since then, membership has grown steadily. Today, over 1400 people have been formally involved with Gesher Galicia over the years, and more participate in the Galicia SIG online discussion group sponsored by JewishGen. In addition to the quarterly newsletter, now available on paper or online, which facilitates information exchange among members, Gesher Galicia publishes an annual directory listing the towns and surnames being researched by members. It also has a website within JewishGen at http://www.jewishgen.org/galicia/.

The current direction of the SIG is to foster the development and dissemination of new information as it develops, to work closely with JewishGen and its hosted organizations, including the Yizkor Book translation project and the Jewish Records Indexing-Poland (JRI) project. You may join the SIG through the website on JewishGen: www.jewishgen.org/galicia, or by contacting geshergalicia@comcast.net.

Acknowledgments

So many people contributed to the information base in this guide over the years that it is impossible to acknowledge all who added their ideas and knowledge. However, some people deserve special mention. Dan Rottenberg and Arthur Kurzweil inspired thousands of Jews to explore their roots. For those with Galician roots, Arthur offered hope that there might be documents in Poland and Ukraine that had survived the ravages of war, fire and time. This hope sparked a handful of people, including this author, Estelle Guzik, the late Nathan "Nat" Abramowitz, the late Ely Maurer, Neil Rosenstein, Florence Marmor and Arye Barkai, to travel to Poland in the mid 1980s to search out records. Miriam Weiner marked the trail in Ukraine, and her bold efforts there and in Poland, have assisted thousand to connect with their ancestry. David Einsiedler, a native of Drohobycz (now Drogobych), has used his knowledge to help others in many ways. He translated material, extended our collective knowledge about written resources, and provided generous assistance to many with respect to rabbinic genealogy.

Fay and Julian Bussgang were instrumental in developing information about Eastern Galician records now housed in two Warsaw archives and the Ukrainian archive in L'viv. Their pioneering work fostered a much fuller understanding of Jewish vital records in present-day Poland and Ukraine. Fay contributed her article about pronunciation of Polish to the first book and it is reprinted here. Both Fay and Julian contributed much needed improvements to the text of the first version of this book.

Mark Halpern, a long time member of Gesher Galicia, has

not only contributed to our ability to fully utilize vital records, but he organized a massive and successful effort to index eastern Galician records housed in Warsaw through Jewish Records Indexing-Poland. He has generously permitted me to include some of the records from his personal collection, and to draw on his expertise, in both Chapter 2 and Appendix C.

Rabbi Meir Wunder of Jerusalem spent many years crafting a multi-volume effort that documents the lives and the religious and literary contributions of Galician rabbis and scholars. His seminal multi-volume work, *Encyclopedia of Galician Rabbis and Scholars*, corrected many errors that had appeared in earlier works and benefitted thousands of descendants of the individuals his work addresses. On a personal level, despite his busy schedule, he always has been available to provide information and guidance. Neil Rosenstein's scholarly works have greatly enhanced our understanding and knowledge of rabbinic families throughout Europe, including those from Galicia.

This book built on the efforts of many other individuals too numerous to mention here, but special acknowledgment must go to those whose written or photographic contributions appear in this book: Susan Gelber Cannon, David Fox, Ada Greenblatt, Ellen Sadove Renck, Alan Roth, David Semmel, Barbara Urbanska-Yeager, Miriam Weiner, Tom F. Weiss, and Geoffrey Weissberg. Additionally, this book has benefitted from the knowledge and expertise of Jeffrey Cymbler, Alexander Dunai, Blossom Glaser, Leon Gold, Peter Jassem, Alexander Kronick, Deborah Raff, and Alexander Sharon. Many members of Gesher Galicia, the Special Interest Group (SIG) for persons researching their Galician-Jewish family history, have contributed their knowledge in many ways through the SIG discussion group on JewishGen, in articles in the SIG's quarterly publication, *The Galitzianer*, and through private communications.

Shelley Pollero deserves special mention because her willingness to succeed me as coordinator of Gesher Galicia, enabled me to spend the necessary time to develop a deeper knowledge base. Shelley steered the SIG with a steady hand through many changes in information technology until her retirement from that role in

2005. Pamela Weisberger, the current coordinator, has pioneered the development of an annual regional meeting of SIG members in New York and a grant program through the SIG to foster new research efforts.

Lorin Wiesenfeld led me to material that added to my deeper understanding of the economics of Jewish life in Poland. Lorin and Dov Rubin cataloged records that they, separately, found in various Polish repositories, and volunteered their valuable research time to conduct research for me in Poland.

All Jewish genealogists owe a debt of gratitude to the volunteer members of the Jewish Genealogy Society of Greater Washington (JGSGW) who compiled the indexes to U.S. resources presented in Appendix D. Don Melman provided technical assistance with *The Galician Gazetteer* that appears in Appendix F.

Finally, my thanks to my husband, Ronald Wynne, and my children, Michael Wynne and Melanie Waldman, who have tolerated my time consuming passion for family history since 1977.

Suzan F. Wynne

Introduction

Organization of This Book

Chapter 1 focuses on various aspects of the Austrian Crownland named Galicia. Presented is a timeline of important historical events and highlights of the geographical, historical, cultural, educational, religious and socioeconomic context of the lives our Galician ancestors lived, as well as some key information about the laws that governed their lives and generated much of the surviving documentation about our ancestors.

Chapter 2 will assist you to identify your ancestral towns and whether they are, today, in Poland or Ukraine. You will first be directed to Appendix F to locate your town(s) and the district and subdistrict in which it was located during the Austrian period. You will then be prompted to return to this chapter for assistance in pinpointing the current location of your town(s) of interest.

Chapter 3 describes the nature and history of vital records (birth, marriage and death) in Galicia, some strategies for determining whether vital records of interest to you have survived in Poland or Ukraine, and, if they did, how to access them. Some examples of these records are in this chapter but many more are in Appendix C.

Chapter 4 focuses on resources and strategies for accessing information and documentary resources other than vital records in Poland, Ukraine and Israel.

Chapter 5 discusses the impact of the Holocaust (or, Shoah), which, effectively, ended Jewish history in most of what had been Galicia, and before that, Poland, where Jews had lived for centuries. The chapter covers some specialized books that were written by survivors after the war and other types of materials that provide information about specific individuals and families in key repositories in Israel and the United States.

Chapter 6 focuses on general and specialized reference materials, including maps, written and audiovisual resources.

Chapter 7 is designed as to aid people who might wish to travel to Poland or Ukraine.

Chapter 8 presents an index to a book written during the Holocaust about important rabbis and scholars in Galicia and Russian Poland; information about little-known records created by the United States government now housed at the U.S. National Archives and Records Administration. A name index to one of these record groups is included in Appendix D.

The appendices in this book are designed to offer assistance to genealogists with the Polish language; a sample letter in Polish to assist with writing a letter of inquiry about genealogical information; examples of vital records with explanations of how to read the information; indexes to collections at the U.S. National Archives and Records Administration; a listing of Galician towns and their administrative districts; an article on 18th- and 19th-century Kraków; a list of *yizkor* books which discuss pre-WWII Galician communities and regions; and an index to Emergency Passport Applications, 1915-1924 at the U.S. National Archives.

The book has no subject index. The Table of Contents is designed to guide readers to important topics. Please refer to the section on References and Bibliography for any material cited in the text. The illustration credits are the final section.

Special Note about Geographical References

The geopolitics of what once was Galicia is complex, and you will be called on to know a great deal about history as well as geography. Because Poland and Ukraine are now the governing bodies of the territory, readers who wish to pursue family research must learn something about the characteristics of the

Polish and Ukrainian languages and be attuned to the nuances of pronunciation in order to move ahead. But because Galicia was once part of the Austro-Hungarian Empire, we also must factor in the influences of the German language on our ancestral names and town names as well as on official forms used by the Austrian government. Indeed, you are likely to be stretched in a number of important ways as you navigate through learning new terms, new ways of looking at your family history, and, indeed, much about Jewish history in Eastern Europe.

The use of town names in this guide requires understanding that a town could have had several names between 1772 and the present time. If the town is in present day Poland, chances are that it is the same as it was in 1772. But, if the town is in modern day Ukraine, you will encounter several challenges, some caused by transliteration of the Cyrillic alphabet, and some caused by the vagaries of political control. When the eastern section of Galician territory reverted to Soviet-controlled Ukraine after World War II, political considerations resulted in the renaming of many towns. And, then after the breakup of the Soviet Union, when Ukraine became independent, nationalistic considerations generated name changes and the differences between Russian and Ukrainian generated transliteration changes. Whenever practical, this guide uses the spellings found in *Where Once We Walked* (Revised Edition, 2001) by Gary Mokotoff and Sallyann Amdur Sack, published by Avotaynu, Inc., because the authors use the spellings of the U.S. Board on Geographic Names, which publishes recognized international standard for place names.

To add to the complexities of the geopolitical situation, many towns had Yiddish-language nicknames—our ancestors often used a different name for their communities the official one so you may have to cope with translating the Yiddish name for the town, which your family knows, to a town name you can find on a map. The late Chester Cohen's *The Shtetl Finder* is useful to guide a researcher from the Yiddish name to the official name(s). Cohen's book does not list every town, but an amazing number of places are included in this small paperback volume. He also included a few facts about and a location guide to the towns as well.

So, having plowed your way through the initial obstacles posed by geographical issues, get ready for he adventure of your life: learning about your Jewish-Galician family history.

Map 1. Partitions of Poland,
1772, 1793, 1795

CHAPTER 1

Galicia: Its History and Jewish Life

Brief Geopolitical History of Galicia

In 1772, the vast territory that was then Poland was carved up by the rulers of the Prussian, Russian and Austrian Empires in the first of three partitions that would take place before the end of the century. Austria's Empress Maria Theresa and her son and co-regent, Josef, absorbed a long horizontal swath of southern Poland and named the new Austrian *Kronland* or Crownland, The Kingdom of Galicia and Lodomeria," after an ancient regional designation of Galych, the ancient capital city. The Crownland was more commonly known as "Galicia. The city of Lwów was renamed Lemberg and made the capital city of the Crownland.
Only Prussia and Russia participated in the second partition in 1775, but in that same year, Austria acquired Bukowina from the Ottoman Empire, a territory adjacent to Galicia, and made it part of Galicia. In the far southeast of Galicia, Bukowina was variously a part of Galicia until 1849 and then again from 1859-1861, when it became an independent Austrian province or *Kronland.*

In the third partition in 1795, Austria's Emperor Franz Ferdinand absorbed more of Poland's territory. Known as West Galicia, the territory soon was overtaken by Napoleon and then, in 1815, was taken by Prussia and Russia in the peace treaty that finally ended the Napoleonic era. In the 1795 partition, Russia and Prussia divided up the rest of Poland. The country, as an independent entity, then ceased to exist until the 1919 peace treaty, that concluded World War I, restored it to independence. In the inter-war years, Poland covered almost as much territory as it had before the first partition, and, so, virtually all of what had been Austrian Galicia, was then under Polish rule.

The roots of the three partitions go back several centuries, as Russia and Poland vied for power and land. By 1768, Poland ruled over Lithuania and a large area of what historically had been, and is again, today, western Ukraine. The region was still mired in feudalism, and Polish society was stratified into a highly rigid class structure. At the top were the 300 or so magnate families who were very wealthy, large landholders who essentially governed whole districts that belonged to them. Below them were various classes of nobility. Together, the magnates and the noble classes, which will be referred to as the "gentry," comprised of 150,000 ethnically Polish nobles. The magnates dominated social, political and economic life, but the lesser nobility supported their power and, collectively, acted as a counter force to any civil government which attempted to rule them. The *Diet*, or Parliament, was composed of the gentry. Rulers of Poland had to accede to the wishes of the gentry in ways that absolute rulers in other European countries did not. Chorzempa (1993) and Subtelny (1988) discuss in detail the friction that existed between the Poles and Ukrainians as a result of this class structure.

Chorzempa said that, in the seventeenth century, about 15 percent of the population were members of the middle class, primarily town and city dwellers who were merchants, traders and craftsmen. Most members of the middle class, including Jews and Germans, were legally considered foreigners. By the middle of the eighteenth century, a small professional or intelligentsia class had emerged from the middle and noble classes. The members of this class were physicians, lawyers, teachers, clergy and writers, and served in other roles requiring education.

Subtelny described the peasant class as constituting about half of the population. At the top of this class were a small number of landowning peasants; at the bottom were those with no resources except that which their daily labor produced. The rest lived on and farmed land owned by the nobility and were obligated to work a fixed number of days each week to pay their rent. Serfs could be sold and needed the landlord's permission to marry or to work in an occupation other than farming.

Against this background, Poland's dissolution began when the peasants revolted in 1768. Russian troops occupied Poland, ostensibly to quell the revolt, but their primary interest was in getting the Polish government to grant religious freedom to members of the Orthodox Church. Though the peasant revolt failed, Empress Catherine of Russia took advantage of the chaos to force the Polish parliament to elect her former lover, Stanisław Antoni Poniatowski (1732–98), to be the new Polish king. Despite his election, he enjoyed only weak support among the nobles. Conditions throughout Poland continued to deteriorate until, in 1772, Catherine turned her back on Poniatowski and joined Frederick of Prussia and Maria Theresa of Austria in dividing Poland in the first of the partitions.

Stanisław Augustus, as Poniatowski was known, fought bitterly against this first partition, which left him with some land but little power. He attempted, unsuccessfully, to gain support from other European powers, but lacked organized support among the noblility and the peasants over whom he ruled. In 1793, Russia and Prussia absorbed additional Polish territory. Austria did not participate in that second partition. Stanisław Augustus finally admitted defeat and abdicated after that third and final partition in which Austria, Prussia and Russia participated in. Russia had absorbed 62 percent of Poland's land and 45 percent of the population; Prussia had taken 20 percent of the land and 23 percent of the population; and Austria had acquired 18 percent of the land and 32 percent of the population (Subtelny 1993).

In the final partition, Austria retained its hold on southern Poland, which had been known officially as Lesser Poland (Małopolska). Part of the territory had, historically, been Ukraine, also known as Ruthenia and Red Russia and the population of the eastern portion of Galicia was, therefore, comprised of ethnic Ruthenians, also known as Ukrainians. Bukowina, adjacent territory taken by Austria from the Ottoman Empire, was comprised of various ethnic groups. The relatively large Jewish population of Bukowina lived mostly in the urban areas.

The late Ronald Sanders, in his landmark book, *Shores of Refuge: A Hundred Years of Jewish Emigration*, described Galicia:

Map 2. Galicia

> This geographically ill-defined province formed a right-angled triangle whose base and side, to the east and to the north, backed onto the Russian Empire, and whose hypotenuse was a northwest-to-southwest line of some five hundred miles running from Cracow to Bukovina along the foothills of the Carpathian Mountains. Beyond the Carpathians, to the south and west, was all the rest of the Habsburg Empire, to which this forlorn province, its largest and poorest, remained a kind of stepchild.

The region was, desperately poor and primarily populated with peasants who were uneducated and economically mired in feudalism. As a result, there were relatively few urban centers and a low rate of agricultural or any other kind of productivity. Jews tended to cluster around the cities and towns, but economic restrictions meant that most Jews were engaged in occupations that did not measurably add to the overall economy.

Austria, prior to the absorption of Galician Jews, had a very small Jewish population by choice. By imposing severe residence laws, extremely high taxes, prohibitions against constructing synagogue and ritual buildings, restrictions on daily activities and movement, and highly restrictive marriage laws, Austria had made it very difficult for Jews to thrive. Austrian Jews had long suffered from occupational restrictions and were, periodically, required to adopt distinctive dress. The exception was a small group of Sephardic Jews residing in Hungary who received more protections because of their important economic and political role with respect to the Ottoman Empire. It was through this lens that Maria Theresa viewed her newly acquired Jews. Shortly after the first partition, Maria Theresa ordered the expulsion of Galician Jews who had failed to pay the high taxes imposed on them. Presumably, as a result, the Jewish population fell in the early years of her rule over Galicia.

Maria Theresa and her son Josef, her co-regent, installed a governor and a bureaucracy in the ancient city of Lwów and renamed the city, Lemberg. Lemberg was a relatively sophisticated city, boasting both a university and a healthy economy. The bureaucracy was composed largely of imported German workers because the Austrian rulers perceived Austrians to be lazy and inefficient, more interested in café life than working. The Germans were charged with attracting fellow Germans to colonize and farm in the territories not controlled by the Polish nobility. Though Galicians were, generally, subject to Austrian laws and taxes, certain local matters were under the jurisdiction of locally elected governments. The Jewish community, as will be discussed in some detail below, was mandated by the 16 July 1776 *Galizische Jüdendnung* to govern itself, initially with six districts, headed by 12 men, six of whom would be elected and six who would be appointed.

When Maria Theresa died in 1780, Josef, became ruler, styled as Josef II. He naively believed that because he was an absolute ruler, he would be able to command and changes would be made. Josef was attracted to Western forms and philosophy of government and sought to use his growing and diverse empire as a laboratory for those ideas. He attempted to promote improvements to the social and economic conditions of all of his subjects. For instance, he first attempted to mandate universal education in 1774 and instituted major reforms in 1781 that were designed to reduce the impact of feudalism. Among his significant "reforms" was a measure in 1788 ensuring that Jews could be conscripted into military service. In his view, this would offer Jews an opportunity to participate more fully in the general society and, thereby, weaken the hold of Judaism. The initial decree limited Jewish service to the transport corps, but the following year, this was expanded to service in the infantry (Schmidl, 1989).

Josef underestimated the importance of gaining popular and political support for his reforms. Even before his death in 1790, much of his reform package had already had fallen apart and within the next five years, his successors had dismantled virtually all of his efforts to bring Austria in line with more progressive European societies. One of his "improvements," according to Henisch (in Fraenkel, 1970), was that Josef dismantled the *Gemeinde* structure and, along with it, the *Bet Din*, Jewish court system. However, he officially recognized 141 Jewish communities in Galicia and 2 in Bukowina. With Josef's death only a year later, and the reestablishment of the *Gemeinde*, it seems likely that *Bet Din* in these communities continued informally. The mandate for military service was suspended after Josef's death in 1790.

Jewish life in Galicia can best be discussed in three distinct phases: that of the initial period of 1772 to 1869 when Jews lived under high taxes and severe economic and social restrictions; from 1869 to 1900 when Galician Jews were reaping the benefits of Emperor Franz Josef's reforms; and 1900 to 1918 when Franz Josef's policies, which granted greater local control to his Crownlands, undermined the benefits of those reforms.

1790-1869

Josef's brother Leopold II ruled only briefly, from 1790 to 1792. He was deeply opposed to Josef's reform efforts and acted quickly to begin dismantling them. Like his mother, Leopold was, particularly, opposed to efforts to integrate the Jews into Austrian society.

At his death, Leopold's son, Franz Ferdinand I, became emperor. He participated in the third partition of Poland three years after coming to power. Like his father, Franz Ferdinand opposed his uncle Josef's reform efforts, and acted to continue Leopold's efforts to reverse the remaining reform initiatives. The Jews fared poorly under his long rule, which lasted until 1835. He encouraged harsh measures concerning Jewish occupations, taxes, marriage and military service. During his reign, Napoleon seized much of the territory that once had been Poland. After Napoleon's defeat in 1815, Poland was restructured again by the Congress of Vienna. The territory known as West Galicia, that had been acquired in the 1795 partition, was split between Russia and Prussia.

Franz Ferdinand was followed on the throne by the extremely weak and, probably, retarded, Ferdinand, who ruled until he abdicated in 1848. Ferdinand ruled with the assistance of regents and ministers, who favored Franz Ferdinand's harsh policies with respect to the Jews. But this regime also miscalculated the strength of the growing nationalism gripping Hungary. Revolutionary tensions were erupting in several quarters of the Hapsburg Empire, as well as in other regions of in Europe. When the Hungarians revolted against Austrian rule, Ferdinand was persuaded to abdicate in favor of his young nephew, 18-year-old Franz Josef.

Franz Josef ruled from 1848 until his death in 1916. During his 68-year reign, the world changed dramatically, but Austria was unable to adapt to these changes. As a result, the Austrian Empire, never well organized or managed, deteriorated under increasing demands for autonomy and control from its many nationalities and ethnic groups. When Franz Josef was assuming his role as emperor, in 1848, the Hungarians were engaged in a full blown revolution, demanding independence from Austria. Although Austria managed to retain its weak hold on Hungary, while at the same time staving off other groups seeking national identity, the issue continued to plague Franz Josef until 1867. In that year, he, reluctantly, agreed to reorganize and recast the Austrian Empire into the dual monarchy known as the Austro-Hungarian Empire. Bukowina, too, was an unruly member of the Empire. Parliament twice granted Bukowina autonomy from Galicia and gave it special status, only to rescind the arrangement. Franz Josef finally granted Bukowina autonomy from Galicia in 1861, though many Bukowinian Jews continued to think of themselves as Galitzianers, which has important implications for those engaged in family research.

1869-1900

In 1869, Franz Josef emancipated Galician Jews, the last in his empire to be granted this status. This dramatic move cancelled the special taxes and most of the economic restrictions that the central Austrian government had imposed on the Jews, and, if they chose to take advantage of the changes, enabled Jews to move more easily into the mainstream society. Emancipation transformed Jewish access to universities and professional education, required Jews to be educated in a core of secular subjects, and lifted the remaining special marriage laws.

Following Emancipation, and, even before that, Franz Josef was widely considered a benevolent ruler by his Jewish subjects. Many Jewish families with roots in Galicia, relate romanticized stories about Franz Josef hunting in nearby woods and visiting their towns and, even, homes and synagogues. Franz Josef had moved early in his reign to reform some of the restrictive and harsh policies of his predecessors. Like Josef II, he sought to Germanize the Jews and to make them his allies in combating the revolutionary fervor among other ethnic groups in his empire. As Henisch (in Fraenkel, 1970) noted, he sought to "make them useful to the State." He held the view that the Jews' adherence to their traditional customs and practice kept them from being productive citizens.

The period following Emancipation to about the turn of the century, was something of a Golden Age for Galician Jews. Franz Josef had ended feudalism in Galicia and this had a generally positive effect on the economy. With increased access to education, Jews and others in the society who aspired to a better life, were able to take advantage of new opportunities in Galicia and other parts of the empire. Although most people continued to be very poor, their sense of hope is evident in the literature that was written in that period. However, at the same time, the Zionist movement was picking up adherents and strength among young people who saw the only lasting hope for Jewish safety and progress in a Jewish homeland, though where that would be, was not yet settled.

1900-1918 and Beyond

Around the turn of the century, Franz Josef began to respond to local demand from political and Catholic leaders in Galicia for greater autonomy and control over local affairs. This resulted in a series of Austrian initiatives which gave more power to local government. The effect of this greater degree of local control was to strengthen the influence of those with strong anti-Jewish feelings among the lay and Catholic leaders in Galicia, and to diminish the degree to which the central Austrian government could provide protection to Galician Jews. There had been a few small scale pogroms in Galicia during the period of 1880-1900, but the number and intensity of these pogroms increased after 1900, as Catholic priests encouraged their parishioners to strike out against Jews in both violent and economic ways. Most damaging were the organized economic boycotts of Jewish businesses and agricultural products, as well as formal legislation generated by the Galician Diet, which outlawed Jewish involvement in any aspect of the production or sale of alcoholic beverages.

These negative events sparked increasing interest in emigration to Hungary, which had long liberalized its policies regarding Jews, as well as European capital cities, such as Vienna, Paris, and Berlin, and, of course, Palestine and the United States. Typically, the head of the household or the older children left first to establish themselves and then, gradually, other members of the family joined them.

By the time long simmering tensions resulted in the outbreak of World War I in 1914, the aging Franz Josef, was no longer the powerful figure he once was. The ostensible excuse for the war was the murder of Franz Josef's only son and heir, Archduke Ferdinand and his wife, by a Serbian nationalist in Sarajevo. But the assassination was only the excuse for Franz Josef's ministers and advisors to entice Germany into a military alliance against Russia. Franz Josef's nephew, Charles, became his successor, though Franz Josef did not favor this move. However, there seemed no option and so, when the Franz Josef died a sad and lonely man, on 21 November 1916, Charles became the last emperor of a vast but doomed empire, styled as Charles I.

During World War I, much of Galicia was ravaged by opposing armies fighting across its territory, particularly in what is now southern Poland. The Jewish population was expelled by the Russians when they had control of the territory and, indeed, the Jews scattered to safety in Hungary and elsewhere where fighting was less apparent. The Austro-Hungarian Empire did not survive the war and the allies who defeated Austria and Germany left Austria bereft of all but the country known as Austria. After the war, Jews returned to their communities in large numbers, though some communities had been destroyed or so badly damaged, that they were uninhabitable and the people moved to the nearest large community that was reasonably intact. Some Jews who had moved to Vienna, then the capital city of the empire, to better themselves financially, worried about Vienna's vastly reduced status and power, and returned to their home towns in what had been Galicia.

By the summer of 1918, the Austro-Hungarian Empire was a shambles and, by that Fall, when it was evident that Charles could not continue as emperor, he abdicated. On November 3, 1918 Polish deputies to the Austrian parliament declared their independence from Austria. Austria also transferred political control to the Ukrainian Committee in Lemberg/Lwów. The empire was formally dismantled as a condition of the Treaty of Versailles in 1919, but that Treaty only settled the western boundary, not that of the east. Within days after the Treaty of Versailles was signed by the victorious Allies, armed conflict broke out between Poland and Russia over rival claims to the territory that had been eastern Galicia. During that conflict, the Jews of Lemberg were victims of a terrible pogrom perpetrated by the Polish *Soldateska* (Henisch, in Fraenkel, 1970). Continuing armed conflict between Poland and Russia, war-related damage to many communities, and the poor state of the post war economy, caused very difficult times for most people living in Poland. Meanwhile, the United States had taken measures to discourage immigration, diminishing opportunities for people to find a more secure future in that country.

In 1923, the Treaty of Riga ended the conflict between Poland and Russia, with an agreement that Poland should hold, not only the vast majority of what had been eastern Galicia, but Vilna, as well. But, the unruly territory continued to boil with Ukrainian (Ruthenian) nationalist fervor and continued conflicts over Poland's control in part of Lithuania. Lemberg was again called Lwów.

Following World War II, the borders were once again redrawn, giving what had been eastern Galicia to the Ukrainian Soviet Socialist Republic, then a part of the Soviet Union. Western Galicia remained within Polish territory. The name of the city of Lwów was Russianized to L'vov. Today, Ukraine is an independent country, and L'vov is called L'viv. Soviet controlled Ukraine changed many other town names as well. Since Ukraine became an independent entity, the official transliteration into English of place names, has changed to incorporate the slightly different Ukrainian pronunciation from that of the Russian pronunciation.

Kraków: Special Status

Although never the capital of Galicia, Kraków (also spelled Krakau under Austria and Craców) played an important role in Galicia's history. Kraków became a sub-provincial center of government for Western Galicia in the late 19th century. In the 1795 partition, the city was granted status as an independent city-state. As part of the Treaty of Vienna in 1809, Napoleon absorbed the city into his then growing empire. In 1814–15, the Congress of Vienna made Kraków an independent ward of Austria, Germany and Russia. This tripartite arrangement lasted until 1831, when Russia invaded the city. When the dust had settled, Austria was the sole overseer of the city which returned to a semi-independent status. In 1846 the Polish nobility attempted to mobilize an army to oust Galicia's Austrian government. Austria countered by arming the Polish peasants, who had long been furious about their feudal status. Before the nobles' revolt broke down, peasants had massacred a number of them in the region of Tarnów. Austria capitalized on this revolt, using it as their justification for fully annexing the city to Galicia and renaming it Krakau, in the German style.

Jews had been invited to live in Kraków in the early years of the 15th century to bring their trading and banking skills to the service of the king, but in 1495, King Jan Olbracht, expelled Kraków's Jews. Most relocated outside the city walls to nearby Kazimierz, where a small number of Jews had already established a community. Though separate from the main city by geography, the Jews of Kazimierz were permitted to trade in Kraków's main market and, from that time until the Holocaust, they prospered. See Appendix E for more about 18th- and 19th-century Kraków.

Kraków street scene

Galicia: Significant Events

The above broad brush account of Galicia's history provides the backdrop for a more thorough understanding of significant events in that history. The following presents a more detailed account of important events, particularly as they impacted Galician Jews.

1772: First Partition of Poland: Austria absorbs much of southern Poland and names the Crownland "The Kingdom of Galicia and Lodmeria." Lwów is renamed Lemberg, made the capital city and co-Regents, Empress Maria Theresa and her son, Josef, begin to send Germans to Lemberg to create a bureaucracy to assist the governor of Galicia with managing governmental affairs. Austrian special taxes are imposed on the Jews with respect to marriage permits, kosher meat, synagogues, protections, etc. Marriage is restricted to the oldest son and there are quotas on the number of Jewish families that can live in an area. The many restrictions on the Jews of Austria are now extended to Galicia: when they could shop, be on the street, what occupations they could participate in, etc. Many occupational restrictions and special taxes had existed under Poland, but they were more restrictive and more rigorously applied under Austrian rule. Jews who were unable to pay the Austrian "head tax" were expelled.

1775: The Second Partition, but Austria does not participate. Austria acquires Bukowina from the Ottoman Empire and annexes the territory to Galicia.

1776: 16 July the *Galizische Jüdenordnung* is issued, establishing the *Jüdischen Kultus Gemeinde* (Jewish Culture Committee), a Jewish system of self-governance, roughly modeled on the old Polish self-governance system that had been discontinued by Poniatowski in 1764. There are to be six officially recognized Jewish districts, headed by a president and twelve other men. Initially, half were to be elected and half appointed, but this later changed to election for all representatives.

1780: Maria Theresa dies. Josef assumes the throne as Josef II. He proposes massive reforms to encourage assimilation of Jews throughout the Empire. Although the reforms are either never implemented or eventually fail, Josef is perceived as a benign ruler.

1781: Edicts are issued to centralize Austrian rule over the Crownlands; the first attempt to dismantle the feudal system. The Jewish *Leibmaut* or "body tax" is abolished and there are decrees establishing Jewish rights to education, military service and professions. Marriage restrictions remain intact.

1783: Austria legislature confirms Josef's mandate for civil marriage and orders Catholic registration of Jewish births, marriages and deaths. Tax on kosher meat is increased.

1787: Josef appoints Herz Homberg to head the new Jewish school system. Homberg embarks on a major initiative to close Yeshivas, causing a massive revolt among the Hassidic majority. Homberg established underused 107 schools and a teachers' seminary before Franz Ferdinand abandons the effort in 1806.

1788: January 1 deadline for Jewish surname adoption. Jewish military service is mandated but controversy causes modification.

1789: May 7 *Judenpatent* (Patent of Toleration): establishes 141 recognized Jewish communities in Galicia and 2 in Bukowina, but abolishes the Kahal structure set up in 1776. Leopold II, subsequently, reinstates the structure, retaining the 141 communities as the framework (Universal Jewish Encyclopedia 5: 493, 1939). With minor modifications, this structure remains in place until 1918. The kosher meat tax is further increased.

1790: Josef II dies and is replaced by his brother, Leopold II, who undertakes reversal of most of Josef's reform efforts.

1792: Leopold II dies and is replaced by his son, Franz Ferdinand I, who soon completes his father's efforts to dismantle all of Josef II's remaining reforms, replacing them with harsh and restrictive laws and heavy special taxes. He rules until 1835.

1795: Third Partition adds "West" Galicia territory north of Lublin; Kraków is declared an independent City-State.

1797: Confirmation of secular education for Jews is mandated, sparking a small movement toward acceptance of Herz Homberg's German-language schools throughout the Empire, along with small development of reform Jewish movement in a few cities in Galicia. Almost no restrictions are lifted in new *Judenpatent.*

1800: Census in Galicia shows 250,000 Jews, the largest in the Empire.

1804-1815: Napoleon's military campaigns impact Galicia. "West" Galicia becomes the Duchy of Warsaw in 1809. After 1815, the Duchy becomes part of Russia and Prussia. Kraków becomes the ward of Austria, Prussia and Russia.

1806: Franz Ferdinand concedes defeat over mandated education for Jews in the face of massive resistance and is moribund until 1849. Hassidism is firmly entrenched in Galicia.

1809: Count Clemens von Metternich appointed as key advisor to Franz Ferdinand to bring order to his shattered regime. Metternich is to become a major player in enforcing reactionary policies and strong resistance to change for many years (McCagg, 1989).

1810: Herz Homberg, a strong opponent of Talmudic Judaism and extreme reformist, writes *Bene Zion* which rails against Hassidism and Orthodox Judaism. The book points out that 90% of the Jews had ignored a government mandate to participate in civil marriage, which convinces the government to change the marriage laws. Henceforth, until Emancipation in 1869, Jews wishing to marry legally had to pass an exam on the contents of the book to qualify for permission. Homberg was, subsequently, hounded out of Galicia by religious leaders. He fled to Prague, where he died in 1841. Shortly after arriving in Prague, Homberg and a friend proposed that Austria impose a tax on candles used by Jews for Shabbat.

1814: Prohibition against publishing or importing Hebrew or Yiddish books.

1816: Candle and kosher meat taxes are increased.

1820: January 22 decree that worship in official synagogues is to be in the German or local language (i.e., Polish or Ukrainian).

1827: Of the 115,000 Jewish males in Galicia, 50,000 are of working age. Less than 60% are gainfully employed (Nachum Gross, "Galicia," in Encyclopedia Judaica, 16: 1327, 1972).

1829: Galician Jews are prohibited from participating in occupations of medicine and pharmacy. A result of Emancipation in 1869 is that, by 1890, Jews comprise 25% of physicians and 48% of lawyers in Galicia.

1831: Krakow comes under full Austrian control.

1835: Franz Ferdinand I dies. His retarded son, Ferdinand, becomes emperor with a regent and a team of advisors who continue targeting Jews with harsh and restrictive laws.

1836: The Galician Haskalah (Enlightenment) movement is established in Galicia, sparking the beginning of a secularization among a small portion of the Jewish population and an interest in higher education, philosophy, literature, theater and the arts. Thereafter, there is increasing tension between adherents of the Haskalah and Hasidism. Decree requires that official rabbis would have to have taken and passed certain academic courses by 1846.

1840: The Hungarian Diet voids existing restrictions on Jewish residency, generating the first significant trickle of Jewish emigration across the border to Hungary.

1845: Austria rejects the proposal of the *Sejm* to end feudalism.

1846: Peasant uprising that begins in Kraków results in the deaths of 2,000 Polish nobles.

1848: Revolution throughout the Empire and in other regions of Europe; *Sejm* (Parliament) grows in power. Ferdinand is persuaded to abdicate in favor of his 18 year old cousin, Franz Josef in December. Franz Josef and members of the Metternich government flee Vienna. Hungary's revolutionary Parliament emancipates the Jews through a revised Constitution. When Franz Josef returns to Vienna, he refuses to recognize the Constitution but begins diplomatic contact with Hungary.

Many Jews side with the Poles in the Revolution, despite opposition from Hasidic leaders; some join the National Guard and become officers. The liberal Chief Rabbi, Abraham Kohn, is poisoned in Lemberg (Universal Jewish Encyclopedia: 5: 495, 1939)

Franz Josef officially ends feudalism, though the system continues for many years in Galicia. The internal customs bureaucracy is dismantled and Galician Jews begin to migrate to Hungary (McCagg, 1989)

1849: For the first time, Bukowina is made a separate Crownland. This is reversed a few years later. The Hungarian *Sejm* (Parliament) confirms emancipation of Hungarian Jews. Franz Josef initiates new legislation to encourage Jewish assimilation, including universal education for children ages 7-14. Some restrictions on Jews are lifted.

1851: Compromise Austrian Constitution continues some restrictions on Jews, including bar on land ownership but this is not well enforced, and increasing numbers of Jews begin to buy land.

1859-72: Railroad connecting Galicia with Bukowina and Russia is developed.

1861: Galician local self-governance is strengthened. Four Jews elected to the Galician Diet and some residence restrictions are lifted. Bukowina becomes a separate *Crownland.*

1863: Effective January, Jewish vital records include maiden names, witnesses, midwives but record collection remains with the Catholic Church and Jewish resistance to registration is widespread.

1865: Polish language school for Jewish children opens in the city of Przemśyl.

1867: Dual monarchy of Austro-Hungarian Empire is created as Franz Josef gives into the pressure to grant Hungary more autonomy. Jews are emancipated everywhere in the empire but Galicia. Jewish support for Polish nationalism declines due to weak support for Jewish emancipation and continuing Polish anti-semitism (Univeral Jewish Encyclopedia, 5: 495, 1939). Polish and Ukrainian language can be officially used in public schools. Unions forming as labor unrest increases. The *Sejm* elects a Jewish deputy to the Parliament in Vienna (Nachum Gross, "Galicia," in Encyclopedia Judaica 16: 1327-1328, 1972).

1869: Franz Josef emancipates Galician Jews. Orthodox Jews begin political involvement. Of the 820,000 Jews residing in Austria, 575,433 live in Galicia, about 10.6 of the population, the largest religious group after Roman and Greek Catholics.

1874: A Zionist movement in Galicia begins in Przemśyl. The movement is to spread rapidly after the Russian pogroms of 1880-1882. Jewish political involvement: 5 of 155 deputies are Jewish; 98 Jews sit on 71 regional councils; 261 Jews serve on various municipal councils; 10 cities have Jewish mayors; and, in 45 cities, Jews comprise the majority of the population (Nachum Gross, "Galicia," in Encyclopedia Judaica, 16: 1327-1328, 1972).

1875: Austrian legislation passes mandating that, by 1877, each district *Jüdischen Kultus Gemeinde* nominate for government approval, a registrar to collect and maintain registration of births, marriages and deaths in a standard format on printed forms in German and Polish or German and Ukrainian

1877: Publication of regulations for administering vital event registration, with a list of the districts and subdistricts of the *Jüdischen Kultus Gemeinde*.

1880: The Jewish population of Austria reaches over 1 million, the majority from Galicia. In the city of Przemyśl, one of Galicia's largest, 60% of Jewish children attend Jewish schools, with the rest in Polish and Catholic schools.

1882: The *Jüdischen Kultus Gemeinde* passes a resolution, which gives full voting rights only to those who follow the *Shulkan Arukh* in an effort to discourage the *Haskalah* and Zionist movements from drawing Jews away from orthodoxy. The Austria government mandates that German become the official language of prayer. Ukrainian is no longer acceptable as an official language. Blood libels trigger pogroms in western Galicia, with resulting loss of life and growing uneasiness with the Poles.

1885: Emigration begins in earnest to Hungary, Vienna, Berlin and the US.

1890: The Progressive Temple in Przemyśl opens.

1893: A Catholic convocation in Kraków declares a economic boycott on Jews (Nachum Gross, "Galicia," in Encyclopedia Judaica, 16: 1330, 1972).

1900: Poles and Ukrainians unite in Galician Diet to prohibit sale of Jewish agricultural products and to exclude Jews from the network of agricultural cooperatives..

1905: Goldmann schools in the German language founded by Jews interested in more secular education for their children.

1906: Zionism enters local politics and the labor movement gets underway.

1908: There are 689 Jewish cooperative lending funds in Galicia, many of which are supported by Jews living elsewhere (Nachum Gross, "Galicia," in Encyclopedia Judaica, 16: 1330, 1972).

1910: The census does not include Yiddish as a choice of primary language but one half of Jews register the language in protest. The Galician Diet prohibits Jews from engaging in any aspect of the production or sale of alcoholic beverages, impacting 15,000 Jews. The restrictions were later softened.

1911: Galician Jews are excluded from occupations in the salt and wine industries. 16,000 more Jews lose their incomes.

1914: 28 June, Franz Josef's son and heir, Archduke Franz Ferdinand and his wife are shot and killed in Sarajevo by a Serbian nationalist, setting off events that led to World War I. On 28 July, Austria declared war on Serbia, after Russia begin mobilizing her troops in defense of Serbia. On 1 August, Germany joins Austria in opposing Russia. The involvement of other countries in Europe and Asia quickly follows. Much of western Galicia becomes a major battleground as hostile troops battle for control of the territory. Many Galicians flee to safer territory.

1916: Franz Josef dies and, his nephew, Charles I, with whom Franz Josef had a difficult relationship, assumes the throne.

1918: World War I begins winding down in summer. The Armistice on 11 November officially ends the war. Refugees begin to return to Galicia.

1919: Late January, the peace conference comprised of the victorious Allies, convenes in Paris. The Treaty of St. Germain dismantles the Austro-Hungarian Empire and confirms that Vienna is to lose all of its territories. The Treaty of Versailles determines the western borders of Poland and confirms Poland as an independent country. What had been western Galicia is part of Poland. Bukowina is given to Romania.

1920-1923: In the absence of clear boundaries between Poland and its neighbors to the east, Ukrainian nationalists move against take possession of predominately Polish Lwów. At the same time, Russia moves to secure Vilna in Lithuania. Under the leadership of General Piłsudski, who feared Russia's Marxist government and Russian designs on the region, Poland then moves militarily against Russia to take as much of Ukraine and Lithuania as possible. After bitter fighting, the 1921 Treaty of Riga gives Poland the Ukrainian territory that had been eastern Galicia. In 1923, Piłsudski occupies and holds Vilna, a move that is upheld in a treaty that year.

Przemyśl's Plac na Bramie

Organization of the Jewish Community

Jewish life in Galicia revolved around religion for the vast majority of Jews. Virtually every aspect of daily and weekly life was tied to the rhythm of religious observance. The celebration of Shabbat gave a focus to the week, just as observance of Jewish festivals, holidays and fast days were central to the cycle of the seasons and the passing years. Although there were people in every community who considered themselves traditionally Orthodox, and a small number of "Reform" Jews in a few of the larger cities, Galicia was heavily influenced by the Hasidic movement and most Jews living in towns and villages were affiliated with one of the several Hasidic "courts." Regardless of their frequent disagreements over matters of religious observance, when Austrian action threatened to negatively impact the Jewish community, Jewish leaders tended to act in concert. Those leading the various Hasidic communities marshaled considerable influence over the degree to which their followers accepted or resisted civil law and authority.

Under Polish rule, the Jewish community had been self governing from 1553-1764. The system, informally known as the *kehillah*, but formally recognized by the Polish government as the *Va'ad Arba Aratzos*, enabled the civil rulers to use Jews to enforce Polish law and tax collection. But, the system also enabled Jewish leaders to ensure that Jewish laws were being followed in a reasonably standard way throughout Poland and to use the Polish government to reinforce their authority, when necessary. Part of the *kehillah* structure was a court system, known as the *Bet Din*, which consisted of three well-respected rabbis in each district whose responsibility it was to resolve local religious issues, based on Jewish law. The administrative system had oversight of Jewish institutions and infrastructure. Although Poniatowski formally disbanded the *Va'ad Arba Aratzos* in 1764, the *Bet Din* had continued to, informally, rule on matters of Jewish and law without interruption.

When Maria Theresa and her son Josef established Austrian rule over Galicia, they decreed the reestablishment of the *Kahal* in 1776, calling it *Jüdischen Kultus Gemeinde* (The Jewish Culture Committee), hereinafter known, variously, as the *kehillah* or *Gemeinde*. The initial *Gemeinde* structure set up six districts headed by elders from those areas with six additional at-large representatives to be elected by Jews from those districts and a chief rabbi (Universal Jewish Encyclopedia, 4: 1941). At a later point, the six appointed leaders were also elected by the community. The very concept of self governance carried within it, a double edged sword.

On the one hand, the *Gemeinde* would represent and advocate for the community's interests but, on the other hand, the *Gemeinde* was expected to ensure enforcement of Austrian law among the Jews, including collection of taxes.

In 1782, Josef II, then ruling in his own right, attempted to decentralize the *Gemeinde* in the interest of better communication and efficiency. He divided the Jewish population in Galicia into 18 districts. In 1781, McCagg (1989) said that Josef had acted to dismantle many monasteries in the Empire and late in his reign, he attempted to dismantle the *kehillah*, both moves in keeping with his philosophy that religious and civil affairs should be separated and religion should play no role in governing civil society. In 1789, Josef acted to dismantle the *Gemeinde*, but recognized 141 Jewish communities. This structure was retained when his successor, a year or so after Josef's death, reinstated the *Kahal* in the 141 communities. Thereafter, the number of districts varied over time. For instance, by 1877, there were 73 main districts and, within them, 160 subdistricts. In what was its final form under Austrian rule, March 1890 legislation revamped the Jewish community structure into 257 Jewish communities with no central governing body.

At the head of each *Gemeinde* was the *rosh hakahal* or president. This man was usually a business man, who spoke the local language and had good relations with local authorities, church leaders and the magnates and the lesser gentry. It was the president's role to serve as a liaison between the Jewish community and those entities to advocate for his Jewish constituents. The president was supported by an elected body of 12 men. Elections took place every four years. Although all Jews, by Austrian law, were members of the Jewish community, judging from voters lists seen on microfilm at the Central Archives for the History of the Jewish People in Jerusalem, it appears that the voters were men over the age of 13 and women who were widowed householders or who owned land. *Gemeinde* membership could only be changed with the permission of the elected council in their district. Even when people moved away from their districts and actually lived elsewhere on a full time basis, they had to obtain permission to change their membership. It was in the financial interest of the home district to retain its members since the *Gemeinde* benefitted from both the number of members in the district and the amount of taxes collected from them.

Josef II sought to Germanize and assimilate the Jews. Had he lived, he might have emancipated them about 80 years before Franz Josef did. Josef wanted the Jews to accept that Judaism was a religion, like other religions that existed in the Austrian empire. Although he didn't lift the egregious marriage restrictions, he did eliminate some restrictions on Jewish trade and Jewish real estate purchases were simplified. He even made a number of efforts to encourage Jews to become farmers. Also, as part of his plan to Germanize the Jews, he insisted on legislation that required them to serve in the military and adopt German surnames. By his mandate, all children, including Jewish children, were required to attend public schools and to learn secular subjects. But, it must be remembered that Josef's initiatives were overturned and his successors only maintained the structure of the *Gemeinde* as a means of ensuring tax collection and accountability, without offering any of the benefits that Josef had intended. The Jewish religious leaders, both Hasidic and traditional Orthodox, in Galicia viewed Josef's efforts as a disaster and they united in fighting against many of the measures. They viewed Josef's reforms as dangerous to their efforts to maintain a distinct Jewish identity, safely separate from the polluting influences of the larger community. Of particular concern was the mandate of military service, which fortunately, was overturned upon Josef's death only two years after he issued it. But, among the many issues of concern were soldiers having access to food that would enable them to keep the laws of *kashrut* and their separation from the many requirements and rhythms of Jewish life. It should be noted that military leaders met this mandate with considerable resistance and dismay. Avoidance of military service could be arranged by paying a rather stiff fine.

The community again had to cope with military service requirements during the Napoleonic wars. At first, the requirement was for life-long service, but this was shortened to 12 years. The first Jewish officers in the military were appointed in 1808.

Following Napoleon's defeat, the ambivalence of military leaders again became an issue that discouraged Jews from entering military service, but from 1849 on, Jews either voluntarily or involuntarily served in the military (Schmidl, 1989).

In political matters, Galicia was governed by the state authorities; in non-religious legal matters, they were governed by the secular law and courts. But, in matters of religion throughout the Empire, sectarian entities were the governing force. In general, activities of each religious community was regulated by general authorizing statutes approved by Austrian authorities and overseen by the governor in Lemberg. The *Gemeinde* had many roles that consisted of: representing the Jewish community's interests to the authorities; defending the legal rights of Jews; taking care of the poor; satisfying the religious needs of the community; supporting institutions for religious needs; making reports to the state; preparing a budget for the community's needs; and collecting taxes. Each community was mandated to organize its own governing body, statutes and bylaws. The statutes of each community were to govern such matters as the procedures for electing a rabbi and other officials of the communities, methods of obtaining funds, methods of resolving controversies, religious education, and regulations regarding private and public religious practices.

It might be instructive to examine more closely the way that the *Gemeinde* in the Przemyśl district, which in 1890, consisted of 110 towns, was organized. Based on the statute approved in Lemberg on December 31, 1874, the obligations of the Jewish religious community were outlined in paragraph 2:

The Przemyśl Jewish community is to maintain and conduct all rituals, serve God, teaching and charitable organizations that are completely or partially supported by it and exist under its supervision and approval. It is satisfy the religious needs of members, help with burial, help the poor and sick within allowable funds.

The Przemyśl Jewish community owned three synagogues

and several houses of prayer. Various Jewish institutions and asso-
ciations existed in the city, such as Jewish Hospital and the *Bikur
Cholim* Society, which supported poor and ill Jews (Krochmal,
1993).

The *Gemeinde* had a particularly important role from the
standpoint of genealogists. After 1877, in every main and subdistrict in the *Gemeinde* system, a man nominated by the *Gemeinde*
and confirmed by the government served as a registrar for the
purposes of collecting and maintaining the registers of birth,
marriage and death records. Of course, the marriage register only
included those marriages that had taken place under the provisions of civil law, not religious law. This issue will be discussed in
some detail later in this chapter.

Each *Gemeinde* had an "official" rabbi who was nominated by
the community. He had to be confirmed by the government and
it is easy to see that this "official" rabbi sometimes satisfied the
needs and desires of the government more than the Jewish community. The rabbi filling this role was the person designated to
perform civil marriages between Jews, to oversee religious and
administrative activities in the "official" synagogue in the district
and to play a major role in disputes about religious matters such
as the laws of *kashrut* that govern the slaughter and consumption
of meat and poultry products and the mixing of meat and dairy
products. Until 1892, rabbis in these roles needed only graduation
from a program of religious training, but national legislation in
that year, required the rabbis leading the 20 largest communities to have earned at least a diploma from the gymnasium. The
rabbis in the rest of the communities were required to have had
four years of elementary school education. Two years later, on
August 6, 1894, the Austrian government published a sample
of the statutes for reorganized Jewish communities, particularly
those governing eligibility of voters for the governing board that
had the power to appoint or dismiss the rabbi. Over the next 15
years, statute changes increasingly emphasized the importance of
financial status of voters, which effectively reduced the number of
eligible voters (Krochmal, 1993).

Depending on many factors, internal to a particular *Gemeinde*, there might have been administrative oversight of all kosher butchers and ritual baths (*mikvot)* in the district and some regulation of charitable efforts and groups. This was not uniform in all districts. In one *yizkor* (memorial) book written by survivors of a town after the Holocaust, there was discussion of how the *Gemeinde* eventually organized and centralized charitable efforts to avoid door to door begging that had resulted in inequitable giving to the poor. That same account described that the district was too poor to heat the town's only ritual bath in the winter or to provide oversight for the several kosher butchers. The latter was assumed to be a matter for the several Hasidic communities to regulate for their own members.

Jews conducted religious activities in the synagogue that was recognized by the government in each district and where services were conducted by rabbis and support personnel paid from Jewish tax funds. But, the official synagogue was not necessarily where ordinary people prayed or learned on a daily basis. In a typical community, there might be multiple houses of study where men gathered daily to learn together and to pray the required number of times from sunrise to sunset. These houses of study, or *Bet haMidrash*, were often located in small houses with benches and study tables. They were generally associated with the various Hasidic groups in the community.

Additionally, there was a *mikvah*, the ritual bath that every community where Jews lived had to have. There were men who specialized in circumcising boys; men who prepared the matzo eaten by everyone during the eight days of Passover, according to exact specifications; men who slaughtered animals according to Jewish law; men who alerted the community to the coming of the Sabbath each Friday, rounding up the men to ensure that there would be the required 10 men necessary for prayers to begin; men who made kosher wine and kosher candles; and men who were scribes for the purpose of creating new Torahs; men who inspected eggs to ensure that they met kosher standards; men who inspected food and kitchens to ensure that the laws of *kashrut* were being followed; and men who fashioned ritual wear. All of these individuals played an important role in the maintenance of a Jewish way of life. People who deviated from accepted practice were shunned and, even subject to excommunication.

As World War I progressed, and it became likely that Poland would again become an entity, the Jewish Religious Union was created on November 1, 1916. After the war ended in 1918 and Poland, indeed, became independent, the previously existing Jewish communities of Austria, were incorporated into this structure. The Jewish Religious Union was formally legalized on February 7, 1919. The laws governing the Union remained in effect until their repeal in 1927, when the Jewish community was so badly split that it could not agree on its role and structure. Zionist groups wanted religious institutions to be self-governing; Orthodox representatives opposed this format. Finally on March 6, 1928, the Polish president decreed that all of Poland's Jewish community would be governed by regulations that restricted religious institutions to religious and commercial activities that would be managed by county boards responsible for selecting rabbis and other religious officials and for overseeing the budget of the community. In the 1930s government interference in internal conflicts reduced the authority of these district boards. Post World War II legislation established Jewish congregations that reassumed the role of providing religious and charitable functions for the survivors of the Holocaust.

Socioeconomic Framework

The feudal agrarian society, which provided the context for the larger society in which the majority of the Galician population lived, had kept most people poor, and, in the case of the peasants, tied to their noble masters. Feudalism was actually banned by successive Austrian rulers but, each time, until Franz Josef was finally successful, the strength and resistance of the gentry would undermine efforts to overturn this evil system. Even after Franz Josef dismantled the structures of feudalism, the remnants of that system crippled efforts to build a modern, industrialized society. Trades and crafts were generally learned through tightly controlled apprenticeships; guilds were similarly, difficult to enter. Today, it is difficult to imagine that our ancestors lived in places where everyone had an assigned societal role that was so resistant to change.

Although some Galician Jews were engaged in subsistence farming on fairly small plots of land, and a very small number of Galician Jews became wealthy landowners, they were a generally non-agrarian population. During the years of 1772 to 1869, the Jews of Galicia were subjected to numerous restrictions on the occupations in which they could engage. Because of occupational restrictions, Jews sought niches where they could engage in economically productive activities without violating the restrictions or inviting the wrath of the non-Jewish community. Minor trading and non-regulated crafts were attractive because they required individual initiative outside of the guild system and often required little more than a small investment and sweat labor.

Some Jews had, historically, during the years of Polish rule, served as tax collectors for the landowning nobles. This role continued under the early period of Austrian rule until feudalism was banned. Under the Polish system, Jews who had established relationships with the gentry, were able to negotiate leases or *arenda* arrangements, with them for the products of the land, such as using the trees for lumber, the grain used to make liquor products, or the hides of the cattle for leather products. But the economic role of Jews as middlemen came at a price that was to prove high. The jealousy and resentment that the peasants felt toward the Jews was generously fanned by the Catholic clergy (Brook-Shepherd, 1996; Subtelny, 1988). Not only were Jews collecting taxes and rendering, sometimes harsh, sanctions for those unable to pay them, but the Jews had access to the land that they had been denied as a result of their station in society. The uneducated peasants were easily led to believe by the clergy that the Jews in their midst killed children for their blood and consorted with the devil.

On the other hand, the vast majority of Jews were poor, even though they were classified as members of the burgher, or middle class. Jews typically engaged in certain occupations, such as peddling goods to non-Jews who lived in villages and rural areas and bringing back home agricultural products for resale and personal use. Jews were also merchants with established stores and stalls, craftsmen or artisans in various trades, traders of horses, cattle and other goods. Their economic base was in small crafts, trade, precious metals, leather goods, clothing, printing, all aspects of the production and sale of alcoholic beverages, specialty foods and the provision of goods and services needed or desired by Jews and non-Jews alike, such as innkeeping. But, according to the *Encyclopedia Judaica*, in 1827, of the 115,000 Jewish males in Galicia, 50,000 of whom were of working age, fewer than 60 percent were gainfully employed. Some men devoted much of their time to religious matters: daily prayer meetings, Torah study and, of course, the celebration and observance of the Sabbath and the Jewish holiday cycle. Women provided for their families by doing or overseeing all of the household chores. In addition, many engaged in a variety of occupations to increase the family income. In fact, the wives of religious scholars were often the main source of income so that their husbands would be free to study, visit with other scholars in distant towns and, sometimes, to teach children and/or adults.

In the late 19th century, the Jewish occupational profile was: 15 percent leaseholders and tavern-keepers, 35 percent merchants, 30 percent artisans and 20 percent miscellaneous occupations. Most Jewish traders were petty merchants, but a tiny minority was exceedingly wealthy and influential and carried on much of the large-scale trade in Galicia. (Subtelny, 1988)

Subtelny (1988) maintains that Jewish involvement in trade and small, capital-producing enterprises was key to Galicia's emerging, if primitive, prewar economy. Jews dominated trade between the towns and villages. Jewish peddlers brought modern products to isolated villages, and Jewish merchants bought up peasant crops for sale in the towns. In the towns themselves, almost all the shops and stalls in which a peasant could buy finished products, such as cloth, boots or iron pots (which were produced by Jewish artisans), were owned by Jews. If the peasant lacked cash to buy these products, the Jewish merchant would offer credit. In short, it was the Jews who pulled the peasantry into the money economy centered in the towns.

Because Hungary moved toward liberalization more quickly than Galicia, trade between Galician and Hungarian Jews increased, as did emigration to Hungary. Emigration fostered family ties and trade between the two Crownlands. For instance, Hungary was known for its fine Tokay grapes and these grapes played a large role in the production of kosher wine for home and ritual use in Galicia, as well as in Hungary.

Jews visiting what had been Galicia today are surprised to find towns that resemble those in Austria and Germany. The typical town had a market square in its center. On market days, when the peasants came to town to sell their produce alongside the Jews who were selling and trading their products, the market square was a central meeting place. Market days also attracted ancillary activities, such as political and community meetings.

Market scene outside the Old Synagogue in Przemyśl

Although Jews were not major players in producing food in either eastern or western Galicia, it was common for Jews living in towns to raise chickens and to tend vegetable gardens. Indeed, this was an economic necessity for people whose incomes were uncertain. A small number of Jews were engaged in the production of goods and services that served only the Jewish population. Jewish involvement in the professions was slow to develop and became more common only in the last quarter of the nineteenth century. Metzler (1997) notes that Galician Jews were forbidden to practice law until 1890.

In the eastern portion of Galicia, the discovery that petroleum could be distilled from oil by Ignacy Lukasiewicz in 1853, sparked a minor industry in petroleum products. Oil had long been known to exist in the regions of Bobrka, Boryslaw and Drohobycz. Lukasiewicz opened the first mine in 1854 and, thereafter, using petroleum for lighting became popular, not only in Galicia, but many other places. Having no alternatives at hand, the early oil wells were dug and operated manually, a dirty, dangerous and inefficient way of extracting oil. Eventually, a few operators went to Canada to learn new methods of drilling and extraction and returned to refine those methods. A few Jews became wealthy from oil enterprises, but the amount of oil turned out to be quite modest and most of those who set out to become rich, were disappointed in the outcome. By the end of the 19th century, oil wells were operating in the regions of Ulaszowice, Krosno, Jaslo, Gorlice, Ustrzyki Dolne, Trzebinia, and Limanowa.

Horse and cattle trading in eastern Galicia was also a Jewish occupation that, again, made a few people quite wealthy, and disappointed the vast majority of those engaging in the occupation.

Jews and the Liquor Trade

Many Jews engaged in some aspect of the liquor trade: growing the grain, making barrels for distilling it, distilling and refining it into drinkable alcohol, or running a tavern where mostly Poles and Ukrainians consumed it. In 1900, however, the Poles and Ukrainians pushed through laws that excluded Jews from selling their agricultural products, and in 1910, Jews were forbidden to sell alcoholic beverages. It has been estimated that 15,000 Jews were impacted by that exclusion, and that probably doesn't include those engaged in the various related occupations. The other side of the picture is that public drunkenness had become a major societal problem and, because it was the Jews who produced the liquor, the clergy had an easy target for blame.

Lorin Wiesenfeld, an early Gesher Galicia member, brought this author's attention to a book by Hillel Levine, a professor of sociology and religion at Boston University's Center for Judaic Studies. *Economic Origins of Antisemitism: Poland and Its Jews in the Early Modern Period* (New Haven, CT: Yale University Press, 1991) which extensively describes and analyzes Jewish economic participation in Poland. Levine earlier had written a *New York Times* op-ed piece in which he mentioned the occupation of *propinator*, and Wiesenfeld, knowing that his ancestor had been a *propinator*, wrote to Levine. Much of Levine's scholarly book discusses the essential role of this occupation.

Quoting Levine (1991, 9), the term *propinacja* refers to the "site and the institution of the trade in alcohol . . . after the small hovel that generally served as drinking room, hostel, barn, and storage room for this enterprise." Thus, the *propinator* was the proprietor of this establishment. According to Levine, "The Jewish tavern, the *kretchme* or 'shenk,' was found in even the smallest village in . . . Poland." Levine's book, which explores the complex economic and sociological role of this societal arrangement, offers a fascinating, if controversial, view of the economic conditions and lives of some of our ancestors, documents the Polish system of feudalism and the role of Jews in managing the use of the nobles' land and in collecting taxes.

In a letter to Wiesenfeld, Levine states that his basic argument is that " . . . the manufacture of vodka saved the Polish economy, at least for the Polish gentry who were calling the shots." Because Jews could not own land, they could gain access to grain only by a complex system that was something like sharecropping in the United States. Once harvested, "Jews were then heavily engaged in distilling the grain, making the barrels that held the grain (*kupfer*) and selling the liquor at the consumer level." Levine went on to say that, "...in mid-eighteenth century Poland, as much as 85 percent of rural Jewry . . . was involved in some aspect of the manufacturing, wholesaling, or retailing of beer, mead, wine, and grain-based intoxicants like vodka."

Georges Rosenfield, a SIG member from Neuchatel, Switzerland, who investigated the occupations of family members, found that his ancestor has been involved in the liquor trade. He wrote in a letter to this author:

> As for the tavern the Lermer family held in Buszkowice (a suburb in Przemyśl), mother told me it had white-washed walls. The roof, after suffering from a fire, was covered by plated metal or tiles (mother wasn't sure which). The tavern stood directly at the end of a road. There a field path began that went to the River San. To cross the river to Przemyśl, one had to use a boat (a ferry?).

This author's own paternal great grandfather was a "vertically integrated" *propinator* who barely made a living for his large family in Bukowsko. Through an *arenda* or lease arrangement, he used wood to make barrels, and he used grain for distilling vodka and making beer. At some point, he also owned a tavern. Unable to make ends meet, he moved his family to the large city of Przemsyl, where he shortly thereafter, died of tuberculosis at age 44.

Surname Acquisition

On 20 February 1784, Josef II became the first European ruler to decree that all births, marriages and deaths be registered under a civil procedure. However, it soon became evident to Josef that, since most of the Jews in his far flung empire did not have surnames, that law was rendered somewhat irrelevant. Josef also recognized that lacking surnames made it easier for Jews to evade taxes, being counted in censuses and avoiding the military service that Josef wished Jewish men to participate in. Thus, Josef decreed, on July 23, 1787, that before January 1, 1788, all Jews in the empire must adopt German-language forenames and family names. (*Jewish Encyclopedia*, V, 549–53, 1925). By a subsequent patent, however, the choice of forenames was relaxed in all regions of Austria except Bohemia and Moravia. Legislation mandating that surnames be adopted by the Jews was passed in 1789 to confirm Josef's order, presumably meant to reinforce the requirement of complying with Josef's decree. It certainly would have delivered a clear message for those Jews who had failed to appear before the authorities to register a fixed surname.

Josef's decree was in keeping with his intention to encourage Austrian Jews to assimilate and become Germanized. The lack of surnames had long had certain advantages for Jews. For instance, when the Austrian government conducted its first census of its newly acquired Galician Jews, some of the Jews who were supposed to have been expelled due to nonpayment of taxes, were able to fool authorities by claiming to be someone else. At least, that's the way the old tale goes. Was it true? Who knows, but having fixed surnames ensured that each *Gemeinde* could be held thoroughly accountable for its members, putting an end to various suspicions about the identity of an individual.

Prior to this time, most Jews in any part of Eastern Europe had not adopted fixed surnames, unless they were from an important rabbinic family that had a high degree of awareness that their surnames meant something in the wider Jewish community, well beyond their town of residence, and among other rabbis and scholars. Some Jews had adopted a surname elsewhere and carried it with them when they settled in Poland. There were a few other exceptions, such as families that had played important historic roles as bankers or physicians to royalty or in major commercial establishments. However, it is relatively rare to find a person who traces his surname's roots back to Galicia who carries other than a German-based surname.

But, aside from the small number of Jews who had adopted fixed surnames prior to 1787, ordinary Jews were known more or less officially by their father's name or patronymic. Informally, they might also be known in the community by their mother's name, if she was a well known merchant, or by some personal, geographic or occupational characteristic that distinguished them from their neighbors. Thus, men named Moses in a given town might be identified uniquely by: a patronymic, such as Moses Aronowicz or Aron's son; or by a matronymic, such as Moses Sara's; by some personal characteristic, such as "Roiter Mendel" for a Mendel with red hair; by a geographic description, such as Moses Dynower meaning that he moved from the town of Dynow; by a geographical landmark in the community that would help people identify where his dwelling was; or an occupational association. While these early surnames and nicknames helped fellow townspeople to distinguish one person from another, they were not fixed or hereditary surnames, that is, surnames passed down from father to child. Even long after the adoption of fixed surnames, accounts in books compiled after World War II to commemorate towns decimated of their Jews, described people in the old informal ways. Some of the authors of these books noted that surnames in small towns were simply not important in daily life.

It was, perhaps, this lack of importance ascribed to fixed surnames, that contributed to the continuing resistance of so many Galician Jews to civil marriage. In fact, it didn't really matter, to most people, what a person's surname was. And, it certainly didn't matter that the government considered them illegitimate because they had married only under the *huppa*, the marriage canopy used in Jewish marriages. Unless the lack of a paternally inherited surname was a problem in some official way, the concept of a surname was, after all, simply a made-up name that the government had imposed on a family between 1787–1789.

How did people acquire their surnames? The law, referenced above, prescribed the procedures for surname adoption. The head of a household was to present himself before authorities to select and register a surname based in the German language unless the family already used a fixed surname. If the individual or family already had a fixed surname, the family did not have to select a new one. There was a fee involved with registration. We know that some Jews came out of the process with unpleasant, insulting and, even vulgar, surnames and so, the presumption is that either they were slow in complying with the law or had been unable to pay the fee. On the other hand, it is suspected, though not proven, that certain pleasant-sounding names like Goldman, Goldberg, Rosenbaum, and Lillienthal might have been granted, subject to a payment of more than the official fee to the official.

Michael Honey (1994/5) described the development of surnames in Tarnobrzeg in an article in *The Galitizianer*. A record of names of the early Jews of Tarnobrzeg is found in the *yizkor* book *Kehilat Tarnobrzeg—Dzików sefer zicharon veedut* (Witness and memorial book Tarnobrzeg—Dzików). The names in the book illustrate the naming pattern of Jews in Poland before the requirement to adopt surnames. In 1718, the Jewish community of Tarnobrzeg/Dzików borrowed 100 Polish florins from the local Dominican friar Antoni Dembowski to build a synagogue. On behalf of the Jewish community, the responsible signatories used the patronymics Aronowicz, Abramowicz, Berkowicz and Zeinderowicz. A further loan of 2,000 Polish złotys was made in 1741 by the Dominican friar Stanisław Lipski to men with the patronymic Levkowicz.

The Central Archives for the History of the Jewish People in Jerusalem, holds microfilmed records that list license fees paid by Jewish businessmen in many places, including Tarnobrzeg *propinacja*—innkeepers and refiners of spirits.

The *propinacja* list of 1779 is as follows. Note the patronymics.

Wolf Tyma	Motko Bogaty (Rich) Itzkowicz
Jankiel Motkowicz	Josef Itzkowicz
Leyzor Izraelowicz	Icek Motzkowicz
David Dawidowicz	Leybush Nysynowicz
Jakob Skotricki Majorowic	Wolf Strzypek
Szmal (Shmuel) Leybowicz	Moisek Dawidowicz
Dawid Jakubowicz	Zeylik Leyzerowicz
Leybusz Chaimonowicz	Abraham Nutowicz
Chaim Bornchowicz	

An 1814 list of konsynacja (wholesale distributors) demonstrates the adoption of surnames among the Jews of Tarnobrzeg/Dzików. Note that most names are rooted in the German language, though some are spelled in the Polish style.

Leybusz Nusbaum	Chaimka wdowa (Chaim's widow)
Herszek Szalmonowicz	Simcha Handler
Leybusz Cwirn	Herszel Cynamon
Gimpel Gurfinkel	Klimanowa wdowa (Kliman's widow)
Susman Lorbaum	Szmul Galman
Wolf Ender	Lewi Morgenlender
Szmul Wahl	Eyzik Fegier
Wolf Pomeranz	Dawid Eched
Motka Klemer	Nuta Spicer
Moysesz Stainhard	Leyba and Bona Forgang

The following individuals were named in the 1822 *propinacja* list:

wdowa Esterka (the widow Ester)	Leybusz Hoffort
wdowa Ita Cwirn	Motka Klemer
wdowa Pepsia Wisenfeld	Dawid Kramer
Wolf Ber	Nisan and Nusen Nusbaum
Leybusz Cytrin	Israel Nusbaum
Wolf Ende	Wolf Pomerancz
Wolf Erlich	Josek Safir
Eyzyk Fegier	Judak Schnat
Liba Fortgang	Mila Spicer
Baruch, Samuel, and Isaak Garfünkel	Mosesz Staynard

Samuel Greher	Moysesz Stern
Szloma Goldmann	Leyzor Szekin
Simcha Handler	Dawid Umfang
Hersz Hartmann	Moyszesz Wahl
Israel Hauzer	Samuel Wahl
Dawid Hecht	Samuel Wisenfeld
Motka Henich	Herzek Wizenfeld
Lewi Morgenlender	Dawid Wisenfeld
Motka Wisenspil	

It is important to remember that when Franz Ferdinand absorbed more of Polish territory in 1795, the Jewish residents of what he called, West Galicia, had been under Polish rule, which had not required surname adoption. Therefore, the Jews of this new territory had to adopt surnames under the Austrian law of 1787. West Galicia included a large swath of land north of Krakow, east and west of the Vistula River, but not including the city-state of Gdansk/Danzig. West Galicia was soon taken by Napoleon, and after his final exile in 1815, West Galicia was ceded to Prussia and Russia. But, the brief connection with Austria left the Jews of Lublin and other important communities of what had been West Galicia, with German surnames.

Education

Josef II perceived Galicia's Jews as potential allies against the Crownland's Polish gentry and their Polish and Ukrainian peasants, as well as nationalists who were unhappy about coming under Austrian rule. Among Josef's key initiatives to Germanize and secularize the Jewish population in his Empire, was his plan for universal education. He sought to introduce religious agents, such as Herz Homberg in 1787, and organizations that would liberate the Jews from what he perceived as their narrow and parochial lives. He also felt that encouraging the use of the German language would further his aims to bring the Jewish population closer to an appreciation for what Austria had to offer (Henisch, 1967; Metzler, 1997). Although Josef's plan was set into motion before his death and continued by Leopold and Franz Ferdinand, the main features of it were abandoned, as unworkable, in Galicia as early as 1806. It is interesting to note that in other parts of the Empire, this educational program had a major impact on the Jews and largely achieved the goals that Josef had envisioned. For instance, in Austria, Bohemia, and Moravia, within one generation, the general economic and social condition of the Jews had begun to improve, despite their living under the same occupational restrictions that pertained to Galician Jews. What was the difference? The major difference was that Galician Jews were tied so closely with Hasidism that so effectively resisted Josef's "reforms" that would have exposed Jewish children to secular learning. It wasn't until Franz Josef's mandate for universal education that what Josef II had hoped for, began to be realized in Galicia.

One of Josef's initiatives was to use more secularized Jews to set up the Jewish schools which would employ Jewish teachers from Bohemia and Bavaria. Homberg's first role for the Hapsburgs was to serve as general inspector of a Jewish school system headquartered in Lemberg, called the *Jüdisch-deutsche Schulen* or German Schools, in three categories: lower, normal and main.

In 1789, most Galicians were illiterate. Even some of the gentry were illiterate. On the other hand, almost all male Jews, had some familiarity with basic mathematics and could read Hebrew, at a minimum. Boys started their religious learning in the *cheder*s (religious school) at the age of three, or, generally, just after their first haircut. They were usually taught by a poorly paid teacher in a group with other boys, where they were expected to sit attentively for long hours. Because children of that age are not developmentally ready for such a regime, it is not surprising that obedience was often enforced by harsh physical discipline. Girls were exempt from learning Torah. In fact, most girls did not formally learn any Hebrew other than basic prayers. Few girls were exposed to Jewish learning, except that which enabled them to manage a Jewish home and to teach their children fundamental ritual observances.

In 1855, Franz Josef gave into pressure from Catholic leaders in Galicia, and signed legislation prohibiting Jews in Galicia from either attending or teaching in public schools. However, when he emancipated the Jews in 1869, he mandated universal education for Jewish children, ages 7-14, and lifted all occupational restrictions.

The mandated Austrian system of education included provisions for parochial schools in which Jewish children could focus on religious subjects, such as Bible studies, the *Talmud* and preparation for rabbinic duties, as well as the required core secular subjects. However, judging from the memoirs of people who grew up in the World War I–II era, as depicted in *yizkor* (memorial) books and books about individual experiences during the Holocaust, many Jewish children went to secular schools with non-Jews. After elementary school, students attended four-year schools that prepared them for the gymnasium (roughly equivalent to high schools in the United States though more rigorous). Jewish attendance in high schools, universities and the professional schools was far in excess of their proportion to the population. For example, in 1890, though only about 10% of the total population, Jewish scholars in the gymnasiums represented 18 percent, and in the universities 21 percent. As a reflection of their educational status, Jews composed 25 percent of the physicians and 48 percent of the lawyers (*Jewish Encyclopedia*, V: 549–53, 1925).

In *The Boys*, Martin Gilbert (1997), interviewed a number of former Galitzianers who began their own education in *cheder* at three or four. They recalled that some of the secular schools were actually run by Jewish organizations. Others were run by the Catholic church. It seems that a typical school day for boys involved attending secular school from about 8 a.m. to 1 p.m. After lunch, boys would go on to *cheder* until 6 or 7 p.m. Some boys from very observant homes would go to *cheder* before as well as after secular school!

One of Gilbert's interviewees stated that, as a boy, he attended a secular school with non-Jews and was frequently taunted by his non-Jewish school mates about killing God, "something which I could never understand, but since it was told to me, it must

have been true. I never actually learned Jewish history as such. I
learned first of all to pray, then *chumash* and Rashi and from then
on I went to *gemara*. . . . but I never actually went through the
Tanach."

Another described his cheder classroom as the rabbi's
kitchen. At the age of seven, he entered the local school, while
continuing his Jewish studies after secular school, where he, too,
encountered hostile schoolmates. The family of a third boy, who
was more orthodox, preferred that he attend the Catholic junior
school so that he would not be exposed to learning "a distorted
view of the Bible." His account of the vicious treatment there
appears to be fairly typical of how Jewish children fared in such
a setting.

Finally, a fourth man was fortunate in that a Hebrew-language
school associated with the Jewish organization of Tarbut, opened
for secular purposes in Opatów when he was seven. He, too,
remembered starting *cheder* at an early age and described the experience of being brought, with other youngsters, to the *malamud*
(teacher) by "the Belfer, a type of Pied Piper figure" in his community. The Belfer was charged with announcing the coming of
sundown to signal the start of the Sabbath and was sometimes
involved in carrying news through the streets.

Language

Because Galicia's territory spanned regions that had been historically both Polish and Ukrainian, the issue of what was to be
the official language of Galicia had to be dealt with, and documents at different periods reflect the internal struggles on this
issue. Early in Austria's rule of Galicia, no apparent effort was
made to impose German as the official language of the country.
In fact, there was a high degree of autonomy in such matters. In
1869, however, German was designated the official language of all
governmental offices in Galicia. In 1872, this order was revoked
and Polish and Ukrainian were restored as official languages,
in addition to German. Polish was the official language used in
universities in Kraków and Lemberg. After 1877, official documents were printed in both German and Polish. The Ukrainian

language had lost out. Following WWI, independent Poland permitted some forms to include Ukrainian instructions.

As for the Jews, well, everyone spoke Yiddish and, over time, the Yiddish they spoke differed from the Yiddish spoken in Russia so that there is a distinctive sound to the way they spoke the language. And, of course, the language itself in Galicia, being an amalgamation of several languages, became more rooted in German than Russian. Some non-Jews knew how to speak Yiddish as well, just as many Jews learned some Polish and Ukrainian in order to be able to function in commercial interactions, in school or for other reasons.

Population and Emigration

The table below shows the percentage of the Jewish population in the various censuses taken during the Austrian era.

Table 1.1. Population of the Jews of Galicia

Year	Jewish Population	Pct	Total Population
1772	224,980	9.6	2,159,808
1773	171,851	6.5	1,117,031
1785	212,002	N/A	N/A
1789	178,072	6.0	3,039,391
1827	246,146	6.0	4,382,383
1850	317,227	7.0	4,734,427
1869	575,433	10.6	N/A
1880	686,596	11.5	N/A
1890	768,845	11.6	N/A
1910	811,103	11.0	8,025,675

(Sources: Nachum Gross, "Galicia," in *Encyclopedia Judaica*, 16: 1325, 1972; "Migration," in *Encyclopedia Judaica*, 16: 1520, 1972; "Galicia," in *Jewish Encyclopedia*, 5:549–53, 1925 Edition; Krochmal, 1993.

At the time of the first partition of Poland in 1772, when

224,980 Jews comprised 9.6 percent of the population of Galicia, Jews lived in 187 cities, 93 small towns and 5,467 smaller jurisdictions. Note that, in the following year's census, either a large number of Jews had left Galicia or there were errors in the data collection. In fact, Empress Maria Theresa's harsh tax policies with respect to the Jews were severe, and she had made it clear that those who could not pay, were unwelcome in her Empire. By the middle of Josef's reign, it appears that the Jewish population of Galicia began to increase, but only 4 years later, the census reflects a decided decrease. Again, this may be due to errors in collection or attribution.

In 1869, the year of Emancipation of the Jews of Galicia, of the 820,000 Jews residing in all of Austria, 575,433 lived in Galicia, about 10.6 percent of the total population. Jews then comprised the third largest religious group after Roman Catholics and Greek Catholics. By 1880, the Jewish population of Austria had grown to 1 million, a majority of whom lived in Galicia. The censuses of 1880 and 1890 showed that the proportion of Jews had grown, though very slightly, but then by 1910, one might interpret the results as reflecting a downward trend in the proportion of Jews. However, in that census, families were designated by language spoken and, though most of the Jewish population was Yiddish speaking, the census did not include Yiddish as a recognized language. This may have altered the resulting assessment of how large the Jewish population was in that year even though it is said that many Jews attempted to add Yiddish for language on their census forms.

It should be noted that Jews in Eastern Galicia were more numerous than in western Galicia, both in real numbers and in percentage terms. This was true because there were more cities in eastern Galicia, whereas western Galicia had more small towns and rural areas.

Population estimates for the early period of Austrian rule are controversial among historians. Censuses were conducted under new and more reliable rules beginning with the census of 1869 (Krochmal, 1993). In 1874, 3 percent of the Galician population was then Austrian, 45 percent Polish, 41 percent Ruthenian

(Ukrainian), and 11 percent Jewish. According to Pogonowski (1987):

> There were 200,000 public officials ruling over 180,000 Jewish merchants and 220,000 Jewish innkeepers and a mass of undersized Jewish businesses and equally undersized Polish and Ukrainian farms supporting 81 percent of the population. Only 400 families had enough land to be considered wealthy.

Citing 1931 census data, Metzler (1997) in talking about the general condition of the Jews, said that though "one out of every ten persons in the [former] Galician provinces was Jewish, in cities, nine out of every ten households or businesses were owned by Jews. . . . In the province of Stanisławów, 94 percent of the stores, 96 percent of the distributors, and 82 percent of the cafes and restaurants belonged to Jews."

Galician poverty and backwardness had a major impact on the population as a whole. Indeed, the Crownland had both the highest birth and death rates in Europe and rated as the most backward area in its industrial and agricultural technologies. Tuberculosis was a major killer. Between 1830 and 1850, the death rate in Galicia exceeded the birth rate. Heavy floods in 1836 and famines in 1846–55 and 1907, along with typhus and cholera outbreaks in 1847–48, 1854, 1866, 1873, 1884 and 1892 were heavy burdens on the Galician population. (Subtelny, 1988; Chorzempa, 1993)

With this background of poverty, disease and disaster, it is no wonder that between 1881 and 1910, 236,000 Jews left Galicia. But Jews were not alone in leaving this region. The *Encyclopedia Judaica* cites Austrian emigration figures indicating that about two million Galicians emigrated from the area by 1914, most to the United States. Galician Jews began coming to the United States in the 1880s. Most settled for at least some period of time in a small area of the Lower East Side of Manhattan, where they established synagogues and many social, cultural and welfare organizations known as *landsmanschaftn*. As word spread that the community had synagogues and burial space, young people began

to join those who had emigrated before. This stream become a
flood that would not end until World War I effectively ended
large scale emigration from Galicia.

Because most Jews spoke German in addition to Yiddish,
Vienna, Berlin, Budapest, and Prague were also popular cities for
Galician Jews, although Paris and London had small populations
of Jews from Galicia. Large numbers of Jewish families moved
to Hungary, some for religious reasons, to join those who were
encouraging the development of Hasidic communities throughout
Hungary, and some for social and economic reasons, since it was
far easier to make a living and live more freely in Hungary. After
World War I, when the United States acted to severely limit immigration from Eastern and Southern Europe, Galician Jews turned
their attention to opportunities in Palestine, Hungary, South
America and the Caribbean countries. Those who chose to stay in
Europe, were among the millions of Jews lost in the Shoah.

Jews as Town and City Dwellers

Although there were some differences in the proportion of
urban Jews in the eastern and western portions of Galicia, in
general, Jews were over represented in the towns and cities of the
the Crownland. In 1900 only 10 percent of Galicia's population
lived in towns and cities, yet Jews comprised 40 to 45 percent
of the urban population. This tendency was undoubtedly due to
a number of economic and social factors. But, certainly safety
must have been a factor in the clustering of Jews in cities and
towns. Although pogroms were less prevalent than they were in
Russian Poland, there are accounts of scattered violence generated by blood libels, false accusations of murder and incitement
by priests. However, clergy-sanctioned pogroms became more of
a problem after 1900, and, of course, the Jewish community was
keenly aware of what had been going on in Russia, so there was
a high degree of vigilance and concern throughout Galicia that
continued until well after World War II.

In the years between 1880–1890, more than 70 percent of all
Galician Jews lived in towns, 20 percent in villages and 8 percent
on royal (rural) grounds. In 1880, in 19 of 102 cities and towns

Market scene, Stryj market

in western Galicia, Jews comprised more than 50 percent of the total population, with the highest proportions in Dukla and Tarnobrzeg (80 percent). In eastern Galicia in the same year, Jews were a majority in 65 of the 205 cities and towns, with the highest proportions in Lubycza Królewska (83 percent), Borysław and Zaleszczyki (79 percent) (Krochmal, 1993). In Brody, 70 percent of the population was Jewish (Subtelny, 1988).

In Przemyśl district, the Jewish population residing in urban areas held steady at about 76–77 percent from 1880 to 1900. In the city itself, the numbers of Jews increased but the proportion declined, as the city increasingly became an economic magnet for non-Jews from surrounding areas. Whereas, in 1880, the percentage of Jews in the city was 34.7 percent, by 1900, it had declined to 30.4 percent (Krochmal, 1993).

Taxes on Jews

Taxes under Polish rule had been very heavy for the Jews who paid head or capitation taxes and sales taxes on many commodities, but when the Jews of Poland came under Austrian rule, the type and amount of taxes increased dramatically.

Pogonowski noted that the people of Galicia, the largest and the poorest province of the Austrian Empire, paid the highest rate of income taxes in Europe and the taxes paid by Jews were disproportionately higher than they were for non-Jews. Indeed, from Empress Maria Theresa to Emancipation in 1869, the Jews suffered under special taxes that their, already tax-burdened fellow countrymen did not have to endure. Among the special taxes on the Jews, was the infamous "candle tax." This tax was conceived by the infamous Herz Homberg, whom we have already encountered as the head of the German schools. Homberg and a friend proposed this tax, no doubt, as a means of further ingratiating himself with his royal patron. This tax directly impacted the religious custom of lighting candles to celebrate the coming of the Sabbath on Friday evening. Candle taxes were to be collected weekly and failure to pay had serious consequences. The tax was higher on rabbis because it was assumed that they used more candles than ordinary families.

There were many other taxes, including the following list from the Universal Jewish Encyclopedia (4, 1941): synagogue, repair permits, kosher meat, trading, marriage, protection/toleration, also known as a "head" tax. In her discussion of European tax lists, Alice Solovy (1991) said that of the marriage tax:

> A Jewish marriage tax in Galicia in the late 1700s was so heavy that it was meant to discourage legal marriages of Jewish couples. It did not, however, discourage Jewish marriages because Jewish couples simply had ritual marriages and bypassed the tax regulations.

Citing Isaac Lewin's book, *The Jewish Community of Poland*, Solovy noted that Empress Maria Theresa doubled the "head tax" and renamed it *Toleranzgebuehr* (payment for tolerance). Those unable to pay it, were expelled from the Austrian Empire. In addition to the purely Jewish taxes, there were other fees and taxes, such as income and property taxes, fees for licenses in connection with conducting business, and travel documents. Though not a tax, Jews, along with everyone else, had to pay notaries, who were licensed by the government, a fee for the notarized statements and documents that were needed for school admission, travel and business related purposes. For most of the years between 1772–1869, Jews were barred from becoming notaries. Jews had higher ferry and bridge tolls, as well (Universal Jewish Encyclopedia , v. 4, 1941).

The kosher meat tax was particularly burdensome for Jewish families. Instituted in 1784, it was increased in 1789, 1810 and 1816 (Universal Jewish Encyclopedia, v.4, 1941). Additionally, in 1847, the government of Ferdinand, decreed what appears to have been a one-time, special tax on all Jews.

The synagogue tax posed an interesting dilemma for the Jewish community. Every district had an officially recognized synagogue where Jews were required to pray at least annually. The tax was based on the number of members of the *kehillah*. The Hasidic "courts" avoided synagogue taxes by using houses and commercial buildings for daily study and communal prayer.

The *Gemeinde* had the annual duty to prepare and submit to the Austrian government, a budget for all anticipated expenses for administrative and religious purposes. This included upkeep of the synagogue and the other buildings associated with Jewish ritual observance and study, social services, and education. Taxes were collected by a person employed by the *Gemeinde.* All tax receipts were paid to the Austrian government which, based on the budget submitted, disbursed funds for the budgeted expenses. If there was a shortfall in collections, the community simply received less than hoped for or raised the funds in some other way.

So, how was it determined who would pay taxes to a particular *Gemeinde?* It is evident from the tax lists on microfilm at the Central Archives for the History of the Jewish People in Jerusalem, from census lists, and from regulations governing vital record registration, that every individual was tied to an ancestral *Gemeinde*, regardless of where he actually lived. Unless the individual received permission from a *Gemeinde* to transfer one's membership, the membership was fixed for life. It makes sense that, since operating funds were based on membership, every effort was made to retain members.

Jewish Religious Observance

For the most part, Galician Jews were expected to conform to community standards of religious practice and ritual. Deviance was rare, and community pressures operated to enforce compliance with Jewish law. In general, when there was controversy, it usually related to the "other group's" failure to adhere sufficiently to Jewish law. Marriage to someone who was not Jewish was rare, though certainly not unheard of. It was generally expected that the child who had "married out," would be shunned, at a minimum, and more commonly, treated as though he or she had died. Families even sat *shiva* for children who so overtly dishonored them.

In 1772, the Jews of Galicia could be classified in religious terms as Orthodox and Hasidic. Hasidism was still in its early stage then, and so, a majority would have characterized themselves as Orthodox. But, very soon, the influence of the Hasidic movement became extremely strong in Galicia. Many of the early leaders of the movement lived in towns that became part of Galicia, but Hasidism found fertile ground in the region. In part this was due to the fact that traditionally Orthodox Judaism in Poland had become associated with dry observance of the laws, with little in the way of the mysticism that had, for some time, attracted Jews from Southern Poland. The Messianic fervor that characterized the period just before the birth of the *Besht*, was particularly strong in this region. The leaders of the Polish *kehillah* were mostly wealthy Jews who had become remote from the problems of ordinary people, drawing the populace into identification with religious leaders who prayed with joyful singing and dancing and were of the same class and condition. Hasidism, therefore, had enormous appeal to ordinary Jews. The movement was well on its way to becoming established when the region came under Austrian rule.

Early in the Hasidic movement, a small group of men, who had studied with the movement's founder, Rabbi Israel (1698-1760), known as the *Baal Shem Tov* or the *Besht* began to spread the teachings and philosophies of the *Besht* by teaching their followers. And so, the movement grew, but with a number of schools of thought arising from the personalities, styles and personal philosophies of the later leaders. Despite intermarriage between members of the groups and fundamentally similar philosophies and belief systems, gradually, a competitive atmosphere set in among them.

Each of the various Hasidic groups was headed by a "Rebbe," who was an extremely influential figure. Male followers would leave their homes and families and travel long distances to visit the Rebbe associated with their particular group, sometimes staying for weeks, as they learned with other followers and grew in commitment and fervor. Promising followers were encouraged to organize groups of followers in their towns or, even to move to a new community to establish a group there. Many communities had multiple Hasidic communities which vied for followers and local influence. Thus, a rebbe's influence could extend far and wide through whole regions. The role of Rebbe was generally hereditary, if there was a son who was acceptable to key followers, or a son-in-law, or a favored student. In these ways, each group grew in numbers and influence in a region. The leader in each town would be perceived as having a direct line from the Rebbe, thus giving him referred authority.

Rebbes established communities throughout western and eastern Galicia, as well as in Hungary in the late 19th and early 20th centuries. Towns, though some of them were very small, including Łancut, Bukowsko, Bełż, Nowy Sącz , Ropczyce, Rymanów, Dynów, Brzesko and Bóbrka, were important centers of Jewish religious life because an influential Hasidic rebbe had established a what is roughly translated into a "court" in those towns. The influence of these leaders radiated into surrounding towns and villages, and sometimes into distant towns.

Hassidic groups competed for the position of "government" rabbi(the rabbi recognized and paid by the government as the chief rabbi of a *Gemeinde*) in order to cement their influence over the purity and piety of the Jews in the community. Marriage partners were generally found within the family's affiliation with a particular Hasidic group, though not necessarily in the same town. Sometimes the different "courts" would arrange marriages to forge positive ties between them.

Though early in the Hasidic movement, relations between the various groups were civil and cooperative, as time went on, bitter animosity and jealousy characterized relations between a few

Kahal of Strzyzów

"courts." Some of the leaders became extremely wealthy as a result of donations from their poor members, which caused criticism by the leaders of other Hasidic groups that disapproved of the acquisition of wealth in this fashion. Some of the disagreements arose from relatively minor ideological or observance differences that eventually blew up into passionate ideological battles, sometimes even generating violence between adherents of different groups in the same town.

A majority of the elected leaders of the *Gemeinde* and members of the religious court, the *Bet Din*, were most often drawn from the Hasidic community. This was not always the case with the government rabbi. The fact that the Austrian government had to approve his appointment, often led to the appointment of a man more acceptable to the authorities. The criteria for selection of the president of the *Gemeinde*, might suggest that he would be less observant or more closely associated with traditional Orthodox Judaism but, surprisingly, *yizkor* books and other accounts of Jewish life in Galicia, suggest that the head of the *Gemeinde*, too, was often involved with a Hasidic community, despite his relative wealth and status. The collective strength of Hasidism occasionally prevented Austrian or local government from implementing policies and measures that would have had negative religious impact on the Jewish community. It was widely understood that Jewish leaders would use organized resistance as a strategy. Resistance to civil marriage was one such example. The government was relatively helpless to require Jews to undergo civil marriage, even though it was mandated. The sanctions were not perceived as severe enough to overcome the resistance, which will be discussed in greater detail later.

By the late 19th century, particularly in the larger cities of Galicia, the confluence of Emancipation's impact, Zionism, the growth of the *Haskalah* (Enlightenment) movement, and the influence of the German movement to reform Judaism, gradually took hold. Progressive synagogues and schools opened in the larger cities. Young people began to identify themselves with Zionist youth movements rooted more strongly in socialism than Judaism. These forces eroded the strength and power of Hasidism, though it remained the dominant type of Jewish observance in Galicia until World War II. Despite the trend toward secularization among young people in Galician cities, there were only a few Galician synagogues associated with the religious reform movement that was sweeping Germany, Hungary and elsewhere in Europe and the U.S.

Josef II had been well ahead of his time in his efforts to secularize and Germanize the Jews of Galicia. He proposed a series of measures designed to encourage a Jewish religious reform movement. While never strong, two of his successors encouraged the development of Jewish secular schools, called "Herz Homberg" or German schools, as part of that overall effort. By 1806, though there were 107 of these schools, throughout Galicia, they were poorly attended and the source of much contention between the government and *Gemeinde* leaders, particularly in the larger urban areas where these schools were located. Homberg, himself, generally reviled by Orthodox and Hasidic leaders, fled Galicia in 1806, in fear for his life. He never returned to Galicia, though he continued his destructive and disruptive work in Prague and Vienna. Under pressure, Emperor Franz Ferdinand subsequently gave up support of this secularizing movement, but some of the schools survived and later educated youngsters whose parents opted for a more secular education after Emancipation. In fact, they educated small but significant numbers of men who were ready and eager for university education, when that became possible after 1869.

Although, as a religious phenomenon, the reform efforts do not appear to have had deep roots in Galicia, two Scottish missionaries who wrote about their travels through Galicia to "investigate the condition of the Jews" in 1839, made frequent mention of Jews attracted to this movement. For example, in describing Brody, they noted:

> There are many adherents of the New School, although
> they have only one synagogue. Most of the rising genera-
> tion are giving up the study of the Talmud; and several
> have been baptized. There is some learning among them;
> for in one synagogue we met with several lads who under-

The Temple in Przemyśl

stood and spoke Hebrew. many of the young men are beginning to attend the Government schools, in which they are taught Latin, and acquire general knowledge. The rabbi of the New School speaks Latin and French.

Marriage: The Cornerstone of Jewish Society

Marriage under Austrian rule in Galicia must be thoroughly understood by those wishing to pursue genealogical research, in order to fully appreciate how civil law impacted the documentation of family life and the surnames of Jewish children. Indeed, Austrian marriage laws, and the resistance of the Jewish population to those laws, had dramatic impact on the surnames that our ancestors carried in Europe and in later places of emigration. This section will first address marriage from a legal point of view and then address how marriages were arranged and carried out.

In the early days of Austrian rule, Galician Jews came under what had long been Austrian *familiant* regulations, which specified what constituted a legitimate Jewish household. These rules had been successfully used to discourage Jews from living in Austria and to maintain the Jewish population at very low levels. These laws stemmed from Charles VI who had issued an order on September 23, 1726, that gave only one male of a Jewish family the right to establish a legitimate household. That person was required to register as a legitimate household and, of course, to pay a substantial tax. Until that household was terminated by death or a substantial fine was paid, no other male in the family was eligible to establish a legitimate household. Legitimate households were only permitted within the quota allowed for each community. That system limited the total number of Jewish households in Austria, proper and its territorial holdings. Therefore, well before Austria's establishment of Galicia, religious marriages were much more common in Austria than the civil and legitimate form. At the same time, individuals whose marriages were religious and not civil found it difficult to conduct official business with the government, including applying for business licenses, permission to engage in certain occupations or to move to another jurisdiction. Additionally, those wishing to move from one community to another had to obtain permission and permission was only granted to legitimate households.

A law on May 13, 1734 had set forth the minimum age for Jewish brides and grooms as 15 and 18, respectively. The couple had to document their ages with births registered with the Catholic parish, circumcision registers, or the attestation of a local nobleman. It would appear that registration with the Catholic parish was not being done because, despite numerous documents which confirm this requirement, this was done in only a handful of large cities, based on the absence of Jewish births, marriages and deaths in Catholic registers from most parishes.

By the time that Josef II, in his 1782 Toleration Patent, confirmed the mandate for civil marriage for all Austrians, Jewish religious leaders in Galicia were well organized to respond to this mandate with forceful resistance. They viewed marriage to be a purely religious matter, in which the state had no business meddling. Moreover, Josef had failed to rescind most of the restrictions established under the old *familiant* laws, nor had he lifted the tax on Jewish brides and grooms lifted.

When Josef issued his 1789 *Judenpatent* for Galicia, the restriction on the number of marriages had been lifted, but with his death only a year later, there was too little time to determine if this change would have made a difference in the attitude of Jewish leaders. Then, two years after Josef's death, Franz Ferdinand reinstated all aspects of the *familiant* regulations, confirmed the tax on brides and grooms, and the requirement for civil registration of births, marriages and deaths with the Catholic parish. The latter was particularly provocative and vexing to Jewish leaders.

Despite these negative acts, the residence quotas that pertained to communities within the country of Austria, did not apply to Galician Jews, except in Lemberg. There, the number of Jews who could live in the boundaries of the city, was restricted until 1869. Generally, Jews were free to move internally to new communities as long as the *Gemeinde* approved of the change in residence. There is no evidence in the historical literature or existing documents that this was ever an issue.

Returning to the problem of with Jewish civil marriage, from 1810-1869, Jews wishing to marry had to pass an examination based on Herz Homberg's reviled book, *Bene Zion*, which most Galician Jews shunned as heretical and dangerous. Then, too, was the marriage tax which varied over time, but the fact of the tax was both a deterrent and an irritant.

Reforms in 1848 abolished the *familiaten* in Bohemia and Moravia but it was not until Emancipation in 1869, that these harsh marriage laws were finally abolished in Galicia. In most parts of the Empire, the reduction of marriage restrictions was greeted with enthusiasm since removing these restrictions were seen as a form of acceptance and a precursor to new freedoms. But, in Galicia, under strong Hasidic influence, this aspect of Emancipation was widely greeted with continuing resistance because of the view that governmental regulation of marriage was unacceptable.

This attitude and the long history of Austrian restrictions and taxes on marriage among Jews goes a long way toward explaining why there are so few Jewish marriages registered in Galician civil registers. In a series of efforts to force the issue of compliance in Galicia, a law passed in Vienna in 1875 strongly reiterated the requirement for civil marriage. The law set forth, for the first time, the requirement that the, then, 73 main *Gemeindes,* and their subdistricts nominate a registrar from among their members to be responsible for collecting and maintaining registers of Jewish births, marriages and deaths. Two years later, the government issued regulation governing the qualifications and appointment of registrars, the content of the forms to be used, and the procedures to be followed by both registrars and Jewish citizens under normal and special circumstances. Marriages were to be performed by the official rabbi of the *Gemeinde* or an approved substitute. The registration procedures included how the registrar was to address various scenarios, including the registration of births to couples who had not complied with civil marriage laws. The towns under the jurisdiction of each main and sub *Gemeinde* were listed in at the end of the booklet of regulations published in 1877. There was an immediate and marked change in the quality of civil registration records after publication of the regulations. No longer were babies listed without parents when they were born or died and there was a definite improvement in listing the parents of individuals who had died. Marriages? Well, that took a lot longer to take hold.

Up until 1877, the register books for marriages were generally very thin and covered many years because there had been so few civil marriages, relative to the number of births and deaths, which were documented in much thicker registers. Surely, Austrian officials must have anticipated that these new arrangements for internally documenting Jewish vital events would satisfy the objections of religious leaders and, it is the case that civil marriages did gradually become more common but for reasons unrelated to the sanctions in the regulations.

And, in terms of current thinking about the matter, there were fairly unpleasant sanctions for those who did not comply with civil marriage laws. The regulations required that a child be registered under the surnames of the mothers, without the father being identified at all, unless he complied with the requirement to appear in person with two witnesses who could attest to his being the father of the child. Another sanction involved the presumption of inheritance. For children who were the product of "illegitimate" unions, they would not automatically inherit property from the father. After the regulations went into effect, the registrars were under scrutiny by government officials and, apparently, there were periodic crackdowns, judging from the records which suddenly follow procedures to the letter, as opposed to other periods when registration might be somewhat lax. In fact, it is interesting to note that documents such as censuses and birth records reflect wide variability in compliance from district to district and from registrar to registrar. Sometimes the daughters were given the surnames of the father but the males were given the surnames of the fathers. Although initially, the form for the birth record had a column for the child's surname but this was eliminated at some point. Readers are left wondering what surname the child used when the father appeared with two witnesses, as required. Of course, when only the mother is listed on the record, it is clear that the child would officially carry the name of the mother.

The regulations implied that, in the course of a person's lifetime, unless there had been a civil marriage, official documents were to be in the surname of the individual's mother. This meant that travel documents might reflect that the person was the product of an illegitimate marriage when entering another country. What seemed normal in Galicia might not be seen in the same light in the US and elsewhere when trying to prove to an immigration official that one's children were legitimate. The acquisition of business licenses to conduct business at a level above minor trade, or to own property or land, required that paperwork be in order. These obstacles may well have propelled some couples into civil marriage, particularly since Emancipation enabled these kinds of freedoms.

If a civil marriage took place at any time before the death of the parents, the parents could petition for the birth records of their children to show that there had been a legal marriage and, at that time, surnames could be changed, if the parties requested it. Too, an adult child of these unions, could also petition for a change in surname and for adding the marriage information to his record.

After emigration from Galicia began in earnest in the early 1880s, the civil registers reflect an increase in civil marriage, as couples began to confront the necessity to regularize their relationships so that they could obtain travel documents and be accepted into other countries. Individuals and couples wishing to obtain travel documents, also had to be in compliance with other laws and regulations such as owing no taxes and completing military service (or payment of a fine as an alternative). By the early years of the 20th century, the marriage registers reflect a sharp increase in the number of couples, who had long been religiously married and long past their childbearing years, had civil marriages, often along with their children who were seeking to emigrate. This would enable the father's surname to be added to the birth register so that passports would be in the "correct" name and the individual would be listed as "legitimate." All of this has caused enormous confusion for family historians seeking to find their ancestors and relatives in Galician records. One can never be sure that the correct surname is being researched so that all possibilities must be considered. Many people have been surprised to find that their surname was actually derived from the maternal side of the family, not, as is expected, from the paternal side. Indeed, many have learned the names of their paternal relatives only from clues in birth or death records.

Sometimes the individual's surname, in instances where civil marriage was lacking, would be hyphenated with the father's name or would be styled to include the word *false*, or *vel*, as in *Spira false Kahan* or *Spira vel Kahan*, meaning "Spira also known as Kahan." On some birth records, the word "*recte*," appears, which means "rectified." This word was apparently used under different circumstances, such as when the father had appeared with two witnesses, or when the surname was corrected from the mother's to the father's.

It is also unfortunate that many registrars, in the absence of a civil marriage, did not record the names of spouses when someone died so that, without a marriage record and with only the name of the mother on birth records, it is sometimes impossible to determine the name of the spouse.

Turning our attention, now, to marriage customs, Jews typically married in their late teens and early twenties in Galicia, and, in virtually all cases until World War I, marriages were arranged by parents and a matchmaker. After World War I, marriages that were not arranged became more common, particularly among young adults involved in one of the 40 or so Zionist groups that arose in the interwar period. Participation in the Zionist movement became a way for Jewish boys and girls to have legitimate interaction, although many older Jews saw such contact as shocking and immoral. These casual interactions and the common interests, ideology, and activities that the youngsters shared, increased the likelihood that they would want to marry each other.

It was extremely rare for a Jew and a non-Jew to marry in Galicia. Social norms simply did not support extensive social interaction between young unmarried Jewish girls and boys, much less between Jews and non-Jewish peers. After Emancipation, children attending secular schools with non-Jews did have such interaction but both Jewish and non-Jewish parents acted to discourage relationships that could become romantically problematic.

Virtually everyone married. There must have been people who were attracted to members of the same gender, but this author has seen nothing written about this issue in any of the literature written by individuals who lived in Galicia. As in most places in the world, even today, Jewish men and women generally led quite separate lives. Some men would spend much of their married life away from their families, traveling for religious or economic reasons. Women managed their domains of the home and, often, the marketplace. Men were not expected to participate in housework or in child rearing apart, from religious and moral instructions and guidance. Men who were drawn to a life of study were marginal participants in making a living, sometimes because they were supported by their wife's father as a matter of pride and honor to have a scholarly son-in-law and sometimes because it evolved that the wife became the primary breadwinner.

Though relatively rare, divorce seems not to have carried the level of social stigma that characterized divorced persons in other societies. Indeed, if a woman did not bear a child within a few years of marriage, Jewish law virtually required the husband to divorce his wife so that he would be free to seek a new wife. (It was assumed to be the woman's fault when there were no children.) On the other hand, wives whose husbands were impotent or uninterested in fulfilling their sexual obligations were also within their rights to request a *get*, a Jewish divorce. A woman could not, however, obtain a divorce without the willing participation of the husband, even if he was missing, or had abandoned her, or if the husband was unable or unwilling to perform his sexual obligations. If the husband disagreed with the divorce or was missing or unreachable, even for many years, as in any observant Jewish community, the wife's marital status could be left in limbo indefinitely.

There were very frequent marriages between relatives in Galicia, even between first cousins and uncles and nieces. This tendency to marry relatives has implications for family historians in terms of how we search and how we make sense of what we find. In fact, a good assumption at the outset is that every spouse should be investigated as a potential link to another part of the biological family. Although today, we might view intrafamily matches with concern about undesirable genetic outcomes, particularly in light of the various genetic disorders that we now know occur among Ashkenazi Jews, in fact, matches between relatives were perceived by our ancestors as desirable for many good reasons. Relative marriages ensured that the religious backgrounds of the parties was a known quantity. Too, such marriages ensured that family money and property would be retained within the family. The latter would have been a concern since the lack of civil marriage made inheritance a less certain proposition.

Weddings were great occasions for families to gather, often for up to a week, to celebrate. Bridal clothing and the canopy or *huppah* under which couples married, were often heirlooms, passed down through families. There was much singing and dancing, though men and women did not dance together and the dancing took place in separate rooms. If brides and grooms were allowed to meet before their marriage, it was not to engage in extended courtships. Some parents allowed their daughters to decline an engagement if the prospective groom was not to her liking. However, if a father wanted his young daughter to marry an elderly man, he was within his rights to insist on the marriage taking place. Some engagements, which had the force of marriage in a contractual sense, were arranged between families when the parties were infants. If a young man wanted to learn full time, parents attempted to arrange a marriage with a girl whose father was able to support and, even, house the couple. Indeed, it was an honor for the father to support his son-in-law so that he would be free from worldly cares.

Typically, if the bride and groom were young and didn't live in the same town, the groom moved to the bride's town. If the groom was already established, the bride was more likely to move to his town. Marriages usually occurred between people who lived in the same or adjacent districts. Thus, when searching for records, if you are unable to locate records for your district, consider searching in available, adjacent districts.

Tarnopol street scene

CHAPTER 2

Jewish Geography in Galicia

The most important fact to learn about your family, regardless of where they originated, is the name of your ancestral town. Knowing the name of an ancestral town significantly increases the chance that you will be successful in searching for documentary evidence about your family. This is true, even when vital records no longer exist due to wars, fires and other catastrophes that wiped out all or parts of communities and their records. Knowing the name of the town will enable you to connect with others searching for the same or nearby communities. In addition to vital records (birth, marriage and death), there may be other documentary proof of your relative's existence in the form of notary, court, land, tax, military, school, and census records. The Central Archives for the History of the Jewish People (CAHJP) in Jerusalem has been acquiring microfilmed records from the Polish government, which include some scattered documentation from various *Gemeindes*, including membership, tax, and voter lists, lists of contributors to the Galician community in Palestine, and official documents confirming appointments of individuals, such as official rabbis and registrars to functions within the community. Additionally, there are some documents affirming land leasing (*arenda*) arrangements, which were commercial contracts subject to government oversight and taxation.

Identifying Your Ancestral Town and its Main and Subdistrict

So, before we go any further on this journey of discovery, you are advised to consult Appendix F to locate your ancestral towns and the districts and subdistricts in which they were located. Appendix A offers a guide to pronouncing and recognizing Polish towns and family names if you know how the name of a town sounds but you don't know how it might be spelled. For example, the city of Rzeszów looks impossible to pronounce but when you know that the Rz is pronounced as though you are saying Sh and that a "w" is always pronounced with the sound of "v," then it is easy to add the rest of the letters to sound like Sheshov. Or take Przemyśl, which looks even more impossible to say. The Poles say this with a soft "P" so that it sounds like P-shem-ish-l. The Jews skipped over the P and called this town "Shemish" or "Shemishl." It is likely that an ancestor from this town used the Jewish version. Or, take the example of the town of Brzozów. Saying the town sounds like "Broshov." So, not so hard once you get some basic principles about the sound of letter combinations!

If you are confronted with multiple towns of the same name and you do not know how to know which among them is yours, for now, note district information about all of them. At some point, you may learn something significant about a river, mountain or some other important landmark that will guide you to the right town. Often, when there are towns with the same name, you may find that one was in eastern Galicia and the other in the western portion so this, too, may help you identify the correct place.

Take Dolina as an example: There were five towns with that name in Galicia. One was a community in eastern Galicia large enough to be the administrative center of the whole district; one was in the Czortk w district and subdistrict in eastern Galicia and another, also in the Czortk w district, but located within the subdistrict of Jagielnica; and, two, oddly enough, were located in the district and subdistrict of Sanok, in western Galicia (one was a tiny village called Dolina ad Zaluz, which means that it was near Zaluz). Checking the index map below, we see that the largest Dolina is in square 4472. The Czortkow district, where two other eastern Galician Dolinas are located is somewhat northeast in square 4375. The other two, near Sanok, are in square 4168. Sanok is on the River San, which may provide a clue.

The other thing to keep in mind is that when people left Galicia, they assumed that their towns would not be known to others and tended to give the name of a larger town, just as today, you might live in a suburb or small town near the U.S. city of Baltimore, Maryland and you would simply tell people living in Kansas, that you live in Baltimore, a place about which they are more likely to have heard. If you can identify a city near where your family lived, this will give you a good starting place.

Readers who don't know the name of their ancestral town, will find very little in the way of records or relevant materials until this essential piece of information can be found. You may be able to find such information from distant relatives or from government records generated in the country where your relatives emigrated to after leaving Galicia. Consult a good general genealogy guide for hints about possible sources for this type of information. In the United States, this might include ship passenger records, the 1920 Federal census, which was supposed to list town of birth, death or cemetery records, and naturalization documents.

Please go to Appendix F now.

Make note of your towns and then return to this Chapter.

Welcome back! If you know the name of the town and the district and subdistrict, you will need to locate your main district in the following alphabetical arrangement. You will note that the districts have two pieces of information: 1) the designation of Poland or Ukraine, which tells you where the district is today and 2) a four-digit number beside the district. That number corresponds to the four digit number on the index map below. Match the numbers and you will have a good idea of where in Galicia the town was located. Each main district below is coded with a number that matches the index map.

Say that you are seeking a town in Ciesanow district. Find Ciesanow in the alphabetical list below. Note that it is in square 3970. Finding square 3970 on the index map will give you a rough idea of where the town was located. For more precise location information, such as longitude and latitude, you can go to JewishGen.org and use the ShtetlSeekers feature. *Where Once We Walked*, which was published by Avotaynu, Inc. and will be discussed later in greater detail, is also an excellent source for geographic information.

Now, assuming that you have correctly identified the main and sub Gemeinde or kehillah district for each town of interest, you will be able use the information in subsequent chapters to determine what vital records might exist about your family, since this is the way that all vital information about Jews was collected and maintained. There were some minor changes in districts, particularly in the eastern part of Galicia in 1890 and later, but district designations held for most towns for the period of 1877-1918 and beyond, into interwar Poland (from 1919-until Jewish records were no longer being kept at the time of WWII).

Main Districts and Their Subdistricts

The following, is a list of the *Gemeinde* districts and their subdistricts, as they were constituted in Galicia in 1877. As noted above, there were minor changes in the composition of districts after 1877, but those changes are not reflected here. Main districts appear in uppercase letters. Subdistricts are in lower case

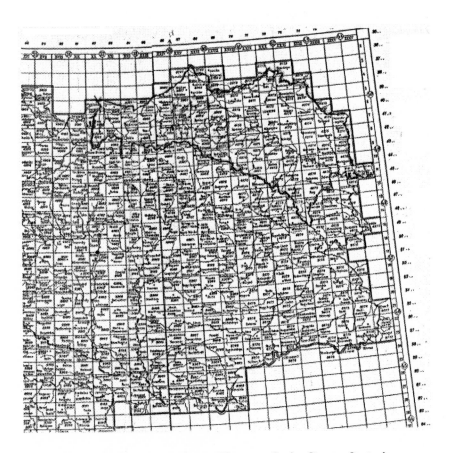

Map 3. Index map to Austro-Hungary Series G6480 S75 .A8.

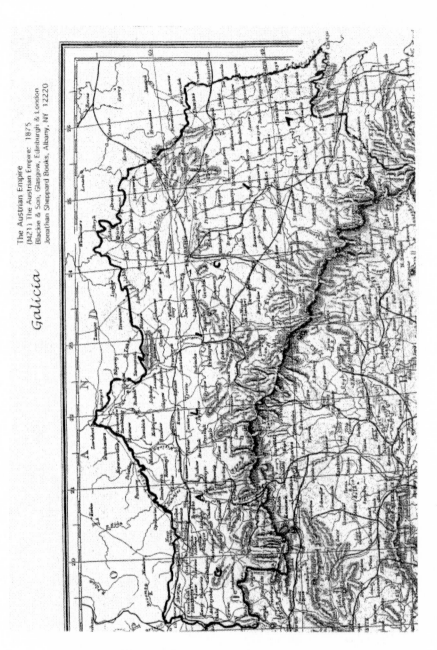

Map 4. The Austrian Empire, 1875

letters. The main and subdistrict town names are spelled in this list as they were under Austrian rule.

You will note that, in some districts, there is a subdistrict by the same name as the main district. For instance, in Gorlice district, the registrar had responsibility for overseeing the whole district and for the collection and maintenance of the records for the Gorlice subdistrict, as well. But, although the head registrar in Gorlice had oversight responsibility for the whole district, a different registrar was responsible for collecting and maintaining the records in the subdistricts of Rzepiennik Strżyzowski and Biecz.

In the listing below, where the main district is today in Ukraine, the name is spelled (and alphabetized) as it was under Austrian rule, and then the current Ukrainian name is shown. After 1890, when districts were redrawn, some of the larger cities in what is currently Ukraine, kept their own vital records and some records were moved to new districts.

BIAŁA DISTRICT 4062 Poland   Biała
Kęty
Lipnik
Oświęcim

BIRCZA DISTRICT 4169 Poland   Bircza
  Dobromil
Nowe Miasto (This town and most of the towns in the old district are within Ukraine)
Rybotycze

BOCHNIA DISTRICT 4172 Poland
Bochnia.
Wiśnicz Nowy

BRZESKO DISTRICT 4065 Poland
  Brzesko
Czchów
Radłów

Szczurowa
Wojnicz

BRZOZÓW DISTRICT 4168 Poland
Brzozów
Dynów (The Germans burned both synagogues with the town's Jews inside. It is assumed that the records for the subdistrict were in one of the buildings).
Jasienica

BÓBRKA DISTRICT (also known as Boberka) 4172 UKR
Bóbrka
Brzozdowiec (now Berezdivtsi)
Chodorów (now Khodoriv)
Mikołajów (now Mykolaiv)
Strzeliska Nowe (now Strilychi Novi)

BOHORODCZANY (now BOGORODCHANY) DISTRICT 4572 UKR
Bohorodczany (now Bogorodchany)
Lysiec (now Lisets)
Solotwina (now Slotvina)

BORSZCZÓW (now BORSHCHEV) DISTRICT 4476 UKR
Borszczów (now Borshchev)
Mielnica (now Melnytsia). Some records for the town of Mielnica are held with records of Krzywcze and Kudryńce. Includes towns of Germakówka, Olchowiec, Okopy. There are separate books of records for Krzywcze and Kudryńce,
Skała (now Skala Podolskaya)

BRODY DISTRICT 3974 UKR
Brody
Leszniów (now Leshnev)
Podkamien (now Podkamen)
Sokolówka (now Sokolivka)

Stanisławczyk (now Stanislavchyk)
Szczurowice (now Shchurovichi)
Toporów (now Toporov)
Założce (now Zalzitsi). Includes records from the towns of
Ratyszcze and Zagórze.

BRZEŻANY (now BEREZHANY) DISTRICT 4274 UKR
    Brzeżany
    Kozłów
    Kozowa (now Kosova)
    Narajów (now Narayev)

BUCZACZ (now BUCHACH) DISTRICT 4375 UKR
    Buczacz (now Buchach)
    Barysz (now Barysh)
    Jazłowice (now Pomortsy)
    Monasterzyska (now Manastryska)
    Potok (now Potik Zoloty)

CHRZANÓW DISTRICT 3963 Poland
    Chrzanów
    Trzebinia

CIESZANÓW DISTRICT 3970 Poland
    Cieszanów
    Lipsko
    Lubaczów
    Oleszyce
    Narol

CZORTKÓW (now CHORTKOV) DISTRICT 4375 UKR
    Budzanów (now Budanov)
    Czortków (now Chortkov)
    Jagielnica (now Yagelnitsa)
    Ulaszkowce (now Ulashkovtsy)

DABROWA DISTRICT 3966 Poland
Dąbrowa
Szczucin

DOLINA DISTRICT 4472 UKR
Bolechów (now Bolekhov)
Dolina
Rożniatów (now Rozhnyuv)

DROHOBYCZ (now DROGOBYCH) DISTRICT 4271 UKR
Borysław (now Borislav). Includes towns of Dołhe, Kropiwnik
Stary, Mrażnica, Rybnik, Schodnica, Tustanowice, Wolanka.
Drohobycz (now Drogobych)

GORLICE DISTRICT 4166 Poland
Gorlice According to the head of the USC in Gorlice (letter
dated May 1977), many books of records were destroyed by the
Germans after the liquidation of the Gorlice ghetto.
Rzepiennik Strżyzowski
Biecz

GRÓDEK JAGIELLOŃSKI (now GORODOK) DISTRICT) 4071 UKR
Gródek Jagielloński (now Gorodok)
Janów (now Janiv)

GRYBÓW DISTRICT 4166 Poland
Grybów. Researcher Georges Rosenfeld, who wrote to the
mayor of this town, was informed that the USC holds some pre-
1900 birth, marriage and death registers. Rosenfeld also received a
book, Studia z dziejów miasta i regionu (Studies in the history of the
town and region), an interesting historical study written by Danuta
Quirini-Poplawka and published by Universitas in Kraków in 1992.
A second volume was slated to discuss the Jews of Grybow. The late
Pauline Horwitz wrote to the civil registry office in Grybow and
was informed that Jewish birth and marriage registers for 1820–30
and 1860–70 were destroyed in World War II.

Bobowa. Researcher Georges Rosenfeld was told that the records were destroyed during World War II, but Miriam Weiner shows some records after 1882 for this district.

HORODENKA (now GORODENKA) DISTRICT 4575 UKR
Horodenka (now Gorodenka)
Czernelica (now Chernilitsa)
Obertyn (now Obertin). Includes towns of Chocimierz, Czortowiec, Niezwiska, Piotrow.

HUSIATYN (now GUSYATIN) DISTRICT 4376 UKR
Chorostków (now Khorostkov). According to researcher Andy Tenenbaum, "The 1830–71 birth register has only one entry per line. The 1874–77 register is in terrible condition. It may have once been under water. Starting in 1877, the records are much more extensive and are in better shape than the older records."
Husiatyn (now Gusyatin)
Kopyczyńce (now Kopychintsy). Includes records for Suchostaw (now Sukhostav).
Probużna (now Probezhna)

JAROSLAU/JAROSŁAW DISTRICT 3969 Poland
Jaroslau/ Jarosław
Radymno
Sieniawa
Pruchnik

JASŁO DISTRICT 4167 Poland
Jasło
Frysztak
Olpiny

JAWORÓW (now YAVOROV) DISTRICT 4071 UKR
Jaworów. Includes towns of Czerczyk, Kurniki, Laszki, Ożmla, Rogozno, Starzyska, Troscianiec, Wierzbiani, Zaluze, among many others.

Krakówiec
Wielkie Oczy

KALUSZ/KALISH (now KALUSH) DISTRICT 4372 UKR
Kalusz/Kalish (now Kalush)
Wojnilów (now Voynilov)

KAMIONKA STRUMIŁOWA (now KAMENKA BUGSKAYA)
DISTRICT 3973 UKR
Busk, Chołojów (now Uzlovoye)
Dobrotwór (now Dobrotvor)
Kamionka Strumiłowa (now Kamenka Bugskaya)
Radziechów (now Radekhov)
Stojanów (now Stoyaniv)
Witków Nowy (now Novyy Witkiv)

KOLBUSZOWA DISTRICT 3867 Poland
Kolbuszowa. Vital records no longer exist
Majdan
Raniżów
Sokolów (now called Sokolow Małopolski)

KOŁOMEA (now KOLOMYYA) DISTRICT 4574 UKR
Gwoździec (now Hvizdets)
Jabłonów (now Yablonov)
Kołomea (now Kolomyya)
Peczeniżyn (now Pechenezhin)

KOSSÓW (now KOSOV) DISTRICT 4674 UKR
Kossów (now Kosov)
Kuty and Pistyn
Żabie (now Verkhovina)

KRAKAU (now spelled KRAKÓW or CRACÓW) 3964 Poland

KROSNO DISTRICT 4161 Poland
Krosno.

Dukla.
Żmigrod
Korczyna

ŁANCUT DISTRICT 3968 Poland

Łancut. Except for 1883-9 birth records at the Rzeszow Archives, vital records were destroyed in a fire. A 1910 census was recently found.
  Żolynia
  Leżajsk
  Kańczuga

LEMBERG (also known as L'VOV, LWÓW, now L'VIV) DISTRICT 4072 UKR

Jaryczów
Lemberg (also known as L'vov, Lwów; now L'viv)[
Nawarya (now Naviriya). Includes towns of Glinna, Kahajów, Lesniowice, Ludwikówka, Milatycze, Miloszowice, Mostki, Podciemne, Podsadki, Porszna, Sokolniki, Solonka, Tolszczów, Wolkiew.
  Szczerzec (now Shchyrets). Includes towns of Chrusno, Ostrów, Piaski, Zagrodki.
  Winniki (now Vinniki). Includes towns of Czyszki, Czyżków, Dawidów, Gaje, Gliniany, Głuchowice, Kozelniki:, Lesienice, Miklaszów, Mikołajów, Swirz.
  Zniesienie. Includes towns of Kulparków and Zimnowoda (now Zimna Voda).

LIMANOWA DISTRICT 4165 Poland

  Limanowa
  Mszana Dolna

LISKO (now LESKO) DISTRICT 4268 Poland

  Lisko (now Lesko)
  Baligród The town was repeatedly ravaged by wars; only records after 1951 survive.
  Ustrzyki Dolne

Wola Michowa
Lutowiska

MIELEC DISTRICT 3867 Poland
Mielec
Radomyśl Wielkie. Records for the subdistrict were
destroyed.

MOŚCISKA (now MOSTISTKA) DISTRICT 4070 UKR
Mościska (now Mostistka). Includes towns of Buchowice,
Czyżowice, Lacka Wola, Radenice, Starzawa.
Hussaków (now Gusakov)
Sadowa Wiśnia (now Sudovaya Vishnya)

MYŚLENICE DISTRICT 4064 Poland
Myślenice
Maków
Jordanów

NADWORNA (now NADVORNA) DISTRICT 4573 UKR
Nadworna (now Nadvorna).
Delatyn (now Delyatin)
Lanczyn (now Lanchyn)

NISKO DISTRICT 3768 Poland
Nisko
Rudnik
Ulanów

NOWY SĄCZ (was known as NEU SANDEZ) DISTRICT 4165
Poland
Krynica
Łabowa
Lacko
Muszyna
Nowy Sącz/Neu Sandec
Piwniczna

Stary Sącz/Alt Sandec
Szczawnica

NOWY TARG DISTRICT 4264 Poland
Nowy Targ
Krościenko

PILZNO DISTRICT 4066 Poland
Pilzno
Dębica. Dov Rubin visited the USC which has only 10 birth records, reconstructed after World War II.
Brzostek
Jadlowa

PODHAJCE (now PODGAYTSY) DISTRICT 4274 UKR
Podhajce (now
Zawalów (now Zavaliv)
Zlotniki (now Zolotnyky)

PRZEMYŚL DISTRICT 4069 Poland
Dubiecko
Krzywcza
Niżankowice
Przemyśl
Sosnica

PRZEMYŚLANY (now PEREMYSHLYANY) DISTRICT 4173 UKR
Przemyślany (now Peremyshlyany)
Dunajowce (now Dunaiv)
Gniany (now Glinyany)
Swirż (now Svirzh)

ROPCZYCE DISTRICT 3967 Poland
Ropczyce
Sędziszów
Wielopole

RAWA RUSKA (also known as RAWA; now RAVA RUSSKAYA)
DISTRICT 3971 UKR
  Rawa Ruska (also known as Rawa; now Rava Russkaya)
  Lubycza Krolewska (now Liubycha)
  Magierów (now Mageriv)
  Niemirów (now Niemirov)
  Uhnow (now Ugnev)

ROHATYŃ (now ROGATIN) DISTRICT 4273 UKR
  Rohatyń (now Rogatin) Includes Knihynicze.
  Bursztyn (now Burshtyn) Includes Bolszowce & Bukaczowce

RUDKI DISTRICT 4171 UKR
  Rudki.
  Komarno

RZESZÓW DISTRICT 3968 Poland
  Błazowa
  Czudec
  Głogów
  Niebylec
  Rzeszow
  Strzyżów
  Tyczyn.

SAMBOR (also known as ALTSTADT) DISTRICT 4170 UKR
  Sambor (also known as Altstadt). Includes towns of Biskowice,
Dublany, Głęboka, Hordynia, Torczynowice, Wojcietycze, Wola
Blazowska, Wolszcza, Wykoty.

SANOK DISTRICT 4168 Poland
  Bukowsko. Records for this town existed after World War II
but are now missing.
  Nowotaniec
  Rymanów. Dov Rubin determined that the USC has birth and
death records amounting to about 100 entries, for 1939–41. Older

records may have been in the synagogue which was burned by the Germans.

Sanok

Tyrawa Woloska

SKAŁAT DISTRICT 4276 UKR

Skałat (main and subdistrict). Includes towns of Chmieliska, Iwanówka, Józefówka, Kamionka, Kaczanówka, Kołodziejówka, Orzechowiec.

Podwołoczyska (now Pidvolochyska)

Grzymałów (now Grimaylov)

Tarnoruda (now Ternoruda)

Touste (now Tovste)

ŚNIATYN (now ŚNYATYN) DISTRICT 4675 UKR

Śniatyn (now Śnyatyn)

Zabłotów (now Zabolotov)

SOKAL DISTRICT 3872 UKR

Sokal. Includes towns of Baranie Peretoki, Jósefówka, Steniatyn, Wojsławice, Zawisznia.

Bełż (now Beltsy)

Krystynopol (now Krystonopil)

Tartaków (now Tartakiv)

Warcz/also known as Warez (now Variazh)

STANISŁAWÓW (ALSO KNOWN AS STANISLAV; NOW IVANO-FRANKOVSK) DISTRICT

4473 UKR

Stanisławów

Halicz (now Galich), Jezupol (now Zhovten), Maryampol (now Mariampil Miasto). No records have been found.

STAREMIASTO (ALSO KNOWN AS ALT SAMBOR) DISTRICT

Staremiasto

Chyrów (now Khirov)
Felsztyn (now Skeliva)
Starasól/ Stara Sól (now Staraya Sil)

STRYJ (now STRYY) DISTRICT4272 UKR
    Stryj (now Stryy)
    Skole (now Skolie

TARNOBRZEG DISTRICT 3767 Poland
    Baranów
    Radomyśl. Sometimes called Radomysl nad Sanem.
    Rozwadów and No records have been found..
    Tarnobrzeg

TARNOPOL (now TERNOPOL) DISTRICT 4175 UKR
    Tarnopol (now Ternopol). Includes towns of Hluboczek,
Kuskowce, Podwołoczyska (see also Skałat district for some years),
Zagrobela.
    Mikulińce (now Mykulyntsi)

TARNÓW DISTRICT 3966 Poland
    Ryglice
    Tarnów
    Tuchów
    Zabno

TŁUMACZ (now TLUMACH) DISTRICT 4474 UKR
    Tłumacz (now Tlumach)
    Chocimirz (now Khotimir)
    Niżniów (now Nizhnev)
    Ottynia (now Otynya)
    Tyśmienica (now Tysmenytsia)
    Uście Zielone (now Ustia Zelene)

TREMBOWLA (now TEREBOVLYA) DISTRICT 4275 UKR
    Trembowla (now Terebovlya)
    Janów (now Janiv)

Strusów (now Stusiv)

TURKA DISTRICT 4370 UKR
    Turka

WADOWICE DISTRICT 4063 Poland
    Andrychów
    Kalwarya
    Wadowice
    Zator

WIELICZKA DISTRICT 4064 Poland
    Wieliczka.
    Podgórze
    Klasno

ZALESZCZYKI (now ZALESHCHIKI) DISTRICT 4575 UKR
    Zaleszczyki (now Zaleshchiki)
    Gródek (now Horodek)
    Korolówka (now Oleyevo Korolevka)
    Tłuste (now Tovste)
    Uścieczko (now Ustechko)

ZBARAZ (now ZBARAZH) DISTRICT 4175 UKR
    Zbaraz (now Zbarazh). Includes records for many town, including Czernichowice, Dobrowody, Klebanówka, Medyń, Obodówka, Romanówka, Terpilówka, Zaluze.

ZLOCZOW (NOW ZOLECHEV) DISTRICT 4074 UKR
    Bialy Kamień (now Belyy Kamen)
    Gołogóry (now Holohory)
    Jezierna (now Ozernyany).
    Olesko (now Olesko)
    Pomorzany (now Pomoryany)
    Sassów (now Sasiv)
    Zborów (now Zboriv)

ZOLKIEW (now ZHOVKA) DISTRICT 3972 UKR
Zolkiew (now Zhovka)
Kulików (now Kulikov)
Mosty Wielki (also called Gross Mosty; now Velikiye Mosty).
Includes towns of Batiatysze, Kupiczwola, Rozanka.

ŻYDACZÓW (now ZYDACHOV) DISTRICT 4272 UKR
Żydaczów (now Zydachov)
Rozdol (now Rozdil)
Żurawno (now Zhuravno)

ŻYWIEC DISTRICT 4063 Poland
Żywiec
Zabłocie

CHAPTER 3

Jewish Vital Records

Historical Overview

This chapter seeks to provide you with information currently known about vital records collected and maintained by Austria during 1772-1918 and by Poland from 1918-1942. The following chapter will address how to gain access to other forms of documents and records.

When the Austrian government, under Josef II, began requiring civil registration of births, marriages and deaths in 1784, responsibility for registration of Jewish events was given to the Catholic Church. Very few records have been found for Jewish events among Church records so it is assumed that compliance was poor. Duplicate records were required, according to the 1784 law, but no duplicates of Jewish records have been located thus far, from this period or any other.

In the years that followed until the publication of the 1877 regulations placing registration in the hands of a Jewish registrar employed by a district *Gemeinde*, some Jewish records were maintained by the Jewish community, but the forms used to record the information and the procedures used to collect and maintain records varied widely, as reflected in the arbitrary manner in which information was documented. While some towns and districts maintained records, others did not. Some communities have records from 1790, while other have no records until 1877, with wide variation in between.

The 1875 legislation was intended to restructure and standardize the collection of Jewish records. An 1877 manual entitled

Führung Der Geburts-, Ehe- und Sterbe-matrikeln für die Israeliten in Galizien, developed by the Austrian justice ministry, set forth official requirements for maintaining vital records in the Jewish communities of Galicia. The manual provided for 73 major administrative districts, most of which were divided into subdistricts. The administrative districts appear to have substantially overlapped with Austrian judicial districts and parish districts, but the Jewish administrative districts, which were created with sensitivity to religious politics, sometimes differed substantially.

As was discussed in chapter one, the official registrar for each main district oversaw the collection and maintenance of all vital records in his district, but might have also responsible for actually documenting vital events that occurred in a subdistrict town, where he lived, as well. Births, marriages and deaths were recorded in separate volumes in the order in which they were recorded. In districts with small Jewish populations, the volumes sometimes covered a number of years. Forms for collecting birth information provided for: documentation of the child's name (although, at some point, the column for the child's surname was eliminated); names, birthplaces and occupations of the parents (including maiden name of mother if she and the father were legally married); date of birth; date and place of circumcision for boys and naming for girls; whether the child was considered legitimate or illegitimate; names of the two witnesses, and the name of the midwife. The last column had space for comments; this space often included relevant genealogical data about the child or family, as well as information about the parents' civil marriage. If the parents were not married under civil law, the last column might provide the father's name and the names of the two witnesses attesting to his acknowledgment of paternity. Occasionally, birth records provide some information about the maternal grandparents.

Marriage records are the most useful since they provide, not only the names of the bride and groom, but their ages or years of birth, where they were born and where they were living at the time of marriage, the occupation of the groom, the names of the parents and their residences and occupations. Some even document that a parent was deceased. The name of the rabbi performing the ceremony and the names of witnesses and other important information is included.

Death records were recorded more haphazardly, despite clear regulations and columns for capturing appropriate information. Death records commonly have missing information and may include nothing more than name, gender, place and date of death, and cause of death. In the death of a woman, the name of the spouse was supposed to be included, but when the couple had not been married under civil law, the spouse was generally missing. She could be listed under her maiden or married name. For some period of time, the names of the parents of the deceased were supposed to be listed, but even when required, this information was often missing, even when the deceased was a young child.

Regulations of 1877

The 1877 regulations governing the collection and maintenance of records included the following:

» Registrars were to be males of Austrian citizenship residing in the district where they were to work. Confirmation of the Gemeinde's nominated candidate was to be made by the governors in Lemberg or Krakau.

» Births or deaths were to be reported

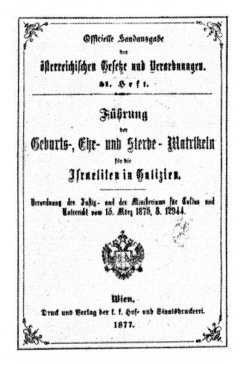

Figure 1. Cover of 1877 regulations for the collection and maintenance of vital records

within eight days of the event. The father was primarily responsible for reporting births, but, in his absence, or if the birth were illegitimate, the midwife or mother was responsible. Stillbirths were required to be reported.

» Rabbis were to report all information about marriages in accordance with legal requirements.

» Those who circumcised boys and who blessed/named girls, as well as the administrators of cemeteries, were required to report their activities to the registrar. Discrepancies in information were to be reported to the authorities. The leader of each *Gemeinde* was to provide the political authorities with the names of all religious supervisors, *mohels* (ritual circumcisers), and synagogue and cemetery administrators.

» Vital records were to be maintained in duplicate. Indexes were to be constructed and maintained in duplicate. Each registry book was to have standard headings in German. In 1877, headings could also be in Polish or Ukrainian (Ruthenian), but this was later changed to just Polish. The regulations provided a sample of the proscribed headings.

» Proof of a civil marriage was to be submitted in order to certify that a child was legitimate. The nature of the proof was to be specifically cited on the birth record. If no documentary proof of marriage was available and the marriage was simply attested to by witnesses, the entry was to read "reportedly married." If the mother had never married or married according to Jewish ritual without complying with legal requirements, the child was to be declared illegitimate.

» If the child was illegitimate, the name of the father could be registered only if the alleged father so declared personally to the registrar, in the presence of a witness, or two witnesses if the registrar did not know him, or if the father had appeared before a notary or court to so declare. If an illegitimate child were later made legitimate through the civil marriage of the parents, the date of the marriage was to be registered. This could occur only if the man acknowledged that he was the father. Even if the father acknowledged paternity, this was not a guarantee that the child would carry the father's surname.

» The registrar was to receive the registry books from the political authorities, with numbered pages and connected by a string. The last page was to list the number of pages, and the end of the string was to be sealed with an official seal.

» Annual compilation of a surname index was mandated. Unfortunately, this mandate was loosely enforced and so many books were not indexed.

Accessing Records Today: Vital Records & Censuses

When *Finding Your Jewish Roots in Galicia: A Resource Guide*, this author's first book about Galicia, was published in 1998, access to records from what had been Galicia, was quite limited. Obtaining vital records was haphazard, very costly and dependent on cooperation from reluctant Polish civil servants in two ministries, one of which oversees the national archival system and the other, which oversees the local records offices that house records less than 100 years old. When Stanley Diamond was confronted with the obstacles in obtaining records from Poland, he put his considerable business and diplomatic skills to work and organized what is now known as Jewish Records Indexing - Poland (JRI-Poland), a 501 (c) 3 nonprofit organization dedicated to facilitating access to Jewish records in Poland.

Diamond's original interest stemmed from his family's genetic disorder. He wanted to locate members of his extended family around the world who might share this disorder in the interest of finding a cure. Although he started by trying to access records from the region of Ostrow Mazowiecka in Poland, he soon understood that thousands of genealogists shared his frustration about lack of access to records all over Poland. In just a few short years, JRI-Poland has dramatically altered access to and understanding of Jewish records. Directed by Stanley and a team of dedicated and highly knowledgeable volunteers, JRI-Poland has fostered cooperative relationships with key people in the two Polish ministries who control access to Jewish vital records.

Diamond and his team made an early decision to focus on Jewish records that had not been filmed by the Mormons. Rather than paying to have records microfilmed, as the Mormons had done, the JRI-Poland team and Polish archival officials settled on projects to have Poles index sets of Jewish records that are housed in the various archival repositories around Poland. As the indices became available online, the Polish officials anticipated that Jews would want to order records, thus increasing their revenue and satisfying a need. Thus, today, JRI-Poland raises money from the genealogical community to support indexing projects. Volunteers within the Jewish genealogy movement, are charged with contacting people who have registered their interest in the town/region on JewishGen's database (JewishGen is the primary online source for Jewish genealogical information). Individuals are advised of the availability of the records, the plan to index the record, and are invited to contribute money to the effort, in exchange for early access to the whole index for the records found in the town. The amount of money needed for the various projects varies by the extent of the material to be indexed and the anticipated number of contributors. When funds are sufficient to begin a project, JRI-Poland arranges for an indexer in Poland to begin work. What the JRI-Poland team, with the support of the Gesher Galicia community, has been able to accomplish, is nothing short of miraculous.

Recently, Jewish censuses for a few towns were found and they have been indexed by JRI-Poland workers. The results are not included in the database until they are 100 years old, but some information may be available on a limited basis to qualified researchers who must sign an agreement not to share information obtained about their families until the data is 100 years old.

Eastern Galicia: Ukraine

A few years after JRI-Poland began its work, Mark Halpern, a long time member and Board member of Gesher Galicia, contacted Stanley Diamond about adding the indexing of the primarily eastern Galician records that were stored in the archives for old records in Warsaw, known as the AGAD (Archiwum Główne Akt Dawnych). The history of how these records happened to find their way to Warsaw after World War II, is outlined below. Fay and Julian Bussgang had cataloged these records in the 1990s. Thus, the members of Gesher Galicia had known for some time that the records were there, but only a handful of people had been fortunate enough to receive records from that collection.

Diamond had been working with this author on accessing Galician records for some time and he was well aware of the records in Warsaw. When Mark Halpern approached Diamond, they quickly moved to contact Polish archival officials about incorporating these into the indexing project. In just a few years, the vast majority of existing records from the Galician records collection in Warsaw have been indexed under what has been titled, the "AGAD Project." For precise information about this project, how to support it, and how to search for and interpret the records, go to www.jewishgen.org/jri-pl/agad/index. Read the research guide and the Frequently Asked Questions (FAQ) and then return to the Home screen. Scroll down to Interpreting Your Galician Vital Records and click on "here" to access a complete interpretation of all known forms of vital records, both pre- and post-1877 throughout Galicia.

Western Galicia: Poland

Meanwhile, JRI-Poland has nearly completed indexing Jewish vital records found in branches of the Polish National Archives system. Only a few districts in either eastern or western Galicia have not attracted sufficient financial support to enable indexing efforts to move forward. As these and other records in Poland become 100 years old, indices to them will be available, and, so, it is anticipated that indexing, and, thus, the need for continual fund raising, will be an ongoing project until the last records of 1942 are indexed.

Some servers do not allow JRI-Poland to be accessed directly. But, since it is hosted on JewishGen, this may be the most direct route for all to use. Go to www.jewishgen.org and find JRI-P in the list of hosted organizations. The Home page will direct you to what you want to know, but you will need to view the AGAD section cited above to see "Interpreting Your Galician Vital Records."

The JRI-Poland system permits users to know what has been found among the vital records and facilitates ordering a copy of the original entry. There are ordering instructions within the JRI-Poland website and the system really works remarkably well, at a very reasonable price that is comparable to ordering records from North American or other European countries. Each record includes location information that is used when ordering to ensure that you receive the correct record. Although the information contained in the index provides a few pieces of information, the full record, particularly for births and marriages, is likely to yield additional information.

With the cooperation of some directors of local records offices (Urząd Stanu Cywilnego or USC), The JRI-Poland indexing effort has recently been extended to include some records that are less than 100 years old and stored in USCs. Unfortunately, not all of the directors of these offices around the country have agreed to cooperate, and because of the way Poland is politically organized, they can not be compelled to cooperate. However, in any event, because of privacy restrictions that pertain to records less than 100 years old, any indices from USC records will not be available to the general public until they are 100 years old. Under the agreement with the Polish Ministry of Justice, JRI-P is authorized to release some limited information to qualified supporters.

What Records Exist Today?

You are strongly advised to begin your research for records in Poland or Ukraine with a search for what is available for your towns and districts in Miriam Weiner's Routes to Roots website: http://www.rtrfoundation.org. Routes to Roots lists, not only vital records, but other types of documentation when it is available. Weiner's site summarizes official information, in English, from both the Polish and Ukrainian governments. She obtained her information directly from officials in those countries and updates the site, as new inventories uncover newly available records, both vital and otherwise and both less than 100 years old and more than 100 years old. Beginning your search with Weiner's site will tell you at a glance whether relevant records survived. If they did and they are in Poland, then JRI-Poland's site is the next step for you. If they survived and they are in Ukraine, Weiner's site will provide specific guidance as to how to access the information. Although Weiner has published wonderfully illustrated books summarizing the data on her website, the information in the books is not as current as the website. Further information about the books, *Jewish Roots in Poland: Pages from the Past and Archival Inventories* and its counterpart for Ukraine, will be included in Chapter 5.

Fate of Eastern Galician Jewish Records

When Poland became an independent country at the end of World War I, Poland was given all of what had been western Galicia, but the eastern boundaries of Poland were not settled without continuing armed conflict between Poland and Russia. When the dust settled, the 1921 Treaty of Riga gave Poland virtually all of what had been Galicia. After World War II, with Ukraine and Poland under Soviet control, Poland negotiated an exchange of records with the Soviet government to have records created in what had been Poland, transferred to their custody. In the 1960s, this negotiation resulted in Poland being given vital records from the districts that had once been eastern Galicia. These records had been stored in the archives in L'viv (once Lemberg). Known as the Zabużański Collection (*zabużański* means "other side of the River Bug," which separates Poland from Ukraine), this collection was deposited in two archives in Warsaw. The older records, those over 100 years old, are housed in the repository for old records called AGAD, while the records less than 100 years old, are stored in the Warsaw city archives (Archiwum Akt Nowych), along with records from Warsaw. Records are moved from AGAD to the AAN as they age.

Regardless of the agreement's intent, we now know that not all records from Eastern Galicia were transferred in this exchange. Researchers have found that records, both vital and communal, remain in Lviv. Chapter 4 covers what is known about the existence of communal records due to the above-mentioned efforts of the Bussgangs and Alexander Kronich, who cataloged the Jewish records in Lviv. Unfortunately, no equivalent effort such as JRI-Poland has been organized to accomplish a similar outcome in Ukraine and, even if such an effort were to be attempted, it is unlikely that it would be successful in the near future.

The Zabużański Collection in Warsaw includes banns published before marriage, birth records that were entered late, birth certificates from Israelite Rabbinical Offices kept in connection with establishing patrimony, correspondence with administrative offices and private persons, books listing members of various *Gemeindes* and other organizations, evidence of disbursements to the poor, documents of activities, communal statutes, and books documenting the income and expenses of deceased persons. This material is not being indexed by Jewish Records Indexing-Poland. You may request permission to research the materials in person or to employ a professional researcher in your place by writing to the addresses below. It is best to have the letter typewritten in Polish. You will receive a response in Polish.

For information about material less than 100 years old:
    Urząd Stanu Cywilnego-Warszawa Srodmiescie
    Archiwum Akt Zabużańskich
    ul. Jezuicka 1/3,
    00-281 Warszawa, Poland

For information about material more than 100 years old:
    Archiwum Główne Akt Dawnych
    ul. Długa 7
    00-263 Warszawa, Poland

Not all eastern Galician vital records were transferred into the Zabużański Collection. Some older vital and communal records remain in the main archives in L'viv, along with some school, *Gemeinde*, and other types of community records, such as those for Zionist and other communal organizations. There are also old vital records from a few western Galician districts or towns, such as Jaworów and Tyczyn. At this writing, the main Archive in L'viv, Ukraine is closed to visitors and requests for research are also suspended so that the archivists can complete a complete inventory of their holdings. The Archive should reopen sometime in 2006. At that time, both individuals and professional researchers will be able to visit the Archive under much tighter security guidelines than previously existed. When the Archives in L'viv reopens, you may visit there to research in person or hire a private researcher to assist you. New guidelines have not been published but, under the old guidelines, one had to notify the archival officials in advance. The name and address of the main L'viv Archives is:

Tsentral'n yi Derzhavnyi Istoryehnyi Archivum L'vovi
290004 Lviv 4, Ukraine
pl. Vozz'iednannia 3'a.

Although it is not necessary for you to know the current name and spelling of your town in Eastern Galicia for the purposes of accessing vital records, you may want to learn this information for travel and other reasons. After Eastern Galicia came under Soviet rule following World War II, many town names were changed. Additional town names have changed since Ukraine declared its independence. Peter Zavon, a long time member of Gesher Galicia and the person responsible for publishing the SIG's annual membership directory, has compiled a list of current names of some towns in the former eastern part of Galicia. This listing is available to members who receive the directory and on the Gesher Galicia website within JewishGen (under Special Interest Groups). Consulting post WWII maps will probably require you to be familiar with the Cyrillic alphabet, but maps created before then will generally show your towns in our alphabet.

Fate of Western Galician Jewish Records

Western Galician records have not fared as well as those from the eastern Galician districts. Western Galicia was on the front line of attack from German forces in World War I and again in

World War II. In this region, many synagogues, where Jewish records were often stored, were deliberately burned (sometimes along with the town's Jews) or were destroyed in the course of the fierce fighting that raged throughout the area. Postwar fighting in this region, after World War I and again after World War II, between the Poles and Russians, further damaged towns and the records that were located there.

Just after the end of World War II, Polish archival officials grappled with the issue of what to do with surviving Jewish vital records. This author's visit to Poland in 1986 uncovered evidence that between 1948 and 1968, vital records were collected and moved a number of times. In 1968, Polish anti-Semitism again surfaced, and the small number of Jews who remained in Poland found themselves thrown out of jobs and subject to both official and unofficial persecution. Sometime in that period, Jewish vital records were to be redistributed to the appropriate branch of the state archival system. In the course of these moves and in light of the various war-related catastrophes, records from many districts and subdistricts either did not survive or have not been located. Just recently, some records, long thought to have been missing, along with some census records for those places, were discovered and they are targeted for indexing by JRI-Poland.

Records less than 100 years old: The *Urząd Stanu Cywilnego* (USC), civil registration offices, are administered by the Polish Ministry of Justice which oversees the various administrative districts within Poland called powiats. In general, these records are difficult to access, even in person. It is best to request information in writing since privacy laws prevent public access and you may be asked to submit documentation proving your relationship to the individual of interest and the death of the person. The document you receive will be on a form which selectively provides demographic information but does not give you a copy of the record.

You can expect that the USC will send the results of its research via Warsaw to the Polish consulate closest to you. The consulate will write to you in your language and ask for a fee of (currently) $35 per record to release the information. The fee is owed whether or not the record is found. When the consulate receives payment, you will receive the communication from the UCS in Polish. The address below will serve for all towns unless there are multiple towns of the same name. In that case, be sure to list the current powiat where the town is located, which you can find in the official Polish website.

Urzad Stanu Cywilnego
Name of town, Poland

Records more than 100 years old: Polish statute requires that when vital records are 100 years old, they are to be transferred to the Polish state archives branch covering their district. The state archival system is under a different ministry and administrative system from the USCs. If you find information about surviving records in Miriam Weiner's Routes to Roots website cited above, check with JRI-Poland's site to determine if surviving records have been indexed. The end of this chapter lists the few western Galician sets of records that have been filmed by the Mormons. Stanley Diamond announced at a regional Gesher Galicia meeting in November, 2005 that it appeared that JRI-Poland has identified all of the records in state archives brances that house Galician records. However, in December, 2005, Mark Halpern announced that new records have been found in the Kraków Archives and its branches in Bochnia, Nowy Sącz and Nowy Targ. This development offers hope that yet more records will be found in the future. If you believe that old vital records have survived, and you do not find them in JRI-Poland's listing of records either completed or in progress, you can contact JRI-Poland to inquire if JRI-Poland is aware of the records and has plans to index them.

Considerations for Interpreting Vital Records

Vital records created before 1877, may be on Latin-language forms, on forms written in old German script, or on any form that was made up by the local parish or political district. Following the 1877 publication of regulations for carrying out the 1875 law governing the collection of Jewish vital records, all forms were to be standardized.

The records were collected and maintained in very large bound volumes. Events for marriages, births and deaths were kept in separate books. This system continued throughout Austrian rule over Galicia and then in the interwar years, by Poland, until 1942 or 1943. In 1877, the forms were in both German and Polish or German and Ruthenian/Ukrainian, though the handwritten entries were in Polish, sometimes with signatures of witnesses in Hebrew, Yiddish or, very occasionally, the Cyrillic alphabet in eastern Galicia. On the off-chance that you do encounter Cyrillic, there are a few things that you will need to know. Ukrainian is similar linguistically to Russian. Both are written in the Cyrillic alphabet. Thus, when translated into languages in the Roman alphabet, some adjustments must be made. For instance, the equivalent of *H* does not exist in the Cyrillic alphabet. Generally, the letter for *G* is substituted, but this is not always the case. The Roman letter *J* sometimes becomes the Cyrillic alphabet equivalents of *Y* or *O*..

Franz Josef much later decided to punish the pesky, restless and intensely nationalist Ruthenians by prohibiting the use of their language for any official purpose, including school instruction. Except for the fact that the forms were all in Polish, inter-war Poland seemed to have retained the Austrian system for collecting Jewish vital information. The columnar format remained in use until the collection of Jewish records ended. The exception is the records for Kraków that are in the narrative style that Napoleon introduced in Europe. The format of the column headings changed very little over time. For instance, birth records were organized as follows:

Column 1. Number of the record in the book. Events were recorded in the order in which they were reported.

Column 2. Date of birth. This is often written out in the Polish words for the months and days.

Column 3. Date of *brit milah* (circumcision) or naming, in the case of a female child.

Column 4. Name of child.

Column 5. Whether civilly married or not married (not married is *nieślubny*).

Column 6. Name of father, place of birth, occupation.

Column 7. Name of mother, place of birth, names of parents.

Column 8. Witness.

Column 9. Name of *mohel* (circumciser) for a male child.

Column 10. Name of midwife, nurse or doctor.

Column 11. Stillborn children.

Column 12. Remarks. Headed *Anmerkung* in German and *Uwaga* in Polish, this column was used for remarks and/or for signatures attesting to the fact that the father had acknowledged paternity in the company of two witnesses when the parents were not married under civil law, or for noting when a civil marriage had taken place, thus legitimizing the child. Sometimes the individual petitioned to have a surname changed even in the absence of a civil marriage of the parents and this is also noted in this column. In fact, this seems to be the only place that such name changes were recorded.

It is important to note the house number where the family lived, since this information may help build a record of who lived in a particular household. The placement of the house number on the forms changed from time to time. Seek the words *Ort u. haus N.* (German) or *miejsce i dom* (Polish). In small towns, houses were given numbers; in larger communities, you may find street names. Sometimes the house number is in the far left column, and sometimes in the column after the year (*jahr* in German, *rok* in Polish) of the event. Mark Halpern has noted that communities using the house number system did not necessarily mean that house numbers were assigned in any systematic way. It was often the result of a more random assignment process, so that one can not assume that people who lived in houses #4 and #5 were neighbors.

A few other observations, based on recent experience with records from numerous districts. Because individuals were assigned to a Gemeinde, but may have lived elsewhere, they had to register vital events in the place where they resided and the place where they held membership. If husband and wife were members of two different Gemeindes and lived in a third place, presumably birth would have to be registered in all three places.

While this probably didn't always occur, examination of JRI-Poland indices have revealed that, in fact, events were often registered in multiple places. This means that, when you are searching the JRI-Poland database for a surname, consider including all of Galicia in the search to be certain that you haven't overlooked anything. Sometimes you will have to order the record to make a more definitive determination about relevance of an individual record.

For examples of records, and more detailed discussion about the format and interpretation of records, please consult Appendix C.

Holdings of the LDS (Mormon) Family History Library

The Family History Library (FHL) of the Church of Jesus Christ of Latter-Day Saints (otherwise called Mormons), hold very few Jewish records from western Galicia and only one set of old death records from Lemberg. To order the microfilms listed below, go to your nearest Family History Center, usually housed within a parish church or stake of the LDS, and request assistance with obtaining the correct microfilm from Salt Lake City. There is a charge for ordering films and there is generally a wait of 2-3 weeks. Of course, if you visit the main facility in Salt Lake City, you can view the films and more within minutes.

Please note that, although the FHL has a substantial number of microfilms from Poland from districts in western Galicia, this author has confirmed that only the films below contain Jewish records.

A few cautionary notes: Kraków's early records do not list surnames so that their usefulness is limited. Moreover, these early vital records were in narrative format, more similar to Russian records than those of Austria. See the relevant appendix for more about the city's history and its records.

FHL microfilms containing Jewish records for Galicia are almost all within the modern Polish *powiats* of Kraków and Rzeszów, shown in both the FHL catalog and the list below as

KR and RZ, respectively. The exception is the film for 1814-1837 births for Lemberg (LW), now in Ukraine.

The list below shows the record type, followed by the year(s) covered, followed by the microfilm number. B=births; M=marriages; D=deaths. Where a microfilm number is followed by a number in parentheses, the numbers refer to the item number on the film (some microfilms include multiple types of data. For example, the first entry in the list shows that, for the subdistrict of Biecz, the FHL has records of births, 1850-1867 and deaths, 1851-1868, respectively, both on microfilm #718,912, Items 1 & 2.

Biecz (RZ)
      B: 1850–67; D: 1851–68, #718,912 (items 1–2)
Brzesko (KR)
B: 1849–86; D: 1863–76, #948,419
Krakau (listed as Kraków) (KR)
B: 1798–1819; D: 1816–19, #718,912
B: 1820–29, #718,913
B: 1830–36; D: 1848–54, #718,914
B: 1837–43, #718,915
B: 1844–50, #718,916
B: 1851–55, #718,917
M: 1798–1816, #718,918
M: 1817–38, #718,919
M: 1830–39, #718,920
M: 1840–52, #718,921
D: 1811/28, #718,922
D: 1829–38, #718,923
D: 1839–47, #718,924
      B: 1874–76, #1,201,162
BDM: 1876–77, #1,201,163
BDM: 1877 index, #1,201,164
Leżajsk (RZ)
D: 1826–66, #766,021 (item 8)
Lemberg is listed as Lwów (LW)
B: 1814–37, #905,274
  Pruchnik (RZ)
B: 1834–70, #766,039 (item 13)

Tarnów (KR)

    B: 1808–10; 1815–49; D: 1808–55, #742,702

B: 1849–63; D: index, 1863–70, #948,420

B: 1863–70, #948,421

M: 1849–70; D: 1855–70, #948,422

Wadowice (KR)

M: 1877–1929, #127,748

Wisnicz (KR)

    B: 1814–59; M: 1827–70, #936,648 (items 4–6)

CHAPTER 4

Researching Other Than Vital Records

Strategies for Researching Other Than Vital Records

In the years since the demise of the Soviet Union, Jewish genealogists have witnessed much improvement in access to records and to the attitudes of archival officials, some of whom have even been featured speakers at annual Jewish genealogical gatherings. To improve your chances of finding information in records other than vital records, it is important to understand why these records were created and what they might reveal.

First, there are ancient documents, mostly housed in the AGAD in Warsaw, that document royal invitations to and authorizations for Jews to settle in Poland, real property holdings and other such official documents. These are interesting but not useful genealogically.

Another group of records are those collected and maintained by noble families. Some of these documents are in government archives but most are in private hands. Jewish genealogists have only recently begun to investigate these records so there is much that is not known about them. However, there is correspondence and documentation of tax collections, contracts or arendas made between the gentry and Jews (and, perhaps, others) for the use of the land or its products and probably genealogically interesting information for the descendants of these families. Contracts involving land had to be approved by the civil government and much of that type of documentation has survived. The Central Archives for the History of the Jewish People in Jerusalem has some arendas on microfilm. The collection is extremely uneven, but examples of the forms and language used are useful as background and for those who find family members mentioned in the documents, they can be exciting genealogical finds.

There were Gemeinde records generated for the purpose of voting, membership, cemetery ownership, taxes and organizational minutes. However, it appears that very little of that material for western Galicia has been found at this writing. Surviving material for eastern Galicia is in the main Archive of Lviv. The little that has survived, or shall we say, surfaced, from western Poland is in various archival repositories and has been microfilmed for the Central Archives for the History of the Jewish People in Jerusalem.

School records are fairly available since Austria mandated universal education. Children had to be registered and proof of their births had to be presented. There are lists of students by grade and at graduation from various levels. There are some lists of children who received awards.

Everyone who lived in Galicia needed to have documents proving their identities. Prior to the invention of electronic copiers, the task of making copies for official purposes was given to notaries. Notaries, who were licensed by the government, played a very important role in providing copies of documents for a great variety of purposes, including travel, business licenses, educational registration, estate matters and so on. They charged for their services. Some of the books generated by these notaries have survived.

Censuses were conducted periodically early in Austria's rule over Galicia and then settled into every 10 years. It appears that the latter censuses were conducted by employees of the Gemeinde since only Jews were listed on the surviving censuses.

Then there was the matter of business licenses and taxes. There were several classes of businesses. The lowest levels of trade did not require licenses, but professionals and businesses with locations had to be licensed. Applications and records of fee and tax payments may be of interest to genealogists.

The rest of this chapter further describes these various forms of documentation and what is known about accessing them. Since we are dealing with two different countries, there will be some differences in the strategies employed to gain access.

Poland

Poland now has an excellent website for its national archives system: http://www.archiwa.gov.pl//mapa/index.Eng.html. www.archiva.gov.pl. This website is useful for getting a good overview of the archival system, obtaining specific hours, name of the manager of the office and a listing, in English, of the holdings. The relevant archives for western Galicia in Poland are in Kraków, Przemyśl and Rzeszów. Kraków and Rzeszów have branch archives within their regions. Some of the regional archives in the system specialize in certain types of records or maps. For example, the regional branch in Przemyśl houses a substantial collection of 2500 cadastre maps, which are maps that pinpoint land or property ownership in a city, town or rural area. The same Archive houses most of the surviving notary records for Galicia. Kraków houses material that focuses on that city's activities, but also has material pertaining to surrounding communities. Magnate records, those of the landowning nobility are variously housed in governmental and specialized private and public repositories.

Ukraine

Ukraine also has a website that provides similar information about its national archival system: www.archives.gov.us/Eng/. The difference between Poland and Ukraine with respect to records about Jews is that after World War II, Ukraine collected virtually all Jewish records that were created prior to 1942, and sent them to the main archives in what was then Lvóv and is now Lviv. The exception would be non-Jewish school records and civil court records, which, when they survived, presumably remain in their local repositories. There is some limited information in Ivano-Frankivsk (formerly Stanislawów) that is described later in this chapter.

Additionally, local town halls and museums house various types of local records that may be of significance to you.

Contacting Local Government

Some researchers have found information by writing to the town's mayor or local history museum, which most towns of any size seem to have. To ensure that your letter will be read, you should send this letter in typewritten Polish or Ukrainian, depending on where your community of interest is located today. These sources of information are often overlooked. In your letter, consider asking for help in finding a researcher or someone well versed in local history who can become your onsite aide in obtaining information—or even someone who will photograph cemeteries and buildings of significance to you.

JewishGen and other Websites

The most important website for Jewish genealogists is JewishGen at www.jewishgen.org because this site has become the main collection point for Jewish family research results, databases, specific hosted family sites, hosted town sites and dialogue. There are other sites, some done by individuals about their families and a large number of sites dedicated to historical and genealogical matters pertaining to both Poland and Ukraine. Typing in those words, with the addition of Austria-Hungary and Galicia - Jewish, will connect you to an amazing world of relevant and irrelevant information. Websites done by organizations which primarily serve a non-Jewish audience should be viewed but with the caveat that you carefully filter information that may not be pertinent to the Jews of Galicia.

Getting back to JewishGen. There is simply nothing that compares to it for Jewish family historians in either comprehensiveness, relevance or accessibility. You can register the surnames and towns that you are researching, find others with similar surnames and towns, jump around from place to place to sample the many links and sites within JewishGen, such as cemetery information and the ShtetlShleppers travel service. And, you can also sign up for the Gesher Galicia discussion group and share information and get assistance with a host of stumbling blocks, including help with reading and interpreting whole documents or words, identifying individuals in photos, understanding more about your ancestor's occupation, translating the disease that your great grandfather died from, and so on. While there are other organizations that host Jewish conversation and information, nothing begins to compete with JewishGen.

JewishGen hosts the Yizkor Book Project, which seeks to raise funds to translate the many books that were created by survivors of towns and regions after World War II. Such books are still being published, though, now, often by the children of survivors. Most of the books were published in Israel or South America and are written in all Yiddish, all Hebrew or a combination of those languages, sometimes with English sections. For many years, English speaking genealogists were frustrated at their inability to access the important information contained with in these books. Joyce Field, one of hundreds of volunteers with JewishGen, is coordinating the effort to finance the translation of these books. Just as with JRI-Poland, people with an interest in the town or region are asked to contribute financially to these efforts. Meanwhile, the number of people who are comfortable with Yiddish and English is dwindling so there is a real sense of pressure to make headway on this project. The project information on JewishGen is updated frequently so that users can see what has been done, what is in progress, and what is yet to be done.

The site reflects considerable respect for the Special Interest Groups and the valuable role that they have come to play among Jewish genealogists. Consequently, when records become available, whether they are vital records or of other types, volunteers find it easy to make connections to help each other create databases and incorporate the information into the structure of JewishGen. JewishGen hosts a number of websites that have been developed by individuals/families and town leaders. The quality of the town and regional sites vary widely but, typically, they include photos, something about the history of the Jewish community, lists of Jewish residents that may have been translated, travel stories and recollections by Holocaust survivors. As an example, the Bukowsko town site includes the portion of the Sanok yizkor book that was translated by the Yizkor Book Project, that covers Bukowsko. Though the services are free, JewishGen is a nonprofit organization that requires and deserves major support donations from its users.

JewishGen is linked to other sites. For instance, when you are in Shtetlinks, you can link to information that is on the Internet about your ancestral town. Most of those sites, pertinent to Galicia, are accessible through the Gesher Galicia site, but you might want to browse the Internet for a surname or geographic designation. Among the best sites is http://www.haruth.com. This website includes a hosted site that appears to have been abandoned about 4 years ago. It is about the small, but religiously important, town of Bircza in western Galicia. The site includes photos of the town and what had been the synagogue but is now the priest's house as well as a list of people in a pre-1941 phone directory, names in the 1923 business directory, survivors from the town and recollections of one of those survivors. Haruth.com also hosts a number of other, more active town sites with links to JewishGen: Kańczuga, Łancut, Gorlice, Lubasz w, Ulan w, Brody, Dębica, Kraków, Rzeszów, Żmigród, Dukla, Krosno, Strzyz w, Żołynia, Frysztak, Tarnobrzeg, Zolochów and Wojnilów.

Rootsweb.com has a Jewish mailing list for those researching ancestry in Galicia. Polishroots.org and maxpages.com are sites that link to various Polish organizations that, while not specifically Jewish, can provide some articles of interest and some additional geographic resources. Maxpages.com does have a whole section on Jewish information and linkages. Incidentally, maxpages.com includes a list of microfiches from Avotaynu that may look enticing but that company is no longer in the microfiche business.

Additionally, there are specific family websites that stand alone and websites for a few non-Jewish organizations, such as the Federation of Eastern European Family History Societies (FEEFHS) which has active Jewish participation at its conferences and in its publications. FEEFHS website address: www. feefhs.com.

Gesher Galicia members have formed a number of subgroups

for intense focus on specific town as well as regional research. Each subgroup has volunteer leaders who are responsible for coordinating information and research activities for that town or region. You can find out more about these subgroups on the Gesher Galicia website: http://www.JewishGen.org/galicia/

Galician Census Documents

For many years, genealogists hoped that the original census documents would be found in Vienna or in an archive in Poland or Ukraine. In the Winter 1993 issue of Avotaynu, George Bolotenko and Lawrence Tapper reported on their visit to five archival institutions in Lviv. Orest Matsiuk, director of the Ukrainian Central State Historical Archives, showed them through the vault in which Jewish records are preserved. Boletenko and Tapper saw hundreds of records, including Jewish town records of Lwów from the 1700s that appear to be census-like records, according to their description:

> Additionally, there are censuses of Galicia from the 18th and 19th centuries. In the basement storage areas . . . a number of Torahs are kept on top of a tall bookcase, under cover. There are no rollers, just fragments of old Torahs. We also saw record books dating back hundreds of years. Many of these books are so bulky and heavy that they require several people to handle them. We were allowed to photograph everything.

This author contacted authorities in Vienna and the response was disheartening. Austrian law did not require that the original censuses be retained after statistical compilations were completed and published. This meant that the chances of finding other than the handful of surviving censuses was dim. This seemed to be confirmed, as the years went on with few significant findings.

However, recently, census documents have, indeed, been found for several western Galician towns. The hope of finding more is not encouraging since all of the archival repositories that might have held them maintain that they have completed inventories of their holdings. However, some hope exists that additional censuses will surface in the future. The censuses for towns listed below, have been indexed through JRI-Poland. All will eventually be part of the database. The type of information collected in the censuses seemed to vary little. This author has reviewed Jewish censuses from 1869/70 to 1910 and they all list, at a minimum, the number of the people in the household; the name of the head of household and the people living in the residence with their relationships to the head; the gender; the age or year of birth; the birthplace; and, the religious denomination; marital status; and, the Gemeinde to which the person belonged. For Łancut, the 1910 census provides the only available window into the Jewish population in that period, because the vital records for the district were destroyed in a fire.

However, with respect to Sanok, it is interesting that the surnames appearing in the vital records do not match up well with the families listed in the census. Why this is the case, is not clear at this writing. The vital records in the JRI-Poland database appear to have been recreated in the 1920s and 1930s and submitted to Lwów considerably after the fact of the actual events. In any event, there are families that appear in the census that do not appear in the vital records and vice versa.

The following censuses have been recently found:

Brzózow, Poland: 1869, 1880, 1890, and 1900
Kraków, Poland: 1850, 1857, 1870, 1881, 1890, 1900 and 1910
Łancut, Poland: 1910
Nowy Targ, Poland: 1870 and 1880
Podgórze, Poland: 1870, 1880, 1890, 1900 and 1910
Rzeszów, Poland: 1870 and 1910
Sanok, Poland: 1900
Tarnobrzeg: 1772

Tarnopol (Ukraine) censuses for 1890 and 1910 are in the Lviv Archives and, at the moment, there is no plan for them to be microfilmed so the 1890 must be researched in person and it should be kept in mind that the 1910 will not be available for research until 2010, though it is possible that special permission might be obtained to gain access to it by a qualified researcher. Mark Halpern was fortunate in having a researcher locate his family in those records. A copy of a page with an translation of the columns appears here.

Some active members of Gesher Galicia contacted me to tell me that they had copies of censuses in their possession. Israel Pickholtz, for example, has 1801, 1819, and 1826 census records for Rozdol. He is willing to do some research for individuals, within limits. His email address: IsraelP@pikholz.org.

In mid-2004, Moishe Miller received word from Arthur Szyndler at the Centrum Żydowski that censuses for the city of Oświęcim (where Auschwitz was located), for 1880, 1890, 1900 and 1910. There are passport records, including photographs. These records are housed at the branch of the State Archives in Katowice (Archiwum Panstwowe w katowicach) which can be contacted through the Polish Archives website: http://www.archiwa. gov.pl . Select Oświęcim and locate Fond No. 26 Akta Miasta Oświęcimia. You will not have access, online, to the censuses, but you can see (in Polish) what is more is available. Mr. Szyndler might be persuaded to conduct some private research. He can be contacted at:

Centrum Żydowskie (Auschwitz Jewish Center)
Pl. ks. J. Skarbka 5
32-600 Oświęcim
Poland
email: szyndler@ajcf.pl
Tel: +48/33/844-70-02
Fax: +48/33/844-70-03

Geoffrey Weisgard, who authored the article about Kraków in Appendix E, viewed the 1795 German-language census of Kazimierz (the ancient Jewish suburb of Kraków), at the Central Archives for the History of the Jewish People in Jerusalem, as well as the regional archives in Kraków. The less-detailed 1790 census of Kazimierz is also at the Kraków regional archives. Weisgard believes that the 1787 census of Kazimierz, conducted by the Catholic Church, is held at the archives of the Bishop of Kraków. This has not been confirmed by this author.

Fay Bussgang wrote an excellent article for *Avotaynu* (Vol. XII, No. 2, Summer 1996) that sheds light on related records in the Kraków regional archive. She described finding records called *spis mieszkanców* (list of residents), kept by many Polish municipalities, that show the members of a household, date and place of birth, names of parents, religion and occupation, among other information. She wrote that the list seems to have included notations of arrivals, departures, deaths, marriages and other information. She saw *spis mieszkanców* records from 1921. No such Austrian records are known to exist. To research these *spis mieszkanców* records by mail, Bussgang's article indicated that one needs permission from the Polish National Archives (write to Naczelna Dyreckcja Archiwow Państwowych; ul. Długa 6; skr. pocz. 1005; 00-950 Warszawa). However, if visiting Kraków, one can view the indexes without such permission at the regional archive located at ul. Sienna 16, Monday–Thursday, 9 a.m.–2 p.m. and 4–7 p.m.; Friday 9 a.m.–1 p.m. Bussgang's Avotaynu article offers tips on using the index.

Deborah Raff, who had family from Bukowko ("Bukowsk") in western Galicia, has been instrumental in creating a website with information about the community. The website can be found in the ShtetlFinders section of JewishGen. Debbie reported seeing an unusual document from the *Spis Parafialny* (church census) which listed the residents, Jewish and non-Jewish, of the community and the surrounding area. While it is not dated, Debbie feels certain that it was created before World War II. It was probably created in the interwar years since some of the names are also mentioned in the Bukowsko chapter in the Sanok *yizkor* book. The list, which was translated by Deborah Greenlee, provides a house number (sometimes two numbers, one for an old number and the current number), the name of the householder and a column for notes.

Because it was Austrian practice to destroy original census documents after summarizing the data, few of those documents

house # apt.#   name   year of birth gender   place of birth Gemeinde occupation

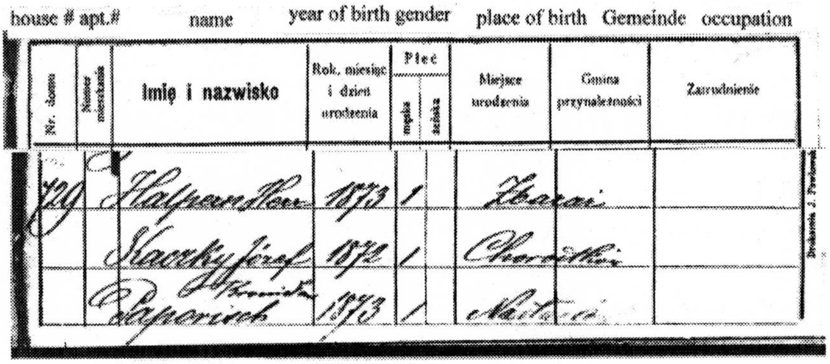

Nr. domu	Numer mieszkania	Imię i nazwisko	Rok, miesiąc i dzień urodzenia	Płeć		Miejsce urodzenia	Gmina przynależności	Zatrudnienie
				męski	żeński			
729		Halpern Herz	1873	1		Zbaraż		
		Stacky Józef	1872	1		Chorostkó		
		Chaporisch	1873	1		Narajó		

Figure 2. Example of an original 1890 Jewish census sheet, Tarnopol

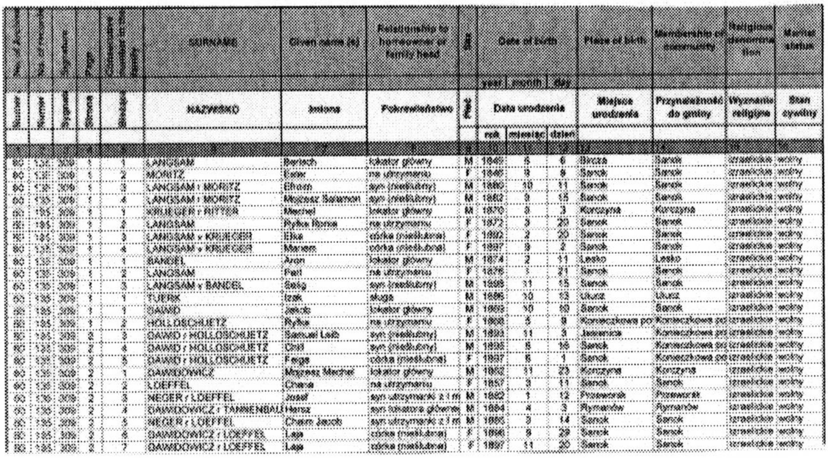

Figure 3. Example of JRI-Poland index to census records,
1900 Jewish Census of Sanok

survived. However, after each census was taken, the Austrian government compiled extensive statistical information about what the
census had revealed. These statistical compilations exist today.
One such compilation was found by Louis Goldman. It was a
German reprint of a book summarizing the 1869 census of Galicia,
*Orts-Reportorium des Konigreiches Galizien und Lodomerien mit dem
Grossherzogthume Krakau* (1874). The census listing included the
number of houses, the number of males, the number of females
and the total inhabitants. The census figures were taken from the
k.k. statistischen Central-Commission. The reprint was published
in 1989 by Helmut Scherer Verlag GmbH Berlin, 1000 Berlin,
Boothstr. 21a (ISBN 3-89433-015-3). The phone number listed
on the title page was 030/773 80 12. Georgetown University
Library in Washington, D.C. has a copy of the original book.

    Pinkas Hakehillot: Poland, vol. 3 (Jerusalem: Yad Vashem, 1984)
provides, among other information, census data for Galician towns.
Although there is some inconsistency with respect to dates, population data are provided for 1563, 1678, 1765, 1808, 1865, 1880,
1890, 1900, 1910 and 1921.

    *The Blackbook of Localities Whose Jewish Population Was
Exterminated by the Nazis* (Jerusalem: Yad Vashem, 1965) offers
1931 summary census data about Jews. However, this source
appears to be of questionable accuracy, since population figures
are sometimes much lower than those indicated in certain *yizkor*
books.

Josephine and Franciscan Maps

    Josephine Metries were maps created by Austria in 1800 and,
revised in 1815, as Franciscan Metries, for purposes of taxing
property owners. Properties were laid out along town streets.
The number assigned to the house/building and the name of
the owner were listed by house number on the map. The house
numbers are those seen in identifying documents from that period
since only a very few large cities used street names. Then, as time
went on, updates were made of these maps. Members of Gesher
Galicia are only beginning to focus on these maps, where they can
be found and how to use them effectively.

The author of this book was given a map from the town of Rymanów but it is undated and the it is not clear if the accompanying list of people by house number refers to the owner or the person actually living there.

Notary Records

The record books of notaries records can be useful for genealogical information. Our ancestors and their governments once relied on notaries to make exact copies. Thus, when someone wanted a passport to travel outside the country or needed to prove one's identity for marriage, school or another official purpose, hiring a notary was the most common method of having copies made. Because notaries were licensed by the government, their records were technically the property of the government. While not all records were collected and stored in archival repositories, some 19th and 20th century notary records survived and are housed in the regional archives in Przemyśl.

However, notary records are covered under privacy laws administered by the Ministry of Justice, which means that you must provide proof that you are descended from the person discussed in the record. If there is a possibility that the person could still be alive, you will also be asked for proof that the person has died.

Apparently, competition for the role of a government licensed notary must have been stiff, because in 1855, the Austrian government issued a ban on Jews becoming notaries. This ban, presumably, continued until emancipation lifted all occupational restrictions.

Richard Schwarzstein succeeded in obtaining notary records from Przemyśl for residents of Nisko and Ulanów. After following their instructions exactly, he received word from the archivists that they had spent five hours in research at $15 per hour and had located several documents. Upon payment, he received good reproductions of the documents. One document related to the transfer of title to the family home, while another related to his great-grandmother's family business.

There are two excellent source of specific information about notary records, by town. One is Miriam Weiner's Routes to Roots

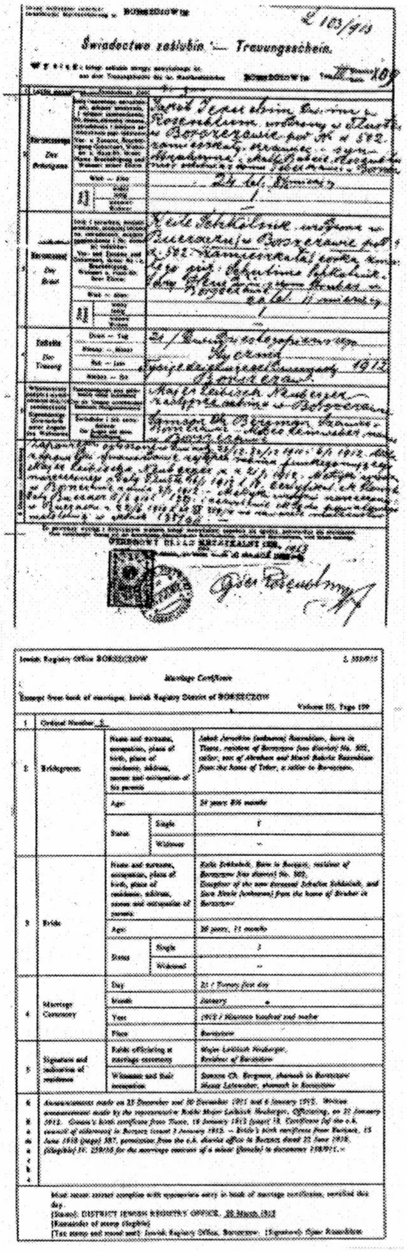

Figure 4. Example of notarized document: original and translation of marriage record.

Foundation online and the other is the website for the Polish national archival system listed above. The website does not describe the limitations on the notary records. These records can not be researched in person.

School Records

School records are also good sources of information. They can, generally, be found in town archives, as well as national archives, in Poland and Ukraine. Miriam Weiner includes school records in her books on records from Poland and Ukraine, as well as her website: http://www.rtrfoundation.org. An example of the types of records that may be available, is illustrated by what Alexander Dunai, a professional researcher who lives in L'viv, discovered in the L'viv archives:

» School year certificates of primary school pupils, Galicia, 1874–1920
» School year certificates of teacher college students, Galicia, 1894–1920

» School year certificates, state secondary schools, Lemberg 1894–1920

» School year certificates, state secondary schools, Galicia, 1871–1920 (only letters B-K and L-Z)

» Documents from Jewish primary school, Lviv, 1881 and 1903 school year certificates, lists of pupils, etc.; some documents have photos.

In the Rzeszów Archives:

» Documents of Jewish private primary school, lists of teachers, 1832–39

» Documents of secondary school, list of pupils, 1879

» Documents of secondary school, list of teachers, 1919–20

» Documents of state secondary school, list of teachers, 1918

» Documents of secondary school, list of pupils, 1836

» Documents of secondary school, 1891–1904

Military Records

[David Fox, Ellen Sadove Renck, Ada Greenblatt and Barbara Urbanska-Yeager contributed to this section. It appeared as is in *Finding Your Jewish Roots in Galicia: A Resource Guide.* which was published in 1998]

In 1789 Austrian legislation mandated universal male military service. In practice, however, Jews did not serve in the military in any great numbers until the 20th century because most Austrian military officers opposed having Jews under their command.

The best source for Austrian military records is the LDS (Mormon) Family History Library (FHL). Rosemary Chorzempa, in her 1993 book, *Korzenie Polskie: Polish Roots*, briefly discusses the LDS holdings of military records. According to Chorzempa, if you have a definite location and year of birth for your ancestor, check film #1186632, item 1 ("Distribution Location Index of the Austro-Hungarian Empire Army and Navy Troops, Regiments, etc."), which lists the Austrian units that recruited in each area and when they were in each locality. Then you can check that unit's records for your ancestor.

Another useful book about the records held by the FHL, according to Ellen Sadove Renck, is *Gesischichte der K. und Wehrmacht*, published in 1901. One can use the *Qualifikationslisten Index des K.U.K. Herres und K.U.K. Marine, 1761–1900*, to follow the locations of the various military units, which remained fairly stable in their deployment, except during a war. After fighting ceased, they generally returned to their original site. The Austrian Army Records are found in the FHL catalog under Austria—Civil Registration. The *Austrian History Yearbook*, vols. 6–7 explains the Kriegsarchiv that began in 1711. Renck found this book through her local Family History Library.

Erwin A Schmidl, author of *Jews in the Habsburg Armed Forces* (Eisenstadt, Germany: Osterreichisches Judisches Museum, 1989) has produced a scholarly work on this subject. Schmidl has been a frequent speaker at IAJGS conferences and is a storehouse of knowledge about this complex topic. The book may be purchased by writing to Schmidl at: A-70 Eisenstadt, Unterbergstr. 6, Austria. German text pages 19–91; English translation, pages 93–189. Photographs are included.

In what seems to be a finding aid to an extensive collection of service records of officers and other military officials of the Austro-Hungarian Empire, *Dienstbeschreibungen und Qualifikationslisten, 1761–1918*, surnames (and some first names) are arranged alphabetically by film number. The English description of the finding aid indicates that the beginning name on each film is shown in this description. Thus, Glaas is the first name on film #1257095, Glanzer is the first name on film #1257096, and so forth. It is listed in the FHL's Locality Search Catalog under "Austria (see Military)."

Ada Greenblatt researched the Hapsburg Military Records for World War I and discovered that for each year there is an alphabetical index of surnames, with a page number after each name. When you find a name, turn to the page that gives details about the person's service.

Film #1506282. The microfilm is labeled 1912–14, but it actually
covers 1911 and 1912. Alphabetical index for 1911 on pages
1479–1737; alphabetical index for 1912, pages 1551–1823.
Film #1506283. Alphabetical index for 1914 on pages 1353–1579;
alphabetical index (A-R) for 1916, pages 1711–1843.
Film #1506284. Alphabetical index (Q-Z) for 1916 on pages 1342–
1421; alphabetical index (A-N) for 1917, pages 1527–1719.
Film #1506285. Alphabetical index (N-Z) for 1917, pages 1718–1853;
alphabetical index for 1918, pages 661–777.

Holdings of Specific Repositories

The Central Archives for the History of the Jewish People

This important repository, affiliated with Hebrew University
in Jerusalem, is currently located in a tiny, cramped space at 46
Jabotinsky Street on the first floor of a building that they share
with various other organizations, just around the corner from the
Israeli president's house. Despite difficult working conditions, the
director, Hadassah Assouline, has been enormously successful in
convincing Polish archival officials to microfilm Jewish documents
of all types. In 2004, Avotaynu, Inc. published a catalog in English
that lists CAHJP's 2001 holdings. Unfortunately, the CAHJP staff
who prepared the catalog for publication did not list the microfilm
numbers so that it is a challenge to sort out the English language
descriptions from the published book against the Polish language
card catalog, particularly since the book does not include newly
acquired material, of which there is a lot. The book provides a fine
overview of the types of holdings at the CAHJP. The holdings are
enormously important and include materials for virtually every
district of what had been Galicia, both east and west.

Though the card catalog for Poland is organized by town, keep
in mind that "town" for former Galician places, means district, so,
you must have a good sense for which districts are of interest
to use their system successfully. The card catalog does not, with
100% accuracy, list all of the towns and villages mentioned within

the film so, if you are looking for a very small place, look at the microfilm(s) for your district.

So, what kind of documents have been microfilmed by Poland and placed with the CAHJP? There is a great deal of correspondence, which is in Polish, and concerns a vast array of official issues, including: attempts to resolve disputes; permissions to contract with members of the nobility for arendas; requests for relief from burdensome taxes or regulations; lists of petititoners requesting approval of an individual for an official appointment of some kind; school matters; minutes of meetings; confirmation of appointments; and, election matters. Much of the later material concerns the Baron Hirsch organization which was helping people to move to Palestine or the business matters of the various Zionist organizations. Legal proceedings surrounding a particular case sometimes appears in very early records from communities, often with no surnames. Virtually none of this type of material is useful from a genealogical point of view.

Then there are lists: lists of teachers; lists of students in Jewish schools; lists of Jews who are working (some with birthdates and the town of residence); communal tax lists; and annual *Gemeinde* tax lists, which include the amounts paid by individuals, synagogues and other buildings used by the Jewish community. Most of the lists in the current holdings appear to be from two time periods: the 1880s and then in the 1920s and 1930s. There are lists of contributors to the Galician religious community, known as the *Kollel* in Palestine from the mid 1930s, as well as lists of male residents. When such lists exist for a town or district, they can be useful for discerning social relationships as well as for confirming the existence of a person's residence. There are random jewels like a telephone list for a district. There are a few censuses from 1765-7, which generated much excitement among those who found them, until we realized that there were no surnames, since this was before surnames were adopted. There are lists of male members of the Kraków Jewish community who were eligible to vote in 1883 and 1929 elections. Though birth dates are not included, some of these lists and other tax lists for other towns, resemble a census for males over age 13. According to CAFHP staffer, Hanna Volovici, the Central Archives has 1856 and 1895 lists of Jews who lived in small towns near Kraków, such as Balice, Czulice, Górka, Grebalowa, Krzeszowice, Liszki, and Mogila among others. They also have 20th-century lists of members of five synagogues in Kraków.

For Brody, there were emigration lists of residents mixed in with refugees from pogroms in Ukraine in the early 1880s. These were the only emigration records found but the lists were on printed forms that clearly indicated that these forms were routinely used for this purpose. Others may yet be found in L'viv and, perhaps, Kraków.

You must go to the CAHJP to do research or employ an outside researcher to do research for you. Staff at the facility can help a bit with language issues and assist with making copies on the ancient microfilm copier, but this even this type of assistance can not be counted on.

Archives in Ivano-Frankivsk, Ukraine

Stanisławów, now Ivano-Frankovsk in Ukraine, was a large Jewish population center. The late Nat Abramowitz in *The Galitizianer*, Vol. 4, No. 2, reported that, while Alexander Dunai had not found vital records in the Ivano-Frankovsk Archives, he did find other types of records in the archives and elsewhere in the city. A partial inventory of what Dunai found follows:

» Census of the Jewish population in Stanisławów for 1857, a 1,200-page list written in Gothic German.
» A portion of the 1900 census of the Jewish population in Stanisławów, written in Polish.
» List of real estate owned by Jews.
» Population information from Stanisławów district, 1923.
» Census of the Jewish population in Stanisławów, August 1939. It consists of about 10,000 pages, each of which contains information about the people in a household: birth dates, occupation, place of work, relationship and, in some cases, property holdings. The census is organized by

street, and, within each apartment building, the records are in alphabetical order.

» List of lawyers, doctors and merchants. The list includes all religious denominations, but most are Jews.

» Lists of Jews deported by the Germans.

Central State Historical Archives in L'viv, Ukraine

As mentioned in earlier sections, Julian and Fay Bussgang visited Lviv and compiled an inventory of the Jewish information that they found in the main archives there. This listing, originally appeared in Vol. 4, No. 2 of *The Galitizianer*. It has been supplemented here by information susequently supplied by Alexander Dunai and Alexander Kronich. A fond is a record group.

Fond 44. Magistracy of the town of Sanok, Sanok lands, *Rusynian Wojewódstwo* (province of Rusynia) since 1783. Sanok region: 1366–1939. Sanok received the Magdeburg Right of self-government in 1366. The Sanok Magistracy had jurisdiction over legislative, civil, commercial and criminal affairs. The fond contains documents for 1685–1864, written in Latin, Polish and German. The holdings include court documents, contracts for sale and purchase of land and chattel, testaments, settlements, real estate affairs and account books for 1787–90.

Fond 141. 26 files 1667–1854. Collection of documents about finances and properties of the Jewish population in Galicia. Town and district implementation of new taxes; benefits to various population groups from towns of Chełm, Bełż, and Czchów; rabbinical court decrees; register of debts and payments of the Jewish population of Belz.

Fond 186. Documents of the Lemberg Regional Lands and Taxes Commission, 1821–1934. Inventories of land holdings of villages; land registers and land maps of villages; lists of landowners in alphabetical order; lists of real estate owners in villages. According to Alexander Dunai:

The greater part of the fond consists of the land registers and maps of villages, including Bochnia, Chortków, Berezhany, Jasło, Kolomyya, Kraków, Lemberg, Nowy Sącz, Przemyśl, Rzeszów, Sambor, Sanok, Stanisławów, Stryj, Tarnopol, Tarnów, Wadowice, Złoczów and Zolkiew. The other part consists of inventories of land with their owners from Berezhany, Kolomyya, Lemberg, Przemyśl, Sambor, Stanisławów, Stryj, Tarnopol, Złoczów and Zolkiew. Additionally, there are lists of landholders for a small number of villages, including the (now Ukrainian) town of Staremiasto (1853) and the Polish town of Lutowiska (1855–95).

Fond 300. 350 files, 1921–39: Records of the private warehouse of iron tubes and hardware belonging to Szymon Soltz of Lwów.

Fond 332. 128 files, 1924–39. Lwów Branch of Zionist Organization for Immigration to Palestine (headquarters in Warsaw). Letters, documents, statistical data, list of immigrants and members.

Fond 334. 161 files, 1920, 1922–39. Lwów Branch of Central Immigration Society (EAC), covered four voivodeships around Lwów. Activities: gave information to immigrants, prepared documents, helped with employment, gave legal help and funds, scheduled transport to Canada and South America. List of immigrants and members.

Fond 335. 225 files, 1920–39. *Keren Haesod* (Society to Build Palestine). Covers Eastern Galicia branch of worldwide organization. Correspondence, minutes of meetings, lists of members and contributors.

Fond 336. 243 files, 1922–23, 1928–39. Regional Commission for Eastern Małopolska in Lwów. Group raised and distributed funds, organized Jews to go to Palestine, provided public education. List of delegates to 1897 Zionist Congress in Basel.

Fond 337. 123 files, 1919–39. *Hanoar Hatzion* (Young Zionists Organization), which had branches in Galician towns. Rules, correspondence, membership list.

Fond 338. 1,635 files, 1895, 1902–40. Regional Zionist Organization of Lwów. Political party of Jewish bourgeoisie in Eastern Galicia. From 1920 to 1939, active in three voivodeships to buy and sell land in Palestine. List of leaders, members, voting places.

Fond 339. 32 files, 1926–39. Society *Keren Kayemet* (Jewish National Fund) of Lwów established in Galicia, 1914. Headquarters in Warsaw. Its purpose was to raise funds for colonization of Palestine. Rules and regulations of society in Lwów and Kraków, correspondence, list of members, 1936–39.

Fond 341. 17 files, 1931–37. Publication and administration of *Zionist Weekly*, newspaper of the worldwide Zionist movement. List of subscribers and ledger book of receipts.

Fond 342. 129 files, 1926–39. *Achba* (Jewish Youth Organization) of Lwów, Eastern Małopolska. Closely tied to Zionist organizations in Poland, Western Europe, America and Palestine. Correspondence with Warsaw, Jerusalem, Tel Aviv, London and Prague. List and application forms of members. List of delegates to conventions.

Fond 346. 288 files, 1929–39. Lwów Branch of Association of Jewish Veterans who Fought for Polish Independence. Covered three voivodeships, reported to headquarters in Warsaw and branches in Poland, Denmark and elsewhere. Employment and financial assistance, loans, care of veterans' graves, Youth Cadre, rules/regulations, projects, memoranda, protocols, news bulletins, conditions in Poland, membership dues and lists and correspondence.

Fond 432. 49 files, 1924–39. Central Jewish Cooperative Bank of Lwów. Bank documents and activity reports.

Fond 441. 17 files, 1928–32. *Hanoar Haivri* (Jewish Boy Scouts) in Lwów and voivodeship. After 1930, it covered all of Małopolska and Silesia. In 1932, it was closed by decision of committees of Zionist organizations in Kraków and joined with *Agudat Hanoar Haivri* in Kraków. Files, correspondence and reports.

Fond 454. 41 files, 1933–39. *Tzion Baoley Miktzoa* (Central Committee of Jewish Zionist Craftsmen) in Małopolska. Activities: educated Jewish craftsmen, promoted Jewish culture, offered lectures. List and card files of members.

Fond 455. 82 files, 1930–39. *Hechalutz HaKlal Tzion* (Jewish Society of Zionist Youth). In 1935, joined with another society, General Zionist *Halutz*, which was active in Eastern Galicia and all of Poland. Correspondence, application forms, membership lists, card file of members going to work on the *kibbutz*.

Fond 456. 15 files, 1930–33. *Gmilat Chesed*. Headquarters for Eastern Galicia. Provided financial aid for poor Jewish craftsmen and merchants. Financial documents.

Fond 457. 10 files, 1925–39. *Hechalutz* (Pioneer) of Lwów (Society for the Education and Training of Jewish Youth for Immigration to Palestine). Card files of members.

Fond 458. 47 files, 1926–39. Lwów Branch of Jewish Cooperative Association. Reported to Warsaw, activities throughout Galicia. Correspondence, reports and financial documents.

Fond 496. 5 files, 1926, 1937–39. Society of Jewish Private Enterprise in Lwów. Payroll records of Geller, president of the society.

Fond 497. 243 files, 1873–1928. Synagogue schools of the Jewish community, chartered under Belgrade statute of 1866. Original founders were Jews expelled from Spain and Portugal during the Inquisition. Goal was to support religion, charity and education of Jews. Drafts of laws regarding religious societies, work plans, memoranda from clergy in Serbia, Croatia and Slovenia; financial activities. List of electors and abstracts of some metrical data.

Fond 498. 5 files, 1929–38. *Ahavat Chesed* (Society of Credit, Self-Help). Was active in three voivodeships in Eastern Małopolska. Applications of members for loans.

Fond 499. 5 files, 1929–38. Society for Assistance to Jewish Students in Poland, Lwów Branch. Applications for financial aid, financial reports.

Fond 500. 9 files, 1930–33. *Hanoteach* (Lwów Society of Farmers to Work in Palestine). Help with care of citrus trees in Palestine for owners in Poland; maintained a citrus plantation in Netanya.

Fond 501. 5 files, 1931–39. *Makkabi* (cultural and physical growth of Jewish youth,.

Fond 502. 9 files, 1925–39. Society of Jewish Women, Eastern Małopolska. Office of job search and placement, shelters for working women, kindergartens, child care, help to runaways.

Fond 503. 222 files, 1921–39. TOZ (Health Care Society for Jews, Society for Promoting Good Health Among Jews). Lwów branch of organization headquartered in Warsaw. List of members of committee, medical card files.

Fond 505. 296 files, 1898–1931. Committee for Assistance of Jewish Population in Lwów. Active in Lwów after pogroms there on November 22–23, 1918. In 1923, changed name to Central Jewish Rescue Committee. List of committee members.

Fond 639. Handwritten and illegible.

Fond 701. 5,672 files 1785–1942. Jewish Religious Community of Lwów.

» Metrical Books. Births, marriages and deaths of Jewish communities in Galicia. Documents are organized alphabetically by town. Within a town, events are listed in chronological order. Sets are incomplete. Most common are birth, marriage and deaths in Lwów and vicinity (56 books), Tarnopol (29 books), Narajew (28 books), Podhajce (21 books) and Mikulince (21 books). Seven books are alphabetical indexes.

» One book lists Jews living in Tarnopol 1850–1900, with indication of birth date and profession.

» One book includes drafts of abstracts from metrical records of Horodenka from the second half of the 19th century to the beginning of the 20th century.

» Seven books are copies of metrical records, 1789–1942 (oldest documents are from a marriage book from Kamionka Strumiłowa, 1781–1861, and marriages from Stanisławów, 1789–1871).

» Correspondence between Lwów voivodeships about various activities: permits for marriage, dowries, taxes; selling kosher meat at auction; assistance to poor; construction and repair of synagogues; establishment of Jewish morgue; Jewish population census; Jewish goods and money for charity; applications from Jewish immigrants from Russia, 1785–1907; Jewish activities with hospitals and synagogues; list of Jewish families with debts (in 18 books), 1791–95, 1796–1850 (still in cataloguing stage).

» Financial documents, applications for aid, financial assistance, reports. List of committee reports. Case files. (Still in cataloguing stage)

» Reports and a list of members of an organization relating to financial assistance (still in cataloguing stage).
» List of deaths. Case files (Ed. note: Still in cataloging stage when this inventory was compiled).

YIVO Institute for Jewish Research

YIVO Institute for Jewish Research, which has the world's largest library and archival collection pertaining to Eastern European Jews, is located at 15 West 16 Street, New York, NY 10011. Enter at 20 West 17th between 5th and 6th if you are going there in person. It is best to phone ahead to confirm hours of operation since they close for many Jewish holidays: (212) 294-6100.

YIVO has the largest collection of *yizkor* books in the United States, lists of Holocaust survivors who registered with various agencies, and hundreds of volumes of books that were rescued from its original location in Vilnius (Vilna), Lithuania, as well as an impressive collection of books and materials acquired since its establishment in the US.

One aspect of YIVO that is less well known is its archival collection, which includes an extensive photo collection on laser disk and a *landsmanschaftn* archive. *Landsmanschaft* organizations were burial, social, religious and welfare societies established in the late 19th and early 20th centuries by people who emigrated from Eastern European towns and wanted to continue their association with others from their old towns in their new countries. In the U.S., these *landsmanschaftn* were established in a few large cities, New York most prominent among them. Several of these groups served all Galician Jews. Additionally, many were composed of Jews from particular Galician towns or regions. *Landsmanschaftn* were organized to address the needs of Jewish Galicians in New York and other major cities in U.S., Europe and Palestine. These were multi-faceted organizations serving religious, social service, and charitable needs of immigrants. Most had affiliated burial societies. Some were only for immigrants from one community, while others were more regional in nature. Two such organizations in New York were for Galitzianers, regardless of where they had come from. Eventually, some of these organizations merged for financial reasons and because of dwindling membership, but in the late 19th and early 20th centuries, they were vibrant and active. The Galician neighborhood of the Lower East Side had many synagogues, large and small, study houses and shops devoted to the particular foods and goods favored by Galician Jews. The mixing of Litvak and Galitzianer in marriage, commerce and in other areas of life in New York, was not something that commonly happened at the height of pre-World War I immigration. While much of the old Galitzianer section of the Lower East Side has been torn down and replaced, the city directories, coupled with the New York City censuses of and the Federal censuses, offer a window into that world. This insularity began to change during World War I, not only because of the effects of the war itself, but because migration from the Lower East Side to Brooklyn, the Bronx and elsewhere accelerated during that period.

Rosaline Schwartz, at the time, a YIVO staff person, became alarmed when she learned that New York-based *landsmanschaftn*, which were going out of business because their members were dying out or no longer interested, were simply throwing away their records. She and some colleagues at YIVO, mounted a campaign to inform that all known *landsmanschaftn* that YIVO would be happy to have their records, in the event of dissolution.

YIVO published a catalogue of their holdings in 1986, *A Guide to YIVO's Landsmanschaftn Archive* by Rosaline Schwartz and Susan Milamed. More current information can be found on their website. Most records are administrative in nature. They consist of minutes, lists of members, lists of cemetery plot holders, and similar types of information. Towns are listed with current names so use that name when inquiring. Although these societies started in the 1890s, most of the records at YIVO begin after 1920 because earlier records were discarded. Check out YIVO online at www.yivo.org. If you do not find the specific information you are seeking, you can contact staff through the website.

Jewish National and University Library in Jerusalem

On the campus of Hebrew University, Givat Ram campus in Jerusalem, the library has material on microfilm and in their

Department of Manuscripts and Archives. The primary focus of their holdings is on Israel but there are a very few interesting resources for Galitizianers, particularly for Bukachevtsky, Ivano-Frankvisk, Kozlów, Kraków and Śnyatyn.

Jewish Historical Institute in Warsaw

The Ronald S. Lauder Foundation's Genealogy Project is housed at the Jewish Historical Institute. Yale Reisner is the Genealogy Project's executive director. The project's priorities have been to preserve the Institute's archival material and to address inquiries from people who are Holocaust survivors or Poles who have discovered that they were either hidden children (during the Holocaust) or whose parents chose to hide the fact of their Judaism.

Most of the Institute's holdings for Galicia concern Kraków and towns surrounding that city. Additionally, the Institute holds master's and doctoral theses on Jewish themes from the prewar and postwar periods among which are histories of Jewish communities. It also holds Jewish communal records, including cemetery records, documents from synagogue authorities that include lists of Jewish residents eligible to vote, and similar types of lists. The Institute also has lists of Polish survivors compiled in 1945–46. Their rich collection of material from Kraków, 1701–1942, includes marriage bann books for the liberal congregation of Kraków and twelve prewar *yahrzeit* (anniversary of death) calendars for the Remu synagogue that list the *yahrzeit* dates for members of the congregation each month.

Yale Reisner has many responsibilities with a small staff. He is not in a position to correspond with people wanting information about the Institute's holdings, but, if you are in Warsaw, you can go to the Institute and research their collection with the assistance of staff there.

The address for the Institute is:
  Zydowski Instytut Historyczny w Polsce
  00-900 Warszawa
  ul. Tlomackie 3/5

Reisner's project welcomes financial assistance to continue its work in preservation and cataloging of fragile material. Additionally, he spends a good deal of time assisting people who believe that they were either Jewish at birth and were given to Poles by their parents for their safekeeping at the beginning of WWII, or who believe that they are otherwise, of Jewish ancestry. He has helped many Poles find information about their Jewish roots. If you do contribute, be sure to note on your check that the money is intended for the Polish Genealogy Project. Send your checks to:

Ronald S. Lauder Foundation
767 Fifth Avenue, Suite 4200
New York, NY 10153

Assistance with Translations

Many genealogists become discouraged when they can not translate the documents that they find. There are several options for addressing this issue. The least expensive option for people who need translation of a Polish word or document is to go online with the Gesher Galicia SIG Discussion Group and ask participants to help you, either by posting the document on ViewMate, within JewishGen, or mailing the document to someone for that purpose. Several people who frequent the discussion group are native Poles and they are generally more than happy to help out if the document is of reasonable length and is legible.

Of course, there are dictionaries that might help out. Anyone conducting serious research about their Galician family will probably do well to invest in a Polish dictionary or two.

Two sites have been well recommended by users: www.poltran. com and www.foreignword.com. Most large cities have commercial translation services, but, unless the material to be translated is a handwritten letter, a diary, or a manuscript, most people will find this to be a prohibitively more costly route. I have had some success finding university students and faculty members with foreign language departments who have translated such materials at a fraction of the cost that commercial translation services would have charged. Some communities have Polish and Ukrainian populations who might be contacted through organizations and churches. There are also Polish and Ukrainian genealogical societies and researchers who can be accessed through FEEFHS at www.feefhs.org.

Finding people: Past and Current

The Gesher Galicia website at http://www.jewishgen.org/ Galicia/databases.html has a number of databases that have been developed over the years. Some are specifically Jewish and some are links to Polish websites that may provide some interesting information. But, first let's look at the range of directories that are available. This is a quick way of seeing who lived in an area.

1891 All Galicia Business Directory

Prior to widespread phone service, commercial publishers in many parts of the world, published directories of individuals, so that businesses could find them, and business directories, so that individuals could find them. These directories were particularly common in the U.S. but they existed in Galicia and Poland, as well. The earliest known business directory for all of Galicia was created in 1891. To be included in a business directory, one had to pay an advertising fee ,which means that the vast majority of Jewish businesses, which could not afford such a fee, are not listed in this directory. However, the directory was organized by type of occupation or business and then, within each category, were listed communities and the individuals who were engaged in that type of occupation or business. You can search the database for your surnames.

JewishGen has posted a surname index to this directory on its website. The information can be accessed through entering a surname. All mentions of that surname will appear in a list, along with towns where they lived and their occupations.

1916 Lemberg Business Directory

A residential/business directory was published in 1916 in Lemberg. The Library of Congress filmed this directory and the microfilm is available for purchase. The directory will soon be indexed and the results will be part of the Gesher Galicia database collection. The directory is in four small chapters: the first chapter is an alphabetical list of males with their occupations and street addresses; the second chapter is organized by occupations with the names and addresses of those engaging in those occupations; and the third chapter appears to be mostly professions such as education, law and medicine, with a list of those engaging in those professions. The fourth chapter is a section of paid advertisements. The directory was, undoubtedly, by subscription and included only those who could afford to be listed. About 10-20% of those listed were Jewish. To order, request film #506331: The Library of Congress, Photoduplication Service, Washington, DC 20540-5234.

Efforts are underway at this writing to create a surname index to this directory with the occupation.

1913 All Galicia Business Directory

There was a 1913 Galician business directory, which is considerably larger than the 1891 directory and much more inclusive of small merchants and tradesmen. This directory is on microfilm and is available for purchase or on interlibrary loan from the University of Illinois at Urbana. It can also be found at a number of major research libraries.

Interwar Polish Business, Residential and Phone Directories

Following the end of the Austrian empire, when Galicia became part of Poland, a number of business directories and residential directories were published in the 1920's and 1930s. The residential directories were called Ksiega Adresowa Polski (Polish address register). Phone directories were also being published by the 1930s. In the U.S., some of these directories are available on microfilm at the Library of Congress and New York Public Library. The Library of Congress also has microfilmed a 1930 phone directory (film #506171) for Kraków and Katowice districts. There is a *Ksiega Adresowa Miasta Krakowa* for 1926 that lists occupations as well as addresses for individuals.

The Polish business and residential directories tend to be organized by provinces, or *voivoides*. Within each voivoide, towns are listed alphabetically. If it is a business directory, then the next subcategory is occupation or type of business. It is surprising how many very small towns are included in these directories. Each community listed was described, depending on the publisher, in Polish alone or in Polish and French, with demographic, business and religious data, as well as the number of residents from the most recent census. At the end of each directory is a listing of occupations translated into severa languages but there are also translated lists at various sites on the Internet. Some of the occupations are obsolete and can not be found in current Polish dictionaries. For instance, many Jews were engaged in selling what translates from Polish as "diverse articles." In the U.S. at that time, many Jews were engaged in operating similar businesses known as "dry goods" or what the peddler carried on his back around the countryside until there was enough money to open a store.

U.S. City and Business Directories

United States city and business directories exist on microfilm and, still, in some libraries, on paper. The city directories (sometimes more regional in nature or for multiple adjacent communities) are alphabetical and the business directories are organized by type of business. The U.S. directories sometimes listed multiple members of a household, noted when someone was widowed or had left the area within the past year since the last publication, and, occupational information. The value of these directories can not be overstated. In years where there is no census or when the family was not in the census, the directories provide an alternative way of documenting where people lived, their relationships to one another and so on. Knowing that groups of people with the same name lived in the same building or two doors away is an important clue to the past, even when current family has no knowledge of who the other family was. On the Lower East Side of New York, where many of our Galician families first settled, there was a section of that neighborhood that housed our ancestors, as opposed to the Litvaks who lived on

adjacent blocks but rarely within the Galician section. As soon
as these Galitzianers settled in New York, they began to recon-
struct the infrastructure that had given them support at home.
These *landsmanschaftn* discussed above under YIVO's resources,
organized various types of welfare organizations, burial societies, synagogues, and so forth.

Newspapers and Periodicals

Newspapers and periodicals are good sources of general information about what was going on at the time and the details of
situations that years later are placed by history in a larger context
since we know the outcomes of events. Obituary sections of papers
should not be overlooked, but keep in mind that most obituaries
are in newspapers because someone paid for them to be there.
Most of our relatives did not have that kind of money. However,
one little known newspaper source might well be extremely
valuable if you had relatives who remained in interwar Poland.
A newspaper called "Monitor Polski: The Government Gazette
of the Republic of Poland," published the names of people known
to have died during the war. The paper published from France
between September-December 1939 and resumed publishing from
Poland in 1945. In the 1946-1948 period, the paper, which was
actually an arm of the government, published motions filed with
the courts to recognize deaths for legal purposes. Motions were
filed by relatives, friends and neighbors. The listings included date
and place of birth, town of residence, names of parents, maiden
names of married women and probably cause of death. Also listed
in the paper were inheritances and mortgages. Jewish Records
Indexing-Poland has created a database of 8400 of those names at
this writing. Judy Boston is the coordinator. See monitorpolski@
jri-poland.org. If you are unable to access JRI-Poland directly, go
to JewishGen and find them under hosted organizations. When
you get to the first screen, you will see "thumbnail." Click on that
and you will see Monitor Polski.

Money and volunteers are needed to complete the indexing
project. The Library of Congress has copies of the newspapers,
themselves. The JRI-Poland database includes edition and page

number to facilitate seeing the whole article. Moreover, JRI-Poland's site includes an order form so that you can request a copy of the legal file behind the notice in the paper from the Polish State Archives.

Cemeteries

Cemeteries can be a rich source of information. Unfortunately, most Jewish cemeteries in Poland and Ukraine have either been destroyed, seriously affected by neglect, or the tombstones have been damaged by the acid rain due to industrial output. There are, of course, some surviving cemeteries and there are numerous projects underway to restore and preserve Jewish cemeteries in those countries. If cemetery records were systematically maintained, they have not been found except for a very few of the largest cities. However, while visiting Poland or Ukraine, it is a worthwhile experience to seek out Jewish cemeteries, regardless of whether your visit will result in any genealogical information. Keep in mind that males and females were, generally, buried in separate sections and it is rare to find old Galician tombstones with surnames, with the exception of cemeteries in larger cities with more secular/modern Jewish communities in the 20th century to the present. Cemetery art can still be seen on some surviving stones. During this author's 1986 visit to numerous towns in western Galicia, a number of cemetery sites were visited. The result was often distressing.

When the Nazis or the local townspeople broke off tombstones, there was evidence of the base of the stone in the ground, even through tall grass. The stones were used for paving and other building purposes so it is not unusual to find that you are walking on a path made of tombstones, often with faded letters and designs still visible. Or, to turn a corner and find that pieces of tombstones were used as part of a building. Even when cemeteries were not vandalized in the war or in modern times by local residents, the condition of most cemeteries is abysmal because there is no one responsible for their upkeep. Some remnants of cemeteries are now buried deep in the woods, covered with underbrush and nettles and thorny vines.

Depiction of the bases of broken gravestones

Path to house comprised of broken gravestone

However, cemeteries in the United States and elsewhere where our relatives went to when they left Galicia, can be mined for their genealogical information. Some cemeteries have good records, while others have none at all. Some tombstones, particularly those made from limestone, can no longer be read because of acid air and rain, but when the tombstone exists and can be read, much can be learned from where it is and who is buried nearby. Since many older Jewish cemeteries were associated with burial societies, synagogues, *landmanschaftn* and family clubs, the identity of the cemetery or cemetery section may provide the context for family information. The condition of some old Jewish cemeteries is little better than those of Poland and Ukraine, but they should always be considered as a source of new knowledge.

The International Association of Jewish Genealogical Societies fostered a cemetery information project conceived and initiated by Arline and Sidney Sachs. This effort resulted in an extensive list of thousands of Jewish cemeteries around the world and information on hundreds of thousands of individual burials. Ellen Sadove Renck has been the Project's coordinator since 2000. For the past couple of years, she has been ably assisted by Kitty Munson Cooper. The IAJGS Project has been redefined to focus on cemetery location, status, and contact information. As of mid-2005, over 22,000 Jewish cemeteries were cataloged at the Project's website: www.jewishgen.org/cemetery/.

The task of collecting and maintaining information about individual burials is now the responsibility of JewishGen's Online Worldwide Burial Registry (JOWBR). Joyce Field is currently coordinating the JOWBR project in her role as JewishGen's Vice President of Data Acquisition.

Censuses in the New Country

Censuses in the country where your relatives emigrated to are an excellent source of information, outside of vital records and residential directories. They can help with tracking relatives and making connections. They can also offer a tool for establishing a time frame for when a person might have arrived, moved, had children, and died. A prime example is the United States censuses

Jewish cemetery in Galicia

for the period of 1880-1930. Let's look specifically at the Lower East Side of Manhattan, where almost every Ashkenazi Jew had relatives, if they came to the United States.

This section of New York City housed, if not well, most Jewish immigrants, at least for a brief period after they first arrived. Galician (and, to some extent, Hungarian) Jews congregated in a small corner of that neighborhood, apart from the Irish and the Jews from Romania, Russia and elsewhere, who also tended to congregate in their own sections. From 1880 to about 1910, it is possible to examine relatively few microfilms for the enumeration districts covering this area and see virtually every Galician Jew living in New York! The area of focus began at the East River and moved to the western boundary of Chrystie Street. The northern boundary was S. Houston Street and the southern boundary was Division Street leading into Broadway. The streets within this area were: Allen, Broome, Cannon, Clinton, Lewis, Goerck, Columbia, Sherriff, Pitt, Stanton, Mangin, Eldridge,

Forsyth, Rivington, Attorney, Willet, Essex, Norfolk, Suffolk,
Grand and Ridge.

Map 5. Portion of Lower East Side, New York City,
where Galician Jews Lived

The slums housing the immigrants in that section, already
terrible when Jews began coming to the area in the 1880s, have
mostly been torn down, along with most of the synagogues,
communal buildings and study houses dotting the area. Visiting
the area now will not be particularly fruitful because little of what
was there when our families lived there is still there, although
some adjacent areas of the Lower East Side have changed little.
YIVO and other large Jewish libraries in the U.S. have copies of
a communal directory that was published in 1915 and this directory lists the location of the various buildings and organizations
central to Jewish life at that time.

When you find a name of interest in any census listing, be sure to look at the whole sheet and those before and after. You might find other people of interest because families tended to live on the same block if not the same building. Although the above focuses on the Lower East Side of Manhattan, early Galician immigrants living in London, Chicago, Pittsburgh, Cleveland and Newark and so on, tended to cluster together as well.

Finding Live People

Finding live people involves several different strategies, none of which are peculiar to Galician research. Before you go to other sources, register the surnames and towns that you are researching with JewishGen in the main database that will connect you with others researching those surnames and/or towns.

Additionally, there are Internet sites now that sell access to huge amount of information about living people (including you). As appalling as some may find these services, because they invade our privacy, they can be used strategically, by family historians. For instance, Google.com and Switchboard.com are among those that offer users free access to very limited information about people. Subscribers can obtain other types of information, such as email addresses, Social Security numbers, credit information, background checks, marriage records, etc.

Some major libraries have hard copies or microfilmed telephone directories from many places around the world.

Consider contacting a Jewish genealogy society, Jewish Federations, synagogues, or Jewish newspapers around the world for assistance with locating "missing" relatives.

Other Internet Resources for Genealogical Research

Estelle Guzik, a long time member of the Jewish Genealogical Society of New York has not only compiled and edited a revised edition of the Society's excellent book, fully referenced elsewhere, and entitled, *Genealogical Resources in New York*, but the Society has created a wonderfully useful website full of pertinent information for those who are researching New York family members, including Burial Societies, cemeteries, landsmanschaftn and other Jewish organizations.

JewishGen has created an "All Poland Database" that should be consulted to see the various types of databases that cover Poland. This offers an index to 2.4 million vital records, census records, legal notices, passports and newspaper announcements. See www. jewishgen.org/databases/Poland.

Both Ancestry.com and Genealogy.com offer similar services by subscription. Ancestry.com offers 14 days of free access so that you can judge for yourself the value of the site. In truth, they are very similar in what they offer to genealogists and they are similar in their subscription prices. Neither caters specifically to Jewish genealogists, but they are terrific sources of information about U.S. government-generated records and documentation of all kinds, plus some linkages to newspaper articles about individuals, Social Security records, World War I draft board records, some cemetery information, and so on. Both of these commercial services offer excellent access to databases of live people for an additional fee.

Say you are interested in finding a record of a passenger who arrived in the U.S. by ship. You have no information except for a surname and a first name that you know as Herman but you don't know what name he used in Europe. You have a vague idea that Herman arrived in New York in about 1900 but it could have been a few years before or after. The search engine allows you to enter what you know or to enter only the initial "H" as Herman's first name. You can also ask for a search between 1897-1903. You find a man named Hirsch from the right town. Since men named Hirsch often adopted the Americanized name of Herman, this is probably the man you are seeking. Finding this record of interest, you click on "image" and in a brief moment, there it is.

Some groups of records are not available as images, but at least you have a citation for where the record can be found on microfilm so that you can follow up with doing the research yourself, or you can request that staff at the National Archives find the record at the citation you provide and provide a copy for a small fee.

These commercial services also offer databases of U.S. and

British censuses. Like the ship records, while some censuses can be viewed on screen, others provide location information to facilitate followup. However, in all cases, again, you have a citation that enables you to pursue more complete information from the source. The technology involved with viewing these records is still not quite perfected, but even fuzzy images are far better than what genealogists had a few years ago!

Ancestry.com is working on compiling an obituary database gleaned from newspapers, while Genealogy.com is compiling a tombstone/cemetery database from individual and organizational contributors. Other resources within one or both sites: some directories, newspapers and periodicals; very limited court, land and probate records; maps; and military records.

Using these types of resources can quickly propel you from knowing little about your family to knowing a great deal, assuming that relatives came to the U.S., Canada, or parts of the United Kingdom. The commercial services are continuously adding to their collection and, having access to such a service, as you progress from novice to expert, is a great investment.

Steve Morse, a very active Jewish genealogist, has created a number of remarkable "One-Step" webpages to facilitate access to these various complex databases such as ship passenger records, censuses, Social Security records, New York naturalization and vital records, and some highly specialized databases, such as changed street names and New York records of incarcerated individuals. Morse has also developed numerous aids to assist Jewish genealogists with such diverse problems as converting dates from the Jewish calendar, searching for refugees from Siberian camps after World War II, and dealing with Hebrew and Russian characters in documents. In any event, you should check out his site because chances are, you will be needing at least one of his aids sooner or later. Go to http://www.stevemorse www.stevemorse. org. Believe it not, Morse does this for fun. He doesn't charge a fee for the use of any of his One-Step webpages.

CHAPTER 5

Holocaust-Related Sources

Events during the Holocaust not only resulted in the destruction of approximately six million Jewish lives but also the destruction of a way of life and many of the records documenting the existence of our ancestral lines. The once vital Jewish communities were crushed, especially those in Eastern Europe. It is no longer possible to visit towns in Ukraine and Poland to see living, thriving Jewish communities that produced our ancestors.

Jews engaged in researching their families find themselves confronting the reality that they lost relatives in the Holocaust. We do honor to ourselves and to the memory of our ancestors when we research the lives of those who were martyrs to the Nazi war machine. But there is the reality that when records and other material relative to genealogical research were destroyed, our task in researching our ancestral heritage is made more difficult.

The resources for conducting such research are continually growing. Records maintained by the German government regarding military operations during World War II (including mass killing operations of Jews and other "undesirables") and records of concentration camps have been available for some time. These microfilmed, German-language records are at the U.S. National Archives and Records Administration in a facility on the campus of the University of Maryland. The collapse of the Soviet Union enabled the U.S. Holocaust Memorial Museum to obtain microfilmed records from Soviet archives that document the fate of Jews in countries associated with the former Soviet Union during World War II. Some of these records are testimonies of eye witnesses; others are administrative records of German management of prisons, camps and other facilities located in Poland and Ukraine.

Although many Jews who survived the Holocaust chose to be silent for decades about their experiences during that period, there are now hundreds of published memoirs and oral testimonies about these experiences. In 2004, Yad Vashem placed their remarkable database and catalog to their holdings online so that everyone with Internet access can now view this database. *Yizkor* books, those compiled by groups of survivors around the world are becoming more accessible to English speakers now that a JewishGen project is working on raising funds to translate the books from Hebrew or Yiddish, or a combination of both.

People fleeing across the railroad bridge crossing the San River, Przemyśl

Yizkor Books

Yizkor books were written by Holocaust survivors about the towns or regions from which they came. Of the known 1,000+ *yizkor* books, the list below cites those that have been written about Galician communities or regions. Most are written entirely in Hebrew and/or Yiddish; a few include English-language sections. Although most books were written within 20 years of the end of the war, some new *yizkor* books have been published more recently, some by children or relatives of Holocaust survivors.

Yizkor books vary widely in content, quality and style, but they generally include photos of places and people, hand-drawn maps of the town, personal memories of what it was like to live in the community, and a list of those who were killed in the Holocaust. Some books include information about community residents who survived and went to Israel, the United States, Canada, or South or Central America, or who remained in Europe. Most of these books include surname and/or topic indexes. A few English-speaking contributors to *yizkor* books, recognizing that people who only speak English, were eager to have access to the information contained within them, have translated and republished whole books, complete with photos.

JewishGen is making major effort to translate all or parts of these books through the *Yizkor* Book Project which was organized in 1994 by Leonard Markowitz and Martin Kessel. Susannah Juni developed the translation effort and Joyce Field is now coordinating this massive effort. On the JewishGen website there is a list of *yizkor* books and the status of translation efforts. Part of the project has resulted in a database, called the Necrology Index, that enables users to search for the names of Holocaust victims mentioned in the translated books. The site also lists libraries where books can be found and suggests commercial establishments that handle these types of materials. A few books or parts of books have been translated by volunteers, but most translation efforts have required payment to the translators. The success of the project is dependent on private donations so please consider donating money toward this effort. You will be instructed within the project site about how to do that so that you are sure that your donation will support translation of a particular book of interest.

Some of the books include some mention of, or even articles about, surrounding villages and towns. Another feature of *yizkor* books is that they include photos of the community and people, and may include lists of residents, school children, taxpayers or other types of listings extracted from archival or local records. For instance, the *yizkor* book for Nowy Sącz includes an 1866 list of Jewish taxpayers, which effectively, amounts to a census of Jewish families living there.

While Yad Vashem in Jerusalem claims to hold the most complete set of *yizkor* books anywhere in the world, in North America, YIVO Institute for Jewish Research in New York City, the Holocaust Memorial Council Library and Archives, the Library of Congress in Washington, DC, and the New York Public Library, have the largest collections. Large collections of these books are held by major Jewish libraries and some public and university libraries in Canada and the U.S.

The books were, generally, published in limited quantities in the, understandable but mistaken, belief that only they and members of their families would be interested. In fact, once the Jewish genealogy movement developed, there was keen demand for copies of these books. By the early 1980s, most of them were out of print. As a result of this, copies of books that come onto to the used market by collectors, specialized book dealers and Judaica auction houses, charge a high price. This author purchased two out of print *yizkor* books that were "extras," one misprinted in several places in the book and the other, bound upside down. The price for each was $75 and this was some time ago. Vendors at annual IAJGS conferences always have a few used *yizkor* books to sell. You may also be able to find the book you are seeking online with dealers who specialize in Judaica, or on E-Bay. Book dealers in Israel, particularly in Jerusalem, and in Brooklyn, are other potential sources.

In addition to formal *yizkor* books, identified as such, there are hundreds of memoirs written by survivors and others who lived in Eastern European towns. Doing an online search for the name of a community is an excellent way to see what might be available.

One book that offers brief English-language translations of excerpts from some of these books, so that readers can better understand the range of information that these books offer, is From a Ruined Garden: Memorial Books of Polish Jewry by Jack Kugelmass and Jonathan Boyarin (New York: Schocken Books, 1983). The book contains an annotated, alphabetical listing of towns for which there were *yizkor* books published to that date.

Appendix B of the revised edition of Genealogical Resources in New York, compiled and edited by Estelle Guzik and published by the Jewish Genealogical Society, Inc., P.O. Box 286398, New York, NY 10128 in 2003, offers a list of *yizkor* books in various libraries in the New York City area.

The following is a list of *yizkor* books that were written about Galician towns or which mention neighboring communities. The latter are given in parentheses. This list is, no doubt, missing some relevant *yizkor* books. In addition, two memorial books cover many towns in Galicia: Gedenkbuch Galicia and Pinkas Galicia, both edited by N. Zucker and published in Buenos Aires, in 1964 and 1945 respectively.

Language code: H=Hebrew; Y=Yiddish; E=English; P=Polish; O=other

Andrychów (see Wadowice)
Baligród (see Lesko)
Baranów, 1964 (H/Y/E)
Baryłów near Brody (see Radziechów)
Bełż, 1974 (H/Y)
Biecz, 1960 (H/Y)
Bielsko-Biała, 1973 (H/O)
Bóbrka, 1964 (H/Y/E)
Bolechów, 1957 (H/Y)
Borszczów, 1960 (H/Y)
Borysław (see Drohobycz)
Brody (see Arim, vol. 6)
Brzesko, 1980 (H/Y)
Brżezany, 1978 (H/Y/E)
Brzozów, about 1985 (E/Y/H)
Buczacz, 1956 (H)
Budzanów, 1968 (H/Y/E)
Bukowsko (see Sanok)
Bursztyn, 1960 (H/Y)
Busk, 1965 (H/Y/E/P)
Chołojów (see Radziechów)

Chorostków, 1968 (H/Y)
Chrzanów, 1948
Cieszanów, 1970 (H/Y)
Czarny Dunajec (see Nowy Targ)
Czortków, 1967 (H/Y/E)
Dębica, 1960 (H/Y)
Dobromil, 1964 (H/E)
Drohobycz, 1959 (H/Y)
Dubiecko (see Dynów)
Dynów, 1949/50 (Y)
Dynów, 1979 (H/Y)
Felsztyn, 1937 (Y/E)
Gliniany, 1945, 52 pages (Y);
    1950, 307 pages (H)
Gorlice, 1962 (H/Y)
Gródek Jagielloński, 1981 (H)
Hordenka, 1963 (H/Y)
Husiatyn, 1977 (H/Y)
Jabłonka (see Nowy Targ)
Janów (near Trembowla; see
Budzanów and Trembowla)
Jarosław, 1978 (Y/E)

Jasło, 1953 (H)
Jaworów, 1950 (Y/E)
Jaworów, 1979 (H/Y)
Jezierzany, (H/Y)
Jordanów (see Nowy Targ)
Kalusz, 1980 (H/Y/E)
Kalwarja Zebrzydowice (see
    Wadowice)
Knihynicze (see Rohatyn)
Kolbuszowa, 1971 (H/Y/E)
Kolomyya, 1957
Kolomyya, 1971/2 (H)
Kopyczyńce (see Husiatyn)
Korczyna, 1967 (H/Y)
Kossów, 1964 (H/Y)
Kossów, 1981 (Y)
Kraków, 1959 (H)
Kraków (see Arim, vol. 3)
Krakówiec (see Jaworów)
Kuty, 1958
Łancut, 1963 (H/Y/E)
Lemberg (see Lvov)
Lesko/ Lisko, 1965 (H/Y)
Leżajsk, 1970 (H/Y)
Łopatyn (see Radziechów)
Lutowiska (see Lesko)
Lvov (see Arim Vol. 1)
Lvov, 1956, (H)
Maków Podhalański (see Nowy
    Targ)
Medenice (see Drohobycz)
Mielec, 1979 (Y)
Mikałajów (see Radziechów)
Monasterzyska, 1974 (H/Y/E)
Mosty Wielki, 2 vols. 1975, 1977
    (H/Y/E)
Myślenice (see Wadowice)
Nadwórna, 1975 (H/Y/E)
Narajów (see Brzeżany)
Nowy Sącz, 1970 (H/Y)

Nowy Targ, 1979 (H/Y/E)
Oświecim, 1977 (H/Y)
Perehińsko (see Rozniatów)
Podhajce, 1972 (H/Y/E)
Przecław (see Radomysl Wielkie)
Przemyśl, 1964 (H/Y)
Rabka (see Nowy Targ)
Radomyśl Wielki, 1965 (H/Y/E)
Radziechów, 1976 (H/Y)
Rawa Ruska, 1973 (H/Y/E)
Rohatyń, 1962 (H/Y/E)
Rożniatów, 1974 (H/Y/E)
Rozwadów, 1968 (H/Y/E)
Rudki, 1978
Rymanów, 198? (H)
Rzeszów, 1967 (H/Y/E)
Sambor, 1970 (H)
Sambor, 1980 (H/Y/E)
Sanok (see Dynów)
Sanok, 1970 (H/Y)
Sassów, 1979 (Y)
Sienków (see Radziechów)
Skała, 1978 (H/Y/E)
Skałat, 1971 (H Sokal, 1968
    (H/Y)
Skole (see Gedenkbukh Galicia)
Stanisławczyk (see Radziechów)
Stanisławów (see Arim vol. 5)
Stary Sambor (see Sambor)
Stojanów (see Kokal)
Strusów (see Trembowla)
Stryj, 1962 (H/Y/E)
Strzemilcze (see Radziechów)
Strzyżów, 1969 (H/Y)
Strzyżów, 198? English transla-
    tion of and additions to above
    by Harry Langsam, 745 N.
    Croft Avenue, Los Angeles,
    CA 90069
Sucha (see Wadowice)

Swaryczów (see Rozniatów)
Szczurowice (see Radziechów)
Tarnobrzeg, 1973 (H/Y)
Tarnopol, 1955 (H/Y/E)
Tarnów, vol. 1, 1954; vol. 2, 1968 (H/Y)
Tłumacz, 1976 (H/Y/E)
Tłuste, 1965 (H/Y)
Toporów (see Radziechów)
Trembowla, 198? (H/E)
Trzebinia, 1969 (H/E)
Turka, 1966 (H/E)
Tyśmienica, 1974 (H/Y)
Uhnów, 1981 (H)
Ustrzyki Dolne (see Lesko)

Wadowice, 1967 (H/Y)
Wieliczka, 1980 (H/Y/E/P)
Wiszniew, 1972 (H/Y)
Wiśniowa, 1972 (H/Y)
Witków Nowy (see Radziechów)
Zabłotów, 1949 (H/Y)
Zagórz (see Sanok)
Zakopane (see Nowy Targ)
Zarszyn (see Sanok)
Zawidcze (near Brody) (see Radziechów)
Zborów, 1975 (H/Y)
Złoczów, 1967
Żołkiew, 1969 (H)

Slave laborer, 1942

Town Name Index to *Pinkas Hakehillot*

Yad Vashem in Jerusalem has completed its publishing project to document the Jewish presence in Central and Eastern Europe from the earliest times to the Holocaust. Known as *Pinkas Hakehillot* (Encyclopedia of Towns), three include articles relevant to Galicia:

» Poland vol.1 Łódź and its Region
» Poland vol. 2 Eastern Galicia, 1980
» Poland vol. 3 Western Galicia and Silesia, 1984

The *Pinkas Hakehillot* series can be purchased through Rubin Mass, Ltd., P.O. Box 990, Jerusalem 91009. Phone: (02) 632-565; fax: (02) 632-719.

The following list includes the Galician towns described in the *Pinkas Hakehillot* (Encyclopedia of towns). The articles focus on Jewish life in these towns. George Sackheim translated and published a list of the towns in *Search* vol. 8, no. 3 in 1988. He designated in which volume on Poland the article appeared. In some cases, there appears to be more than one article.

Sackheim's translation (or perhaps that of the *Pinkas* authors, since some books include English-language indexes) spells the name of the town as it was spelled by the Austrian government. While not generally a problem for towns in Poland, many towns in Ukraine are now spelled differently in their transliterated form. Since there are multiple towns of the same name in Poland and Ukraine, there may be confusion for some towns. Some towns may have been missed from Sackheim's original list.

Table 8.1. Galician Towns Described in Pinkas Hakehillot

Baligród 3	Bielsko 1	Bolechów 2
Baranów 3	Bielsko Biała 3	Bolszowce 2
Barycz 2	Bircza 2	Borysław 2
Bełż 2	Błazowa 3	Brody 1 and 2
Bełżc 1 and 2	Bóbrka 2	Broszniów 2
Bialy Kamień 2	Bochnia 1 and 3	Brzesko 3
Biecz 3	Bohorodczany 2	Brzezhany 2

Brzeżnica Stara 1
Brzostek
Brzozów 3
Buchach 2
Budzanów/Budanow 1, 2
Bukaczowce 2
Chodorów/Khodorov 2
Chołojów 2
Chorostków 2
Chrzanów 3
Chyrów 2
Cieszanów 1 and 2
Cisna 3
Czarny Dunajec 3
Czchów 3
Czortków 2
Czortowiec 2
Czuduc 3
Dąbie 1
Dąbrowa 1
Dąbrowa Tarnowska 3
Dębica 1 and 3
Delatyn 2
Dobczycze 3
Dobra 1
Dobromil 2
Dobrotwór 2
Dolina 2
Domaradz 3
Drohobycz 2
Dubiecko 3
Dukla 3
Dunajów 2
Dynów 3
Stary Dzików 2
Dzików 1
Gliniany 1 and 2

Gołogóry 2
Gorlice 3
Grabów 1
Grebów 3
Grójec 1
Gromnik Grybów 3
Grzymałów 2
Halicz 2
Horodenka 2
Ilnik 2
Iwanowice 1
Jankowice 1
Janów 1 and 2
Jarosław 1
Jaryczów 2
Jasienica Ros. 3
Jasliska 3
Jasło 3
Jawornik Polski 3
Jawornik Szklar. 3
Jaworów 2 and 3
Jazłowice 1 and 2
Jedlicze 3
Jezierzany 2
Jeżow 3
Jezupol 2
Jordanów 3
Kalusz 2
Kamionka Strum. 2
Kańczuga 3
Kęty 3
Kłodowa 1
Kolaczyce 3
Kolbuszowa 3
Kołomea 2
Kopyczyńce 2
Korczyna 3
Kozłów 2
Kozowa 2
Kraków 1 and 3

Krechowice 2
Krościenko 2
Krosno 3
Krukienice 2
Krynica 3
Krystynopol 2
Krzeszowice 3
Krzywcza 3
Kulików 2
Kuty 2
Łabowa 3
Łacko 3
Łańcut 3
Lanczyn 2
Lesko 2
Lesniów
Lezhanovka 2
Leżajsk 3
Limanowa 3
Lipsko 2
Lomna 2
Lopatyn 2
Lutowiska 2
Lemberg 1 and 2
Magierów 2
Mielec 3
Mielnica 2
Mikołajów 2
Mikuliczyn 2
Mikulińce 2
Monasterzyska 2
Mosciska 2
Mszana Dolna 3
Muszyna 3
Myślenice 3
Nakło 1
Narajów 2
Narol 2
Niebylec 3
Niemirów 1 and 2

Niepolomice 3
Nowy Dwór 1
Nowy Sącz 3
Nowy Targ 3
Obertyn 2
Olesko 2
Oleszyce 2
Olpiny 3
Osiek 1 and 3
Otrówek 1
Oświęcim 3
Peczeniżyn 2
Pilzno 3
Piwniczna 3
Plazów 1
Podbuż 3
Podhajce 2
Podwołoczyska 2
Pomorzany 2
Potok 2
Probuzna 2
Pruchnik 3
Przecław 3
Przedbórz 1
Przemyślany 2
Przemyśl 2
Przewórsk 3
Rabka 3
Radgoszcz 3
Radlow 3
Radomyśl nad Sanem 3
Radomyśl Wiel. 3
Radoszyce 1
Radymno 3
Radziechów 2
Raków 1
Rawa Ruska 2
Romanów 1
Ropczyce 3

Równe 1
Rożniatów 2
Roznów 2
Rozwadów 3
Rybnik 3
Rybotycze 2
Ryglice 3
Rymanów 3
Rzepiennik Strz. 3
Rzeszów 1 and 3
Sambor 2
Sanniki 1
Skała 2
Skałat 2
Skawina 3
Skole 2
Śniatyn 2
Sokal 2
Sokołów 2 and 3
Sokolówka 2
Solotwina 2
Sosnowice 1
Stanisławczyk 2
Stanisławów 2
Stara Sól 2
Starachowice 1
Stary Sącz 3
Stary Sambor 2
Stebnik 2
Stojanów 2
Stratyń 2
Strusów 2
Stryj 2
Strzeliska Nowe 2
Strzyżów 3
Suchostaw 2
Swięciany 1
Świrz 2
Szczakowa 3
Szczawnica Wyżna 3

Szczerzec 2
Szczurowice 2
Tartaków 2
Tarnobrzeg 3
Tarnopol 1/2
Tarnoruda 3
Tarnów 1/3
Tłumacz 2
Tłuste 2
Touste 2
Trembowla 2
Truskawiec 2
Trzebina 3
Tuchów 3
Turka 2
Tyczyn 3
Tylicz 3
Tyrawa Woloska 3
Uhnów 2
Ujazd 1
Ulanów 3
Ulaszkowce 2
Urycz 2
Uście Zielone 2
Uścieczko 2
Ustrzyki Dolne 2
Wesola 1
Wieliczka 3
Wielkie Oczy 1/2
Winniki 2
Wiśnicz Nowy 2/3
Witów 1
Żabie 2
Zabłotów 2
Zabno 3
Zagórz 3
Zagórze 1
Zakliczyn 3
Zakopane 3
Zaleszczyki 2

Załoźce 2	Zbaraż 2	Żołynia 3
Zarnowiec 1	Złoczów 2	Żurawno 2
Zator 3	Zlotniki 2	Żywiec 3
Zawada 1	Żmigród Nowy 3	
Zawalów 2	Żołkiew 1/ 2	

Jewish cemetery

Holocaust-Related Institutions and Collections

[Jeffrey Cymbler contributed substantially to the information in this section]

Yad Vashem

In recent years, there have been many important changes at Yad Vashem, The Holocaust Martyrs' and Heroes' Remembrance Authority in Jerusalem, in both the depth of their resources and the public's access to their information. Those attending the 2004 annual International Association of Jewish Genealogical Societies (IAJGS) in Jerusalem, were able to use the yet-to-be publically released Central Database of Shoah Victims' Names, compiled from many sources, including Pages of Testimony submitted by survivors and witnesses to atrocities committed throughout Europe. Shortly after the conference, this database was placed online and so, it became available to anyone with Internet access. Simply by entering a surname or a town name, one will be able to see everything in the database which mentions that surname or town. Though most of the information was derived from Pages of Testimony, many other sources of documentation have been used, such as compiled lists of victims from various camps and ghettos. By clicking on a name, you can see and print out the actual Page of Testimony and other documentation on that individual. One can see, at a glance, the source or sources for the information. Researchers may also conduct searches by the name of the submitter. The search engine permits entry of soundex spelling or exact spelling. In addition to this resource, Yad Vashem has computerized its highly accessible library and archival holdings, which include microfilms and photos.

A Guide to Jewish Genealogical Research in Israel: Revised Edition by Sallyann Amdur Sack and Israel Genealogical Society (Teaneck, N.J.: Avotaynu, 1993), though now somewhat dated, offers excellent background on Yad Vashem and its holdings. In addition to an exhaustive collection of yizkor books and Holocaust testimonials, the library has acquired a modest collection of published and unpublished genealogies.

An example of the type of material acquired by Yad Vashem was a list of 10,000 Jews who died in the Lwów ghetto. The list was acquired by Yad Vashem from the Ukrainian archives in L'viv. The material in Record Group M37/88, was prepared by officials of the Jewish cemetery during 1941–42. It is in chronological order and includes the descendent's age, date of death and residence in Lwów (once Lemberg and now L'viv).

The website is: www.yad-vashem.org.il

U.S. Holocaust Memorial Museum, Library and Archives

The library and archives housed on the top floor of the U.S. Holocaust Memorial Museum in Washington, D.C., 100 Raoul

Wallenberg Place SW, Washington DC 20024-2150, has an extensive collection of material about the Holocaust on paper, microfilm and microfiche. Much of their material duplicates what is available at Yad Vashem. The archives holds microfilmed records from German records captured by the Allies as the war was ending. Other material was held by the Soviet Union and the demise of that entity enabled the U.S. Holocaust Memorial Museum to acquire material from various archives of the former Soviet Union and microfilms of records generated in Warsaw after the war by the Main Commission for the Investigation of Crimes Against the Polish Nation and its counterpart in the Soviet Union, the Extraordinary Commission to Investigate German-Fascist Crimes Committed on Soviet Territory. Both contain much of interest to those interested in what had been Galicia. The Extraordinary Commission records are in Russian (Cyrillic alphabet). Easier to manage are Main Commission records, since they are Polish but names are easy to spot. This author reviewed portions of Record Group 31 covering Ukraine and Record Group 15 for Poland. They are described in some detail below.

An email by Renee Steinig on 26 December 2005 to the Gesher Galicia discussion group indicated that Extraordinary Commission records cover 180 communities, many of them formerly Galician. She stated that there were 15,000 entries for the district of Stanislaw w, now Ivano-Frankivsk. Peter Lande, a member of the Jewish Genealogy Society of Greater Washington, has long coordinated extensive volunteer efforts to index the names of individuals appearing in various groups of records. To date, Lande has not organized an indexing project for these record groups. The microfilms are on the fifth floor of the Museum in the archives located next to the library. The library and archives are open seven days a week. However, if you plan to use the facilities on the weekend, you must notify the staff in advance because the material must be pulled for you on Friday. Weekend staffing is very limited. Although the facilities are excellent, keep in mind that you will probably encounter material from these collections in languages other than English and, unless you can read the material or a staff member has time to help you, you may need to either make copies or bring a translator with you.

An agreement between the museum and the International Committee of the Red Cross (ICRC) has facilitated the transfer of microfilms of more than 25,000 pages of Holocaust-era material to the museum's archives. According to *Washington Jewish Week* (26 December 26 1996, page 6), the documents "contain official reports on ICRC rescue missions, delegation visits to concentration camps and ghettos, deportation operations, and Jewish emigration before and after the war. Many of the pages include photographs relating to World War II and the postwar years in Europe." Microfilms of some documents were also deposited, under this agreement, with Yad Vashem and the Center for Jewish Documentation in Paris.

Although efforts to catalog the vast and growing holdings of the archives are ongoing, there is still much that remains uncataloged. However, one may view what has been cataloged online. Additionally, there are finding aids to manuscript and microfilm holdings. A full-word indexing search engine is available to query both the library and archives catalog. Contact the archives staff by e-mail at archives@ushmm.org. The website is: www.ushmm.org.

Ukraine, Record Group 31

The Polish form of the towns names are used in describing this record group since that is the way they are listed in the catalog of holdings.

RG31.002M. Selected records from the Ukrainian Central State Archive in Kiev. Name lists of persons killed in various villages (in Cyrillic). (14 reels, probably not from areas once Galicia)

RG31.003M. Selected records from what at the time of filming was the L'vov Oblast Archive (1 reel). This reel includes a list of names of about 13,000 Jews, most of whom were men born or resident in Lwów or neighboring towns. Plans have been cited for this list to be placed on the museum's website. These records were created when individuals applied for German passes to leave their ghettos to work in factories and other establishments, in an effort to prevent their deportation to camps. In most cases, the list provides only names and local addresses.

Fond 24. Records documenting the creation of ghettos on November 25, 1942, in Gródek, Jaworów, Rudki, Szczerzec, Bóbrka, Jaryczów Nowy and Zolkiew; disposition of registers for Jews in Lwów; correspondence; name lists of Jews (including birthplaces and dates from several towns in the vicinity of Lwów), 1942–43.

Fond 31. Order establishing Lwów ghetto, July 22, 1941.

Fond 35. List of Jewish physicians in Lwów.

Fond 37. Population statistics for Gródek Jagielloński, Janów, Jaworów, Sadowa Wiśnia, Rudki, Mosciska and Komarno regions, by community, nationality and Jewish population; Jews employed by Lwów city departments; labor utilization of POWs and Jews in labor camps and ghettos; Jewish workers in city agencies, etc.

Fond 56. Jews employed in Bolechów, Drohobycz, Skole and Broszniów.

Fond 85. Transit permission for Jews employed in Borysław and insurance matters for Jews working for German firms in Lwów.

Fonds 2042 and 1951. Records from the Drohobycz city administration.

Fond 1952. Material about Stryy and more transit passes for Jews in Drohobycz; work permits for Jews in Skole.

RG31.005*01. Records relating to Ukrainian Jews in Lwów.

RG31.006M. Selected records from what, at the time of filming, was the Czernovitz Oblast Archive (11 reels).

Poland, Record Group 15

RG15.003M. Records of the Office of the Gouvernment Kommissar for the Productivity of the Jewish Population (3 reels).

RG15.008M. Records of German occupation, 1939–45 (8 reels).

RG15.010M. Records of the Institut fur Deutsche Ostarbeit in Kraków. There is little about Jews, but for the town of Jarosław, the family Seitelbach was mentioned in 1943: Abraham, b. 1898; Maria, b. 1900; Sura, b. 1925; David, b. 1928. Numerous charts are included that list surnames taken from birth records dating 1777–1943, with the number of persons with those surnames for either every year, or, in some cases, every 10 years. For instance, for the towns of :

> Biecz: Gotfried, Kraus, Guter, Furst, First, Heller, Horn, Mayer, Muller, Rajman, Salamon, Saidel, Zaydel, Wolff and Schindler.

> Błazowa: an incident in 1943 resulted in the deaths of 23 Jews: Mayer Spiss, age 45, a rabbi; Baruch Wiesenfeld, age 65, merchant; Leib Sturm, age 43, merchant; Moses Katz, age 48, merchant; Ruchla Weiss, age 33, merchant; Leiba Leinhard, age 25, merchant; Symcha Heischuber, age 41; Moses Steppel, age 18; Kelman Wang, age 46; Efroim Sturm, age 39; Berl Horstein, age 45. Also included were 12 others whose names were unknown, with 2 Jews from Kalisz.

RG15.019M. Court inquiries about executions and graves in various places in Poland. A number of reels are of significance to Jews, but considerable effort is needed to extract the relevant information. Reels 3, 4, 10, 11, 14, 15 and 17 seem most pertinent. This record group is composed of questionnaires generated in 1945. Entirely in Polish, they document the knowledge of Poles and Ukrainians about the executions and mass killings of Jews and others. One item specifically seeks to identify, by ethnic group, those who had been victimized. Some of the questionnaires name individuals; others estimate the number killed in the action described. Where mass killings took place in cemeteries and elsewhere, the number of dead was estimated. Within each district, small towns are listed alphabetically. Not surprisingly, most of the individuals mentioned by name were not Jewish. When Jews are mentioned, some information is usually given beyond the name, such as age, occupation, and circumstances surrounding the person's death.

- » Reel 3. Sections 8 and 9 refer to Kraków and the surrounding district: Bochnia, Biała Krakowska, Brzesko, Chrzanów, Dąbrowa Tarnowska, Limanowa and Miechów.
- » Reel 4. Continues with Section 9 communities; Section 10: districts of Myślenice, Nowy Sącz and Nowy Targ; Section 11: districts of Olkusz, Tarnów, Wadowice and Żywiec.
- » Reel 10. Section 33: districts of Rzeszów, Brzozów, Dębica, Gorlice and Jarosław; Section 34: districts of Jasło, Kolbuszowa, Krosno, Lesko and Lubaczów.
- » Reel 11. Section 35: districts of Łancut, Mielec and Nisko; Section 36: districts of Przemyśl, Przeworsk, and Rzeszów; Section 37: districts of Sanok and Tarnobrzeg.

Łancut powiat (district):

Symcha Safier; Izrael Wegier; Markus Weinberg; Golda Goldman;? Kornblau;? Mendel; Fass from Wysoka; Besenstock from Łancut; Weissman, age 60; Maria Wolkenfeld; Josef and Moses Fenig; Lazar Kestcher; Izrael Anmuth; Mendel Feuer; Moses Sauer; Maier Rozmarin and wife; Sara and Frimet Wurm; Kalman Walkenfeld and wife; Feiga Schwanenfeld and three children; Fiege Rosenfeld and two children; Boruch Reichard, his wife, Mala, and daughter Elka; Mira Low, Szulem Low and two children; Serla Speigel; Chana and Scheindel Rosenfeld. In another questionnaire: Josef Kanner, age 45; Mendel Lindenbaum, age 30; N. Bitner, age 40; Majlech Lorberbaum, age 22; Mojeszez Lorberbaum, age 24; N. Cuker, age 26 from Sarzyna near Rudnik.

Town of Żołynia:? Weiss, Isak Schuck, Joel Felter and wife.

Mielec powiat:

Town of Borowa: Moses Hirschfeld; Abraham Horowitz; Moses Birnbaum, his wife and three children; David Kupperman; Haskiel Bluth; Jakub Kass; Pinkas and Aron Spialter; Jakub and Maarkus Horn; Wolf and Joachim Storch; Isaak Klagsburn and wife; Abraham Storch; Leib Grun and wife; Moses Weiser, wife and three children; Josef Storch, wife and 3 children; Kahl family.

Town of Czernia: Mendel Mebsinger (one born 1910, the other born 1912); Raiza Gross, age 60; Matylda Gross, age 35; Hersch Braw, age 60, his wife, age 30; daughter, 15; and son, 12; Leib Kornbluth, age 40, and Cyla Kornbluth, age 60.

Town of Przeclaw: Jakob Jam; April Manes; Male Kopel; Fiege Silber.

Nisko powiat: Josef Rothbard, born 1894; wife, born 1903; Markus and Yenta Krell.

Przemyśl powiat:

Town of Dubiecko: List of 80 people, mostly Jews, killed in Dubiecko, though many came from other communities in the vicinity, including Drohobycz, Kańczuga, Jawornik Polski, Iskan, Hucisko, Nienadowa. Surnames include Frieder, Rubinfeld, Lamper, Ringel, Hofner, Pechter, Kanner, Meller, Eisbart, Unger, Herfenist, Grudzewski, Domb, Baruch, Binder, Zeichner, Jaworniker, Gluksman and Tewel.

Town of Nienadowa, suburb of Dubiecko: Natan Unger, age 16; Etla Glucksman, age 61; Zeiger Gluksman, age 24; Markus Harfenist and numerous other Harfenist family members. Schimmel, Jaworniker, Adler and Hofner. Page 490: Sara and Isak Knoller; page 491: Samuel Landau and Jozef Schimmel; page 492: Aron, Sara and David Domb; Natan Meller; page 493: Simche Tisser, Samuel Strassler, N. and N. Dornbusch; page 495: Moses Harfenist; page 497: Leidnerow; page 498: Kańczuga and the Spitz family from Bacie.

From Przeworsk powiat:

Town of Krzywcza: Rosner, Chaji Hersch; Aron and Srul Freifeld; David Wassner; Mendel and Jankiel Pelner; Moses Fast; Chaim Grumet.
Town of Orzechowice: page 501: Samuel Ehrenfreund.

Town of Rybotycze: David Rubenfeld, age 56; Moses Amster, age 60; Moses Rubenfeld, age 45; Michael Rubenfeld, age 58; Simche ?; Leib Dank.

Town of Kańczuga: Page 514: Berkowa Adler, age 43; Juda Harfenist, age 40; Jankiel Nadel, age 45; Hana Nadel, age 40; Josek Hoch, age 40, and Brandla ?, age 40.

Town of Frysztak: Chune Wolf Zanger, Josef Puderbeitel and Berisch Schlesinger.

Town of Markowa: Gartenhaus family: Kaila, age 38; Szmuel, age 20; Ryfka, age 17; Szmuel, age 15; Jankiel, age 13. Several additional lists.

Town of Jawornik Polski: Page 594: Springer family; Chaje Blau, age 50; Jacob Spitz, age 88; Leib Chiel, age 84; Chaskiel Speigel, age 60; Chaya and ? Speigel; Daniel Gerstler, age 50; Chaja Beck, age 48.

Town of Strzyżów: page 635: David Leiberman, b. August 1, 1884; Dr. Franciszek Rosenthal recte Koppleman, attorney, b. 1894; Samuel Zeinwel Grunblatt, b. June 18, 1893; Samul Grosskopf, b. May 6, 1872; Jakub Rosen, b. July 25, 1892; Moses Scheffler, b. December 6, 1877; Pinkas Klein, b. June 7, 1886; Chaim Salamon Flaumenhaft, b. May 21, 1884.

Town of Kolaczyce: page 636: Nates Stern.

Town of Bukowsko: page 661: 100 Jews listed.

From Rzeszów powiat:

Town of Błazowa: page 535 describes an "action" resulting in the deaths of 23 Jews, among them were surnames: Spiss, Wiesenfeld, Sturm, Katz, Weiss, Leinhard, Heischuber, Steppel, Wang and Horstein.

Town of Rymanów: page 679: Hersch and Ester Pinkas; Josef and Dora Morchower; Ruchel Singer; Abraham and Moses Wolf; Markus Stoff and wife; Eisig Bobik; Jozel Sponder; Isaak Schamroth.

Town of Szczawne: page 690: families Kresch, Kornreich, Fall, Kessler, Feibus, Kiern and Symchowitz.

Town of Bażanówka: page 692: Henia Diller, b. 1922; Gizella Diller, b. 1927.

Town of Jacmierz: page 696: Abraham Wilner, b. 1876; Isela Sturm, b. 1910; Leon Sturm, b. 1938; Henie Sturm, b. 1939; Josef Brand, b. 1904; Abraham Spira, b. 1914; Regina Spira, b. 1919.

Town of Zarszyn: ? Wilner, b. 1902; David Goldstend, b. 193?; Moses Goldstend, b. 1932; Ruchel Brand, b. 1940. On page 790: Aron, Golda and Isak Strenger.

» Reel 14. Section 48: Kraków; Section 48a: Myślenice, Nowy Sącz, Nowy Targ, Olkusz, Tarnów, Wadowice and Żywiec.
» Reel 15. Continuation of reel 14.
» Reel 17. Section 58: the same districts as Reel 10.

Examples of Records from Reel 10:

On Reel 10, there are some inquiries about Jewish deaths in towns in the Rzeszów area. Mentioned as having died in one incident in Dukla: Helena Zajdel, David, Josef and Jakob Krill; Jankiel and Israel Altholz; Benek Scherer; Moses Zehngut, age 48; Naftali Stein, age 32; Feitel Stein, Isak Gutwirt; Israel and Tyla Fries; ? Zimerspitz; Majer Hechtschrifen; Chaim Spira.

In nearby Nadole, Abraham and Herz Hendler, David Blechner and Josef Maum (?) were mentioned. There were also names from other towns in the vicinity. There were numerous lists of Jews with names, ages and occupations for towns around Lubaczów, including Oleszyce. One page included photos of three Grief men and Aba Engel from Oleszyce.

A questionnaire from a Łancut court documented the deaths of Wachs family members along with members of the Stein, Haftel, Leiberman, Gross, Blumenfeld and Turkenkopf families. On the other hand, questionnaires from many towns merely noted the approximate numbers of Jews killed in various *Actions.*

Another type of record on this reel charts the surnames of people born in various towns from 1777 to 1942, listing the number of individuals with each surname.

RG15.020M: Selected records from the Polish State Archive in Tarnów (11 reels).

RG03.017*01 (flat file, drawer 1) consists of paper records relating to Jews from Mielnica.

RG15.024M: Records of Deutsche Strafanstalt Reichshof (German Prison in Rzeszów) and other prisons in the area, including Tarnów, Nowy Wiśnicz, Kraków and Jasło. Included are lists of Jews held in the Rzeszów prison (17 reels).

Other Holocaust-Related Materials

» *The Blackbook of Localities Whose Jewish Population was Exterminated by the Nazis (Jerusalem:* Yad Vashem, 1965). This book identifies some 32,000 towns in Central and Eastern Europe giving town name and population before the Holocaust (exact year of census varies by country). The towns are organized by district within each country.

» *The Einsatzgruppen Reports: Selections from the Dispatches of the Nazi Death Squads' Campaign Against the Jews, July 1941–January 1943,* edited by Yitzhak Arad, Shmuel Krakowski and Shmuel Spector, was published in 1989 by The Holocaust Library of New York in cooperation with Yad Vashem in Jersualem. This 370-page English-language book describes, from Germany's daily reports, what the *Einsatzgruppen* (killing squads) did to carry out the policy of annihilating the Jews in an area that extended from the Caucasus, Crimea and Ukraine in the south through the Baltic states in the north. Four main *Einsatzgruppen*— lettered A, B, C, and D—consisting of up to a thousand soldiers each, killed nearly two million Jews in mass gassings, mass and individual shootings or hangings, or other actions in or just outside of villages. Excerpts from translated German reports, which are arranged chrono- logically, describe their daily activities. These reports depict the German mind set that the killing of Jews was justified because they were Communists and Russian spies who were despised by the [good] Ukrainians who supported the German invasion. The accounts do support that Russians and Ukrainians were involved in massacres of each other in Ukraine and that Ukrainians, as well as Germans, actively participated in killing Jews.

» *I Remember Every Day: The Fates of the Jews of Przemysl During World War II*, edited by John J. Hartman and Jacek Krochmal and translated into English (from Polish) by Agnieszka Andrzejewska. It was published in Przemyśl in 2002 and made available to readers in English in association with Remembrance & Reconciliation, Inc. in Ann Arbor, MI. This author purchased the book at the U.S. Holocaust Memorial Museum bookstore in Washington, DC. The Polish website: http://www.tpn.vt.pl/. This remarkable book is a compilation of memoirs by both Jews and Poles from that city, with important historical articles by the editors, and Anna Krochmal, in the appendices.

» *Be-Ovdan Moladety: yad vashem li-kehilah kedoshah Bardeyov, Tsekhoslovahyah:mi-yom hivasda hurbanah* by Abraham Grussgott (Brooklyn: 1988). This book can be found in the New York Public Library in the Slavic and Baltic Division under PXT-Bardejov 91-400. Moishe Miller found this book to be a good source of birth information for about 2,400 Jews who fled the Germans by going across the Tylicz Pass to Bardejov and Slovakian border towns and who were, for various reasons, not deported from Bardejov in 1942. The book contains name, birthdate, city of birth, occupation, and the reason they were not deported. Many Jews born in Nowy Sącz, Tylicz, Kańczuga, Oświęcim, Sanok and Gorlice, as well as other towns in Galicia are listed.

» *Poland's Jewish Heritage* by Joram Kagan (New York: Hippocrene Books, 1992). This slim volume, though spotty in its information about Holocaust-related events and memorials in certain communities in Poland, occasionally mentioned a community's Jewish history and the

existence of mass graves, and the condition of cemeteries and synagogues. Concentration and death camp sites
are discussed at some length, and drawings and photos of
memorials at these sites are presented. The book has its
primary value as a guide to travelers in the Polish towns
mentioned.

» *The Boys* by Martin Gilbert.(New York: Henry Holt and
Company, 1997). This 500+ page, widely available book,
offers a rich, though deeply disturbing examination of
some of the experiences of 732 children and youth who
had survived the Holocaust and were rehabilitated in
England. It also includes a chapter describing everyday
life in prewar Galicia. Those survivors from Galicia identified by their original names and towns are listed below.

Harry Balsam (Gorlice)
Ken Roman (Gorlice)
Aryeh Czeret (Budzanów)
Simon Lecker (later Gilbert) (Rymanów)
Jan Goldberger (Bielsko Biała)
David Hirszfeld (Biesna and Bobowa)
Leopold "Lipa" Tepper (Dukla)
Salek Orenstein (Opatów)
Michael Perlmutter (Opatów)
Moshe Rosenberg (Kraków)
Jack and Israel Rubinfeld (Bircza)
Zvi Brand (Ulucz near Bircza)
Zisha "Jack" Schwimmer (Stróżówka and Gorlice)
Witold Gutt (Przemyśl)
Toby Trompeter (Mielec)
Nathan and Kurt Lewin (Lvov)
Mark Goldfinger (Rabka Zdrój)
Joseph Moss (Krosno)

Michael Honey (formerly Misa Honigwachs) was one of "the
boys." He was an early and active member of Gesher Galicia. He
has frequently documented his experiences growing up in the
town of Tarnobrzeg. Here, his moving account documents the

difficulties survivors encountered in adjusting to normal life after their horrendous experiences.

Gilbert's index is less than complete. Oddly, the author did not acknowledge the contributions of all of those who provided him with their written or verbal memories, and the index reflects the same sort of spotty organization. Even more surprising was Gilbert's sometimes peculiar characterization of geographical locations. In failing to remember that Galicia had ended following World War I, Gilbert compounded his error by placing towns from what had been western Galicia in eastern Galicia and referred, without explanation, to Ukraine as "Ruthenia," which could confuse readers unfamiliar with the tortured history of Ukraine. Moreover, he incorrectly placed 1930 communities that were in Czechoslovakia in Ruthenia. While these are minor distractions to the overall purpose and theme of the book, Gilbert's extensive publication experience on the subject of geography would have suggested a more accurate account of this topic.

Personal Accounts

While, by no means an exhaustive list of Holocaust memoirs, the following provide accounts of individual experiences and, specifically, deal with communities once in Galicia.

- » Horowitz, Irene and Carl. *Of Human Agony* (New York: Shengold Publishers, 1992) Survival in Borysław and Lwów.
- » Horowitz, Irene and Carl et al. *Holocaust Revisited* (New York: Shengold Publishers, 1994). Focus on Borysław and Drohobycz.
- » Kahane, David. *Lvov Ghetto Diary* (Amherst: Ma.: University of Massachusetts Press, 1990).
- » Kornbluth, William. *Sentenced to Remember: My Legacy of Life in Pre-1939 Poland and Sixty-Eight Months of Nazi Occupation* (Bethlehem, Pa.: Lehigh University Press), in conjunction with the Brookdale Holocaust Center; distributed by Copyright Associates University Presses, Inc., 440

Forsgate Drive, Cranbury, NJ 08512 in 1994. The focus of the book is on Tarnów.

» Lehrer, Shlomo Zalman and Leiser Strassman. *The Vanished City of Tsanz* (New York: Mishnas Rishonim/Targum Press, 1997).

» Mayer, Bernard. *Entombed* (Self published: 2100 NE 207 Street, North Miami Beach, FL 33179). This is an account of how the author, as a teenager, along with others built and survived in a bunker under a house in Drohobycz. Photos and diagrams are included.

» Mogilansky, Roman. *The Ghetto Anthology* (Los Angeles: American Congress of Jews from Poland and Survivors of Concentration Camps, 1985). Includes description of many places in Galicia.

» Rebhun, Joseph. *God and Man: In Two Worlds* (Or Publishing, 1481 LaFayette Road, Claremont, California, 91711, 1985). An account of the author's childhood in Przemyśl and the years that he spent in labor camps and hiding.

» Rosen, Sara. *My Lost World: A Survivor's Tale* (published in the U.S. by Vallentine Mitchell, c/o International Specialized Book Services, Inc., 5602 N.E. Hassalo Street, Portand, Oregon 97213, 1993). The book was published as one in a series of The Library of Holocaust Testimonies under the auspices of the Yad Vashem Committee of the Board of Deputies of British Jews and the Centre for Holocaust Studies of the University of Leicester. The author was originally from Kraków but she and her family were widely scattered at the beginning of the war. The author's account informs the reader about the many strategies that individuals and families used to evade capture.

» Rosenberg, Blanca. To Tell at Last: Survival Under False Identity (Urbana, Ill.: University of Illinois Press, 1993). How two young women from Kolomyya survived the Nazis by masquerading as gentiles in Kolomyya, Lvov, Warsaw and Germany.

» Rothenberg, Samuel. *List o Zagladzie Zydow w Drohobyczu* (Letters about the extermination of Jews in Drohobycz), (London: Poets and Painters Press, 1984). 14 pages.

» Salsitz, Norman and Amalie Petranker. *Against All Odds* (New York: Holocaust Library, 1990). Describes Kolbuszowa, Stanisławów and Kraków under Russian and German occupation.

» and Richard Skolnick. *A Jewish Boyhood in Poland: Remembering Kolbuszowa* (Syracuse, NY: Syracuse University Press, 1992).

» Schiff, Meilach. Lost Borysław (New York: Vantage, 1977).

» Suslensky, Yakov. True Heros The book is a touching account of the Holocaust in Ukraine, during which many Jews were saved by Ukrainians at a risk (and often at the cost) of their own deaths. The book is a combination of oral history by real-life participants of the Holocaust drama and the author's analysis of the events. The book contains numerous photographs, letters, poems dated from the time of the war to the present. To order, contact Tanya Puchkova, 20 College Drive, Roscommon, MI 48653.

» Szende, Stefan. The Promise Hitler Kept (New York: Roy Publishers, 1944). This book offers a detailed description of what happened to Jews in Lwów during the Russian and German occupations.

» Thorne, Leon. Out of the Ashes: The Story of a Survivor (New York: Rosebern Press, 1961). Thorne, now a rabbi in the U.S., was in the Drohobycz and Sambor ghettos until liberation. He also discusses Schodnica and Lwów.

» Well, Leon. Janowska Road (New York: Macmillan Company, 1963). Wells provided an excellent description of Janowska Concentration-Death Camp outside of Lwów.

January 1940: Radiogram

Victor Low of Hanover, New Hampshire, contributed the above Radiogram. Low's father, Sol Low, was born in Sędziszów, near Kraków, in 1895. After emigrating to the United States in 1910, Sol Low became an active member of the *Ershte Shendishover Galitzianer Chevrah*, a *landsmanschaftn*.

The preamble to the *landsmanschaftn's* statement of purpose said, "The goal of the society is to maintain the spirit of fraternity . . . That ideal is to be kept alive among the younger generation born in this land and an attempt must be made to plant in them an awareness of our origins" (translated by Irving Howe).

Victor Low wrote, "With the rise of Fascism in Europe at the turn of the 1930s, Dad founded and became president of the United Galician Jews of America. By the late 1930s, it had some 80,000 members, who twice sent him to investigate the prospects of Galician Jews. On his second return, he urged the delegates to the annual convention to empty the organization's coffers and their own pockets and rescue as many Galitzianers as still could be saved from the gathering Holocaust. He was viewed as an alarmist, voted down and resigned to become an active Zionist.

Dad died in 1959 and Mom lived on until 1982. Among the memorabilia she left is an RCA radiogram sent to my folks by Dr. Abraham Silberschein, a Polish Jew and an ex-member of the Polish Parliament. Datelined Geneva, January 3, 1940, it said:

> Two hundred persons released by our action from co-camp leaving next German. Among them [20 names given]. Passage deposed here by American relatives. Information relatives but not papers. Other names follow. Accelerate action. Danger. Needing urgently passage for 350 other Polish Jews in co-camp and Western Galicia."

When I read this in 1983, I asked, 'Why not inform the papers?' The answer was self-given. A majority of Americans polled in that decade were anti-Semitic and were hostile or indifferent to the chief future victims of the Germans. And almost all Polish Jews stayed home rather than heed the rare voices prophesying a systematic destruction of them if they failed to seek refuge—or failed to find it, as so often occurred—outside of Poland."

Figure 5. Radiogram, 1940

RCA RADIOGRAM
R.C.A. COMMUNICATIONS, INC.
A RADIO CORPORATION OF AMERICA SERVICE
TO ALL THE WORLD — BETWEEN IMPORTANT U.S. CITIES — TO SHIPS AT SEA

Send the following Radiogram *Via RCA* subject to terms on back hereof, which are hereby agreed to

NBC BU 82384   JAN 3 1940

GENEVA 86/80 2 2150 1/50

NLT EUROLOW NEWYORK

TWOHUNDRED PERS US RELEASED BYOUR ACTION FROM COCAMP LEAVING
NEXT GERMANY AMONGTHEM (CHAIM FINGERHUT) STEINBERG) VERSTANDING)
WEISS) MOSZKOWICZ) SCHINDELHEIM) PROPPER) LAST) NEUMANN) AND WIFE GEIER)
FORSCHNER) SZLECHTERMANN) WHOSE PASSAGE DEPOSED WITHYOU AND BLACHMANN)
LEMO) RIEMER) ANDWIFE SCHWARZ) TEITELBAUM) BRACHFELD) INSEL) GRUNNBAUM) LINDER)
MOSES FINGERHUT) PASSAGE DEPOSED HERE BY AMERICAN

Main Office: 66 Broad Street, New York, N. Y. (Always Open)   Phone: HAnover 2-1811

FULL-RATE MESSAGE UNLESS MARKED OTHERWISE
Sender's Name and Address
(Not to be transmitted)   Form 100-20-Ta-800

Figure 5. Radiogram, 1940

CHAPTER 6

Other Books and Resource Materials

Materials cited in this chapter have come from many contributors over the years, including David Einsiedler, Laurence Krupnak, Lorin S. Weisenfeld, Elliott Bernstein, Barbara Urbanska-Yeager, Morey Altman and Georges Rosenfeld. Some materials in this chapter are simply presented, while others are reviewed or annotated in some detail. This is not an exhaustive list of material, but most books listed here include bibliographies that might lead the reader to other sources. Jewish encyclopedias also include articles about Galicia, as well as articles about specific towns and personalities. Most of these materials are also in the References & Bibliography at the end of this book.

General References

Baxter, Angus. *In Search of Your European Roots*. Baltimore: Genealogical Publishing Co., 1985. According to Elliot Bernstein, this book mentions many documents currently in Austria, including census returns, movement registration, military records.

Chorzempa, Rosemary. *Korzenie Polskie: Polish Roots* Baltimore: Genealogical Publishing Co., 1993. This book is a worthwhile investment for anyone interested in research in Poland. However, there is little that is, specifically, useful to the Jewish researcher. Chapter 4 discusses the social and class structure of Polish society, which may offer insights into Polish attitudes toward Jews. Chapters 5 and 6 discuss ethnic groups and geography in relation to these groups. Chapters 10, 11, 13 and 14 comprise the heart of this book for Jewish genealogists. Chapter 10 covers civil and military records. Addresses for every branch office of the Polish

National Archives are listed. Chapter 13 provides an helpful guide to pronunciation of letters and letter combinations, grammatical peculiarities of the Polish language and a helpful, if overly brief, genealogical dictionary in Polish, Latin and German.

Jewish References

www.Littman.co.uk is a site for Littman Library of Jewish Civilization, a publisher in London that was founded in 1965 to keep important Jewish books in print. The company now offers on-demand publishing opportunities for books of Jewish interest that would have an limited audience. Jonathan Webber and Chris Schwarz are in the process of publishing a 320 page book of current photographs from what was western Poland. The book, *The Ruins of Jewish Civilization in Polish Galicia*, is expected to be published in North America by Indiana University in December 2006 (ISBN: 0-235-33449-7).

The eminent-Polish Jewish historian Professor Majer Bałaban (1877–1942) wrote primarily in Polish, Russian and German, with a few books in Yiddish and Hebrew. He used authentic data from Polish and Jewish archival sources and was a reliable historian and genealogist. In 45 years, he published about 70 historical studies and some 200 short papers and reviews. His works on Galicia, all in the Polish language, are as follows:

> » *Dzieje Żydów w Galicji i w Rzeczpospolitej Krakowskiej, 1772–1868* (History of Jews in Galicia and in the Kraków Republic) Lemberg: 1916. Bałaban presents a candid picture of the life of Jews in Austrian Galicia and their political and cultural struggles; much history, no genealogy.
> » *Dzieje Żydów w Krakowie i w Kazimierzu, 1304–1868* (History of Jews in Kraków and Kazimierz, 1304–1868) Kraków: 1913. Library of Congress, DS 135 P6 K72. (Republished in Yiddish in about 1990.) The two volumes of history include 49 family trees of prominent rabbinic and non-rabbinic families. Excellent description of the organization and function of the *Kahal*, the official organization of the Jewish community. Geoffrey Weisgard (*Shemot,*

v. 5, no. 1) notes that Bałaban includes an 1809 map of Kazimierz that shows house numbers. An 1815 map in the book clearly shows the new Jewish cemetery, separated from the town of Kazimierz by a farm and fields.

» *Żydzi Lwowscy na Przełomie XVI i XVII Wieku* (The Jews of Lwów at the turn of the 16th and 17th centuries), Lemberg: 1906.

» *Zabytki Historyczne Żydów w Polsce* (Historical antiquities of the Jews in Poland) Warsaw: 1929. This book is an inventory of Jewish art and artifacts between the two wars, most of which were ultimately destroyed. Bałaban describes the treasures of Galician towns and those of the Jews: exhibits, museums, libraries, archives, synagogues and cemeteries, and secular memorabilia and family relics (portraits, papers, ritual objects, prayer books, bibles, Talmuds). The illustrations include one of the Eastern Wall in the synagogue of Chodorów (circa 1642). Call number at the University of Judaism, Los Angeles, is 937.2 B 1712 1929.

Books by other authors include the following:

» Beider, Alexander. *A Dictionary of Jewish Surnames from Galicia.* Bergenfield, NJ: Avotaynu, Inc., 2004. Beider is a well known expert on Eastern European Ashkenazic names. This is one of several books that Avotaynu has published by Beider on Jewish surname acquisition in Eastern Europe.

» Eisenbach, Arthur. *The Emancipation of the Jews in Poland, 1780–1870.* Oxford: Basil Blackwell, 1991. Sections on Galicia appear on pages 201–06 and 504–13.

» Fuks, Marian, Zygmunt Hoffman, Maurycy Horn and Jerzy Tomaszewski. *Polish Jewry: History and Culture.* Warsaw: Interpress Publishers, 1982. ISBN: 83-223-2002-7. While much of this book concerns Russian Poland, the authors do an admirable scholarly job of presenting Jewish culture, education, art, religious customs and family life.

The second part of the book focuses on Jews in various industries and cultural pursuits in the 19th and 20th centuries. The illustrations that accompany the written text are impressive. The book, in English, purchased in Warsaw in 1986, may be difficult to obtain elsewhere.

» Hausler, Wolfgang. *Das galizische Judentum in der Habsurgermonarchie: Im Lichte de zeitgenossischen Publizistik und Reiseliteratur Von 1772–1848.* Munich: R. Oldebourg Verlag, 1979. ISBN: 3-486-49511-9.

» Henisch, Meir, "Galician Jews in Vienna," in *The Jews of Austria: Essays on Their Life, History and Destruction,* 2d ed. Edited by Josef Fraenkel. London: Vallentine Mitchell, 1970.

» Heshel, Rabbi J., "The History of Hassidism in Austria," in *The Jews of Austria: Essays on Their Life, History and Destruction,* 2d ed. Edited by Josef Fraenkel. London: Vallentine Mitchell, 1970.

» Mahler, Raphael. *History of Modern Jewry,* 1780–1815. New York: Schocken Books, 1971. The chapter on Galician Jews is found on pages 314–40.

» McCagg, William O., Jr. *History of Habsburg Jews,* 1670–1918 (Bloomington: Indiana University Press, 1989). Discussion of Galician Jews appears on pages 105–22, 181–226.

» Mendelsohn, Ezra. *The Jews of East Central Europe Between the World Wars.* Bloomington: Indiana University Press, 1983. Chapter on Poland, including Galicia, pages 11–83.

» Sanders, Ronald. *Shores of Refuge: A Hundred Years of Jewish Emigration.* New York: Henry Holt and Company, 1987. This book is out-of-print, but it may be available for purchase through Amazon.com. It focuses mostly on Russian emigration, but there is much rich description of Galicia and the condition of Galician Jews, as well as a detailed study of the Jewish exodus from Europe to the United States, Palestine and elsewhere.

» Schorr, Mojzesz. *Żydzi w Przemyślu do Końca XVIII Wieku* (Jews in Przemyśl until the end of the 18th century)

Lemberg: 1903. This is an early history, in Polish, of the Jews in Przemyśl.

Geography and Maps

Shtetlinks within JewishGen is, often, the most direct way to quickly and easily gain access to a general map of your ancestral town's location. The maps are much less detailed and descriptive than many of the old maps available through public and commercial sources listed below but, as a start, it is a terrific resource.

The best map series for Galician research can be found at the Library of Congress, the New York Public Library and the University of Toronto library, and, probably other libraries, as well. The series is Map Series G6480 S75.A8. It was created in 1878 by the Austrian government for military purposes. The index map in Chapter 2 of this book is the index to this map series. There is a map for each of the squares on microfilm. There will be a modest charge for making an 11x 17 copy of each square . Write to: The Library of Congress, Geography & Map Division, Washington, DC 20540 to request copies, using the call number and the pertinent 4 digit number on the index map. This map series is also part of the LDS (Mormon) Family History Library collection on microfiche, numbers 6,000,198 through 6,000,339. The index is on fiche 6,000,198. Local LDS libraries do not have the capability of making a large copy of these maps.

Miriam Weiner published a helpful guide to the map collections of the Library of Congress and the U.S. National Archives entitled *In the Footsteps of Our Ancestors*. The guide included information about the town plans of Poland held by the Geography and Map Division of the Library of Congress and World War II aerial photos taken of towns by the Germans, now located at the National Archives II in College Park, Maryland. The town plans of Poland series includes communities in Ukraine, since at the time the series was created, part of Ukraine was in Polish territory. The guide includes a list of all towns included in each of the two series. Some Galician towns are mentioned in two of the three series. Contact Miriam Weiner, 136 Sandpiper Key, Secaucus, NJ 07094 or through mweiner@routestoroots.com about current availability.

Old maps can often be found in good used book stores, antique shows, and from specialized collectors. Vendors selling maps and used books of Jewish genealogical interest at annual IAJGS conferences, are a very good source for these materials. Reproductions are coming on the market in response to high demand for old maps at a reasonable price. Try the following sources:

» Avotaynu, Inc., sells a reproduction of an 1875 map of the Austro-Hungarian Empire. Internet: info@avotaynu.com; Web: http:www/avotaynu.com

» In the July 1995 edition of the newsletter, *Galizien German Descendants*, John Pihach said that Vienna's Kriegsarchiv is a source of Josephinian (*Josephinische Landesaufnahme*) military maps from 1779 to 1782. Send the latitude and longitude of the town or region for which you need a map or send a photocopy of a map showing your village to Kriegsarchiv, Nottendorffer 2, 1030 Wien, Austria, to order or to inquire about fees and postage.

» Kubijouyc, W. *Atlas of the Ukraine and Ethnic Groups of Southwestern Ukraine*. Berlin: Selbst-verlagdern Publikationsstelle, 1942. Includes Jewish population figures for every town in the Ukraine ethnographic region in 1937.

» Lenius, Brian J. *Genealogical Gazetteer of Galicia*. Lenius is an organizer of the Federation of East European Family History Societies. This 375-page book includes 22 maps and more than 13,500 place names. The gazetteer includes non-Jewish administrative and judical district information, and alternative names for villages. The book notes administrative district changes in 1906 and judicial district changes in 1914, both of which are consistent with changes in the administrative districts for Jewish records in those periods. Lenius relied on several sources to compile his book, but *Church in Ruin* by O.W. Iwanusiw, was the primary source. The book has a large section of regional maps. Each map includes the boundaries of the administrative districts within the region and the major town or city within the district. This highly recommended book is available from Brian J. Lenius, Box 18 Grp. 4 RR #1, Anola, Manitoba, Canada R0E 0A0.

» Magosci, Paul Robert. *Historical Atlas of East Central Europe* (Toronto: University of Toronto Press, 1993).

» Mokotoff, Gary, and Sallyann Amdur Sack. *Where Once We Walked.* Revised Ed. (Bergenfield, N.J.: Avotaynu, 2001. This book is a treasure and a major resource for serious genealogists. It is far improved from the first edition from the standpoint of including more formerly Galician communities. The authors used the U.S. Board on Geographic Names, the current international standard, to compile the book's place names. The listings include alternative names, exact latitude and longitude, and other location information. It is well worth owning a copy, but the book can be found in major Jewish and university libraries.

» Pogonowski, Iwo Cyprian. *Poland: A Historical Atlas.* New York: Hippocrene Books, 1987. Although this book emphasizes the history of Russian Poland, interesting maps and facts cover the existence of Austrian-ruled Galicia.

Biographical Compilations

» *Almanach Żydowski* (Jewish almanac). This book reads like a Jewish *Who's Who* of pre-World War II Lwów. It includes biographies of people and lists Jewish communal societies and religious organizations. It is available in major Jewish research libraries.

» Bader, Gershom. *Medinah V'Chachmeyah* (Galician-Jewish celebrities. New York: National Booksellers, 1934. The book is written mostly in Hebrew, with liberal use of Yiddish. Only one volume was published, with the surnames *aleph* to *lamed* (A-L in the Hebrew alphabet). Brief biographies; for authors, their book titles.

» Buber, Solomon. Buber, grandfather of Martin Buber, was a scholar and researcher of note. One of the "enlightened" Hebraists in Poland, he wrote two books of interest in Hebrew:

- *Anshei Shem* (Men of renown). Kraków: 1895. This book presents biographical sketches of 564 rabbis who served the Lwów community from 1550 to 1890. Some distinguished lay leaders are included in this list. Many biographies include family genealogies.
- *Kirya Nisgava* (Lofty city). Kraków: 1900. This is a similar book about Zolkiew.

» Dembitzer, Chaim Nathan. *Klilat Yoffi* (Perfection of Beauty). Kraków: 1888. Dembitzer, a Kraków rabbi, was a historian of Lwów rabbis. In Hebrew, the book contains biographies of 21 Lwów rabbis and other figures.

» Wunder, Rabbi Meir. *Meorei Galicia* (Encyclopedia of Galician Rabbis and Scholars), 5 volumes. This series offers detailed biographical information about rabbis and scholars and their families. Each volume includes indexes in English and Hebrew to family names and the towns mentioned in the biographical sketches. Rabbi Wunder also cites *yizkor* books and bibliographical sources. The Hebrew alphabet is the organizing framework for the volumes. These volumes are held by major Jewish libraries and the U.S. Library of Congress.

A database of surnames appearing in these volumes can be accessed through JewishGen.org. Go to Special Interest Groups and click on Rav-SIG (a special interest group for those interested in rabbis and rabbinic families).

To purchase copies of the volumes, write to Rabbi Wunder, Institute for Commemoration of Galician Jewry, 13 Panim Meiroth Street, 94473 Jerusalem, Israel.

Socioeconomic References

» Gay, Ruth. *Unfinished People: Eastern European Jews Encounter America*. New York: W.W. Norton, 1996. This book is an often amusing and touching analysis of the culture that grew up among Eastern European Jews who came to New York in the late 19th and early 20th centuries. The author offers the perspective of a first-generation American from the Bronx, using such themes as laughter, the Catskills, food, work, Florida, hats, corsets, *landsman-schaftn*, marriage, girls and winter to frame her discussion of the unique culture that arose as young immigrants struggled to make peace with mainstream American culture. The central thesis is that many immigrants, particularly those who came alone or without their parents, were, themselves, "unfinished people," and this impacted their general knowledge and what they transmitted to their children. She cites numerous examples of holes in her own fund of general knowledge of the world around her as she was growing up.

» Levine, Hillel. *Economic Origins of Antisemitism: Poland and Its Jews in the Early Modern Period.* New Haven, CT: Yale University Press, 1991. This dense and scholarly book is well worth reading for an understanding of the socioeconomic underpinnings of antisemitism in Poland and the feudal system which deeply affected all of those living in Poland prior to its partition.

» Mahler, R. *Jewish Social Studies,* vol. 1, 1939:97. This article discusses socioeconomic issues among the 250,000 Jews in what had been Galicia in 1930. Most of the Jews were traders, shopkeepers and artisans. Most lived in small towns which, in Eastern Galicia, were the property of the Polish nobility. Innkeeping had long been a Jewish occupation, but the laws of 1785 and 1789 forbade Jews from engaging in this trade. Although the practice continued, it required Jews to hide their true occupations.

» Moore, Deborah, ed. *East European Jews in Two Worlds: Studies from the YIVO Annual.* Evanston, Ill.: Northwestern University Press; New York: YIVO Institute for Jewish Research, 1990. This book includes a discussion of the economic background of Jewish emigrants from Galicia.

» Opalski, Magdalena. *The Jewish Tavern Keeper and His Tavern in 19th-Century Polish Literature,* published in 1986 by The Zalman Shazar Center, Center for Research on

History and Culture of Polish Jews, P.O. Box 4179, 91041
Jerusalem, Israel. This book includes a discussion of
Galician Jews.

» Potich, Peter J. and Howard Aster, eds. *Ukrainian-Jewish
Relations in Historical Perspective.* Edmonton, Alberta:
Canadian Institute of Ukrainian Studies, University of
Alberta, 1990.

Historical Travel Guides

» Baedeker, K. *Handbook for Travellers for Austria.* Martha
Burg of Houston, Texas, found an 1896 edition of this
work in her local library. The 10-page section on Galicia
and part of the introduction includes background on
money, travel and hotels. The brief section on Galicia
offers valuable historical information on rail travel in the
region.

In the opening "General Remarks," the author comments that
the region is:

........rich in corn, wood, salt and petroleum, but poor in
industries, which are chiefly in the hands of the Jews
(660,000 out of a population of 6 million), to whom most
of the inns, taverns, and shops belong. The horse dealers
and carriage owners are always Jews. They differ in their
dress and the mode of wearing their hair from the other
inhabitants, who despise them but are financially dependent on them.

The author judged that good hotels were in " Craców,
Lemberg, Przemyśl and Czernowitz [in Bukowina]. Otherwise,
in the smaller towns and in the country, the inns are generally
very primitive and dirty, while in the villages as a rule, the only
house of call is the brandy shop." Unsaid was that these shops
were usually owned by Jews.

At that time, two railways, one going east and west, the other
north and south, ran through Galicia. One line went from Bielitz to

Czernowitz and the other from Oświęcim to Tarnopol. The 212-mile trip from Kraków to Lemberg (Lwów) took 7½–10 hours. The 164 miles from there to Czernowitz took 6½ to more than 8 hours. Several branches from towns along the way extended out to towns in the vicinity. At that time, one-third of the population of Kraków were Jews. A small, general map of the town is included. Lemberg then had 21,900 Jews, of a total of 127,638 inhabitants, and was said to have two synagogues.

In describing Stanislau (Stanisławów, now Ivano-Frankivsk), Baedeker mentioned that the town had been "handsomely rebuilt since a great fire in 1868." Both restaurants recommended were owned by Jews. Borysław was known for its petroleum and ozocerite beds, and Truskawice for its sulphur and salt baths. Travel times for other legs of north-south journeys are listed with interesting local features and data.

» Bonar, Andrew A., and Robert Murray M'Cheyne. *Narrative of a Mission of Inquiry to the Jews from the Church of Scotland*. Philadelphia: Presbyterian Board of Publishing, 1842. This book is an account of the travels of two Church of Scotland missionaries in 1839. The two men, who were authorized to visit Jewish communities, traveled through North Africa, Palestine, Turkey, the Balkans, territory now in Ukraine, Galicia, France and Germany. In 1997, Gesher Galicia arranged for the 1997 republication of the book's chapter on the authors' travels through Galicia. To obtain a CD of this book for $10, contact Gesher Galicia.

Bibliographic Aids

» Bacon, Gershon C., and Gershon David Hundert. *The Jews in Poland and Russia: Bibliographical Essays*. Bloomington: Indiana University Press, 1984. Bibliographical essays are organized by historical period and by aspects of life, referenced to a bibliographical checklist. Galicia is integrated in sections on Poland.

» Magosci, Paul Robert. *Galicia: A Historical Survey and Bibliographic Guide*. Published in association with the

Canadian Institute of Ukrainian Studies and the Harvard
University Ukrainian Research Institute. Toronto:
University of Toronto Press, 1985. Morey Altman recommended this book whose main focus is on Ukrainian
history. There are good maps and a chapter on Jewish life.
The bibliographical references are excellent and include
materials on Jews in the Polish, Yiddish and Ukrainian
languages.

Language Aids

» Judith Frazin's marvelous book will aid you in many ways.
Although there are other such aids, Frazin's book is still
the best there is. Although the book focuses on the vital
record formats used in Russian Poland, Frazin includes a
section to guide you through translating terms commonly
used in genealogical documents, including numbers,
months, relationships and Polish phrases often used to
express events with genealogical significance. Frazin also
provides sample letters and phrases that you can use in
your letter writing on pages 33-41. Contact the author
about purchasing a copy of *A Translation Guide to 19th-
Century Polish-Language Civil-Registration Documents.*:
1025 Antique Lane, Northbrook, IL 60062.

Photo Collections and Video Resources

» The Reference & Bibliography section at the end of this
book includes other books, primarily of photos but including some text, as well. The information below provides
information about lesser known resources.

» Bet Hatefutsoth (The Museum of the Diaspora) on the
campus of Hebrew University in Ramat Aviv, outside of
Tel Aviv, has an extensive collection of videos made about
present and former Jewish communities around the world.
The address is P.O. Box 39352, Tel Aviv 61392, Israel.
Copies of some of the videos are for sale. The Museum
can provide a list of the videos currently for sale. Marian
Rubin, a long time member of Gesher Galicia, reported

seeing videos of Rzeszów and Łancut at Beth Hatefutsoth. The videos, which provided some history of the Jewish community and mention prominent members of the community, combine current footage with scenes of the Jewish community before World War II. The Beth Hatefutsoth catalog from several years ago included short, 1939 films about Jewish life in Kraków and Lwów and a 1988 filmed dialogue between former Jewish residents of Tarnów and a group of Poles.

» Marcia Meyers, another Gesher Galicia member, saw a video at Beth Hatefutsoth about the ceiling of the wooden synagogue in Chodorów. She was able to buy a copy, in English, formatted for American video machines. The cost a few years ago was $15.

» Salaminder, Rachael. *The Jewish World of Yesterday*, 1860–1938 (New York: Rizzoli International, 1993). This 320-page book contains fascinating photos of life in Central Europe, including Galicia.

» *A Time to Gather Stones* is a moving 30-minute video of Miriam Weiner's group trip to Poland and Ukraine in 1993. A number of genealogy societies have shown the video at meetings. Copies may still be available from Ergo Media, P.O. Box 2037, Teaneck, NJ 07666.

» *Return to My Shtetl Delatyn*. Dutch filmmaker Willy Lindwer documented his father's trip to Poland and Ukraine in 1991. His father, Berl Nachim Lindwer, was born in Delatyn but left before World War II. In the film, Berl and his granddaughter walk the streets of the towns, interview the local population, and visit some of the remnants of Jewish culture. In addition to Delatyn, towns visited include Bolekhiv, Kraków, L'viv, Przemyśl and Stryj.

» Brandeis Jewish Film Center at Brandeis University in Waltham, Massachusetts, has a 1939 film depicting Jewish life in Warsaw, Lwów, Kraków, Białystok and Wilno (now Vilnius, Lithuania).

» Pamela Weisberger, current coordinator of Gesher Galicia, showed a 1939 film depicting Jewish life in a Galician community at the Fall 2005 regional meeting of the SIG. She knows of other such films and she is, herself, a film maker, who produced a video based on an interview with David Einsiedler about his early years in Drohobycz. Pamela may be contacted through Gesher Galicia's website.

CHAPTER 7

Travel

Everyone seriously interested in knowing more about how our forebears lived, should visit the communities where they lived, worked and prayed. It is an enriching experience and makes places come alive in a way that no other experience can. So much myth has been created about our ancestral towns that, until you see the places with your own eyes, you may have a very distorted view of the way things were. For most of us, returning to ancestral towns will involve confronting the sad reality that are few or no Jews left in the vast majority of communities in what had been Galicia. Virtually everyone was killed, whether by killing squads, in street actions, by being taken to Belzec death camp, transported to other work or death camps, or some other "action" that resulted in death. The territory that had been the western portion of Galicia, was captured by the Nazis in their first assault in early September 1939. Those living in the northern part of Przemyśl and north were, for a brief time, under Russian control, but on the other side of the San River, residents were under Germany control. Some, thinking themselves fortunate to have found themselves under Russian control, moved quickly to go further east, outrunning the Nazis, but finding themselves shipped to camps in Siberia by Stalin. Many Jews met their end there, due to hunger, disease and exposure.

Ukrainian Jews were slaughtered by death squads of Nazis and Ukrainians, either by suffocation in closed trucks or by gunshot. They were buried, sometimes, alive, in mass graves. Jews in a number of communities in southern Poland were rounded up, locked inside their synagogues and burned to death. Only a remnant survived. Those who tried to return to their homes, found that they were not welcome. Their homes and property had either not survived the fighting or had been taken over by non-Jews who did not expect that the Jews would be returning. After a few pogroms, resulting in deaths in a number of communities, most Jews left for safer places after the war was over. Survivors clustered in a fairly small number of large communities in Poland and Ukraine. Many of those who stayed, married people who weren't Jewish, and raised their children outside of Judaism.

Some of the Jews who stayed in Poland after the war, were members of the Communist Party and they, for a time, were protected by their membership and loyalty. However, in 1968, they became targets for new rounds of discrimination and hatred. Priests preached against the Jews, blaming them for the Communist regime and the Communist prohibition against practicing Catholicism. Things were very tense and some chose to emigrate. By the end of the Communist era in Poland, there were an estimated 6,000 acknowledged Jews in the whole country. Since then, some people have followed up on suspicions that they were Jewish by birth or ancestry and have reconnected with their Jewish roots. There is a small but lively Jewish community in Warsaw and a viable community in the Kraków suburb of Kazimierz, with kosher restaurants and stores catering to Jewish visitors who come through on heritage tours, sponsored by both U.S. and Polish tourist agencies, to see the city and visit nearby Auschwitz. Ironically, it has become fashionable to be associated with Jewish culture, particularly in Warsaw and Kraków. There has long been a Yiddish theater troupe in Warsaw (with mostly non-Jewish actors), and now there are Jewish folk and music festivals. Jagiellonian University in Kraków has developed a popular Jewish studies program, where students can learn Yiddish and Jewish history. In Poland, Warsaw and Kazimierz in Kraków, have functioning synagogues and weekly Shabbat services, along with a warm and welcoming community of Jews who are eager to entertain visiting Jews. These cities have become important and easy destinations for Jewish travelers. In Ukraine, the larger communities have Jewish populations. Though the long years of Communist rule prevented people from knowing about their Jewish heritage, there are efforts underway to reconnect Jews to the understanding and practice of Judaism. Kosher food is available in a few places in Ukraine, particularly where the Chabad movement has been most active. Miriam Weiner, whose article on Ukraine, is below, is probably the best person to provide up to date information about developments in Ukraine.

Roads in both rural Poland and Ukraine may be two lanes, and one may still expect to share the local roads with horse-drawn carts or a tractor. As one person put it, "The driving is fierce and crowded; the roads are not well marked. The roads are frequently marked by town instead of route number." This traveler recommended hiring a local driver.

Ukraine is a bit more complex for travelers than Poland, in large measure because the economy is still so fragile and services are less developed than Poland's. This may change over time but , until the 2005 political changes in leadership in Ukraine, the government had not moved Ukraine into modern resources for tourists. On the other hand, there are more Jews living in Ukraine than in Poland and very active efforts to reenergize Jewish life there. But, even in places without Jews and, in the face of confronting the painful reality of what happened to the Jews who came from these towns, there is really no substitute for seeing the places and walking the streets that our relatives walked. Though wars and changing conditions have, in many cases, dramatically altered the communities where our relatives lived, it is important to have visual images of the context, places and landmarks that colored their daily lives.

Before you contact any travel agency or service, check out whether your town or region is part of Shtetlinks within JewishGen because you may find specific articles by people who have traveled there; map links; information about the condition of Jewish sites; books; and links to database information within JewishGen pertaining to the town or region.

*Former study house (*Bet Hamidrash*) of Dynower hasidim,
Bircza, 1986*

Resources

There are many travel guides to Poland available today. These
are a few that this author found particularly helpful in anticipat-
ing what the visitor might seek and find. Several others are mentioned in the References & Bibliography at the end of this book.

» Gruber, Ruth Ellen. *Upon the Doorposts of Thy House: Jewish
Life in East-Central Europe, Yesterday and Today* (New York:

Przemyśl street leading to destroyed old Jewish cemetery

John Wiley and Sons, 1994). A review of the book was originally published in The Galitzianer (v. 3, no. 3). This book
is deeply satisfying because the author, then in her 80s,
infuses every page with her very personal reactions and
observations. Rather than being a travel guide, the book
is more like a journal of Gruber's travels. For some places
she has visited several times, she shares the changes that
she sees, her own changed perspectives and, sometimes,
the frustrations that can accompany travel in that part of

the world. Much of this book covers Galician territory. Gruber became snowbound while visiting Auschwitz and had to become a guest at the convent. We listen in on her conversations about the controversies swirling around the very existence of the convent. She shares her heartbreaking visits to Kraków, where Kazimierz, the ancient Jewish community on the outskirts of the city is crumbling and on the verge of becoming a "pretend" place where few Jews live but many visit. Gruber muses over these issues, inconclusively, because no one quite knows what to do about the issues. The author also takes us through her motor tour of northeastern Hungary and southern Poland, as she makes clear the vital connection between those places because of the cultivation of the Tokay grape, which was used in making wine for ritual and commercial purposes by some of our ancestors.

She describes her visits to the few remaining Jews in villages, crumbling and desecrated synagogues, and the occasional cemetery to bear witness in our behalf. We cry with her. Her ear is wonderful and, although a photo is absent, we see the person she is talking to. This book is valuable to those who want to understand where they came from and where so few of us now live.

» Gruber, Ruth Ellen. *Jewish Heritage Travel: A Guide to Central and Eastern Europe* (New York: John Wiley and Sons, 1992). Poland is included in this guide, but not Ukraine.

» Salter, Mark, and Gordon McLachlen. *Poland: The Rough Guide* (London: Rough Guides Ltd, 1996). Good sections are included on Kraków and what had been Galician territory in southern Poland.

In addition, Gesher Galicia's website within JewishGen and websites for individual towns include travel information and commentaries by people who have experienced their communities first hand. Many issues of The Galitzianer, the quarterly publication of Gesher Galicia, have included travel articles. Back issues may be available in hard copy or online. Further, it is common for people about to embark on travel to Poland and Ukraine to solicit current advice from those involved with the Gesher Galicia SIG discussion group on JewishGen.

» ShtetlSchleppers: is a nonprofit organization affiliated with JewishGen and it does what the title suggests. The web address is: http://www.jewishgen.org/ShtetlSchleppers/
They have some standard trips set up two or three times per year with flights into major cities, including Kraków, a couple of days of touring the city and, perhaps a concentration camp, and then individual or small group visits to ancestral towns with a driver and guide. They will also tailor-make a trip for a group or a family. The current guide fees are about $100 per day plus meals and accommodations. The driver's fee is about $130 per day plus meals, overnight accommodations and parking. You will also be asked to contribute to ShtetlSchleppers for each day you will be traveling with their help. When you contact ShtetlSchleppers, you will be asked to identify the exact coordinates of the towns you wish to visit. You may find this information at: http://www.jewishgen.org/ShtetlSeeker/loctown.htm .

» The Polish National Tourist Office (PNTO, formerly known as ORBIS): has several publications about Jewish-oriented travel in Poland. Their *Map of Jewish Heritage* highlights sites of interest, including centers of Hasidism, death and concentration camps and cemeteries and synagogues. They Lived Among Us: Jewish Heritage in Poland notes that the synagogue in Lesko, formerly known as Lisko, which was built in the 18th century, is now an exhibition hall. Scenes from a handful of Galician cemeteries and other notable sites are mentioned and portrayed. The PNTO is located at 275 Madison Avenue, New York, NY 10016. They can assist independent travelers booking hotels and car rental, and can provide guides and drivers, as well as general advice. Although the site does not offer you an option for booking train travel through the PNTO, you should ask the agent about this if you want to travel by train. Most tourists in Poland do not use the train system, but it is an excellent and relaxing way to experience the country and its people. Find them at their website by entering Polish National Tourist Office into your search engine.

» Heritage Tours: Jewish publications advertise "heritage tours" which focus on visiting Eastern Europe, Holocaust sites and, sometime, Israel. These are general tours, usually operated by commercial travel agencies that specialize in Jewish travel. While they rarely afford the opportunity to visit small towns for individual research and touring, as a way of getting an overview for travel in a foreign country of interest, it is a good introduction.

Nowy Sącz

» PolandVisit.com: a travel service to Poland, the Czech Republic, Slovakia, Hungary, Bulgaria, Romania, Austria, Germany, Switzerland, France, Benelux and the Baltic

States. They provide a full range of travel services, including an English speaking guide and chauffeur driven car. The price is fairly reasonable. They also handle hotel accommodations. For more information, email pgolabek@mail.com or on mobile phone number +48 605 540 831.

» Staypoland.com: this site seems to focus on tours to Kraków and environs. They claim to provide full services for travelers to this city.

» The Polish State Railways system (PKP) for Polskie Koleje Państwowe can also be accessed online and there is an English language section. However, you would do best if you work with a travel agent who understands Polish and the rather complex train system to book intercity transit, overnight accommodations, or to arrange for a Polrailpass, which is a pass for unlimited train travel for 8, 15, 21 days or a month. If you are planning to do some or all of your traveling by train, it will be easier and a lot safer if you do not have a lot of heavy luggage. Try to use a suitcase on wheels or a soft-sided bag. And, beware of your wallet, passport and valuables while in the station and on the train. Pickpockets are on the alert for tourists who are not paying attention to their surroundings. With all of that said, the train is a reliable way to travel in Poland.

Planning a Trip

There are many considerations in planning a trip anywhere but, when visiting ancestral towns in Eastern Europe, you must be well organized and focused on what you will do there and what you want to get out of the experience. Tom F. Weiss and others have contributed some thoughts on what is needed as you ponder the purpose(s) of your trip:

» searching in archives and local records offices;

» walking around and visiting any physical remnants of Jewish life still visible, including cemeteries, synagogues and study or prayer houses, or any other buildings associated with the Jewish community;

» meeting local people who might have known relatives or who have special knowledge about Jews or Jewish matters;

» visiting local historical museums and other cultural sites that might add to your understanding of the place or region.

Major issues to consider are whether to: 1) arrange for a guide and a driver, 2) go with a tour group, or 3) to go on your own. In some instances, you may be able to arrange to break off from a tour group for a day or more to explore on your own or with the assistance of a pre-arranged guide and/or driver. If you can afford it, there are great advantages to having your own guide and driver because this option will provide maximum flexibility to make daily changes.

Going with a tour group will mean that you will have the company of others interested in the focus of the planned trip and the ease of knowing that hotel, luggage and eating arrangements will be managed by someone else. On the less positive side, there will most likely be a set itinerary which may exclude opportunities for personal exploration.

The least expensive arrangement is to rent a car, maybe make a few hotel reservations (essential in the busy summer months in large cities), and just, go. This is fine if you know enough of the language to navigate through complex conversations. Otherwise, you will be missing out on a lot. The early pioneers who traveled in the 1980s, generally traveled on their own or had guides and drivers for part of the time and floundered around on their own for the rest.

If you are on your own, you will have to consider whether to rent a car or travel between towns by bus and train, or even by taxi. Gasoline prices are very high in Europe and it may be less expensive to use local transportation but you will be adding time and uncertainty to your schedule. Some intercity trains in Poland have fairly comfortable sleeping compartments so that you can travel long distances, say from Warsaw to Rzeszów or Kraków to Przemyśl and save on a bit on your hotel bill.

If you want to take photography or video equipment, you will need to take everything that you need because you won't be able to rely on local suppliers. This includes batteries and film. If you plan to visit cemeteries, you will need to bring or purchase equipment for getting through brush, burrs and thorny vines. Some might want to take rubbings of gravestones. You will need equipment for that as well. If you know the addresses where family members once lived, you will need to bring that information with you, but keep in mind that communities are no longer organized by just house numbers, as they once were. Now you can expect street names and a modern house numbering system.

Should you take a cell phone? No, because they won't work in Poland or Ukraine. But, you will probably be able to rent a cell phone, which you should do for reasons of safety, if you plan on being on your own for all or part of the time.

Will you have access to the Internet and should you take a laptop? Larger communities may have Internet access at Internet cafes or some of the more expensive hotels, but don't count on it. If you decide to take a laptop, bring a very light one and remember that you will need a transformer for 50 Hz and 22 Volts. Do not let it out of your sight.

If you plan to do archival research, you might consider placing what you know about the family on large sheets of newsprint because they are light, easily foldable and offer a quick view of what you know in one place. You can even tuck blank sheets in your luggage to capture new information as you go through records. If you travel with a guide, the guide will be able to explain in Polish or Ukrainian what you are seeking.

Although you should not expect to walk into a local records office and have access to records, because of privacy laws governing those records, you can present a list of typed names with possible dates. Some offices will agree to research the information and allow you to return in a few days to collect the information. The advantage to this arrangement is that you will pay local fees instead of the fee you would pay by ordering from abroad.

You will want to be as inconspicuous as possible. Dress conservatively and so that your clothing doesn't offend local sensibilities. It is best not to wear jeans, short dresses or shorts. Rather, dress in simple, neutral colored clothing that will not mark you as a foreigner. Sturdy walking shoes will come in handy, along with a hat and sunglasses in summer.

Take all the toiletries and medications that you could possibly need and, if you have special dietary needs, you may have to take an extra suitcase to take your own food. Packages of dried fruit, crackers and nuts are good snacks that won't spoil and will be reliable food in areas where fresh food is less available. However, even in very small places, you can find break, crackers, cheese, an array of fruit, juices and dairy products. Ice cream and yogurt are widely available in Poland.

Credit cards: Take on VISA card and remember to put your pin number in a separate place to facilitate withdrawing money, if needed, at an ATM in a larger community. If you take money in your own currency, you can change it at the airport, hotel or bank. Small towns may not have modern amenities so be prepared to pay for food, etc. with local cash. Credit cards are accepted at large city hotels and restaurants but you may find it difficult to use your credit card for purchases, the way you do at home.

Hotel selection: The better hotels have become very expensive. It is difficult to find decent accommodations in many small places in both Poland and Ukraine, so many people have adopted the strategy of staying in one or two central locations and traveling daily to the towns of interest. The more adventurous might consider venturing into inns and hostels, often available for travelers, even in out of the way places. Though warned not to do so, I stayed in a very basic hotel, a step above a hostel, in Sanok, Poland, and found it to be small but clean, with a good breakfast (included) and very helpful staff.

Bathroom access: Tom Weiss wisely suggests bringing toilet paper or lots of tissue packs, and some hand disinfectant gel. Consider bring rubber bands to keep your pant legs off the floor. Expect most public toilets to be disgusting and you won't be disappointed.

Weiss also suggests making copies of all of your documents and credit cards and keeping the copy with you at all times, apart from your passport, credit card, driver's license, etc. Be vigilant about your safety and about the safety of your possessions. Leave your jewelry at home.

Medical insurance is highly recommended by Weiss. In the event that you need to be airlifted to a facility in a larger place, this could be extremely costly to pay for on your own.

The rest of this chapter will focus on specific travel advice from people who are experienced travelers in Poland and/or Ukraine. Because conditions continue to be so different in Poland and Ukraine, there is a subsection for each.

Visiting Ancestral Towns in Ukraine: A Report by Miriam Weiner

Miriam Weiner, a certified genealogist, author and lecturer in the field of Jewish genealogy and Holocaust research, has worked with archival officials and staff throughout Poland since 1989 and in the former Soviet Union since 1991. She is the president of Routes to Roots, an international firm offering archival research services in the "old country," customized tours for individuals and families to ancestral towns and "town visits" in behalf of clients. Weiner is the recipient of the 2003 "Lifetime Achievement Award" from the International Association of Jewish Genealogy Societies. She is the author of two award-winning books: *Jewish Roots in Poland: Pages from the Past and Archival Inventories* and *Jewish Roots in Ukraine and Moldova*, both co-published by Routes to Roots Foundation, Inc. and YIVO Institute for Jewish Research. The latter is out of print and is not planned for republication. The Routes to Roots Foundation, Inc. also hosts a website at http://www.rtrfoundation.org, which includes a searchable daatabase by town name of archival holdings in those countries. For further information, you can contact Ms. Weiner at (201) 866-4075 or mweiner@routestoroots.com.

The following report is loosely based upon, but substantially revised and updated from, an article by Miriam Weiner that originally appeared in *The Galitzianer* (v. 2, no. 1, Fall 1994) and subsequently appeared in *Searching for Your Jewish Roots in Galicia: A Resource Guide.*

During the past 15 years, I have visited more than 100 towns and villages in Poland and Ukraine, many of which were once part of Galicia. There are vast differences between these two countries today. The focus of this article is on the part of Ukraine that once was Eastern Galicia, specifically the Ukraine *oblasts* (districts) of Ternopil, L'viv and Ivano-Frankivsk (formerly Stanisławów).

When I first began to visit Ukraine on a regular basis in 1991, it soon became evident that I would need to pack differently and carry goods we take for granted in America. Because I now spend almost half my time in Eastern Europe, I bought an apartment in Ukraine in order to leave my office equipment (computer, fax, printer, cameras, video cameras, copy machines, etc.), reference books, clothing and other essentials in one secure place.

With the last few years, communications have improved signficantly in the large cities of Ukraine. Many people travel with mobile/cell phones now - both local residents and tourists. Additionally, the Grand Hotel in L'viv has a Business Center which offers an Internet connection and their restaurant features a buffet-style breakfast comparable to a Sunday brunch in the finest New York restaurants. Internet connections are available in a few hotels in Ukraine and also in small Internet cafes. Air conditioned rooms are available in some of the larger and more expensive hostels in major cities.

When I go to Poland, I think nothing of renting a car and driving myself, traveling only with my translator. In Ukraine, I do not go anywhere without both my translator and a driver/security guard. The road conditions are not near U.S. standards. The economic situation is such that highways are not repaired, and one must be ever vigilant for potholes, as well as free-ranging animals that wander along the roads. Also, highways are not well lit (or lit at all) for night driving.

The police still stop cars at will, generally for no infraction of the law, but for the purpose of inspecting the car's engine number and to inquire about destination. This is unsettling to those of us who have enjoyed and take for granted the freedom to be undisturbed unless we are suspected of breaking a law.

For the first few years in Ukraine, I carried gasoline in canisters in the trunk of the car because it was almost impossible to find open gas stations. Gasoline is no longer a deficit item, and I am now free of the gas fumes and the ever-present danger of carrying several gallons in the trunk.

Travelers should be aware, however, that frequent service areas along the secondary highways do not exist, as we know them. There are inadequate directional signs in the towns and along the roads. Toilet facilities along the highway could be an occasional outhouse, but more often, they consist of a short walk into the woods. Do not expect to find public telephones or convenience stores along the roadways.

The single most important thing to bring with you is extra patience – more than you ever dreamed you would need. Everything takes longer than expected to accomplish: phone calls, restaurant service, hotel registration/check out and document inspection at checkpoints on the highway and at border crossings.

Some handy items to pack are small tissue packets, film and batteries for camera and video equipment, packets of wet towelettes, aspirin or similar pain medication, first aid supplies, sugar substitutes (if you use them), sufficient supplies of any medications and a spare pair of eyeglasses.

Another important consideration in planning your trip should be the reliability of your transportation in Ukraine. It is essential that your driver carry spare parts and be a reasonably good mechanic. My frequent trips to Ukraine have forced me to learn more about auto maintenance and repairs than I ever thought I would need or want to know. Most cars used for tour transport are Russian made and one must think about their condition. Until recently, I carried a set of spark plug, a tow rope, tire inflator, a spare set of windshield wipers, a can of WD-40, flares, motor oil (I brought a case from the U.S.) and a strong flashlight. However, in early 1997, I bought a Dodge minivan that I shipped by boat to Gdańsk. I picked it up there and drove it through Poland and across the Ukrainian border (with my translator, of course) because I thought it important for the people who book town tours with me to have a strong and reliable vehicle in which to travel. My adventures in crossing the Polish/Ukrainian border in a new American car with New Jersey license plates, a New Jersey car registration, and International driver's license, all in English, would provide material for a stand-up comedian's entire act.

Another item that goes everywhere with me is a small bag, similar in size to carry-on luggage. In this bag, I carry a first-aid kit and an assortment of presents for the many helpful people I continually meet in my travels. These souvenirs from America, consisting of office supplies, gifts for children (dolls, crayons, toy trucks), cosmetics, watches, etc., are one method of return-ing the many kindnesses I receive from government officials, the local people on the street and members of Jewish communities throughout Ukraine.

Although some people choose to do archival research person-ally, the lack of familiarity with local procedures in the former Soviet Union, the difficult living and travel conditions, the time-consuming research process itself, and problems with language and naming patterns cause many more to hire professionals for this job.

Some people have asked me to do archival research that can be conducted in as many as five archives for one town. For example, Jewish documents for Ivano-Frankovsk (Stanisławów) are located in the local ZAGs (civil registration) archive in the town, the Lviv Historical Archives and in two separate archives in Warsaw. Additionally, civil records and 20th-century Jewish records are located in the Ivano-Frankivsk *oblast* (district) archives. It is not uncommon for me to find Jewish documents dating a particular family back into the 1700s. For example, one assignment produced 700 documents on family names from Melnitsa Podolskaya. Research for another client resulted in more than 500 documents about his ancestors who had once lived in Ozeryany, Korolówka, Skala Podolskaya and Borshchev (formerly Borszczów). For the last few years, I have been doing research for a client that has resulted in locating more than 2,000 documents with his family names.

When I first began working with these very old Jewish record books, it was clear that some of the books had not been opened for perhaps 50 years. The pages were stuck together, and the books are very fragile. Since copy machines are the exception in Ukraine, I travel with a Canon copier, transformer/converter, extra cartridge and paper. Since it is not advisable to leave valuables in the car, I must carry all of this equipment in and out of hotels and offices where I travel, along with the two cameras, two video cameras and other equipment that are part of each trip.

I have visited and worked in many towns in Ukraine, including Berezhany, Bolekhiv, Borshchev, Brody, Buchach, Chortkov, Dolina, Drogobych, Gorodek, Gusyatin, Ivano-Frankivsk, Jaworiw, Korolówka, L'viv, Monastyriska, Mostiska, Ozeryany, Podgaysty, Probezhna, Peremyshlyany, Rohatyń, Rozniatów, Sambor, Skala Podolskaya, Snyatyn, Sudovaya Vishnaya, Ternopil, Ugniev, Zabolotiov and Zolochiev.

Jewish Cemetery in Ukraine

My town visits include taking photographs and videos of general views and remaining Jewish sites (cemeteries, synagogues, new Holocaust monuments, Jewish schools and hospitals). I also conduct interviews with government officials and people in the Jewish community, perform local archival research and hold meetings with town historians. Where possible, I obtain maps of the town and mark the Jewish sites, along with any former ancestral homes described during local interviews. To date, I have worked in more than 25 *oblast* archives and branch archives throughout Ukraine. In the winter, heating is scarce, and people often wear coats inside. In the winter, heating is scarce and people often wear costs inside. In the summer, there is no air conditioning, and heat can be stifling. I remember once finding my driver, a man of many talents, on a ladder at the L'viv Historical Archives. He was repairing the wiring. Within a short time, the lights came back on.

Perhaps the most rewarding and fulfilling part of this work is that about 20 percent of the time I find previously unknown living relatives (in the former Soviet Union) for clients. Often the clients then plan a trip to Ukraine to meet their newly discovered cousins. All of this makes me regret that I never purchased stock in Kodak.

Recent Travel in Ukraine by Susan Gelber Cannon

In August 1996, I traveled with my husband and two sons (ages 10 and 17) to the two small towns in Ukraine that I had discovered, through researching family histories and maps from early in the century, to have been the homes of my grandparents, George and Sarah Poliner.

Articles and maps published in the back issues of *The Galitzianer* were instrumental to the success of our trip. Additionally, my request for information published in The Galitzianer resulted in advice from several knowledgeable people. We followed much of their advice—especially about bringing dried fruits and snacks. As vegetarians, we ate a lot of vareniky and blintzes and yogurt. (We actually brought a small plug-in pot with an electrical adapter with which to make instant dried soups each evening in our hotel room—a real help to vegetarians!)

We found that bringing a travel kit of silver duct tape, wire, needle and thread, batteries for cameras, and over-the-counter and prescription medicines was a very practical idea. We got the Hepatitis A vaccine, which eased our minds about eating salads, if nothing else. We brought backpacks in which to carry with us everywhere the 1 ½ liter bottles of spring water we each purchased twice daily.

We highly recommend bringing a compact video camera with a battery recharging system compatible with Ukraine's 220-volt electrical current. Samsung makes one that can adapt from 110 to 220 volts. We used it and were satisfied with its performance. (We have already presented several "video showings" of our travels to eager relatives who were fascinated by the footage even more than by still photographs.)

A guide book we found extremely useful is *Hippocrene Language and Travel Guide to Ukraine* by Linda Hodges and George Chumak (New York: Hippocrene Books, 1994). We also used sections of Let's Go: Eastern Europe. The section on L'viv is very descriptive. We had been told to bring lots of one dollar bills. However, we found it much more useful to exchange about $30 each day for use in small bakeries, shops and taxis. Dollars were not accepted anywhere except the artists' market in L'viv. Then, it was useful to have new, crisp, unmarked bills. Credit cards were not an option, except in the Grand Hotel in L'viv. We had also been advised to be as wary as one would in any big U.S. city, but frankly, we felt safer in Ukraine than in cities in the U.S. Of course, we were careful with our belongings and money and did not appear flashy; except, of course, for our numerous cameras (bring lots of film and videotape).

We found Brody (Brot, in Yiddish), one of the places we visited, a large important city in the late 1800s, is still a large city. There was a sizeable Jewish population. In 1942, the synagogue was destroyed. The shell of the building remains standing and has been under "reconstruction" for about eight years. The task seems daunting. According to Simon's account, about 12,000 Jews were killed in Brody's ghetto and many thousands more in the surrounding towns.

L'viv is still a gem of a city. Untouched by bombs during the world wars, buildings remain standing from the 1500s, with an intact town center and market square. There is a lovely opera house in the center of town and historical churches of various denominations. The Jewish ghetto was liquidated in 1942. After

Ukrainian independence, a monument was erected near the site. There were three major synagogues in L'viv. One, the Golden Rose, was destroyed by the Germans in 1942. A plaque, written in English, Ukrainian and Hebrew, now marks the site. Another synagogue is used today as an active Jewish community center. The third, used as a stable during the war, is now a 300-family synagogue. There are beautiful paintings all around the high ceiling depicting the Twelve Tribes of Israel. Bullet holes are also visible.

We had not gone to Ukraine with the intention of doing archival research and did not do any. We were interested in visiting the towns and cities important to my grandparents, who had come to the U.S. in 1904. In a way, the visit raised more questions than it answered, in that any evidence of the Jewish communities my grandparents had described was so often missing. However, with every bit of our beings, we absorbed the days we spent in Ukraine, a fascinating country full of the feeling of history, age and transition. The intangible impact on our family, especially our sons, was strong and totally worthwhile. Whether you go with an organized tour or on your own, travel to Ukraine for family research purposes may be rewarding for you as well.

Visiting Ancestral Towns in Poland

In recent years, there have been many improvement in road conditions, tourist accommodations and availability of wholesome food in Poland. When this author traveled to southern Poland in 1986, the country was still under the heavy thumb of the Soviet Union and everything was in short supply, the roads were bad, and hotels outside of a few large cities struggled to provide hot water and reliable electricity. Condition today are much improved but the introduction of capitalism and the increase of tourism in Poland, have caused higher prices for hotels. If you want to go in high season, book early and shop around for the best prices on hotels.

Typical house in small-town Galicia

Travel Experience in Poland by David Semmel

In 2002, my family and I traveled to southern Poland with the assistance of Alex Dunai. He was recommended by people associated with JRI-Poland and others. I negotiated with Alex via email and a final phone discussion to clarify our needs and plans. Alex selected the driver and I decided on the more expensive Mercedes van to ensure that we would have enough room. Alex met my conditions for qualities that I wanted in a guide.

» Language skill: ability to translate on the fly" and in context
» Local knowledge: knowing key people and local resources and how to access them
» Jewish empathy: important for context and for the overall experience
» Entrepreneurship: willingness to be flexible, grab an opportunity to get information and keep momentum going

Distances in southern Poland are misleading if you are only going by the map. Driving in Poland will always take longer than you expect. Some narrow roads snake up and down fairly steep mountains and there are often obstacles, such as horses and carts and tractors, on secondary roads, both of which characterize southern Poland. We tried to do too much driving in one day. Our guide was concerned about hotels in Przemyśl and recommended that we stay in

Typical residential street in small-town Galicia

Rzeszów, which significantly cut our time in Przemyśl. In retrospect, we would have done better to give up some comfort and have had more time in that city. On the other hand, our stay at the Hotel Rzeszów was quite adequate. The rooms were small but clean and the breakfast was quite nice.

We found that food was not a major problem. We always had water and snacks in the van so that we didn't have to rely on local truck stops, often the only places to eat in rural areas. On the other hand, we did have a great meal one day at a roadside tavern in the country where we ordered what the locals were eating: trout and soup.

I was glad that I brought sturdy shoes so that I could climb through the ruins of two synagogues. Having a guide and a driver is important when you make a local stop and have to leave luggage and equipment behind while you go off. Our driver was our guard who protected us from theft.

Destroyed synagogue in Dukla

CHAPTER 8

Indexes to Selected Books and Collections

State Department Records in the United States National Archives and Records Administration

Emergency Passport Applications, 1915-24 (see Appendix D)

Protection of Interests of United States Citizens: Record Group 59

The U.S. State Department maintained elaborate correspondence files on everyone who contacted the agency about any matter. Often, the contact was to ask the State Department for assistance with a relative of a citizen who was living abroad or to request assistance with a U.S. citizen who was either living or traveling abroad. The agency would sometimes deny the request, but, when possible, at a minimum, the nearest embassy or consulate was contacted to inquire about how the party might be helped. The Jewish Genealogy Society of Greater Washington (JGSGW) learned about Record Group 59, Series on Protection of Interests of United States Citizens in about 1984. The team that first examined the material immediately saw the value in it and organized a team of volunteers to create a name index of Jews appearing in the records, covering the period of just before and after World War I, a time when most of us had relatives who were caught in Eastern Europe as war broke out.

The team focused on material for Germany, 1910-1929; Poland,

1910-1929; Romania 1910-1929; Austro-Hungary for 1910-1939. About half of the names in the Austro-Hungary documents were linked to Galician place names, with the others from Moravia, Hungary and Bukowina. The Polish series also has a lot of names for people who had lived in Galicia, but, the State Department records reflect the new geopolitical reality that in 1918, Austro-Hungary was no more and former Galicians were then residents of Poland. Teams of volunteers went through the material, selecting names that appeared Jewish.

The State Department indexes were by the name of the person who wrote the letter of inquiry, sometimes a family member, but, more often, an attorney, a Congressman, or someone with more English facility than the family member. Because the material covers the war years, a single case can reflect considerable movement from place to place as people sought safer ground. Some people are in the index numerous times. The the pre- and post-war correspondence usually concerned missing family members and procedures for sending money or boxes of food; war brought a sense of urgency to the correspondence. Letters reflect the concern about family members who had been visiting in Europe when war broke out, relatives who had not been heard from, and relatives who had been heard from and were without funds. The index includes the names of the U.S. citizens (usually naturalized) making the request, as well as the person(s) being inquired about.

These indices are now part of JewishGen's database collection. For Austro-Hungary, it is best to click on Poland. If you find a name of interest and are unable to travel to Washington to visit the National Archives, you may ask for assistance in obtaining copies of the relevant material by writing to the National Archives, Washington, DC 20408. The State Department records are held in Archives II in College Park, Maryland. Provide all of the information listed in the index notation. A small fee is charged for research and copying. See also Appendix E for names of Galitzianers appearing in these records.

State Department Records Reveal Family Drama
by Saul Lindenbaum

When World War I began, my grandfather, Selig Lindenbaum, was in New York City. However, my father, Sam, and his sister, Regina (then ages 6 and 14, respectively), as well as my grandmother, Etel, were still living in Uście Biskupie, a small town in Eastern Galicia. After the Russians burned down their home, the three of them became refugees in a series of small towns around Borszczów (now Borshchev). When the United States entered the war against Austria in 1917, communication between people in the two countries appears to have been difficult to impossible. Conditions in the new country of Poland were chaotic right after the war, too, and Selig lost track of his family for many months. My father has often spoken of Selig's determined letter-writing efforts to locate them in postwar Poland and bring them to America. But my grandfather was a quiet, unassuming man who never seemed quite at ease in America. Though learned in Hebrew and Yiddish, he never mastered English, so I had always wondered just how, exactly, he had gone about trying to find his family. About a year ago, I discovered that Avotaynu, Inc. (P.O. Box 900, Teaneck, NJ 07666) sells on microfiche an index of people who had written to the State Department on behalf of relatives in post-World War I Poland. It was clear that this could be an opportunity to separate family myth from reality, so I bought a copy of the microfiche. When it arrived, I hastened to the local library, slipped the fiche on "Jewish Names in Protection of U.S. Citizens in Austria-Hungary, 1914–1920" into the machine, ran rapidly through the alphabet to "L" and there it was, a file with my grandfather's name. Next, I inserted the microfiche called, "Jewish Names in Protection of Interests of U.S. Citizens in Romania, Germany and Poland, 1917–1920" and was thrilled to find two more files under the names of my grandfather, father and aunt

Town Name Index to Le Toledot ha-Kehillot be Polin

Rabbi Zevi Horowitz, born in Kraków in 1872, was the son of the chief rabbi there. Zevi Horowitz himself became the chief rabbi in Dresden in 1920 and remained there until 1939, when he took refuge in Nice. He lived through the war, but died in Nice just after the war ended in 1945. His book, published posthumously by his son, was entitled *Le Toledot ha-Kehilot be Polin* (On the history of the Jewish communities of Poland). He seems to have used the term "Poland" to describe Eastern Europe generally, since some of the towns were never in Poland.

The book is a compilation of articles, some very brief and some very long, about the communities, with an emphasis on the rabbinic history of the town. Much of the book focuses on the Horowitz family and the families that they intermarried with, so in a sense, it is a genealogy book. But, in a larger sense, it is also a record of some of the rabbinic history of the communities he selected.

The list below represents the work of David Einsiedler, who corrected the list initially published in *The Galitzianer* (v. 1, no. 2). The entire list of Galician towns and the page number in the Horowitz book follows.

The author of this guide has a personal copy of *Le Toldedot ha-Kehillot be Polin.* The book, was published in 1978 by Mosad Harav Kook in Jerusalem. The Library of Congress and the New York Public Library each has a copy. Try Jewish book-stores, Jewish libraries or, if all else fails, send this author a self-addressed stamped envelope, and you will be told the cost for a copy of the article(s) of interest. The address is 3603 Littledale Road, Kensington, MD 20895. For towns in present-day Ukraine, the current name is included after the slash, if it has changed. Each entry shows the town name and the page (in parentheses) in the book where the town description appears.

Bełż, N of Lviv (132)

Biały Kamień/Belyy Kamen, ENE of Lviv (130)

Bóbrka, SE of Lviv (99)

Bochnia, E of Kraków (104)

Bohorodczany/Bogorodchany, S of Lviv (151)

Bolechów/Bolekhov, S of Lviv (105)

Brzesko (Brigel), E of Kraków (154)

Brzeżany/Berezhany, NE of Lviv (155)

Brzostek, W of Przemyśl (157)

Buczacz/Buchach, SE of Lviv (101)

Budzanów/Budanov, SE of Ternopol (100)

Bursztyn/Burshtyn, SE of Lviv (126)

Busk, NE of Lviv (112)

Dobromil, SW of Lviv (195)

Drohobycz/Drogobych, SW of Lviv (229)

Dukla, SW of Przemyśl (199)

Gologóry, E of Lviv (166)

Janów, near Lviv (360)

Jarosław, NNW of Przemyśl (366)

Jaryczów Nowy/Novyy Yarychev, NE of Lviv(361)

Jazłowice/Pomortsy (356)

Kamionka near Przemyśl (491)

Komarno, SW of Lviv (493)

Lesko (Linsk, Lisko), SE of Sanok (379)

Leszniów/Leshnev, NE of Lviv (382)

Narol, NNE of Przemyśl (391)

Niemirów, WNW of Lviv (392)

Nowy Sącz (Sanz), SE of Kraków (477)

Olesko, ENE of Lviv (7)

Oświęcim/Auschwitz, W of Kraków (4)

Podhajce/Podgaytsy, SE of Lviv (432)

Podkamień, ENE of Lviv (437)

Pomorzany/Pomoryany, ESE of Lviv (439)

Przemyśl, E of Kraków (464)

Rawa Ruska/Rava Russkaya, NW of Lviv (516)

Rohatyń/Rogatin, SE of Lviv (508)

Skole, S of Lviv (405)

Stryy, S of Lviv (403)

Swirż, 45 mi. ESE of Lviv (400)

Tarnopol/Ternapol, E of Lviv (324)

Tarnów, E of Kraków (321)

Tyśmienica/Tysmenitsa, near Tlumacz (332)

Ulanów, N of Kraków (1)

Uście Zielone/Uste Zelene, SE of Lviv (2)

Wisnicz Nowy near Kraków (265)

Wojsławice, near Sokal, N of Lviv (262)

Jaworów, W of Lviv (351)

Załoźce/Zalozhtsy, E of Lviv (301)

Zbaraż/Zbarazh, N of Ternopol (298)

Zborów, E of Lviv (299)

Złoczów/Zolochev, E of Lviv (304)

Żmigród Nowy, SE of Kraków (307)

Żurawno/Zhuravno, SE of Lviv (300)

Zuzmir (Kazimierz, Jewish suburb of Kraków) (481)

APPENDIX A

Pronouncing and Recognizing Your
Polish Town and Family Names
by Fay Vogel Bussgang1[1]

One could then recognize that "Brzeziny" and "*w* Brzezinach" refer to the same town but that "Brzeżany" is something totally different. A guide to Polish pronunciation and basic rules of Polish grammar relevant to genealogical research are presented below.

Polish Pronunciation Guide

The following guide gives the essentials for learning to sound out family or town names. When you practice, go slowly, sound all the letters, and put the accent on the next to last syllable.

Polish	English	Sounds Most Like	Polish Example
a	short ah	ha! ha!	Kraków, Radom
ą*	on [om before b/p]	song [trombone]	Nowy Sącz, [Dąbrowa]
e	eh	bet	Mazowiecki, Przemyśl
ę*	en [em before b/p]	Bengal [hemp]	Będzin, [Dębicy]
i	ee	feet	Katowice, Wieliczka

Polish	English	Sounds Most Like	Polish Example
o	o	bought	Drohobycz, Horodenka
ó/u	oo/u (or, see below)	boot, flute	Jelenia Góra, Lublin, Kuźnica
ó/u	short oo/u	book, put	Łódź, Lwów, Kraków
y	short i	fit	Gdynia, Drohobycz
c	ts	eats	Katowice, Kielce, Płock, Siedlce
ć/ci	ch (softened)	cello/cheat	Chęciny, Ciechanów, Tykocin
cz	ch	church	Łowicz, Wieliczka
ch/h	h (aspirated)	Helen	Chęciny, Chelm, Częstochowa
dz	ds	suds	Dzbanów, Radzanów
dzi	dgy	fudgy	Będzin, Działoszyce, Radziejów
j	y	year	Jarosław, Kolomyja, Radziejów
ł	w	wood	Łódź, Białystok, Wrocław
ń	nn	onion	Gdańsk, Poznań, Toruń
prz	psh	pshah!	Przedbórz, Przemyśl
r	r (rolled)	rrroar!	Radom, Rawa Ruska
ś/si	sh (softened)	sh!	Przemyśl, Siedlce, Śląsk

Polish	English	Sounds Most Like	Polish Example
sz	sh	shop	Kalisz, Kolbuszowa
szcz	shch	sh children	Bydogoszcz, Szczecin
w	v	van	Lwów, Warszawa, Wrocław
ź/zi	zh (softened)	cashmere	Kuźnica, Zielona Góra
ż/rz	zh	vision	Łomża, Rzeszów, rychlin

*   ą and ę are nasalized before s, ś, sz, rz, z, ż, ź, f, w, ch; ą is also nasalized at the end of a word. In these instances, such as in Śląsk or Częstochowa, there is no n or m sound after the ą or ę.

Beware: The **final consonant** of a word is **unvoiced**, that is, the larynx (voice box) is not used in craeting the sound. The following letters change to their unvoiced counterpart: b→p, d→t, g→k, w→f, z→ś, ź→s, dz→c, dź→ć, rz/ż→sz, dż→cz. Therefore Kraków sounds like "Krakoof," and Brzeg, sounds like "Bzhek."

Rules of Polish Grammar Useful for Genealogists

Even if you cannot translate a Polish document, understanding the most common forms of the names of people and towns will help you determine if a person or place of interest to you is mentioned in the document.

There are three important concepts to note in learning the Polish language that may be new to English-language speakers: case, gender, and stem. Each of these, explained below, as well as whether the noun is singular or plural, influences the ending (suffix) of the noun.

The *case* of a noun indicates its function in a sentence; it shows whether the noun is the subject, the direct or indirect object or is in a prepositional phrase. There are seven different cases in Polish, but only those commonly seen in genealogical research are described below: nominative, genitive, instrumental (used mainly in marriage documents) and locative. Table A2 gives examples of town named in the most frequently encountered cases.

Town names, like other nouns in Polish, come in different varieties; they have *gender* (feminine, masculine or neuter), and some are even plural.

The *stem* is the basically unchangeable part of a word to which endings are added. The stem is termed soft, velar or hard, depending on the pronunciation of its last letter.

This may sound confusing, but it will make more sense as you go along. It is not necessary to learn all the grammar presented here. Try to get a general understanding of the concepts and then write down the endings that apply to your particular town and family names and become familiar with them.

Nominative Case

The nominative case is used to denote the subject of a sentence. The name of a town or person in the nominative case is spelled as you commonly know it: Płock, Radom, Glasman.

Genitive Case

The genitive case denotes "of" or possession, follows certain prepositions, or is the direct object after a negative verb. In vital records, the genitive is most often used following *z/ze* (from) to identify the town someone is from, as in z Krakowa, and to indicate maiden name, as in z Bussgangów (literally, from the Bussgangs).

Forming the Genitive Case from the Nominative for Town Names

» Feminine town names usually end in *a* in the nominative case: Warszawa, Warta, Horodenka. (A few towns ending in double consonants or ew are also feminine: Bydgoszcz, Łódź, Żółkiew.) The genitive ending for all feminine towns is y or i: Warszawy, Warty, Horodenki, Bydgoszczy, Łodzi, Żółkwi. (Note that ie before a final letter, as in Żółkiew, is dropped in the genitive case before the ending is added.

» Masculine town names end in a consonant in the nominative: Lwów, Gdańsk, Płock, Włocławek. The genitive ending is *a* or u for towns with masculine names:

  - The genitive of most Polish masculine town names is formed by adding *a* at the end: Lwowa, Gdańska, Płocka, Włocławka Note that e before a final letter is dropped before the genitive ending is added.
  - If the town name ends in a soft consonant such as *ń* or a hidden softening (which you learn by usage), ia is added: Poznań→ Poznania; Radom→Radomia; Wrocław→Wrocławia.
  - Most foreign cities and a few Polish towns have the ending *u*: Londynu, Bostonu, Tarnobrzegu, Żmigrodu.

» Neuter town names end in *o* or sometimes e in the nominative: Brzesko, Radomsko, Opole. Neuter town names form the genitive by adding a to the stem: Brzeska, Radomska, Opola.

» Plural town names end in *y*, i, and with a few exceptions, e, in the nominative: Chęciny, Suwałki, Działoszyce, Katowice. To form the genitive, the final letter is dropped to form Chęcin, Suwałek, Działoszyc, Katowic. (If the word thus formed ends in two consonants that make pronunciation difficult, an e is often added before the final letter to separate the two consonants, as in Suwałek.)

Forming the Genitive Case from the Nominative for Women's Surnames

To indicate the maiden name of a married woman, the genitive plural is used after *z/ze*. The usual genetive plural ending is ów: Bussgang→z Bussgangów; Spiro→ze Spirów. If the name ends in cka/ska (feminine of names ending in cki/ski), the ending is ich: Sawicka→z Sawickich, Kowalska→z Kowalskich. To indicate that a woman is unmarried, ówna is added to her surname in the nominative, ównej in the genitive: Glasman→Glasmanówna/Glasmanównej (Miss Glasman). To indicate a woman is married, owa is added in the nominative or

owej in the genitive to her husband's surname: Glasmanowa/
Glasmanowej (Mrs. Glasman).

Instrumental Case

In general, the instrumental case is used to show with whom
or by what means something is done. In a marriage record, it may
be used for the groom who appears *with* the Rabbi. It is formed
simply by adding em for a man (to both first and last names or
just to the first name): Szmuel Kron→wraz ze (together with)
Szmuelem Kronem. For names ending in cki/ski, the ending is m:
Aron Laski→z Aronem Laskim.23 The instrumental case is also
used after "między" (between) to indicate an agreement between
the bride and groom. For a woman, ą is added to the stem of her
first name (Ruchla→Ruchlą): między Aronem Laskim i Ruchlą
Wolf, also to the surname of the ówna form is used: Ruchlą
Wolfówną.

Locative Case

The locative case, which tells where something is located, is
used only after certain prepositions, the most common in vital
records being *w/we* (in).34 The rules for forming the locative
seem very complicated, because there are changes in the stem of
the word, not just the ending. If you go through your list of towns
one by one and apply the rules, however, it should not be too difficult. First, you must determine the gender of the name and also
its type of stem (hard, velar, soft).

---

2   The word ze is used instead of z to indicate "from" or "with"
when the word following it begins with a cluster of consonants which
would make it difficult to pronounce without the added e. This is why
the instrumental ze is used before Szmuel, but only z is used before
Aron.

3   For the same reason, we is used instead of w. Therefore, it is
we Lwowie, but w Warszawie. However, what we think would be difficult may not necessarily be what Poles consider difficult. We might
want we before Przemyśl, but they don't consider the Prze sound to
cause any problems!! Thus, it is w Przemyślu.

» Hard stems. If the last consonant of the word is hard, regardless of gender, it must be softened and then an *e* ending is added.

- Hard stems ending is *p*, b, f, w, m, n, s and z are softened by adding i before the e ending: Warszawa→w Warszawie; Kraków→w Krakowie; Chełmno→w Chełmnie; Lublin→w Lublinie.
- Stem endings *t*, d, r, and ł are softened according to the following pattern before adding e: t→ci, d→dzi, r→rz, ł→l: Łańcut→w Łańcucie; Rajgród→w Rajgrodzie; Zielona Góra→w Zielonej Górze.

» Velar stems. The final consonant of a velar stem has a gutteral sound (k, g, ch).

- Feminine nouns soften velar stems (*k*→c, g→dz, ch→sz) before adding an e ending: Horodenka→w Horodence; Struga→w Strudze; Bierwicha→w Bierwisze.
- Masculine and neuter names with velar stems simply add *u* to the stem: Płock→w Płocku; Przemyśl→w Przemyślu; Tarnobrzeg→w Tarnobrzegu; Włocławek→w Włocławku (drop e before final k); Radomsko→w Radomsku.

» Soft stems. Soft stems end with the consonants *i*, j, l, c, ć, cz, ś, sz, ź, ż, rz)

- Feminine names ending in *ia* or with a soft stem add i or y to the stem: Bochnia→w Bochni, Łódź→w Łodzi, Bydgoszcz→w Bydgoszczy, Dębica→w Dębicy.
- Masculine and neuter names ending in a soft stem consonant add *u* to the stem: Drohobycz→w Drohobyczu; Mielec→w Mielcu; Opole→w Opolu; Zgierz→w Zgierzu.

» Plural names of towns all form the locative case by adding *ach* to the stem: Brzeziny→w Brzezinach; Katowice→w Katowicach; Chęciny→w Chęcinach; Suwałki→w Suwałkach.

Table A1. Sample Declensions of Town Names
(Arranged by Type of Stem)

Type of Stem	Nominative	Genitive	Locative
Fem hard stem	Warszawa	Warszawy	Warszawie
Fem hard stem	Indura	Indury	Indurze
Fem velar stem	Wieliczka	Wieliczki	Wieliczce
Fem soft stem	Dębica	Dębicy	Dębicy
Fem soft stem	Łomża	Łomży	Łomży
Fem soft stem	Kołomyja	Kołomyji	Kołomyji
Fem soft stem	Łódź	Łodzi	Łodzi
Masc hard stem	Kraków	Krakowa	Krakowie
Masc hard stem	Lublin	Lublina	Lublinie
Masc hard stem	Żmigród	Żmigrodu*	Żmigrodzie
Masc velar stem	Gdańsk	Gdańska	Gdańsku
Masc velar stem	Chmielnik	Chmielnika	Chmielniku
Masc velar stem	Tarnobrzeg	Tarnobrzegu*	Tarnobrzegu
Masc soft stem (hidden)	Jarosław	Jarosławia	Jarosławiu
Masc soft stem (hidden)	Radom	Radomia	Radomiu
Masc soft stem	Mielec	Mielca	Mielcu
Masc soft stem	Lubraniec	Lubrańca	Lubrańcu
Masc soft stem	Zamość	Zamościa	Zamościu
Masc soft stem	Tarnopol	Tarnopola	Tarnopolu
Neut hard stem	Grodno	Grodna	Grodnie
Neut velar stem	Radomsko	Radomska	Radomsku
Neut soft stem	Opole	Opola	Opolu
Plural	Chęciny	Chęcin	Chęcinach
Plural	Katowice	Katowic	Katowicach
Plural	Kielce	Kielc	Kielcach
Plural	Suwałki	Suwałek	Suwałkach

For towns with compound names—composed of a noun plus a modifier—the nouns follow the rules above, but the adjectives, such as Nowy (new), Zielona (green), or Mazowiecki (in Mazowiecki region), however, follow the rules for adjectival endings, depending on gender, case, and number. Adjectival endings are underlined in the compound names below to show the pattern of the endings.

Table A2. Declention of Adjectives
Associated With Town Names

Adjective	Nominative	Genitive	Locative
Zielona (f)	Zielona Góra	z Zielonej Góry	w Zielonej Górze
Zduńska (f)	Zduńska Wola	ze Zduńskiej Woli	w Zduńskiej Woli
Mazowiecka (f)	Rawa Mazowiecka	z Rawy Mazowieckiej	w Rawie Mazowieckiej
Mazowiecki (m)	Mińsk Mazowiecki	z Mińska Mazowieckiego	w Mińsku Mazowieckim
Nowy (m)	Nowy Sącz	z Nowego Sącza	w Nowym Sączu
Nowe (n)	Nowe Miasto	z Nowego Miasta	w Nowym Mieście
Biały (m)	Białystok	z Białegostoku	w Białymstoku

[Białystok (m) is treated like a compound word made up of *Biały* (white) and stok (slope).]

APPENDIX B

Sample Letter to Polish Archives

The following is a letter in Polish adapted from Judith Frazin's book, *A Translation Guide to 19th-Century Polish Language Civil-Registration Documents*. (See Chapter 5 for ordering information.) Her book offers a much greater variety of phrases, but the letter below should suffice as an adequate explanation of what most researchers seek.

Poland today is divided into 49 provinces, which are abbreviated *woj.* for voivodeships. When writing to small towns in Poland, it is best to use these designations in the address because there may be more than one town of that name.

The provinces listed below include towns that were once part of Western Galicia. Because of the complexities of the Polish language, they are to be written as follows:

Bielsko-Biała = *woj. bielskie*
Katowice = *woj. katowickie*
Krosno = *woj. krosnienskie*
Nowy Sącz = *woj. nowosadeckie*
Przemyśl = *woj. przemyśkie*
Rzeszów = *woj. rzeszówskie*
Tarnobrzeg = *woj. tarnobrzeskie*
Tarnów = *woj. tarnówskie*

Send your letter to the town civil records office (*Urząd Stanu Cywilnego*):

Urząd Stanu Cywilnego
Name of the province (if you know it)
Name of town, Poland

Civil Registration Office
Name of province (if you know it)
Name of town, Poland

szanowny Panie,

Dear Sir:

W celu uzupełnienia historii mojej rodziny, potrzebne mi są dane z żydowskich ksiąg urodzin, ślubów i zgonow z [name of town].

In order to prepare a history of my family, I need information from the Jewish records of birth, marriage and death from [name of town].)

Jeśli te akta nie są w Waszym posiadaniu, proszę o podanie mi adresu, gdzie się one znajdują.

If you do not have the records, I request that you provide the address where the records may be found.

imię i nazwisko:
data urodzenia (w przybliżeniu):
miejsce urodzenia:
imię i nazwisko ojca:
panieńskie nazwisko matki:
imię matki:
imię i nazwisko męża:
imię i panieńskie nazwisko żony:
data ślubu:
miejsce ślubu:
data emigracji:
wyzanie (żydowskie):

Given name and surname:
Date of birth (approximately):
Place of birth:
Full name of father:
Maiden name of mother:
First name of mother:
First name of husband:
First and maiden name of wife:
Date of marriage:
Place of marriage:
Date of emigration:
Religion: (Jewish)

Interesuje mnie rodzina tej osoby i byłbym wdzięczny [byłabym wdzięczna if you are female] za podanie mi imion, nazwisk, oraz dat i miejsc urodzenia rodzenstwa, jak rownież przesłanie mi odpisu aktu ślubu rodzicow.	I would like to know more about the family of this person, and if you would provide the names and birth dates of the brothers and sisters, and an extract of the marriage record of the parents, I would be very grateful.
Z góry dziękuję.	I thank you in advance for your assistance.
Z poważaniem,	Respectfully,

Polish Date Styles

Dates in Polish can present major challenges to those who are unfamiliar with the pecularities of the Polish language. Dates and, indeed, numbers sometimes appear written out in Polish. In other words, instead of writing a number such as 1899, you might encounter "one thousand eight hundred ninety-nine." Judith Frazin's book, previously referenced, includes a good list of numbers to help translate records with examples of how to read them.

Dates follow the European style with the day first, the month next and then the year, as in 2 November 1997. Months in Polish are as follows:

January: stycznia	May: maja	September: września
February: lutego	June: czerwca	October: października
March: marca	July: lipca	November: listopada
April: kwietnia	August: sierpnia	December: grudnia

APPENDIX C

Examples of Vital Records

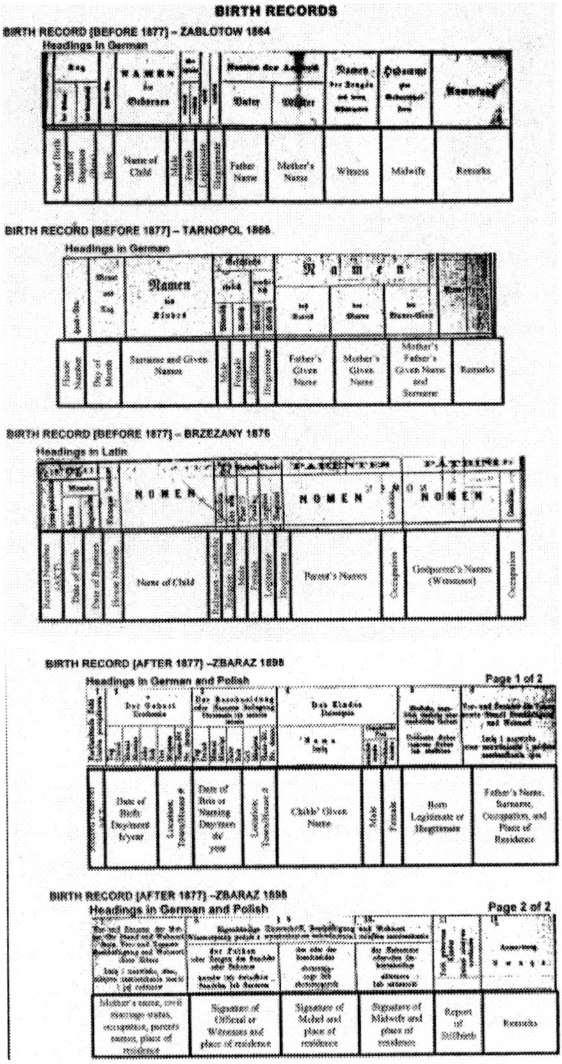

BIRTH RECORDS

BIRTH RECORD [BEFORE 1877] – ZABLOTOW 1864
Headings in German

BIRTH RECORD [BEFORE 1877] – TARNOPOL 1866
Headings in German

BIRTH RECORD [BEFORE 1877] – BRZEZANY 1876
Headings in Latin

BIRTH RECORD [AFTER 1877] –ZBARAZ 1898
Headings in German and Polish — Page 1 of 2

BIRTH RECORD [AFTER 1877] –ZBARAZ 1898
Headings in German and Polish — Page 2 of 2

*Figure 6.
Examples of
birth records
pre- and
post-1877*

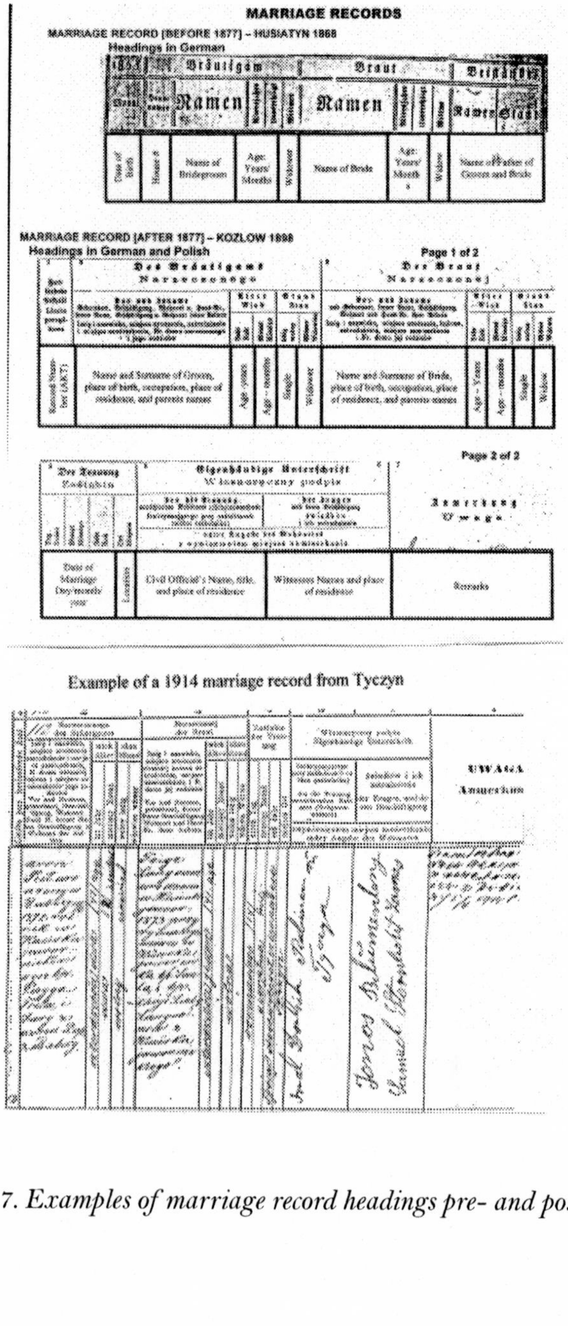

MARRIAGE RECORDS

MARRIAGE RECORD [BEFORE 1877] – HUSIATYN 1868
Headings in German

MARRIAGE RECORD [AFTER 1877] – KOZLOW 1898
Headings in German and Polish

Page 1 of 2

Page 2 of 2

Example of a 1914 marriage record from Tyczyn

Figure 7. Examples of marriage record headings pre- and post-1877

DEATH RECORDS

DEATH RECORD [BEFORE 1877] – TARNOPOL 1876
Headings in German

Haus Nro.	Monat und Tag	Vor = und Bunamen	Alter Jahr/Monat	Geschlecht männlich/weiblich	Todesart	Namen des Vaters verstorben: Kinder	Anmerkung
House #	Date of Death	Name of Deceased	Age at Death Years/Months	Male / Female	Cause of Death	Name of Father for Child	Remarks

DEATH RECORD [BEFORE 1877] – NADWORNA 1876
Headings in Latin

Dies mortis 1876 Mensis mortuus / sepultus	Numerus domus	NOMEN, Cognomen et Conditio Mortui	Religio Catholica / Aci Alba	Sexus Mas. / Femina	Dies Vitae	et Qualitas Morbi
Date of Death / Date of Burial	House #	Name of Deceased	Religion: Catholic / Religion: Other	Male / Female	Age at Death	Cause of Death

DEATH RECORD [AFTER 1877] – ROZDOL 1886
Headings in German and Polish

Page 1 of 2

1	2	3 Des Absterbens Zmierci					4 Der Beerdigung Pogrzeb				5 Des Verstorbenen Zmarłego	6	7
Record Number	Date of Recording, Page of entry, and Name of Examiner	Hour of Death	Day of Death	Month of Death	Year of Death	Place of Death	Day of burial	Month of Burial	Year of Burial	Place of Burial	Name and Surname of Deceased, Marital Status, Occupation, and Town of residence	Town of Residence	House #

Page 2 of 2

8 Geschlecht Płeć		9 Alter Wiek		9 Stand Stan			Krankheit und Todesart Choroba i rodzaj śmierci	10 Anmerkung Uwaga
Male	Female	Age: Years	Age: Months	Single	Married	Widow	Cause of Death	Remarks

Figure 8. Examples of death record headings pre- and post-1877

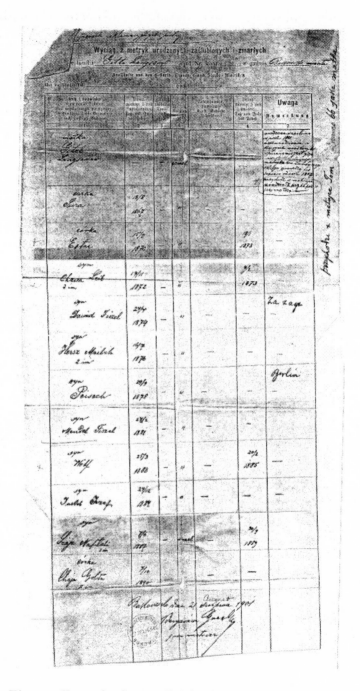

Figure 9. Example of a compiled family record by a notary, 1901

Rare example of a record of the births and deaths of a mother's children. The mother had not been married under civil law to her late husband, Eliezer Ephraim Fischel and so, was not mentioned. Two male children were given the middle names of "Fiszel" in the Polish style. The long note says that the mother claimed 1841 as her birth year but this could not be confirmed because birth records were not kept until 1857. The document was prepared by a notary for travel purposes in August 1901.

Appendix D

Index to United States Emergency Passport Applications, 1915-1924

Emergency passports are usually reserved for United States citizens who lose their passports or whose passport is stolen, while traveling abroad. During the early period of the U.S., when passports were not needed, a second group of applicants included individuals who, while traveling abroad, felt the need for one, either to prove U.S. citizenship or for the imagined protection that such a document would afford. But, there was a third group of applicants that are of primary interest to Jewish genealogists—those who became citizens without ever stepping on U.S. soil because of the laws governing citizenship prior to the 1920s.

Before 1922, women generally could not become U.S. citizens in their own right. With some exceptions, women became citizens by virtue of being the daughter or wife of a U.S. citizen. Minor children also were able to qualify for derivative citizenship from their father. Thus, the wife and minor children of a man who came to this country, who claimed to reside in the U.S. continuously for five years, and who became a citizen, automatically derived citizenship from him. If the family of the new citizen still lived abroad, they were able to enter the U.S. with full rights of citizenship. For some, this curious situation meant that people who had concerns about not being admitted to the U.S.—because of physical, mental or medical conditions that might otherwise have disqualified them at the port of entry—could enter unquestioned. This strategy was put to good use by some Jews.

American citizens caught in Europe when World War I broke

out also applied for emergency passports. Emergency passports had to be renewed annually and so, regardless of where they found themselves during and just after World War I, those who held these documents made their way to the nearest U.S. consulate to ensure that they would be under continuous U.S. protection and would not experience difficulties because they carried an expired passport.

The U.S. National Archives and Records Administration holds passport applications for the period 1789–1924. Bound in volumes, they are filed according to the country in which the U.S. consulate was located. Typically, there are several books in an archival box. The applications are on microfilm but copying the material from microfilm will result in poor quality reproductions. After 1924, the State Department holds the applications and all correspondence relating to the applications. To gain access to this material requires that you write to the United States State Department for assistance.

Because the official index to the 1915–1924 Emergency Passport Applications was missing and, presumed lost, a group of volunteers from the Jewish Genealogy Society of Greater Washington compiled an index of the names of Jews that appeared in the material for the time period.

Individuals wishing to renew their passports in the period JGSGW indexed, were required to submit photos of themselves. If children were to be included on the parent's passport, photos of them were also attached. The photos are pristine since they have rarely been exposed to use or air since the applications were filed and placed in bound books. The applications contain such genealogical information as, place and date of birth, current address (which during the war could have been quite temporary) and occupation. All passport applications include such information, but the Emergency Passport Applications are special in that most of the applicants had never set foot on U.S. soil. Some of the applications required additional documentation of identity and this material is also included, including birth records, documentation of the husband's or father's citizenship, affidavits from people who could attest to the individual's identity.

To access the collection in person, go to the National Archives II, located on the campus of the University of Maryland in College Park, Maryland, or you may write to U.S. National Archives and Records Administration, Washington, DC 20408. Provide the information listed in the index below and request that a reproduction be made of any photographs found, as well as a photocopy of the record(s). This service is provided at a very reasonable cost.

Indexes to regular passport applications and other types of special passports applications for the period 1797–1924 have been microfilmed and are available through your nearest LDS (Mormon) Family History Center, as well as in the first floor microfilm reading room in the main building of the National Archives in Washington, D.C. Since passports were generally not required by the United States for reentry into the country until World War I, the early part of the collection is rather small, but includes a large percentage of Jews.

The names that appear below were identified as Jews from Galicia in the emergency passport applications for 1915-1924. The birthplace, place of issuance, and the location information are given in Table E.1. Note that some birthplaces are not in Galicia, but they are included if any member of the family was born in a Galician town. "Issue" refers to the country where the emergency passport was issued. The location code is divided into three numeric parts, representing the box, book and page number where the record is located. For example, the first entry in the table identifies Adel Adasse, born in Szczucin (Poland), passport issued in Poland, whose file is located in box 1737, book 1, page 385. Do not be put off by the country code. Remember that persons may have been displaced during the war. After the war, Galicia was no more than a memory, and virtually all of Galician territory reverted to Poland until World War II.

Table E-1. Names of Galician Jews in Emergency Passport Applications

Surname	Given Name	Birthplace	Issue	Location Code
Adasse	Adel	Szczucin	Pol	1737 0001 00385
Addasse	Ida	Szczucin	Pol	1737 0001 00392
Alexander	Annie	Zolkiew	Aus	1585 0177 01481
Alexander	Celia	Zolkiew	Aus	1585 0177 01481
Alexander	Esther	Zolkiew	Aus	1585 0177 01481
Alexander	Samuel	Zolkiew	Aus	1585 0177 01481
Alexander	Sara	Zolkiew	Aus	1585 0177 01481
Alter	Chaim	Grebów	Pol	1740 0006 02149
Anderman	Abraham	Buczacz	Pol	1737 0001 00146
Anderman	Abraham	Buczacz	Pol	1738 0003 00807
Anderman	Hanna	Buczacz	Pol	1738 0003 00807
Antler	Isador	Jazłowice	Swt	1759 0178 04394
Antler	Minke	Jazłowice	Swt	1759 0178 04395
Antler	Rubin	Monasterzyska onasterzyska	Aus	1585 0177 01313
Antler	Sadie	Jasłowice	Swt	1759 0173 04396

Surname	Given Name	Birthplace	Issue	Location Code
Ashkenazi	Anna	Tyczyn	Pol	1738 0003 00955
Ashkenazi	Joseph	Tyczyn	Pol	1738 0003 00955
Ausbel	Frimet	Galicia	Aus	1584 0147 00583
Ausbel	Sheva	Galicia	Aus	1584 0147 00584
Ax	Blanche	Stanisławów	Aus	1585 0177 01355
Bader	Chana	Borysław	Pol	1739 0004 01334
Bader	Jenny	Dynów	Aus	1584 0147 00724
Bader	Markus	Borysław	Pol	1739 0004 01334
Balamut	Anna	Wielopole	Pol	1738 0002 00528
Balamut	Chaim	Wielopole	Pol	1738 0002 00528
Balamut	Isak	Wielopole	Pol	1738 0002 00528
Balamut	Rachel	Wielopole	Pol	1738 0002 00528
Balamut	Wolff	Wielopole	Pol	1738 0002 00528
Balamuth	Annie	Rokszyce	Aus	1585 0176 01039
Balamuth	Isaac	Rokszyce	Aus	1585 0176 01039
Balamuth	Isaac	Galicia	Ger	1676 0175 08190
Baldash	Isidor	Tarnopol	Pol	1738 0003 01157

Surname	Given Name	Birthplace	Issue	Location Code
Baldash	Mina	Tarnopol	Pol	1738 0003 01157
Barer	Israel	Turza Wielka	Pol	1737 0001 00043
Barer	Cyllie	Turza Wielka	Pol	1737 0001 00043
Baron	Pauline	Obertyn	Aus	1585 0176 00947
Bau	Abraham	Dombrowa	Aus	1584 0147 00734
Bau	Beile	Dombrowa	Aus	1584 0147 00734
Bau	Breindl	Dombrowa	Aus	1584 0147 00734
Bau	Chaskel	Dombrowa	Aus	1584 0147 00734
Bau	Chiel	Dombrowa	Aus	1584 0147 00734
Baumel	David	Grzymałów	Aus	1584 0147 00716
Baumel	Max	Grzymałów	Aus	1584 0147 00716
Baumel	Regina	Grzymałów	Aus	1584 0147 00716
Bebczuk	Malka	Jezierzany	Pol	1739 0004 01528
Bebczuk	Morris	Jezierzany	Pol	1739 0004 01528
Berg	Malka Kramer	Rawa Ruska	Pol	1741 0009 04443
Berg	Malka Kramer	Rawa Ruska	Pol	1737 0001 04443
Berman	Anna	Radomysl	Fin	1651 0001 00087

Surname	Given Name	Birthplace	Issue	Location Code
Berman	Elisabeth	Radomysl	Fin	1651 0001 00087
Berman	Harry	Radomysl	Fin	1651 0001 00087
Berman	Louis	Radomysl	Fin	1651 0001 00087
Bernhang	Rosie	Galicia	Aus	1584 0147 00573
Bernzweig	Emilia	Stanisławów	Pol	1738 0003 00884
Beyman	Buncha	Czortków	Fr	1660 0165 02887
Beyman	Buncha	Czortków	Fr	1702 0001 00037
Bienenstock	Jacob	Tarnobrzeg	Pol	1737 0001 00302
Bienenstock	Schyfra	Tarnobrzeg	Pol	1737 0001 00302
Biller	Isaac	Zabłotów	Pol	1737 0001 00246
Biller	Molly	Zabłotów	Pol	1737 0001 00246
Birnbaum	Beppi	Widynów	Pol	1738 0002 00491
Birnbaum	Bessie Gewitz	Frysztak	Pol	1741 0009 04638
Birnbaum	David	Widinów	Pol	1738 0002 00491
Birnbaum	David	Zaleszczyki	Aus	1585 0176 01280
Birnbaum	Nathan	Widynów	Pol	1738 0002 00491
Bisgier	Minnie	Galicia	Aus	1585 0176 01083

Surname	Given Name	Birthplace	Issue	Location Code
Bisgier	Pauline	Galicia	Aus	1585 0176 01083
Bisgier	Ruth	Galicia	Aus	1585 0176 01083
Blatt	Anna	Kozowa	Pol	1740 0006 02024
Blatt	Jonas	Brzeżany	Pol	1740 0006 02024
Bloch	Samuel	Dobrowa	Ger	1676 0176 10536
Bloomfield	Clara	Lemberg	Aus	1585 0176 00967
Blustin	Annie	Sanok	Aus	1585 0177 01414
Blustin	Mary	Sanok	Aus	1585 0177 01414
Bodner	Anna	Radom.Wiel.	Ger	1740 0006 02333
Bodner	Aron	Radom.Wiel.	Ger	1740 0006 02333
Brandes	Baruch	Swidowa	Pol	1737 0001 00371
Brandes	Yetta	Swidowa	Pol	1737 0001 00371
Brandriss	Sara	Brody	Aus	1585 0176 00877
Brenner	Kalman	Kraków	Ger	1679 0183 00421
Brodofsky	Annie	Nowy Dwor	Pol	1737 0001 00196
Brodofsky	Max	Nowy Dwor	Pol	1737 0001 00196
Brown	Harry	Kraków	Ger	1674 0172 04226

Surname	Given Name	Birthplace	Issue	Location Code
Bruck	Solomon	Złoczów	Aus	1585 0177 04720
Buchner	Irving	Kraków	Aus	1585 0177 00018
Burn	Emilia	Stanisławów	Pol	1738 0003 00884
Burn	Samuel	Stanisławów	Pol	1738 0003 00884
Calvary	Dora	Tarnów	Bel	1590 0003 00842
Chapkiewicz	Chana	Rzeszów	Pol	1739 0004 01523
Chapkiewicz	Philip	Rzeszów	Pol	1739 0004 01523
Charapp	Drezel	Jezierzany	Pol	1739 0004 01234
Charapp	Max	Jezierzany	Pol	1739 0004 01234
Cohen	Braina	Lemberg	Aus	1585 0177 01415
Cohen	Fannie	Lemberg	Aus	1585 0177 01415
Cohen	Gusia	Galicia	Cz	1644 0001 00205
Cohen	Harry	Lemberg	Aus	1585 0177 01415
Cohen	Mary	Lemberg	Aus	1585 0177 01415
Cohen	Wolf	Galicia	Cz	1644 0001 11205
Cohn	Eva	Brody	Aus	1585 0177 01387
Cohn	Eva	Brody	Aus	1585 0177 01545

Surname	Given Name	Birthplace	Issue	Location Code
Conay	Daniel	Zagórze	Fr	1667 0180 00831
Dachs	Mendel	Delatyn	Fr	1673 0169 01757
Degen	Renie	Galicia	Aus	1585 0176 01092
Deitel	Yetta	Lemberg	Pol	1741 0008 04182
Dembitzer	Emma	Wash DC	Den	1648 0004 00318
Dembitzer	Louis	Kraków	Den	1648 0004 00317
Diamond	Abraham	Miedzyrzecz	Egy	1650 0002 00015
Diamond	Max	Miedzyrzecz	Egy	1650 0002 00014
Diamond	Max	Miedzyrzecz	Egy	1650 0002 00119
Dicker	Joel	Brzeżany	Aus	1585 0177 01354
Dicker	Leah	Brzeżany	Aus	1585 0177 01354
Dinner	Lewis	Bełż	Aus	1584 0147 00704
Dramin	Pauline	Tarnów	Aus	1584 0147 00661
Dreiblatt	Morris	Kraków	Hol	1706 0001 00035
Drucker	Max	Galicia	Aus	1585 0176 01122
Dub	Basia	Bukaczowce	Pol	1741 0009 04597
Dub	Genia	Sędziszów	Pol	1741 0009 04597

Surname	Given Name	Birthplace	Issue	Location Code
Dub	Mechel	Sędziszów	Pol	1741 0009 04597
Eckstein	Feige	Sokolki	Pol	1737 0001 00037
Eckstein	Gershon	Sokolki	Pol	1737 0001 00037
Edelman	Jacob	Włodzimierz	Pol	1739 0004 01493
Edelman	Rose	Włodzimierz	Pol	1739 0004 01493
Eder	Lottie	Mielec	Pol	1749 0005 01883
Eder	Sam	Mielec	Pol	1749 0001 01883
Einhorn	Benny	Kraków	Hol	1707 0003 00793
Eis	Elias	Miechów	Aus	1585 0176 01250
Eis	Malka	Miechów	Aus	1585 0176 01250
Eis	Pinkas	Miechów	Aus	1585 0176 01250
Eis	Ryfka	Miechów	Aus	1585 0176 01250
Eisenberg	Chaja Mincia	Bursztyn	Aus	1585 0177 01309
Eisenberg	Juda Chaim	Bursztyn	Aus	1585 0177 01309
Eisenberg	Leah	Bursztyn	Aus	1585 0177 01309
Eisenberg	Sadie	Bursztyn	Aus	1585 0177 01309
Eisenkraft	Chaim	Russów	Aus	1585 0176 01211

Surname	Given Name	Birthplace	Issue	Location Code
Eisner	Bernard	Kołomea	Pol	1738 0002 00629
Eisner	Max	Kołomea	Pol	1738 0002 00629
Eisner	Fannie	Kołomea	Pol	1738 0002 00629
Elifant	Dora	Pożdzimierz	Aus	1585 0176 01274
Elifant	Joseph	Pożdzimierz	Aus	1585 0176 01274
Elifant	Minnie	Pożdzimierz	Aus	1585 0176 01274
Ettinger	Arnold	Tarnów	Ger	1674 0172 04882
Ettinger	Arnold	Tarnów	Ger	1674 0178 04276
Ettinger	Sabine	Tarnów	Ger	1674 0178 04276
Ettinger	Sabine	Tarnów	Swt	1759 0178 04279
Ewig	Adolph	Stryy	Hun	1708 0001 00279
Ewig	Israel	Stryy	Hun	1708 0001 00279
Fassman	Bertha	Krzywcza	Pol	1738 0002 00427
Fassman	Nathan	Krzywcza	Pol	1738 0002 00427
Fassman	Sarah	Krzywcza	Pol	1738 0002 00427
Faust	Abraham	Zaleszczyki	Pol	1737 0001 00368
Faust	Bessie	Zaleszczyki	Pol	1737 0001 00368

Surname	Given Name	Birthplace	Issue	Location Code
Faust	Rachel	New York	Pol	1737 0001 00368
Feid	Joseph	Dubowica	Pol	1737 0001 00378
Feid	Sarah	Dubowica	Pol	1737 0001 00378
Feingold	Hirsch	Kolbuszowa	Ger	1678 0180 15610
Feld	Sara	Dubowica	Aus	1585 0177 01365
Feld	Sarah	Dubowica	Hun	1709 0162 00850
Feuer	Moritz	Galicia	Aus	1585 0176 01001
Feuer	Rosa	Galicia	Aus	1585 0176 01090
Fink	Chaim	Slone	Pol	1738 0003 01079
Fink	Rosa	Galicia	Aus	1584 0147 00629
Finkel	Julius	Sielce	Pol	1738 0003 01068
Finkel	Rywka	Sielce	Pol	1738 0003 01068
Fishman	Rose	Lemberg	Ger	1674 0171 03480
Flam	Bernard	Tarnów	Pol	1738 0002 00689
Flam	Bernard	Tarnów	Pol	1737 0001 00118
Flam	Camil	Tarnów	Pol	1737 0001 00118
Flam	Celia	Pilzno	Pol	1737 0001 00118

Surname	Given Name	Birthplace	Issue	Location Code
Flam	Joseph	Pilzno	Pol	1737 0001 00118
Flam	Pinkus	Tarnów	Pol	1737 0001 00118
Flam	Camil	Tarnów	Pol	1738 0002 00689
Flam	Celia	Pilzno	Pol	1738 0002 00689
Flam	Pinkus	Tarnów	Pol	1738 0002 00689
Fliegelman	Chiel	Majdan	Pol	1737 0001 00282
Fliegelman	Chiel	Majdan	Pol	1737 0001 00283
Fliegelman	Ethel	Majdan	Pol	1737 0001 00282
Fliegelman	Markus	Majdan	Pol	1737 0001 00283
Fliegelmann	Biele	Majdan	Pol	1737 0176 01273
Fliegelmann	David	Majdan	Pol	1737 0176 01273
Fliegelmann	Elka	Majdan	Pol	1737 0176 01273
Fliegelmann	Golda	Majdan	Pol	1737 0176 01273
Fliegelmann	Jakob	Majdan	Pol	1737 0176 01273
Freimaurer	Anna	Lysaków	Pol	1737 0001 00237
Freimaurer	Louis	Kuty	Pol	1737 0001 00237
Freimaurer	Harry	New York	Pol	1737 0001 00238

Surname	Given Name	Birthplace	Issue	Location Code
Freimaurer	Rosie	New York	Pol	1737 0001 00239
Fried	Isidore	Galicia	Egy	1650 0002 00083
Fried	Tille	Ciechanów	Pol	1737 0001 00075
Friedlander	Cyrla	Woloska Wieś	Pol	1738 0002 00581
Friedlander	Herman	Woloska Wieś	Pol	1738 0002 00581
Friedman	Esther	Radomysl	Pol	1738 0003 01024
Friedman	Morris	Radomysl	Pol	1738 0003 01024
Friedman	Rive	Horodenka	Pol	1737 0001 00169
Friedman	Sam	Horodenka	Pol	1737 0001 00169
Fuchs	Perl	Leszniów	Aus	1585 0177 01303
Fuerman	Dasia	Sieniawa	Pol	1738 0003 00983
Fuerman	Isidore	Sieniawa	Pol	1738 0003 00983
Gaffner	May	Buczacz	Pol	1741 0008 04397
Garfinkel	Mina	Galicia	Cz	1644 0001 00261
Gebel	Rachel	Rymanów	Pol	1741 0009 04603
Gebel	Sadie	New York	Pol	1741 0009 04603
Geffner	Paul	Buczacz	Aus	1585 0177 01435

Surname	Given Name	Birthplace	Issue	Location Code
Geller	Emanuel	Wróblik	Aus	1585 0176 01277
Geller	Joseph	Wróblik	Aus	1585 0176 01277
Geller	Paulina	Wróblik	Aus	1585 0176 01277
Geschwind	Morris	Mielec	Hol	1729 0003 01224
Gevirtz	Malvina	Kalusz	Ger	1674 0172 04307
Gewurz	Bertha	Dębica	Aus	1584 0147 00576
Gewurz	Elias	Dębica	Aus	1584 0147 00576
Gewurz	Elias	Dębica	Aus	1584 0147 00576
Gewurz	Henoch	Dębica	Aus	1584 0147 00576
Gewurz	Joseph	Dębica	Aus	1584 0147 00576
Gewurz	Lena	Dębica	Aus	1584 0147 00576
Gewurz	Sarah	Dębica	Aus	1584 0147 00576
Ginsberg	William	Sambor	Pol	1738 0003 00889
Glatt	Leah	Galicia	Ger	1678 0181 06719
Gluckman	Aron	Sambor	Fr	1664 0174 05295
Gluckman	Golde	Sambor	Fr	1664 0174 05295
Gluckman	Mendel	Sambor	Fr	1664 0174 05295

Surname	Given Name	Birthplace	Issue	Location Code
Gluckman	Golde	Sambor	Eng	1699 0174 07234
Gold	Esther	Galicia	Aus	1584 0147 00784
Gold	Isaac	Baligród	Pol	1749 0005 01933
Gold	Jacob	Lemberg	Ger	1675 0173 05100
Gold	Rose	Baligród	Pol	1749 0005 01933
Goldberg	Cipra Esther	Muszyna	Pol	1739 0004 01494
Goldberg	Rifka	Obertyn	Pol	1740 0006 02025
Goldhirsh	Fanny	Jezierzany	Egy	1650 0002 00052
Goldhirsh	William	Jezierzany	Egy	1650 0002 00052
Goldik	Chaim	Torski	Pol	1738 0002 00563
Goldik	Sophie	Torskie	Pol	1738 0002 00563
Goldmuntz	Michael	Kraków	Hol	1706 0001 00282
Goldmuntz	Michael	Kraków	Hol	1707 0002 00435
Goldmuntz	Sophie	Lemberg	Bel	1590 0003 00658
Goldmuntz	Sylvan	Kraków	Hol	1705 0001 00283
Gottfried	Fannie	Kołomea	Hun	1708 0161 00470
Gottfried	Bessie	New York	Hun	1708 0161 00470

The Galitzianers

Surname	Given Name	Birthplace	Issue	Location Code
Gottfried	Irene	Corona NY	Hun	1708 0161 00470
Gottfried	Rosie	Tarnopol	Pol	1737 0001 00224
Gottfried	Samuel	Galicia	Egy	1649 0001 50/19
Gottfried	Simon	Tarnopol	Pol	1737 0001 00224
Gottlieb	Adolph	Bochnia	Aus	1585 0176 01002
Gredinger	Adele	Galicia	Aus	1584 0147 00695
Gredinger	Dora	Galicia	Aus	1584 0147 00695
Gredinger	Fanny	Galicia	Aus	1584 0147 00695
Gredinger	Herman	Galicia	Aus	1584 0147 00695
Gredinger	Jetty	Galicia	Aus	1584 0147 00695
Gredinger	Moritz	Galicia	Aus	1584 0147 00695
Gredinger	Rebecca	Galicia	Aus	1584 0147 00695
Green	Bessie	Rokitno	Aus	1585 0176 01257
Greenbaum	Morris	Podwołoczyska	Pol	1741 0009 00036
Greenberg	Annie	Glinyany	Pol	1738 0002 00658
Greenbaum	Zelig	Sokolniki	Rus	1744 0003 00035
Greenbaum	Freida	Sokolniki	Rus	1744 0003 00035

Surname	Given Name	Birthplace	Issue	Location Code
Greenbaum	Samuel	Sokolniki	Rus	1744 0003 00035
Greenberg	Louis	Glinyany	Pol	1738 0002 00658
Greenberg	Sophie	Galicia	Pol	1737 0001 00078
Greene	Jacob	Galicia	Aus	1585 0177 01470
Greene	Tillie	Galicia	Aus	1585 0177 01470
Grinberg	Harry	Strzyżów	Pol	1737 0001 00220
Grinberg	Necha	Strzyżów	Pol	1737 0001 00220
Gutreich	Blume	Galicia	Aus	1585 0176 01138
Habenstrut	Anna	Rawa Ruska	Pol	1738 0002 00678
Habenstrut	Joseph	Rawa Ruska	Pol	1738 0002 00678
Habenstrut	Rebecca	Rawa Ruska	Pol	1738 0002 00678
Habenstrut	Samuel	Rawa Ruska	Pol	1738 0002 00678
Haber	Mateusz	Brzozowce	Pol	1738 0004 01034
Haber	Sofia	Brzozowce	Pol	1738 0004 01034
Halpern	Henoch	Lemberg	Pol	1741 0009 04549
Halpern	Sam	Lemberg	Pol	1741 0009 04549
Hauser	Izik	Borysław	Fr	1650 0160 01754

Surname	Given Name	Birthplace	Issue	Location Code
Hecht	Lois	Horodenka	Aus	1584 0147 00515
Hecker	Jennie	Kolbuszowa	Ger	1675 0174 07215
Heischuber	Esther	Tyczyn	Pol	1740 0006 02382
Heischuber	Max	Tyczyn	Pol	1740 0006 02382
Heller	Max	Hałicz	Pol	1737 0001 00263
Heller	Rose	Hałicz	Pol	1737 0001 00263
Hellman	Osias	Dolina	Aus	1585 0176 00991
Heuschuber	Anna	Rzeszów	Aus	1584 0147 00740
Heuschuber	Esther	Rzeszów	Aus	1584 0147 00740
Heuschuber	Herman	Rzeszów	Aus	1584 0147 00740
Heuschuber	Moses	Rzeszów	Aus	1584 0147 00740
Hitzig	Becky	Galicia	Aus	1585 0177 01512
Hitzig	Eni	Galicia	Aus	1585 0177 01512
Hochaus	Lillian	Kraków	Bel	1590 0003 00841
Hochaus	Samuel	Kraków	Bel	1590 0003 00841
Hochaus	Samuel	Kraków	Bel	1589 0001 00032
Hoffman	Minnie	Chorostków	Pol	1737 0001 00206

Surname	Given Name	Birthplace	Issue	Location Code
Hoffman	Sam	Chorostków	Pol	1737 0001 00032
Hollander	Irving	Lemberg	Rus	1744 0008 00034
Hollander	Lena	Lemberg	Rus	1744 0008 00034
Jalb	George	Dukla	Aus	1585 0176 01298
Jonas	Leon	Galicia	Aus	1585 0176 01025
Jonas	Minna	Galicia	Aus	1585 0176 01025
Kudd	Isidor Israel	Kraków	Aus	1585 0176 01025
Judd	Josephine	Kraków	Aus	1585 0176 01025
Judd	Isidore	Kraków	Fr	1662 0170 03885
Kahn	Sarah	Galicia	Aus	1585 0176 01172
Kalb	David Leib	Rymanów	Pol	1737 0001 00173
Kalb	Bessie	Rymanów	Pol	1737 0001 00172
Kalb	David Leib	Komorniki	Swt	1758 0176 03629
Kalb	Liba	Haber, Czech	Pol	1737 0001 00173
Kalb	Benjamin	Haber, Czech	Pol	1737 0001 00173
Kanner	Bennie	Galicia	Aus	1584 0147 00593
Kanner	Bertha	New York	Aus	1584 0147 00593

Surname	Given Name	Birthplace	Issue	Location Code
Kanner	Bine	New York	Aus	1584 0147 00593
Kanner	Leopold	New York	Aus	1584 0147 00593
Kanner	Marcus	Galicia	Aus	1584 0147 00593
Kanon	Lilly	Radomysl	Aus	1584 0147 00659
Kanon	Tessie	Radomysl	Aus	1584 0147 00659
Kantor	Pauline	Lemberg	Pol	1738 0003 01176
Kantor	Tadeusz	Lemberg	Pol	1738 0003 01176
Kaplan	Pesa	Radomysl	Lat	1577 0146 00143
Karol	Julia	Podhajce	Pol	1737 0001 00214
Karol	Adele	New York	Pol	1737 0001 00214
Karol	Justyn	Podhajce	Pol	1737 0001 00214
Karpen	Florence	Kraków	Pol	1741 0008 04192
Karpen	Jennie	Kraków	Pol	1741 0008 04192
Karpen	Lawrence	Kraków	Pol	1741 0008 04192
Katz	Max	Korczyna	Fr	1666 0177 06585
Klein	Rosa	Galicia	Aus	1585 0176 01064
Konig	Benny	Stanisławów	Aus	1585 0177 01431

Surname	Given Name	Birthplace	Issue	Location Code
Konig	Betty	Stanisławów	Aus	1585 0177 01431
Konig	Louis	Kalusz	Aus	1585 0177 01430
Kornhabe	Fannie	Lemberg	Aus	1585 0177 00510
Kornhabe	Julius	Lemberg	Aus	1585 0177 00510
Kornhabe	Samuel	Lemberg	Aus	1585 0177 00510
Kornstein	Annie	Galicia	Aus	1584 0147 00609
Kornstein	Dora	Galicia	Aus	1584 0147 00609
Kornstein	Fannie	Galicia	Aus	1584 0147 00609
Kornstein	Morris	Grzymałów	Aus	1584 0147 00609
Kornstein	Morris	Grzymałów	Aus	1585 0177 01406
Kreiger	Abraham	Tyczyn	Pol	1749 0005 01954
Kreiger	Sally	Tyczyn	Pol	1749 0005 01954
Kruleck	Fannie	Narol	Aus	1584 0147 00725
Kruleck	Israel	Narol	Aus	1584 0147 00725
Kruleck	Sarah	Narol	Aus	1584 0147 00725
Kronstein	Isadore	Żurawno	Aus	1586 0173 00118
Kurzrok	Gitla	Sassów	Pol	1738 0002 00531

Surname	Given Name	Birthplace	Issue	Location Code
Kurzrok	Raphael	Sassów	Pol	1738 0002 00531
Lachner	Celia	Brody	It	1715 0172 00835
Lachner	Henry	Brody	It	1715 0172 00835
Last	Moses	Tarnobrzeg	Ger	1677 0178 00881
Leidner	Golda	Mielec	Hol	1707 0002 00580
Leidner	Samuel	Mielec	Hol	1707 0002 00580
Leidner	Samuel	Mielec	Pol	1737 0001 00123
Leidner	Golda	Mielec	Pol	1737 0001 00122
Leistyna	Bertha	Grybów	Pol	1738 0002 00780
Leistyna	Sophie	Grybów	Pol	1738 0002 00780
Leistyna	Morris	Grybów	Pol	1738 0002 00780
Lechner	Mary	Nisko	Pol	1737 0001 00229
Lechner	Morris	Nisko	Pol	1737 0001 00229
Lerner	Hyman	Krystynopol	Pol	1738 0002 00680
Lerner	Sadie	Ciechanów	Pol	1737 0001 00048
Lewkowitz	Annie	Jaszczurowa	Ger	1679 0183 00350
Lichtenberg	Tachel	Bledowa	Pol	1737 0001 00049

Surname	Given Name	Birthplace	Issue	Location Code
Lieberman	Annie	Tyczyn	Aus	1584 0147 00712
Lieberman	Jacob	Raków	Pol	1740 0006 02152
Lieberman	Regina	Galicia	Aus	1584 0147 00761
Lieberman	Sam	Galicia	Aus	1584 0147 00761
Lieblich	Max	Rzeszów	Aus	1585 0176 01215
Lifscheitz	Morris	Monastyriska	Pol	1740 0006 02261
Lifscheitz	Yenta	Monastyriska	Pol	1740 0006 02261
Linder	Nettie	Rymanów	Aus	1585 0176 01173
Lippman	Ettel	Buczacz	Aus	1585 0177 01513
Low	Anna	Bóbrka	Pol	1739 0004 01347
Low	Berl	Bóbrka	Pol	1739 0004 01347
Low	Heni	Bóbrka	Pol	1739 0004 01347
Lowenthal	Dora	Galicia	Aus	1584 0147 00602
Lowenthal	Lillian	Galicia	Aus	1584 0147 00602
Luks	Pinkas	Wasylkowce	Pol	1738 0002 00575
Luks	Rachel	Wasylkowce	Pol	1738 0002 00575
Mages	Annie	Drohobycz	Pol	1738 0002 00782

Surname	Given Name	Birthplace	Issue	Location Code
Mages	Fannie	Drohobycz	Pol	1738 0002 00782
Mages	Jennie	Drohobycz	Pol	1738 0002 00782
Mages	Nathan	Drohobycz	Pol	1738 0002 00782
Mages	Timothy	Drohobycz	Pol	1738 0002 00782
Mandel	Joseph	Pruchnik	Aus	1585 0176 01143
Manheim	Daniel	Szczakowa	Pol	1738 0003 00924
Manheim	Jacob	Szczakowa	Pol	1738 0003 00924
Manheim	Rose	Szczakowa	Pol	1738 0003 00924
Manheim	Taube	Szczakowa	Pol	1738 0003 00924
Manheim	Wolf	Szczakowa	Pol	1738 0003 00924
Margulias	Abraham	Galicia	Aus	1584 0147 00598
Margulias	Broni	Galicia	Aus	1584 0147 00598
Margulias	Israel	Galicia	Aus	1584 0147 00598
Margulias	Jacob	Galicia	Aus	1584 0147 00598
Margulies	Abraham	Galicia	Aus	1584 0147 00657
Margulies	Broni	Galicia	Aus	1584 0147 00657
Margulies	Clara	Galicia	Cz	1684 0003 00085

Surname	Given Name	Birthplace	Issue	Location Code
Margulies	Mary	Tarnopol	Pol	1737 0001 00054
Margulies	Mary	Tarnopol	Aus	1584 0147 00664
Margulies	Mary	Tarnopol	Pol	1737 0001 00055
Margulies	Rosa	Mikulince	Pol	1737 0001 00054
Margulies	Simon	Mikulince	Pol	1737 0001 00054
Margulies	Simon	Tarnopol	Aus	1584 0147 00664
Messer	Annie	Lubaczów	Pol	1737 0001 00216
Messer	Carl	Lubaczów	Pol	1737 0001 00216
Meyerowitz	David	Glinik	Aus	1584 0147 00708
Meyerowitz	Eva	Glinik	Aus	1584 0147 00708
Meyerowitz	Sophie	Glinik	Aus	1584 0147 00708
Mielnik	Anna	Rohatyń	Pol	1738 0002 00423
Mielnik	Helen	Rohatyń	Pol	1738 0002 00423
Mielnik	John	Rohatyń	Pol	1738 0002 00423
Muschel	Alte	Dąbrowa	Aus	1584 0147 00532
Muschel	Markus	Dąbrowa	Aus	1584 0147 00532
Nagel	Anna	Złoczów	Aus	1585 0176 01275

Surname	Given Name	Birthplace	Issue	Location Code
Nagel	Eva	Złoczów	Aus	1585 0176 01275
Nagel	Harry	New York	Aus	1585 0176 01275
Nathanson	Ida	Grodzisko	Fr	1656 0157 00605
Papernik	Samuel	Zolocze	Aus	1585 0177 01582
Pavlotsky	Boris	Radomysl	Pol	1739 0004 01534
Pavlotsky	Etla	Radomysl	Pol	1739 0004 01534
Perlman	Abraham	Galicia	Hol	1707 0003 00864
Perlman	Abraham	Wieliczka	Aus	1585 0176 01239
Perlman	Abraham	Galicia	Hol	1707 0003 01104
Perlman	Chaskell	Boston	Aus	1585 0176 01240
Perlman	Dora	Brzesko	Aus	1584 0147 00579
Perlman	Fannie	Galicia	Aus	1585 0176 01240
Perlman	Hanna	Boston	Aus	1585 0176 01240
Perlman	Samuel	Galicia	Aus	1585 0176 01240
Perlman	Stefina	Boston	Aus	1585 0176 01240
Perlman	Theresa	Wieliczka	Aus	1585 0176 01240
Perlstein	Sima Parciak	Rzeszów	Pol	1741 0008 04370

Surname	Given Name	Birthplace	Issue	Location Code
Pitzele	Fanny	Kraków	Fr	1658 0162 02388
Pitzele	Rosa	Kraków	Fr	1658 0162 02389
Pitzele	Rubin	Kraków	Fr	1658 0162 02390
Polikuk	Jacob	Buczacz	Pol	1749 0005 01885
Polikuk	Liebe	Zoloty Potok	Pol	1749 0005 01885
Posner	Blima	Nowy Dwor	Pol	1737 0001 00304
Posner	Joseph	Nowy Dwor	Pol	1737 0001 00304
Postaz	Charlotte	Tarnopol	Ger	1676 0175 08676
Postaz	Frieda	Tarnopol	Ger	1676 0175 08676
Postaz	Mollie	Tarnopol	Ger	1676 0175 08676
Potsteve	Clara	Nowy Dwor	Pol	1737 0001 00314
Propper	Gussie	Mokre	Pol	1737 0001 00388
Propper	Hyman	Mokre	Pol	1737 0001 00388
Rabinowitz	Nasia	Radomysl	Pol	1749 0005 01910
Rabinowitz	Chaim	Radomysl	Pol	1749 0005 01910
Rabinowitz	Leiser	Stanisławow	Pol	1738 0002 00608
Rabinowitz	Meshulam	Stanisławow	Pol	1738 0002 00608

Surname	Given Name	Birthplace	Issue	Location Code
Rakower	Fannie W.	Nowy Sącz	Bel	1589 0001 00315
Rakower	Josef	Podgórze	Bel	1589 0001 00269
Rakower	Josef	Podgórze	Bel	1589 0001 00315
Rakower	Sabine	Podgórze	Bel	1589 0001 00315
Rand	Gussie	Sanok	Aus	1584 0147 00711
Rappaport	Ascher Schaye	Strzyżów	Pol	1737 0001 00185
Rappaport	Cyvie	Strzyżów	Pol	1737 0001 00185
Reichenstein	Ethel	Lemberg	Aus	1585 0176 00957
Reisner	Harry	Rzeszów	Aus	1585 0176 00873
Reiss	Joseph	Lemberg	Lat	1577 0147 00055
Renner	Jacob	Stanisławów	Bel	1590 0003 00828
Richter	Max	Lemberg	Aus	1584 0147 00644
Richter	Moses	Lemberg	Aus	1584 0147 00644
Richter	Nettie	Lemberg	Aus	1584 0147 00644
Rine	Victor	Kudryńce	Egy	1650 0002 00156
Ringelheim	Chaje	Jarosław	Aus	1585 0176 04633
Ringelheim	David	Jarosław	Aus	1585 0176 04633

Surname	Given Name	Birthplace	Issue	Location Code
Ringelheim	Osias	Jarosław	Aus	1585 0176 04633
Ringelheim	Mary	Galicia	Aus	1585 0176 04633
Ringelheim	Jacob	Kanczuga	Aus	1585 0176 04633
Ritterman	Abraham	Trzebina	Aus	1584 0147 00683
Ritterman	Abraham	Trzebina	Swt	1759 0173 04397
Rodner	Anna	Radom.Wiel.	Pol	1740 0006 02333
Rosen	Morris	Lesko	Aus	1584 0147 00656
Rosenbach	Sophia	Mikulince	Ger	1673 0169 01400
Rosenbluth	Frederick	Galicia	Eng	1696 0163 04922
Rosenbluth	Hanna	Galicia	Eng	1696 0163 04922
Rosenbluth	Herman	Galicia	Eng	1696 0163 04922
Rosenbluth	Gussie	New York	Aus	1585 0176 01210
Rosenbluth	Minia	Śniatyn	Aus	1585 0176 01210
Rosenfeld	Johanna	Stanisławów	Pol	1738 0002 00615
Rosenfeld	Oscar	Stanisławów	Pol	1738 0002 00615
Rosenfeld	Oscar	Stanisławów	Aus	1585 0176 01183
Rosenfeld	Rose	Stanisławów	Aus	1585 0176 01184

Surname	Given Name	Birthplace	Issue	Location Code
Rosenfeld	Rose	Stanisławów	Pol	1738 0002 00650
Rosenfeld	Salomon	Stanisławów	Pol	1738 0002 00614
Rosenfeld	Salomon	Stanisławów	Pol	1738 0002 00615
Rosenfeld	Taube/ Toni	Stanisławów	Pol	1738 0002 00614
Rosenfeld	Taube/ Toni	Stanisławów	Aus	1585 0176 01183
Rosenman	Celia	Maków	Hol	1707 0003 00979
Rosenstrauch	Sam	Podhajce	Aus	1584 0147 00587
Rosiner	Clara	Sielce	Pol	1738 0002 00697
Rosiner	Max	Sielce	Pol	1738 0002 00697
Roth	Fanny	Tarnów	Ger	1677 0178 14343
Roth	Pauline	Sanok	Aus	1584 0147 00615
Rothman	Henry	Lezajsk	Swt	1759 0178 04469
Rothman	Henry	Lezajsk	Aus	1706 0176 01021
Rubin	David	Kolbuszowa	Aus	1585 0176 01272
Rudolph	Nettie	Galicia	Aus	1584 0147 00604
Sacher	Joseph	Kuty	Ger	1676 0177 12505
Saifer	Anna	Felsztyn	Pol	1738 0003 00986

Surname	Given Name	Birthplace	Issue	Location Code
Saifer	Paisy	Felsztyn	Pol	1738 0003 00986
Salzman	Israel	Niebylec	Rus	1744 0008 00043
Sattler	Annie	Galicia	Aus	1585 0176 01127
Schaffer	Hyman	Dora	Pol	1740 0006 02301
Schafler	Elias	Radymno	Hol	1706 0001 00453
Schatz	Anna	Bialy Kamień	Pol	1741 0008 04155
Schatz	Bronia	Bialy Kamień	Pol	1741 0008 04155
Schein	Cecilia	Stanisławów	Pol	1738 0002 00717
Schiffer	Bruche	Majdan	Pol	1737 0001 00309
Schiffer	Salamon	Majdan	Pol	1737 0001 00309
Schindler	Poli	Galicia	Hun	1708 0161 00482
Schindler	Jack	New York	Hun	1708 0161 00482
Schindler	Meyer	New York	Hun	1708 0161 00482
Schlaff	Frandel	Ropczyce	Pol	1738 0002 00533
Schlaff	Lewis	Ropczyce	Pol	1738 0002 00533
Schlanger	Moses	Rzeszów	Aus	1585 0176 00857
Schmertzler	Fannie	Zaleszczyki	Rom	1743 0001 00002

Surname	Given Name	Birthplace	Issue	Location Code
Schmertzler	Morris	Kasperowce	Rom	1743 0001 00002
Schnall	Max	Galicia	Aus	1585 0176 01101
Schnapp	Rose	Podhajce	Aus	1584 0147 00554
Schwartz	Clara	Lemberg	Aus	1586 0178 00153
Schwartz	Zacharia	Dolina	Pol	1749 0005 01875
Schwarz	Anna	Szcerzec	Pol	1738 0003 01029
Schwarz	Harris	Szcerzec	Pol	1738 0003 01029
Scitumer	Kopie	New York	Aus	1585 0176 01261
Scitumer	Lena	Stanisławów	Aus	1585 0176 01261
Segal	David	Roznów	Pol	1740 0006 02007
Segal	Gertrude	Roznów	Pol	1740 0006 02007
Seidmann	Fannie	Raków	Pol	1741 0009 04613
Seinfeld	Herman	Stanisławów	En	1696 0168 00472
Shuelander	Mariem	Sokolów	Pol	1737 0001 00221
Shuelander	Morris	Sokolów	Pol	1737 0001 00221
Siegel	Regina	Borysław	Pol	1738 0002 00786
Singer	Esther	Gorlice	Ger	1679 0183 00290

Surname	Given Name	Birthplace	Issue	Location Code
Sitzer	Clara	Kalusz	Pol	1738 0003 01154
Sitzer	Leib	Kalusz	Pol	1738 0003 01154
Sojfer	Anna	Felsztyn	Pol	1738 0003 00986
Sojfer	Paisy	Felsztyn	Pol	1738 0003 00986
Sonnenfeld	Mary G.	Jezierzany	Pol	1650 0003 00334
Speigel	Helen	Buczacz	Aus	1585 0176 01250
Speilvogel	Chaim	Tarnobrzeg	Ger	1676 0177 13276
Speilvogel	Jacob	Tarnobrzeg	Ger	1676 0177 13276
Speilvogel	Schiffra	Tarnobrzeg	Ger	1676 0177 13276
Sprunk	Rosa	Galicia	Aus	1585 0176 00925
Stanger	Malka Kramer	Rawa Ruska	Pol	1741 0009 04443
Starer	Brina	Ottynia	Pol	1738 0003 01165
Starer	Pinkus	Ottynia	Pol	1738 0003 01165
Stark	Celia Keller	Kraków	Eng	1699 0175 0139A
Stein	Adele	Kołomea	Aus	1585 0177 01438
Stein	Harry	Kołomea	Aus	1585 0177 01360
Stein	Chaja Feider	Kołomea	Pol	1738 0003 00848

Surname	Given Name	Birthplace	Issue	Location Code
Stein	Samuel	Kołomea	Pol	1738 0003 00848
Steinhauser	Esther	Bochnia	Bel	1590 0003 00880
Steinhauser	Esther	Bochnia	Bel	1589 0001 00282
Sternbach	Isidor	Borysław	Aus	1584 5449 00483
Sternbach	Isidor	Borysław	Cz	1644 0001 00327
Sternfeld	Barney	Sandomierz	Eng	1699 0175 00068
Stevenson	Abe	Nowy Dwor	Pol	1737 0001 00314
Stone	Fannie	Kraków	Pol	1740 0005 01797
Stein	Fannie	Kraków	Pol	1740 0005 01797
Stein	Salo	Kraków	Pol	1740 0005 01797
Stone	Salo	Kraków	Pol	1740 0005 01797
Streich	Clara	Stanisławów	Pol	1741 0008 04362
Streicher	Beril	Kołomea	Pol	1739 0004 01408
Streicher	Sara	Kołomea	Pol	1739 0004 01408
Sturtz	Annie	Jasło	Pol	1737 0001 00264
Sturtz	Elsie	Jasło	Pol	1737 0001 00264
Sturtz	Elsie	New York	Pol	1737 0001 00264

Surname	Given Name	Birthplace	Issue	Location Code
Sturtz	Sophie	Jasło	Pol	1737 0001 00264
Sussman	Fannie	Ruda	Aus	1585 0177 01458
Sussman	Samuel	Ruda	Aus	1585 0177 01458
Sussman	Nehama G.	Tarnopol	Ger	1673 0170 02158
Swartz	Elika	Radomysl	Lat	1577 0147 00061
Teitel	Hyman	Tarnobrzeg	Aus	1584 0147 00729
Thau	Bertha	Galicia	Aus	1585 0177 01583
Thau	Mauritz	Galicia	Aus	1585 0177 01583
Thau	Phillip	Galicia	Aus	1585 0177 01583
Thau	Tilli	Galicia	Aus	1585 0177 01583
Thurshwel	Albert	Galicia	Cz	1644 0001 00395
Thurshwel	Eidel	Galicia	Cz	1644 0001 00395
Thurshwel	Rebecca	Galicia	Cz	1644 0001 00395
Traun	Joseph	Galicia	Aus	1585 0176 01228
Trauring	Aron Benj.	Galicia	Aus	1585 0176 01103
Tischler	Bertha	Zakliczyn	Aus	1585 0177 01134
Tischler	Katie	Zakliczyn	Aus	1585 0177 01134

Surname	Given Name	Birthplace	Issue	Location Code
Tischler	Rosie	Zakliczyn	Aus	1585 0177 01134
Trauring	Isak	Kanczuga	Aus	1584 0147 00589
Tuchschneider	Joseph	Radomysl	Pol	1737 0001 00297
Tuchschneider	Sarah	Radomysl	Pol	1737 0001 00297
Tuerk	Beatrice	Posada Chyr.	Ger	1675 0174 06200
Tuerk	Moses	Posada Chyr.	Ger	1675 0174 06200
Tuerk	Rose Francis	Posada Chyr.	Ger	1675 0174 06200
Unger	Ida	Korczyna	Aus	1585 0177 01530
Uram	Henry	Maniów	Bel	1590 0003 00756
Viertel	Anna	Stanisławów	Aus	1585 0176 01074
Viertel	Bertha	Stanisławów	Aus	1585 0176 01074
Viertel	Calel	Stanisławów	Aus	1585 0176 01074
Viertel	Simon	Stanisławów	Aus	1585 0176 01074
Viertel	Zofia	Stanisławów	Aus	1585 0176 01074
Vogel	Pinkas	Kossów	Aus	1585 0147 00728
Wachtel	Max	Rzeszów	Ger	1676 0173 11383
Wadler	Anna	Kraków	Ger	1673 0169 01020

Surname	Given Name	Birthplace	Issue	Location Code
Wadler	Lucille	Kraków	Ger	1673 0169 01020
Wadler	Mayer	Kraków	Ger	1673 0169 01020
Wadler	Ruth	Kraków	Ger	1673 0169 01020
Wadler	Seymour	Kraków	Ger	1673 0169 01020
Wasser	Bertie	Lemberg	Aus	1585 0176 01071
Wasser	Bertie	Lemberg	Aus	1585 0176 01260
Wasser	Jacob	Lemberg	Aus	1585 0176 01260
Wasser	Jacob	Lemberg	Aus	1585 0176 01071
Wasser	Jacob	Lemberg	Aus	1585 0177 01441
Wasser	Willie	Lemberg	Aus	1585 0176 01260
Weber	Arthur	Slopnice	Aus	1584 0147 00685
Weber	Elias	Slopnice	Aus	1584 0147 00685
Wiedman	Lena	Jezierzany	Pol	1738 0002 00739
Wiedman	Max	Jezierzany	Pol	1738 0002 00739
Weichsel	Tobias	Rzeszów	Pol	1738 0002 00716
Weiner	Emanuel	Kraków	Eng	1699 0175 00048
Weiner	Emanuel	Kraków	Eng	1690 0156 09385

The Galitzianers

Surname	Given Name	Birthplace	Issue	Location Code
Weisgray	Dina	Rohatyń	Aus	1585 0177 01384
Weisgray	Morris	Rohatyń	Aus	1585 0177 01384
Weisgray	Mortimer	Rohatyń	Aus	1585 0177 01384
Weiss	Leah	Krościenko	Aus	1585 0177 01488
Weiss	Marcus	Krościenko	Aus	1585 0177 01487
Weissberg	Bernard	Leżajsk	Bel	1590 0002 00384
Welczer	Max	Galicia	Pol	1738 0002 00518
Welczer	Sara	Galicia	Pol	1738 0002 00518
Werner	Louis	Galicia	Ger	1673 0169 01017
Wilson	Minnie	Nowy Sącz	Ger	1680 0186 01092
Wilson	Emanuel	Philadelphia	Ger	1680 0186 01092
Wohlman	Beatrixe	New York	Hun	1708 0001 00212
Wohlman	Max	Stryj	Hug	1708 0001 00212
Wolfenstein	Clara	Czortków	Aus	1585 0177 00002
Wolfenstein	Philip	Czortków	Aus	1585 0177 00002
Wolkenheim	Amalia	Rzeszów	Pol	1737 0001 00183
Yamenfeld	Basia	Kołomea	Pol	1741 0009 00050

Surname	Given Name	Birthplace	Issue	Location Code
Yamenfeld	Clara	Kołomea	Pol	1741 0009 00050
Yamenfeld	Wolf	Kołomea	Pol	1741 0009 00050
Zahler	Louis	Radomysl	Aus	1585 0177 01408
Zahler	Louis	Radomysl	Aus	1585 0177 01063
Zeichner	Elias	Niżniów	Aus	1584 0147 00673

APPENDIX E

Documents About Kraków Jews: 18th and 19th Centuries
by Geoffrey M. Weisgard

For several centuries until 1939, Kraków was a major center of Jewish life and influence. It is not surprising, then, that numerous books have been published that describe Kraków's Jewish community. In recent years, most new books have concentrated on the Holocaust period but resources do exist for genealogists and historians interested in Kraków Jews of the 19th and 20th centuries. Little is available about the 18th and earlier centuries, however, largely due to fires that destroyed the mostly wooden structures of Kraków. In his *Jewish Monuments of Kraków's Kazimierz: A Short Guide*, Michael Rozek refers to the Kehillah (Jewish community) scribe, Pinchas Szijowicz Horowitz, noting that, in 1773, Kehillah archives were destroyed by fire in his house, along with many valuable documents of the Jews from Kazimierz (the Jewish quarter of Kraków).

By the 18th century, the major center of Kraków's Jewish population and activity was firmly established in Kazimierz, then still considered a separate town. Jews were prohibited from practicing trade and crafts in Kraków and its environs, but these prohibitions did not extend to Kazimierz.

Maps

Maps from the 18th century show that Jews lived in only a part of Kazimierz. A number of maps may be of interest to genealogists and historians, though only one is from the 18th century.

The first is a map that appears in *Miasto Kazimierz* (Town of Kazimierz) by E. Ekielski. This map, which appears to have been dated 1703, illustrates various features of Kazimierz from the 14th to the 17th centuries. The second map, found in Majer Bałaban's book Kraków, Wedrówki w Przeszłosc: Kazimierz (Kraków: A journey in the past), is an Austrian map from 1786. Though small in scale, it shows the city's surrounding rivers and the city walls and identifies the Judenstadt (Jewish city) in the northeast corner.

The third map, which appears in Bałaban's leading academic work, *Historja Zydów w Krakówie i ma Kazimierz, 1304-1868* (History of the Jews of Kraków and Kazimierz, 1304–1868), was probably prepared around 1809. This map is particularly useful because it shows house numbers that correspond to the censuses of 1790 and 1795. A fourth map, published in 1815, shows the new Jewish cemetery separated from Kazimierz by a farm and fields. Kazimierz is clearly shown, virtually surrounded by rivers. In particular, the map shows the Stara Visła (Old Vistula), which ran along the route of what is now ul. J. Dietła. At the time of the first partition of Poland in 1772, Austria occupied the area to the south of the Old Vistula, including Kazimierz, but not the area to the north, Kraków. This map is located in the Kraków archives on ul. Lubcicz.

A fifth map, published in Kraków in 1930 by the *Polska akademia umiejętności*, is of Kraków province, but it includes as an inset a plan of the city of Kraków. This map is in the LDS (Mormon) Family History Library collection under the title Atlas historyczny Polsky: nr. 1. Mapa wojewodztwa krakowskiego z doby sejmu czteroletnego (1788–92)/Karol Buczek. The call number in the Europe Book Area is 943.8, E7h, Ser. A.

Records of Births, Marriages and Deaths

In 1784, the Austrian administration introduced the requirement to register births, marriages and deaths with civil authorities. Some registrations for the end of the 18th century are among the records held on microfilm by the LDS Family History Library. The reader is cautioned, however, that the records for 1798–1800 are incomplete and also that family names were not widely used among Jews at the time.

The Jewish community is likely to have maintained records of births, marriages and deaths prior to 1784, but few have been found. An example of 18th century death records can be seen in a manuscript that is held by the Jewish National and University Library in Jerusalem, which has two manuscripts concerning Kraków. The first (Heb. 8'2332) is a *pinkas hazkarat neshamot* (Book of memorial services for the dead) from the synagogue of Rabbi Meir Dayan in Kraków. This is a 34-page, mostly parchment document from the 17th -18th centuries. The other manuscript is a similar document from another synagogue. The entries in the 19-page pinkas hazkarat neshamot begin in the 19th century and end in 1919.

Burials prior to 1800 took place at the cemetery adjacent to the Remu synagogue. It appears that burial records for the cemetery have not survived, and, in addition, its tombstones suffered extensive destruction during the German occupation. Nevertheless, a number of books list information relating to the surviving gravestones. Further research is being conducted by a team at the Jagiellonian University in Kraków. The team, headed by Dr. Pilarczyk of the Department of Jewish Studies, has undertaken to record the inscriptions on the surviving stones; particularly important work because of continuing damage from erosion and environmental pollution.

The "new" cemetery on ul. Miodowa opened in 1800. A book exists that lists burials from about the 1880s to the present time. This was one of three or four such books, but the others apparently did not survive the Holocaust. The original book is held at the Jewish community office at ul. Skawinska 2, but the staff has no copy machine. Copies can be obtained from the New Cracow Friendship Society (a society of Holocaust survivors and their families), c/o Max Hilfstein, 1523 Dwight Place, Bronx, NY 10465; phone: (718) 972-2224. The society welcomes donations in exchange for information.

Censuses

In 1765 a census was taken of the entire Jewish community of Poland, but the results of that census appear to survive only in aggregate data. In *Historia Żydów w Krakówie i w Kazimierz, 1304–1868* (History of the Jews of Kraków and Kazimierz, 1304–1868), Bałaban maintains that the data resulting from the 1765 census were less accurate than that from the subsequent 1773 census. When Bałaban wrote his book in 1936, the 1765 census was in the main archives in Kraków, but searches there, as well as in other archives, have been conducted without success; its fate is unknown. It may have been destroyed during World War II, or it is buried somewhere at that same archives.

The Roman Catholic Church collected information about the Jewish community of Kraków as described in *Sources for Jewish History in the 18th Century in Church Archives* by Stanisław Litak of the Catholic University in Lublin. One such census was carried out in 1787, but, though it provides general information about the community, no names are included. Copies of this census are believed to be held at the Archives of the Bishop of Kraków.

A 1790 census does not show great detail, but, nevertheless, I was able to find my ancestors in that census using the 1795 census described below as a starting point. Living at house number 96 was Szmul Świecarz (*swiecarz* means candlemaker in Polish), age 45; his wife, Dwora, age 40; and their family, including Isaac, who is featured in the 1795 return.

The first census useful to genealogists was taken by the Austrians in 1795; however, a major difficulty for genealogists with this census is that most of the people listed did not have surnames. The German-language book, *A List of the Jews of the Jewish Town of Kazimierz and the Surrounding Suburbs and Villages*, contains this census. Copies of this book are held by the Centre for Research on the History and Culture of Polish Jews of the Central Archives for the History of the Jewish People at Hebrew University in Jerusalem. A copy of this book is also held by the Archiwum Panstwowe (National Archives), ul. Sienna in Kraków.

As an example, entry number 508 shows that my ancestor, Isaac, son of Samuel, lived at house number 96, and that he was 30 years old. The previously referenced map in Bałaban's book shows that house number 96 was on ul. Ciemna. The entry also shows that Isaac's wife, Ester, age 36, was the daughter of Chaim. They lived with their children, Blume, age 8, and Gittel Lea, age 3. The record of Blume's marriage in 1805 is in my possession.

Central Archives for the History of the Jewish People

The Central Archives for the History of the Jewish People in Jerusalem holds many documents relating to Kraków in the 18th century and even earlier, but few are of genealogical significance. However, the inventory shows that the Central Archives holds fragmentary birth, marriage and death records from the 1788–1855 period, as well as court records concerning the Jews of 1624–1765.

Jewish Historical Institute

The Jewish Historical Institute in Warsaw (as of 1996) has the largest and most accessible number of documents of any collection relating to the Jewish community of Kraków. Although the institute's holdings relate primarily to post 18th century Poland, they also have 45 files of 18th century documents. Each file includes a brief index written in Polish. The documents, also written in Polish, contain a large number of names, which could be of particular interest to genealogists. A list of the 45 documents is available. Send three international reply coupons to Geoffrey M. Weisgard, 18 Daylesford Crescent, Cheadle, Cheshire 5K8 1LH, England.

National Archives in Kraków

The National Archives (*Archiwum Panstwowe*) in Kraków is divided among a number of buildings located in different parts of the city. The map archives is located at ul. Lubicz; 20th century documents are to be found at ul. Grunwaldzka 8; the bulk of 18th and 19th century documents are held at ul. Sienna 16. Non-Polish-speaking researchers are advised to enlist the assistance

of someone who speaks Polish. In addition to the censuses for
Kraków and the district for 1790–92 and 1795–96, the archives
holds a list of Jewish inhabitants compiled for the army in 1795;
a list of Jewish doorkeepers in Kraków, 1796–1808; and a list of
property owners in Kazimierz, 1790–94.

Selected Books on the History of Kraków Jewry

The following works may be helpful to the genealogist or
historian:

» Bałaban, M. *Historia Zydów w Krakówie i w Kazimierz,
  1204–1868* (History of the Jews of Kraków and Kazimierz,
  1204–1868), 2 vols. This is the leading work on the
  history of the Jewish community of Kraków. Published in
  Kraków from 1931 to 1936, the volumes were an update of
  Bałaban's Dzreje Zydów Krakówie i w Kazimierz, 1304–
  1868, published before World War I. The volumes were
  reprinted in Poland in Polish and Yiddish in the 1990s.
  The second volume contains several chapters on the 18th
  century, which include a lengthy index of names, a number
  of family trees and illustrations and maps.
» Bałaban, M. *Przewodnik po Żdowskich Zabytkach Krakowa*
  (Guide to Jewish monuments of Kraków), 1935 (repub-
  lished 1990). The book includes descriptions and plans of
  the Remu cemetery.
» Duda, Eugenieusz. *Krakowskie Judaica* (Kraków Judaica).
  The book is written largely in Polish, but an English section
  sets out the history of the Jewish community in Kraków.
  The book also contains modern maps and photos.
» Rozek, Michael. *Jewish Monuments of Kraków's Kazimierz:
  A Short Guide.* Kraków, 1990. This book may be found in
  Great Britain through Orbis Books Ltd., 68 Kenway Road,
  London SW5 ORD, or Earl's Court Publications, Ltd., 192
  Chiswick High Road, London W4 1PP.
» Exielski, Eustachy. *Miasto Kazimierz i Budowle Akademickie
  w tym mieście* (Town of Kazimierz and its university build-
  ings), Kraków, 1869. This book includes a map from
  1793.

» Friedberg, ?. *Luchot Zikaron.* Drohobycz, 1897. The book offers 122 biographies of rabbis and leaders in the Talmudic Academy of Kraków.

» Wettstein, F.N. *Luchot Zikaron.* Frankfurt, 1904, reprinted Jerusalem, 1968/9. Biographies of rabbis and other community leaders.

» Zunz, J.M. *Ir Hatzedek.* Lemberg, 1874. In Hebrew, this book offers a history of the Kraków rabbinate from 1500 to 1856.

» *Bibliographies of Polish Judaica,* 1993. This book reproduces a number of papers presented at an international symposium in Kraków, July 1988. The symposium was sponsored by the Jagiellonian University, the centre of research on Jewish history and culture in Poland.

» *Guide to Bibliographies of Polish Judaica* edited by Krzystof Pilarczyk. This book lists a number of books worthy of examination. It also contains an inventory of the archives of Kazimierz, entitled, Inwentarz Archiwum Miasta Kazimierza pod Krakowem, 1335–1802 (Inventory of the town of Kazimierz near Kraków, 1365–1802) by Marian Friedberg, published by the National Archives of Poland, Warsaw, 1996.

» Another book relevant to 18th century research is a catalogue of art monuments in Poland (vol. 4, part 6), issued by the Polish Academy of Sciences Institute of Art in 1995. The text, largely in Polish, includes short sections in English, an index of names mentioned in the volumes and a number of photographs, some of which include 18th century tombstones in the Remu cemetery.

» Several *yizkor* books have been published for Kraków. One, Sefer Kroke, includes a section on the history of the Jews in Kraków from 1304 to 1815.

APPENDIX F

Galician Towns Where Jews Lived in 1877

The 1875 Austrian law governing the collection and maintenance of vital records is described in chapter 2. The 1877 regulations, entitled *Fuhrung der Geburts-, Ehe- und Sterbematrikeln fur die Israeliten in Galizien*, set forth the procedures for administering the law. The regulations manual included a list of towns where Jews were known to live in the 1870 census, and the Gemeinde administrative districts and subdistricts to which each town was assigned. Those regulations, for the first time, assigned the Jewish community the right and responsibility for recording and maintaining its own registers of all births, civil marriages and deaths. Prior to this time, responsibility for Jewish record keeping rested with the Catholic parish in the Gemeinde where the family lived. Since there was widespread resistance to registering their events with the Catholic church (and, perhaps, little enthusiasm among Catholic registrars as well), Catholic registration of Jewish events had been almost non-existent. This accounts for the paucity of Jewish records before 1877, except in large cities such as Tarnopol, Kraków, Lemberg and Przemyśl. So, the 1875 law that transferred this responsibility to the Jewish community, was very significant for those of us interested in our family history.

A word about Jewish, as opposed to judicial and parish districts and subdistricts. Austria had broken each of its territories into judicial districts for the purpose of assigning court personnel to administer civil and criminal justice. Austria also created Catholic and Jewish districts. Often the three types of districts overlapped, but not always, and the reader is cautioned not to use non-Jewish districts to determine how Jewish records were organized. Should you happen upon non-Jewish, general material about administrative districts on the Internet or in one of the Polish gazetteers, you may find lists of administrative districts, but these are not Jewish districts, unless they are so identified. Jewish districts were evidently created with some religious politics in mind, since some subdistricts administrative centers are quite distant from their main district center, and are not always formed along natural boundary lines.

After the 1998 publication of *Finding Your Jewish Roots in Galicia: A Resource Guide,* this author was informed by readers that the book was missing some towns. This was probably due to administrative errors in compiling the 1877 listing. This book includes the towns known to be missing, but some villages may still be missing. If you find that your town is missing, and you can identify the nearest town, you can be reasonably sure that the administrative districts will be the same.

Chapter 2 summarizes the complete list of the 1877 administrative districts with information about whether the town is in current-day Poland (POL) or Ukraine (UKR). The four-digit number refers to the 1878 Austrian index map that is in that chapter to provide geographical guidance in locating the general area where your town and districts are located. You may use the four-digit number to order a copy of the map for that area from the Library of Congress, Geography and Map Division, Washington, DC 20540. The map series reference number is: G6480 S75.A8.

Under the Austrians, the German word alt (old) was used, as in Alt Sambor. The Polish equivalent is stary Towns sometimes carry descriptors, such as (old), nowy (new), wielky (large) and mały (small) as masculine forms (also stare, nowe, wielke and małe) or stara, nowa, wielka and mała as the feminine form. Miasto generally denotes the whole town or city. Rynek is the town center or market square. Sometimes towns were divided into sections and the words dolny (lower) and górne (upper) were used, as in Ustrzyki Dolne and Ustrzyki Górne.

Town	Main District	Subdistrict
Abramowice	Limanowa	Limanowa
Adamierz	Dąbrowa	Dąbrowa
Adamówka	Jarosław	Sienawa
Adamy	Kam. Strumiłowa	Busk
Adzary	Dąbrowa	Dąbrowa
Agatówka	Tarnobrzeg	Rozwadów
Akreszory	Kossów	Pistyn
Albigówa	Łańcut	Łańcut
Albinówka	Śniatyn	Zabłotów
Alfredówka	Przemyślany	Gliniany
Alfredówka	Tarnobrzeg	Tarnobrzeg
Alwernia	Chrzanów	Chrzanów
Andryanów	Rudki	Komarno
Andrychów	Wadowice	Andrychów
Andrzejówka	Nowy Sącz	Muszyna
Andrzejówka	Sokal	Tartaków
Anielówka	Tarnopol	Tarnopol
Anielówka	Zaleszczyki	Tłuste
Annaberg	Stryj	Skole
Antonin	Kam. Strumiłowa	Radziechów
Antoniów	Tarnobrzeg	Radomyśl
Antonów	Czortków	Jagielnica
Antonówka	Tłumacz	Niźniów
Arlamów	Bircza	Dobromil
Arlamowska	Mościska	Mościska
Armanice	Przemyśl	Niżankowice
Artasów	Zolkiew	Kulików
Artyszczów	Gródek	Gródek
Augustówka	Brzeżany	Kozowa
Babcze	Borhodczany	Sołotwina
Babianka	Tłumacz	Ottynia
Babica	Rzeszów	Czudec

Town	Main District	Subdistrict
Babice	Biała	Oświęcim
Babice	Chrzanów	Chrzanów
Babice	Przemyśl	Krzywcza
Babice	Wadowice	Wadowice
Babin	Kalusz	Wojnilów
Babin	Kam. Strumiłowa	Chołojów
Babin	Kossów	Kossów
Babina	Sambor	Sambor
Babińce	Rohatyń	Rohatyń
Babińce	Sokal	Sokal
Babińce ad Krzywcze	Borszczów	Mielnica
Babińce ad Dżwinogród	Borszczów	Mielnica
Babuchów	Rohatyń	Rohatyń
Babule	Mielec	Mielec
Bachlówa	Lisko	Lisko
Bachórz	Brzozów	Dynów
Bachórze	Przemyśl	Dubiecko
Bachów	Przemyśl	Krzywcza
Bachówice	Wadowice	Wadowice
Bacza	Nowy Sącz	Łabowa
Baczal Dolna	Jasło	Jasło
Baczałka	Pilzno	Brzostek
Baczów	Przemyślany	Przemyślany
Baczyn	Wadowice	Kalwarya
Baczyna	Staremiasto	Staremiasto
Bagienica	Dąbrowa	Dąbrowa
Bajdy	Krosno	Dukla
Bajkowce	Tarnopol	Tarnopol
Bajowice	Mościska	Hussaków
Bakowce	Bóbrka	Strzeliska Nowe
Bakowe	Tarnobrzeg	Rozwadów

Town	Main District	Subdistrict
Bakowice	Staremiasto	Chyrów
Bałahorówka	Horodenka	Obertyn
Bałazówka	Limanowa	Limanowa
Balice	Mościska	Hussaków
Balicze Podrozne	Żydachów	Żurawno
Balicze Pogórne	Żydachów	Żurawno
Baligród	Lisko	Baligród
Balin	Chrzanów	Chrzanów
Balińce	Kołomea	Gwozdziec
Balnica	Lisko	Wola Michowa
Bałucianka	Sanok	Rymanów
Bandrów	Lisko	Ustrzyki Dolne
Bandrów Narodowy	Lisko	Ustrzyki Dolne
Bania	Kalusz	Kalusz
Bania	Kołomea	Jabłonów
Bania Kotowska	Drohobycz	Drohobycz
Banica	Gorlice	Gorlice
Banica	Grybów	Grybów
Banków	Bochnia	Bochnia
Banowice	Myślenice	Myślenice
Bańska	Nowy Targ	Nowy Targ
Banunin	Kam. Strumiłowa	Busk
Bar	Gródek	Gródek
Bar	Mościska	Sądowa Wisznia
Barańczyce	Sambor	Sambor
Baranie	Sokal	Sokal
Baranów	Buczacz	Monasterzyska
Baranów	Tarnobrzeg	Baranów
Baranówka	Brzeżany	Brzeżany
Baranówka	Nisko	Rudnik
Barczków	Bochnia	Bochnia
Barczyce	Nowy Sącz	Piwniczna

Town	Main District	Subdistrict
Barnowice	Nowy Sącz	Łabowa
Barszczowice	Lemberg	Jaryczów
Bartatów	Gródek	Gródek
Bartkowa	Nowy Sącz	Nowy Sącz
Bartkówka	Brzozów	Dynów
Bartne	Gorlice	Gorlice
Barwałd Dolny	Wadowice	Wadowice
Barwałd Średni	Wadowice	Wadowice
Barwinek	Krosno	Dukla
Barycz	Przemyśl	Sosnica
Barycz	Rzeszów	Błazowa
Barycz	Wieliczka	Klasno
Barycza	Brzozów	Jasienica
Baryłów	Brody	Szczurowice
Barysz	Buczacz	Barysz
Basiówka	Lemberg	Nawarya
Basznia Dolna	Cieszanów	Lubaczów
Basznia Górna	Cieszanów	Lubaczów
Batiatysze	Zolkiew	Gross Mosty
Batków	Brody	Załoźce
Batycze	Przemyśl	Przemyśl
Batyjów	Brody	Szczurowice
Baworów	Tarnopol	Mikulińce
Bayczka	Rzeszów	Niebylec
Bażanówka	Sanok	Rymanów
Bazar	Czortków	Jagielnica
Bęczarka	Myślenice	Myślenice
Bedinka	Sokal	Krystynpol
Bedinka Poturzycka	Sokal	Krystynopol
Bediuchy	Sokal	Sokal
Bednarka	Gorlice	Gorlice
Bednarów	Stanisławów	Stanisławów

Town	Main District	Subdistrict
Bedrykowce	Zaleszczyki	Zaleszczyki
Będziemyśl	Ropczyce	Sędziszów
Będzieszyna	Brzesko	Czchów
Bekersdorf	Podhajce	Podhajce
Bełchówka	Sanok	Bukowsko
Bełdno	Bochnia	Wiśnicz Nowy
Bełejów	Dolina	Bolechów
Bełeluja	Śniatyn	Śniatyn
Bełż	Sokal	Bełż
Bełżec	Cieszanów	Lipsko
Bełżec	Rawa Ruska	Lubycza
Bełżec	Złoczów	Biały Kamień
Benczyn	Wadowice	Zator
Berdechów	Tarnobrzeg	Rozwadów
Berdikau	Jaworów	Jaworów
Berdychów	Gorlice	Gorlice
Berdychów	Grybów	Bobowa
Berdychów	Jaworów	Jaworów
Berehy Dolne	Lisko	Ustrzyki Dolne
Berehy Górne	Lisko	Lutowiska
Berenowce	Złoczów	Zborów
Bereska	Lisko	Baligród
Berest	Grybów	Grybów
Berestek	Zaleszczyki	Uścieczko
Bereżanka	Borszczów	Skała
Berezki	Lisko	Lutowiska
Bereżnica	Sambor	Sambor
Bereżnica	Stryj	Stryj
Bereżnica Krolewska	Żydaczów	Żydaczów
Bereżnica Niżna	Lisko	Lisko
Bereżnica Szlachecka	Kalusz	Kalusz
Bereżnica Wyżna	Lisko	Baligród

Town	Main District	Subdistrict
Bereżów	Kołomea	Jabłonów
Bereżów	Staremiasto	Starasól
Bereżów Nizny	Kołomea	Jabłonów
Bereżów Wyzny	Kołomea	Jabłonów
Bereżówka Bortniki	Buczacz	Monasterzyska
Bereżówka Monaster.	Buczacz	Monasterzyska
Berlin	Brody	Brody
Berłohy	Kalusz	Kalusz
Bernadówka	Trembowla	Strusów
Berniany	Zaleszczyki	Uścieczko
Berteszów	Bóbrka	Strzeliska Nowe
Berwinkowa	Kossów	Żabie
Berzowica Wielka	Tarnopol	Tarnopol
Besko	Sanok	Rymanów
Besów	Bochnia	Bochnia
Bestwina	Biała	Lipnik
Bestwinka	Biała	Oświęcim
Betwin	Przemyśl	Przemyśl
Bezapy	Złoczów	Złoczów
Bezejów	Sokal	Bełż
Bezmiechowa Dolne	Lisko	Lisko
Bezmiechowa Górne	Lisko	Lisko
Biała	Biała	Lipnik
Biała	Czortków	Czortków
Biała	Myślenice	Maków
Biała	Nowy Sącz	Nowy Sącz
Biała	Rawa Ruska	Magierów
Biała	Rzeszów	Tyczyn
Biała	Tarnopol	Tarnopol
Biała	Tarnów	Tarnów
Biała Niżna	Grybów	Grybów
Biała Wyżna	Grybów	Grybów

Town	Main District	Subdistrict
Białaskorka	Tarnopol	Tarnopol
Białdoliny Szlacheckie	Brzesko	Brzesko
Białe	Przemyślany	Dunajowce
Białka	Nowy Targ	Nowy Targ
Białka	Rzeszów	Błazowa
Białka Dunajec	Nowy Targ	Nowy Targ
Białkowce	Złoczów	Jezierna
Białobereska	Kossów	Kuty
Białobiernica	Złoczów	Zborów
Białoboki	Łańcut	Kańczuga
Białoboznica	Czortków	Czortków
Białobrzegi	Krosno	Dukla
Białobrzegi	Łańcut	Żolynia
Białodoliny Rodlowskie	Brzesko	Wojnicz
Białokiernica	Podhajce	Podhajce
Białowoda	Nowy Sącz	Szczawnica
Białowoda Polska	Nowy Sącz	Nowy Sącz
Biały Potok	Czortków	Budzanów
Białykamień	Złoczów	Białykamień
Biczyce Niemieckie	Nowy Sącz	Nowy Sącz
Biczyce Polskie	Nowy Sącz	Nowy Sącz
Biecz	Gorlice	Gorlice
Biedaczów	Łańcut	Żolynia
Biegonice	Nowy Sącz	Stary Sącz
Bielanka	Gorlice	Gorlice
Bielanka	Myślenice	Jordanów
Bielany	Biała	Kęty
Bielawce	Brody	Brody
Bielawince	Buczacz	Buczacz
Bieliczna	Grybów	Grybów

Town	Main District	Subdistrict
Bielina	Nisko	Ulanów
Bielowce	Borszczów	Mielnica
Bielowy	Pilzno	Pilzno
Bieniawa	Podhajce	Złotniki
Bieniów	Złoczów	Złoczów
Bienków	Kam. Strumiłowa	Kam. Strumiłowa
Bieńkowa Wiznia	Rudki	Rudki
Bieńkowce	Rohatyń	Rohatyń
Bieńkowice	Bochnia	Bochnia
Bieńkowice	Wieliczka	Klasno
Bieńkówka	Myślenice	Maków
Bierlowice	Myślenice	Myślenice
Bierna	Biała	Lipnik
Bierówka	Jasło	Jasło
Bierzanów	Wieliczka	Klasno
Biesiadki	Brzesko	Brzesko
Biesiady	Żólkiew	Żólkiew
Biesna	Gorlice	Gorlice
Bieśnik	Gorlice	Gorlice
Bieżdziatka	Jasło	Frysztak
Bieżdziedza	Jasło	Frysztak
Bihałe	Cieszanów	Lubaczów
Bilcze	Drohobycz	Drohobycz
Bilcze	Zaleszczyki	Korolówka
Bilczyce	Wieliczka	Klasno
Bilicz	Staremiasto	Starasól
Bilina	Sambor	Sambor
Bilinka	Sambor	Sambor
Bilinka	Sambor	Sambor
Bilitówka	Skałat	Grzymałów
Biłka	Przemyślany	Przemyślany
Biłka	Skałat	Touste

Town	Main District	Subdistrict
Biłka Królewska	Lemberg	Jaryczów
Biłka Szlachecka	Lemberg	Jaryczów
Biłków	Borhodczany	Sołotwina
Biłohorszcze	Lemberg	Zniesienie
Bilsko	Nowy Sącz	Nowy Sącz
Binarowa	Gorlice	Gorlice
Binczarowa	Grybów	Grybów
Biołoszowa	Tarnów	Ryglice
Bircza	Bircza	Bircza
Biskowice	Sambor	Sambor
Biskupice	Dąbrowa	Dąbrowa
Biskupice	Wieliczka	Klasno
Biskupice Lanckoronskie	Brzesko	Czchów
Błaszkowa	Pilzno	Jodłowa
Błazów	Sambor	Sambor
Błazowa	Rzeszów	Błazowa
Blechnarka	Gorlice	Gorlice
Bledowa ad Tyczyn	Rzeszów	Tyczyn
Blich	Brody	Załoźce
Blicza	Brzesko	Brzesko
Blizianka	Rzeszów	Niebylec
Blizna	Ropczyce	Ropczyce
Blizno	Brzozów	Jasienica
Błonie	Mielec	Radomyśl Wielkie
Błonie	Tarnów	Tarnów
Błotnia	Przemyślany	Przemyślany
Błotnia	Stryj	Stryj
Błozew Dolna	Rudki	Rudki
Błozew Górna	Sambor	Sambor
Błudniki	Stanisławów	Hałicz
Blyszczanka	Zaleszczyki	Zaleszczyki

Town	Main District	Subdistrict
Błyszczywody	Żólkiew	Żólkiew
Bobiatyn	Sokal	Tartaków
Bobowa	Grybów	Bobowa
Bobrek Dolny	Chrzanów	Chrzanów
Bobrek Górny	Chrzanów	Chrzanów
Bóbrka	Bóbrka	Bóbrka
Bóbrka	Krosno	Dukla
Bóbrka	Lisko	Lisko
Bobrowa	Pilzno	Dębica
Bobrówka	Jarosław	Jarosław
Bobrowniki	Tłumacz	Uście Zielone
Bobrowniki Małe	Tarnów	Zabno
Bobrowniki Wielkie	Tarnów	Zabno
Bobulińce	Buczacz	Buczacz
Bochnia	Bochnia	Bochnia
Boczów	Bochnia	Wiśnicz Nowy
Bodaki	Gorlice	Gorlice
Bodnarówka	Rzeszów	Strzyżów
Bodzanów	Wieliczka	Klasno
Bodziwoj	Rzeszów	Tyczyn
Bodzów	Wieliczka	Podgórze
Bogdanówka	Myślenice	Jordanów
Bogdanówka	Złoczów	Jezierna
Bogoniowice	Grybów	Bobowa
Boguchwala	Rzeszów	Rzeszów
Bogucice	Bochnia	Bochnia
Bogucice	Wieliczka	Klasno
Bogumilowice	Brzesko	Wojnicz
Bogusza	Grybów	Grybów
Boguszówka	Bircza	Bircza
Bohatkowce	Podhajce	Złotniki
Bohordczany	Bohordczany	Bohordczany

Town	Main District	Subdistrict
Bohordczany Stare	Bohordczany	Bohordczany
Bohordyczyn	Tłumacz	Chocimirz
Bohutyn	Złoczów	Pomorzany
Bojańczyce	Wieliczka	Klasno
Bojanice	Sokal	Warez
Bojanice	Żólkiew	Gross Mosty
Bojanów	Nisko	Nisko
Boków	Podhajce	Zawałów
Bolanowice	Mościska	Mościska
Bołdury	Brody	Brody
Bolechów	Dolina	Bolechów
Bolechów Ruski	Dolina	Bolechów
Bolechówce	Drohobycz	Drohobycz
Bolęcin	Chrzanów	Chrzanów
Bolesław	Dąbrowa	Dąbrowa
Bolestraszyce	Przemyśl	Przemyśl
Bołochów	Dolina	Dolina
Bolomyja	Rzeszów	Niebylec
Bołozynów	Brody	Sokolówka
Bolszowce	Rohatyń	Bursztyn
Bonarówka	Krosno	Korczyna
Boniowice	Bircza	Dobromil
Boniszyn	Złoczów	Złoczów
Bonów	Jaworów	Jaworów
Bór Łodygowski	Biała	Lipnik
Bór Witkowski	Biała	Lipnik
Boratycze	Mościska	Hussaków
Boratycze	Przemyśl	Przemyśl
Boratyn	Brody	Brody
Boratyn	Jarosław	Jarosław
Boratyn	Sokal	Krystynopol
Borchów	Cieszanów	Oleszyce

Town	Main District	Subdistrict
Bordulaki	Brody	Stanisławczyk
Boreczek	Ropczyce	Sędziszów
Borek	Bochnia	Bochnia
Borek	Krosno	Dukla
Borek Fałecki	Wieliczka	Podgórze
Borek Mały	Ropczyce	Ropczyce
Borek Nowy	Rzeszów	Tyczyn
Borek Stary	Rzeszów	Tyczyn
Borek Szlachecki	Wadowice	Zator
Borek Wielki	Ropczyce	Sędziszów
Borkanów	Podhajce	Złotniki
Borki	Dąbrowa	Szczucin
Borki	Mielec	Mielec
Borki	Nisko	Ulanów
Borki Dominikańskie	Gródek	Janów
Borki Janowskie	Gródek	Janów
Borki Małe	Skałat	Touste
Borki Wielkie	Tarnopol	Tarnopol
Borodczyce	Bóbrka	Chodorów
Borowa	Brzesko	Czchów
Borowa	Mielec	Radomyśl Wiel.
Borowa Gora	Cieszanów	Lubaczów
Borowe	Żólkiew	Gross Mosty
Borowna	Bochnia	Wiśnicz Nowy
Borownica	Bircza	Bircza
Borszczów	Borszczów	Borszczów
Borszczów	Śniatyn	Zabłotów
Borszów	Przemyślany	Przemyślany
Borszowice	Przemyśl	Niżankowice
Bortiatyn	Mościska	Sądowa Wisznia
Bortniki	Bóbrka	Chodorów
Bortniki	Tłumacz	Chocimirz

Town	Main District	Subdistrict
Borusowa	Dąbrowa	Dąbrowa
Borwałd Górny	Wadowice	Kalwarya
Boryczówka	Trembowla	Trembowla
Boryków	Podhajce	Podhajce
Borynicze	Bóbrka	Brzozdowce
Borysław	Drohobycz	Borysław
Borysławka	Bircza	Rybotycze
Boryszkowce	Borszczów	Mielnica
Borzęcin	Brzesko	Radłów
Borzęta	Myślenice	Myślenice
Boszyry	Husiatyn	Husiatyn
Bouszów	Rohatyń	Bursztyn
Bouszów	Stanisławów	Halicz
Boża Wola	Jaworów	Wielkie Oczy
Boznów	Nowy Sącz	Nowy Sącz
Braciejowa	Pilzno	Dębica
Brandwica	Tarnobrzeg	Rozwadów
Bratkowce	Stanisławów	Stanisławów
Bratkowce	Stryj	Stryj
Bratkowce	Tłumacz	Tyśmienica
Bratkowice	Gródek	Gródek
Bratkowice	Rzeszów	Rzeszów
Bratówka	Krosno	Korczyna
Bratucice	Bochnia	Bochnia
Bratyszów	Tłumacz	Niźniów
Brelików	Lisko	Lisko
Breń Osuchowski	Mielec	Radomyśl Wiel.
Brigidyn	Drohobycz	Drohobycz
Brnik	Dąbrowa	Dąbrowa
Brodki	Lemberg	Szczerzec
Brodła	Chrzanów	Chrzanów
Brody	Brody	Brody

Town	Main District	Subdistrict
Brody	Wadowice	Kalwarya
Brody Stare	Brody	Brody
Bronica	Drohobycz	Drohobycz
Bronisławówka	Złoczów	Zborów
Broniszów	Ropczyce	Ropczyce
Broszniów	Kalusz	Kalusz
Browary	Buczacz	Jazłowice
Bruchnal	Jaworów	Jaworów
Bruckenthal	Rawa Ruska	Uhnów
Brunndorf	Gródek	Gródek
Bruśnik	Brzesko	Czchów
Bruśnik	Grybów	Bobowa
Brusno Nowe	Cieszanów	Narol
Brusno Stare	Cieszanów	Lipsko
Brustury	Kossów	Pistyn
Brykoń	Przemyślany	Przemyślany
Brykuta Nowa	Trembowla	Strusów
Brykuta Stara	Trembowla	Strusów
Brylińce	Przemyśl	Przemyśl
Bryły	Jasło	Jasło
Bryńce Cerkiewne	Bóbrka	Bóbrka
Bryńce Zagóne	Bóbrka	Bóbrka
Bryszcze	Żólkiew	Żólkiew
Brząszowice	Wieliczka	Klasno
Brzana Dolna	Grybów	Bobowa
Brzana Górna	Grybów	Bobowa
Brzaza	Dolina	Bolechów
Brzczowa	Wieliczka	Klasno
Brzeczyczany	Gródek	Gródek
Brzegi	Nowy Targ	Nowy Targ
Brzegi	Sambor	Sambor
Brzegi	Wieliczka	Klasno

Town	Main District	Subdistrict
Brześciany	Sambor	Sambor
Brzesko	Brzesko	Brzesko
Brzeszcze	Biała	Oświęcim
Brzeżanka	Rzeszów	Strzyżów
Brzeżany	Brzeżany	Brzeżany
Brzeżawa	Bircza	Bircza
Brzezice	Rudki	Komarno
Brzezie	Wieliczka	Klasno
Brzezina	Żydaczów	Rozdól
Brzezinka	Biała	Oświęcim
Brzezinka	Chrzanów	Chrzanów
Brzezinka	Wadowice	Andrychów
Brzezinka ad Kopytówka	Wadowice	Zator
Brzeziny	Nowy Sącz	Nowy Sącz
Brzeziny	Ropczyce	Wielopole
Brzezna	Nowy Sącz	Nowy Sącz
Brzeżnica	Bochnia	Wiśnicz Nowy
Brzeżnica	Pilzno	Dębica
Brzeżnica	Wadowice	Zator
Brzezowa	Bochnia	Wiśnicz Nowy
Brzezowa	Brzesko	Czchów
Brzezowa	Krosno	Dukla
Brzezowice	Brzesko	Brzesko
Brzezówka	Dąbrowa	Szczucin
Brzezówka	Jasło	Jasło
Brzezówka	Kolbuszowa	Kolbuszowa
Brzezówka	Rzeszów	Tyczyn
Brzodzowce	Bóbrka	Brzozdowiec
Brzostek	Pilzno	Brzostek
Brzostowa Gora	Kolbuszowa	Majdan
Brzoszkowice	Biała	Oświęcim

Town	Main District	Subdistrict
Brzoza	Tarnobrzeg	Radomyśl
Brzoza Królewska	Łańcut	Leżajsk
Brzoza Stadnicka	Łańcut	Żolynia
Brzozów	Brzozów	Brzozów
Brzozówa	Tarnów	Tuchów
Brzozowice ad Czaszyn	Sanok	Bukowsko
Brzozówka	Ropczyce	Ropczyce
Brzuchowice	Lemberg	Zniesienie
Brzuchowice	Przemyślany	Przemyślany
Brzuska	Bircza	Bircza
Brzusznik	Żywiec	Zabłocie
Brzyna	Nowy Sącz	Łącko
Brzyna	Ropczyce	Ropczyce
Brzyście	Jasło	Jasło
Brzyście	Mielec	Mielec
Brzyska Wola	Łańcut	Leżajsk
Brzyski	Pilzno	Jodłowa
Brzyszczki	Jasło	Jasło
Brzyszyna Dolna	Wieliczka	Podgórze
Bubniszcze	Dolina	Bolechów
Bubszczany	Złoczów	Pomorzany
Buchowice	Mościska	Mościska
Bucniów	Tarnopol	Tarnopol
Buców	Przemyśl	Przemyśl
Buczacz	Buczacz	Buczacz
Buczaczki	Kołomea	Gwozdzice
Buczały	Rudki	Komarno
Bucze	Brzesko	Brzesko
Buczki	Skałat	Grzymałów
Buczków	Bochnia	Bochnia
Buczkowce	Czortków	Budzanów

Town	Main District	Subdistrict
Buczkowice	Biała	Lipnik
Buczyna	Bochnia	Wiśnicz Nowy
Buczyna	Brody	Brody
Buda	Nisko	Nisko
Budki Nieznanowski	Kam. Strumiłowa	Chołojów
Budków	Bóbrka	Bóbrka
Budomierz	Jaworów	Wielkie Oczy
Budy	Rzeszów	Głogów
Budy ad Rajsko	Biała	Oświęcim
Budy Łancuckie	Łańcut	Łańcut
Budy Przeworskie	Łańcut	Przewórsk
Budyłów	Brzeżany	Kozowa
Budyłów	Śniatyn	Śniatyn
Budynin	Sokal	Bełż
Budzanów	Czortków	Budzanów
Budzisz	Ropczyce	Wielopole
Budzów	Wadowice	Kalwarya
Budzyn	Jaworów	Krakówiec
Budzyn	Tłumacz	Tłumacz
Bugaj	Dąbrowa	Dąbrowa
Bugaj	Gorlice	Gorlice
Bugaj	Wadowice	Kalwarya
Bugaj	Wieliczka	Klasno
Bujaków	Biała	Kęty
Bujanów	Żydaczów	Żurawno
Bujawa	Sokal	Tartaków
Bujne	Nowy Sącz	Nowy Sącz
Buk	Lisko	Baligród
Bukaczowce	Rohatyń	Bursztyn
Buków	Brzozów	Brzozów
Buków	Wieliczka	Podgórze
Bukowa	Pilzno	Brzostek

Town	Main District	Subdistrict
Bukowa	Sambor	Sambor
Bukowice	Lisko	Baligród
Bukowiec	Grybów	Bobowa
Bukowiec	Kolbuszowa	Kolbuszów
Bukowina	Bóbrka	Chodorów
Bukowina	Nisko	Ulanów
Bukowina	Nowy Targ	Nowy Targ
Bukówna	Tłumacz	Niźniów
Bukowsko	Sanok	Bukowsko
Bulowice	Biała	Kęty
Bunary Nizne	Grybów	Grybów
Bunary Wyzne	Grybów	Grybów
Burakówka	Zaleszczyki	Tłuste
Burcze	Rudki	Komarno
Burdziakowce	Borszczów	Skała
Burgthal	Gródek	Gródek
Burletka	Wieliczka	Klasno
Bursztyn	Rohatyń	Bursztyn
Burzyce	Rudki	Rudki
Burzyce Nowy	Rudki	Rudki
Burzyce Stary	Rudki	Rudki
Burzyn	Tarnów	Ryglice
Busk	Kam. Strumiłowa	Busk
Buskupice Radłowskie	Brzesko	Radłów
Busowisko	Staremiasto	Staremiasto
Buszcze	Brzeżany	Narajów
Buszkowice	Przemyśl	Przemyśl
Buszkowiczki	Przemyśl	Przemyśl
Butyny	Żólkiew	Gross Mosty
Buzek	Złoczów	Białykamień
Bybło	Przemyśl	Niżankowice

Town	Main District	Subdistrict
Bybło	Rohatyń	Bursztyn
Byczyna	Chrzanów	Chrzanów
Byków	Mościska	Hussaków
Byków	Przemyśl	Przemyśl
Byków	Sambor	Sambor
Bykowie	Sanok	Sanok
Bylice	Sambor	Sambor
Bysina	Myślenice	Myślenice
Bystra	Biała	Lipnik
Bystra	Gorlice	Gorlice
Bystra	Myślenice	Jordanów
Bystra	Żywiec	Zabłocie
Bystre	Lisko	Baligród
Bystre	Staremiasto	Staremiasto
Bystrowice	Jarosław	Jarosław
Bystrzyca	Drohobycz	Drohobycz
Bystrzyca Dolna	Ropczyce	Sędziszów
Bystrzyca Górna	Ropczyce	Sędziszów
Byszki	Brzeżany	Brzeżany
Byszów	Podhajce	Zawałów
Byszów	Sokal	Tartaków
Bytomska	Bochnia	Wiśnicz Nowy
Bzianka	Sanok	Rymanów
Caporocz	Zaleszczyki	Tłuste
Caryńskie	Lisko	Lutowiska
Cebłów	Sokal	Bełż
Cebrów	Tarnopol	Tarnopol
Cecory	Brzeżany	Kozłów
Cecowa	Złoczów	Zborów
Celejów	Husiatyn	Chorostków
Ceniawa	Dolina	Rożniatów
Ceniawa	Kołomea	Kołomea

Town	Main District	Subdistrict
Ceniów	Brzeżany	Kozowa
Ceperów	Lemberg	Jaryczów
Cerekiew	Bochnia	Bochnia
Cergowa	Krosno	Dukla
Cerkowna	Dolina	Bolechów
Cetula	Jarosław	Sienawa
Cetula	Jaworów	Jaworów
Cewków	Cieszanów	Oleszyce
Chabówka	Myślenice	Jordanów
Chałupki	Łańcut	Przewórsk
Chałupki Dusowskie	Przemyśl	Sosnica
Chartanowce	Zaleszczyki	Uścieczko
Charzewice	Brzesko	Czchów
Charzewice	Tarnobrzeg	Rozwadów
Chaszczowanie	Stryj	Skole
Chechly	Ropczyce	Ropczyce
Chełm	Bochnia	Bochnia
Chełm	Myślenice	Myślenice
Chełmek	Chrzanów	Chrzanów
Chełmice	Nowy Sącz	Nowy Sącz
Chełmice Niemiecki	Nowy Sącz	Nowy Sącz
Chełmice Polski	Nowy Sącz	Nowy Sącz
Chilczyce	Złoczów	Złoczów
Chiszewice	Rudki	Komarno
Chlebiczyn	Śniatyn	Zabłotów
Chlebiczyn Lesny	Kołomea	Kołomea
Chlebna	Krosno	Dukla
Chlebowice	Bóbrka	Bóbrka
Chlebowice Swirskie	Przemyślany	Świrz
Chlewczany	Rawa Ruska	Uhnów
Chlewiska	Cieszanów	Lipsko
Chlewiska	Sambor	Sambor

Town	Main District	Subdistrict
Chliple	Rudki	Rudki
Chłopczyce	Rudki	Rudki
Chłopiatyn	Sokal	Bełż
Chłopice	Jarosław	Jarosław
Chłopówka	Husiatyn	Chorostków
Chłopy	Rudki	Komarno
Chmiel	Lisko	Lutowiska
Chmieliska	Skałat	Skałat
Chmielnik	Rzeszów	Tyczyn
Chmielno	Brody	Stanisławczyk
Chmielów	Tarnobrzeg	Tarnobrzeg
Chmielowa	Horodenka	Czernelica
Chmielowa	Zaleszczyki	Uścieczko
Chmielówka	Borhodczany	Sołotwina
Chmielówka	Trembowla	Strusów
Chobot	Bochnia	Bochnia
Chocen	Lisko	Lisko
Chochłów	Sokal	Warez
Chochołów	Nowy Targ	Nowy Targ
Chochoniów	Rohatyń	Bursztyn
Chochorowice	Nowy Sącz	Nowy Sącz
Chocimirz	Tłumacz	Chocimirz
Chocin	Kalusz	Kalusz
Chocznia	Wadowice	Wadowice
Chodaczków Mały	Tarnopol	Tarnopol
Chodaczków Wielki	Tarnopol	Tarnopol
Chodaczów	Łańcut	Kańczuga
Chodaczów	Łańcut	Żolynia
Chodenice	Bochnia	Bochnia
Chodnowice	Mościska	Hussaków
Chodnowice	Przemyśl	Przemyśl
Chodorów	Bóbrka	Chodorów

Town	Main District	Subdistrict
Chodorowa	Grybów	Bobowa
Chodowice	Stryj	Stryj
Chojnik	Tarnów	Tuchów
Cholewiana Góra	Nisko	Nisko
Chołojów	Kam. Strumiłowa	Chołojów
Chołowice	Przemyśl	Przemyśl
Chomczyn	Kossów	Kossów
Chomiakówka	Czortków	Jagielnica
Chomiakówka	Kołomea	Gwozdziec
Chomiakówka	Tłumacz	Tyśmienica
Chomranice	Nowy Sącz	Nowy Sącz
Chomrzyska	Nowy Sącz	Łabowa
Chorągwica	Wieliczka	Klasno
Chorderkowce	Bóbrka	Bóbrka
Chorkówka	Krosno	Dukla
Chorobrów	Brzeżany	Kozłów
Chorobrów	Sokal	Sokal
Chorocowa	Kossów	Kuty
Choronów	Rawa Ruska	Uhnów
Chorosiec	Brzeżany	Kozłów
Chorosnica	Mościska	Sądowa Wisznia
Chorostków	Husiatyn	Chorostków
Chorostków	Rohatyń	Bursztyn
Chorowiec	Wieliczka	Podgórze
Chorzelów	Mielec	Mielec
Chorzów	Jarosław	Pruchnik
Chotowa	Pilzno	Pilzno
Chotowice	Przemyśl	Krzywcza
Chotylub	Cieszanów	Cieszanów
Chotynice	Jarosław	Radymno
Chrabuzna	Złoczów	Zborów
Chraplice	Mościska	Hussaków

Town	Main District	Subdistrict
Chraplice	Przemyśl	Przemyśl
Chreniów	Kam. Strumiłowa	Busk
Chrewt	Lisko	Lutowiska
Chromohorb	Stryj	Stryj
Chronów	Bochnia	Wiśnicz Nowy
Chrość	Wieliczka	Klasno
Chrostowa	Bochnia	Wiśnicz Nowy
Chruślice	Nowy Sącz	Nowy Sącz
Chrusno Nowe	Lemberg	Szczerzec
Chrusno Stare	Lemberg	Szczerzec
Chryplin	Stanisławów	Stanisławów
Chrzanów	Chrzanów	Chrzanów
Chrząstów	Mielec	Mielec
Chrząstowice	Wadowice	Zator
Chrząstówka	Jasło	Jasło
Chudykowce	Borszczów	Mielnica
Chudyowce	Zaleszczyki	Korolówka
Chwalibog	Kołomea	Gwozdziec
Chwałowice	Tarnobrzeg	Radomyśl
Chwatów	Złoczów	Olesko
Chyrów	Staremiasto	Chyrów
Chyrzyna Kortyniki	Przemyśl	Krzywcza
Chyszów	Tarnów	Tarnów
Chyżówka	Limanowa	Limanowa
Cichawa	Wieliczka	Klasno
Cichawka	Bochnia	Wiśnicz Nowy
Ciche Miętustwo	Nowy Targ	Nowy Targ
Ciechania	Krosno	Dukla
Cięcina	Żywiec	Zabłocie
Cieczyna	Jasło	Frysztak
Cieląż	Sokal	Sokal
Ciemierzowice	Przemyśl	Sosnica

Town	Main District	Subdistrict
Ciemierzyńce	Przemyślany	Dunajowce
Ciemieżypce	Złoczów	Gologory
Cieniawa	Grybów	Grybów
Cieplice	Jarosław	Sienawa
Cierpisz	Ropczyce	Sędziszów
Cieszanów	Cieszanów	Cieszanów
Ciezacin Mały	Jarosław	Jarosław
Ciezacin Wielki	Jarosław	Jarosław
Cieszyna	Jaslo	Frysztak
Ciężkowice	Chrzanów	Chrzanów
Ciężkowice	Grybów	Bobowa
Ciężów	Stanisławów	Stanisławów
Cikowice	Bochnia	Bochnia
Cisna	Lisko	Baligród
Cisów	Dolina	Bolechów
Cisowa	Przemyśl	Przemyśl
Cisowiec	Lisko	Baligród
Cisowlas	Kolbuszowa	Ranizów
Ciszec	Żywiec	Zabłocie
Ciszki	Brody	Sokolówka
Cmolas	Kolbuszowa	Kolbuszów
Cucułowce	Żydaczów	Żydaczów
Cucyłów	Nadwórna	Nadwórna
Cuniów	Gródek	Janów
Ćwików	Dąbrowa	Dąbrowa
Ćwitowa	Buczacz	Jazłowice
Ćwitowa	Kalusz	Wojnilów
Cygany	Borszczów	Skała
Cygany	Tarnobrzeg	Tarnobrzeg
Cyranka	Mielec	Mielec
Czabalina	Brzesko	Czchów
Czabarówka	Husiatyn	Husiatyn

Town	Main District	Subdistrict
Czaczów	Nowy Sącz	Łabowa
Czahrów	Rohatyń	Bursztyn
Czajkowa	Mielec	Mielec
Czajkowice	Rudki	Komarno
Czaniec	Biała	Kęty
Czanyż	Kam. Strumiłowa	Busk
Czaplaki '	Jaworów	Wielkie Oczy
Czaple	Sambor	Sambor
Czarna	Grybów	Grybów
Czarna	Łańcut	Żolynia
Czarna	Lisko	Ustrzyki Dolne
Czarna	Pilzno	Pilzno
Czarna	Ropczyce	Sędziszów
Czarne	Gorlice	Gorlice
Czarnokońce Małe	Husiatyn	Probużna
Czarnokońce Wielkie	Husiatyn	Probużna
Czarnokońiecka Wola	Husiatyn	Probużna
Czarnołożce	Tłumacz	Tyśmienica
Czarnorzeki	Krosno	Korczyna
Czarnowoda	Nowy Sącz	Szczawnica
Czarnuchowice	Wieliczka	Klasno
Czarnuszowice	Lemberg	Jaryczów
Czarny Dunajec	Nowy Targ	Nowy Targ
Czartorya	Bóbrka	Brzozdowiec
Czartorya	Tarnopol	Mikulińce
Czasław	Wieliczka	Klasno
Cząstkowice	Jarosław	Jarosław
Czaszyn	Sanok	Bukowsko
Czatkowice	Chrzanów	Trzebina
Czchów	Brzesko	Czchów
Czechów	Buczacz	Monasterzyska

Town	Main District	Subdistrict
Czechowa	Kołomea	Gwozdziec
Czechówka	Wieliczka	Klasno
Czechy	Brody	Sokołówka
Czechy	Złoczów	Olesko
Czekaj Pniowski	Tarnobrzeg	Radomyśl
Czekaj Wrzawski	Tarnobrzeg	Rozwadów
Czelatycze	Jarosław	Pruchnik
Czelowice	Rudki	Komarno
Czeluśnica	Jasło	Jasło
Czepiele	Brody	Podkamień
Czerchawa	Sambor	Sambor
Czercze	Rohatyń	Rohatyń
Czerczyk	Jaworów	Jaworów
Czeremcha	Sanok	Rymanów
Czeremchów	Bóbrka	Chodorów
Czeremchów	Kołomea	Kołomea
Czeremosznia	Złoczów	Białykamień
Czerepin	Lemberg	Nawarya
Czerhanówka	Kossów	Kossów
Czerkasy	Rudki	Komarno
Czerkawszczyzna	Czortków	Czortków
Czerkowatyce	Kam. Strumiłowa	Stajanów
Czerlany	Gródek	Gródek
Czermin	Mielec	Radomyśl Wiel.
Czermna	Jasło	Olpiny
Czerna	Chrzanów	Chrzanów
Czernelica	Horodenka	Czernelica
Czerniatyn	Horodenka	Horodenka
Czerniawa	Mościska	Mościska
Czerniawka	Jarosław	Radymno
Czernica	Brody	Podkamień
Czernica	Żydaczów	Rozdół

Town	Main District	Subdistrict
Czernice	Nowy Sącz	Łącko
Czernichów	Rudki	Rudki
Czernichów	Tarnopol	Tarnopol
Czernichów	Żywiec	Zabłocie
Czerniejów	Stanisławów	Stanisławów
Czernilawa	Jaworów	Jaworów
Czernilów Mazowiecki	Tarnopol	Tarnopol
Czernilów Ruski	Tarnopol	Tarnopol
Czerniów	Rohatyń	Bursztyn
Czerniszówka	Skałat	Skałat
Czerteż	Sanok	Sanok
Czerteż	Żydaczów	Żurawno
Czertynie	Żółkiew	Kulików
Czertyżne	Grybów	Grybów
Czerwonogród	Zaleszczyki	Uścieczko
Czesniki	Rohatyń	Rohatyń
Czołhańszczyzna	Tarnopol	Tarnopol
Czołhany	Dolina	Bolechów
Czołhynie	Jaworów	Jaworów
Czorsztyn	Nowy Targ	Nowy Targ
Czortków	Czortków	Czortków
Czortków Stary	Czortków	Czortków
Czortowiec	Horodenka	Obertyn
Czuczmany	Kam. Strumiłowa	Busk
Czudec	Rzeszów	Czudec
Czudowice	Jarosław	Pruchnik
Czukiew	Sambor	Sambor
Czupernosów	Przemyślany	Przemyślany
Czyrna	Grybów	Grybów
Czystohorb	Sanok	Bukowsko
Czystopady	Brody	Zaloczce

Town	Main District	Subdistrict
Czystopady	Brody	Zalocze
Czystylów	Tarnopol	Tarnopol
Czyszki	Lemberg	Winniki
Czyszki	Mościska	Mościska
Czyszki	Złoczów	Olesko
Czyżki	Sambor	Sambor
Czyżów	Dąbrowa	Dąbrowa
Czyżów	Wieliczka	Klasno
Czyżów	Złoczów	Pomorzany
Czyżowice	Mościska	Mościska
Czyżówka	Chrzanów	Chrzanów
Czyżyce	Bóbrka	Bóbrka
Czyżyków	Lemberg	Winniki
Dąb	Chrzanów	Chrzanów
Dąbie	Wieliczka	Klasno
Dąbki	Horodenka	Czernelica
Dąbrowa	Chrzanów	Chrzanów
Dąbrowa	Cieszanów	Lubaczów
Dąbrowa	Dąbrowa	Dąbrowa
Dąbrowa	Kalusz	Wojniłów
Dąbrowa	Kam. Strumiłowa	Radziechów
Dąbrowa	Łańcut	Żolynia
Dąbrowa	Nowy Sącz	Nowy Sącz
Dąbrowa	Ropczyce	Sędziszów
Dąbrowa	Sambor	Sambor
Dąbrowa	Wieliczka	Klasno
Dąbrowa Rzeczycka	Tarnobrzeg	Rozwadów
Dąbrowa Wrzawska	Tarnobrzeg	Rozwadów
Dąbrowica	Dąbrowa	Szczucin
Dąbrowica	Gródek	Janów
Dąbrowica	Jarosław	Sienawa
Dąbrowica	Nisko	Ulanów

Town	Main District	Subdistrict
Dąbrowica	Tarnobrzeg	Baranów
Dąbrowica Chrostowa	Bochnia	Wiśnicz Nowy
Dąbrówka	Bochnia	Bochnia
Dąbrówka	Borszczów	Borszczów
Dąbrówka	Brzesko	Szczurowa
Dąbrówka	Jasło	Jasło
Dąbrówka	Nisko	Ulanów
Dąbrówka	Wadowice	Wadowice
Dąbrówka Infułacka	Tarnów	Tarnów
Dąbrówka Luchowska	Tarnów	Tuchów
Dąbrówka Pniowska	Tarnobrzeg	Radomyśl
Dąbrówka Polska	Sanok	Sanok
Dąbrówka Ruska	Sanok	Sanok
Dąbrówka Starzeńska	Brzozów	Dynów
Dąbrówka Szczepans.	Tarnów	Tarnów
Dąbrówki Górzyckie	Dąbrowa	Dąbrowa
Dąbrowkibreńskie	Dąbrowa	Dąbrowa
Dachnów	Cieszanów	Cieszanów
Dalastowice	Dąbrowa	Szczucin
Daleszowa	Horodenka	Czernelica
Daliowa	Sanok	Rymanów
Dalnicz	Żólkiew	Gross Mosty
Damienice	Bochnia	Bochnia
Danilcze	Rohatyń	Rohatyń
Daniłowce	Złoczów	Jezierna
Danina	Żydaczów	Rozdól
Dankowice	Biała	Oświęcim
Darów	Sanok	Nowtanice
Darowice	Przemyśl	Niżankowice
Darszyce	Wieliczka	Klasno

Town	Main District	Subdistrict
Daszawa	Stryj	Stryj
Daszówka	Lisko	Ustrzyki Dolne
Dawidkowce	Czortków	Czortków
Dawidów	Lemberg	Winniki
Dęba	Tarnobrzeg	Tarnobrzeg
Dębelówka	Dolina	Dolina
Dębesławce	Kołomea	Kołomea
Dębica	Pilzno	Dębica
Dębina	Kam. Strumiłowa	Radziechów
Dębina	Łańcut	Łańcut
Dębina Letowska	Brzesko	Wojnicz
Dębna	Sanok	Sanok
Dębnik	Chrzanów	Trzebina
Dębniki	Wieliczka	Podgórze
Dębno	Brzesko	Brzesko
Dęborzyn	Pilzno	Jodłowa
Dębów	Łańcut	Przewórsk
Dębowa	Pilzno	Jodłowa
Dębowice	Jasło	Jasło
Dębowiec	Tarnobrzeg	Rozwadów
Dębówka	Borszczów	Skała
Dehowa	Rohatyń	Rohatyń
Delatyn	Nadwórna	Delatyn
Delawa	Drohobycz	Drohobycz
Delawa	Tłumacz	Tłumacz
Delejów	Stanisławów	Maryampol
Dembno	Nowy Targ	Nowy Targ
Dembów	Łańcut	Leżajsk
Demenka Lesńa	Żydaczów	Rozdół
Demenka Poddniestrzańska	Żydaczów	Rozdół
Demeszkowce	Rohatyń	Bursztyn

Town	Main District	Subdistrict
Demeszkowce	Stanisławów	Halicz
Demianów	Rohatyń	Bursztyn
Demianów	Stanisławów	Halicz
Demidów	Bóbrka	Chodorów
Demków Grabie	Brzesko	Czchów
Demków Pusty	Brzesko	Czchów
Demnia	Brzeżany	Brzeżany
Demnia	Dolina	Rożniatów
Demycze	Śniatyn	Zabłotów
Denysów	Tarnopol	Tarnopol
Deputaty	Nisko	Ulanów
Derczyce	Drohobycz	Drohobycz
Dereniówka	Trembowla	Janów
Derewlany	Kam. Strumiłowa	Kam. Strumiłowa
Derewnia	Żółkiew	Żółkiew
Dernów	Kam. Strumiłowa	Kam. Strumiłowa
Derzów	Żydaczów	Rozdół
Desznica	Krosno	Dukla
Deszno	Sanok	Rymanów
Deutschbach	Cieszanów	Narol
Diatkowce	Kołomea	Kołomea
Ditkowce	Brody	Brody
Ditkowce	Tarnopol	Tarnopol
Długie	Gorlice	Gorlice
Długie	Krosno	Dukla
Długie	Sanok	Rymanów
Długoleka	Nowy Sącz	Stary Sącz
Długopole	Nowy Targ	Nowy Targ
Długoszyn	Chrzanów	Chrzanów
Dłużniów	Sokal	Warez
Dmuchawiec	Brzeżany	Kozłów
Dmytrów	Kam. Strumiłowa	Chołojów

Town	Main District	Subdistrict
Dmytrów Duzy	Tarnobrzeg	Baranów
Dmytrów Mały	Tarnobrzeg	Baranów
Dmytrowice	Lemberg	Winniki
Dmytrowice	Mościska	Sądowa Wisznia
Dmytrowice	Przemyśl	Sosnica
Dmytrze	Lemberg	Szczerzec
Dobcza	Jarosław	Sienawa
Dobczycze	Wieliczka	Klasno
Dobiczye	Tarnów	Zabno
Dobieszyn	Krosno	Dukla
Dobne	Nowy Sącz	Muszyna
Doboków	Pilzno	Pilzno
Dobra	Jarosław	Sienawa
Dobra	Limanowa	Limanowa
Dobra Rustykalna	Bircza	Bircza
Dobra Szlachecka	Bircza	Bircza
Dobraczyn	Sokal	Krystynopol
Dobranowice	Wieliczka	Klasno
Dobrocierz	Brzesko	Czchów
Dobrohostów	Drohobycz	Drohobycz
Dobromil	Bircza	Dobromil
Dobroniów	Limanowa	Limanowa
Dobropole	Buczacz	Buczacz
Dobrostany	Gródek	Janów
Dobrotwór	Kam. Strumiłowa	Dobrotwor
Dobrowlany	Bóbrka	Chodorów
Dobrowlany	Drohobycz	Drohobycz
Dobrowlany	Kalusz	Kalusz
Dobrowlany	Stryj	Stryj
Dobrowlany	Zaleszczyki	Zaleszczyki
Dobrowódka	Kołomea	Kołomea
Dobrowody	Podhajce	Podhajce

Town	Main District	Subdistrict
Dobrucowa	Jasło	Jasło
Dobrynin	Mielec	Mielec
Dobrzanica	Przemyślany	Przemyślany
Dobrzanka	Bircza	Bircza
Dobrzany	Gródek	Gródek
Dobrzany	Lemberg	Szczerzec
Dobrzany	Mościska	Sądowa Wisznia
Dobrzany	Stryj	Stryj
Dobrzechów	Jasło	Frysztak
Dołega	Brzesko	Szczurowa
Dołha Wojniłowska	Kalusz	Wojniłów
Dołhe	Drohobycz	Borysław
Dołhe	Drohobycz	Drohobycz
Dołhe	Stryj	Stryj
Dołhe	Tłumacz	Uście Zielone
Dołhe	Trembowla	Janów
Dołhe Kałuskie	Kalusz	Kalusz
Dołhomosciska	Gródek	Gródek
Dołhomosciska	Mościska	Sądowa Wisznia
Dołhopol	Kossów	Żabie
Dolina	Czortków	Jagielnica
Dolina	Dolina	Dolina
Dolina	Sanok	Sanok
Dolina	Tłumacz	Tłumacz
Dolina ad Zaluz	Sanok	Sanok
Doliniany	Gródek	Gródek
Doliniany	Mościska	Sądowa Wisznia
Doliniany	Rohatyń	Rohatyń
Dolnawieś	Myślenice	Myślenice
Dołobów	Rudki	Rudki
Dołpotów	Kalusz	Wojniłów
Dołuszyce	Bochnia	Wiśnicz Nowy

Town	Main District	Subdistrict
Doły	Brzesko	Brzesko
Dołżanka	Tarnopol	Tarnopol
Dołżka	Dolina	Bolechów
Dołżka	Kalusz	Wojnilów
Dołżyca	Lisko	Baligród
Dołżyce	Sanok	Bukowsko
Domacyny	Mielec	Mielec
Domalkówka Wola	Kolbuszowa	Kolbuszów
Domaradz	Brzozów	Jasienica
Domaszer	Lemberg	Zniesienie
Domaszów	Rawa Ruska	Uhnów
Domatków	Ropczyce	Ropczyce
Dominikowice	Gorlice	Gorlice
Domosławice	Brzesko	Czchów
Domostawa	Nisko	Ulanów
Dora	Nadwórna	Delatyn
Dorbrosin	Żólkiew	Żólkiew
Dornbach	Łańcut	Leżajsk
Dornfeld	Lemberg	Szczerzec
Dorochów	Trembowla	Strusów
Dorofijówka	Skałat	Podwołoczyska
Dorohin	Stanisławów	Hałicz
Doroszów Mały	Żólkiew	Kulików
Doroszów Wielkie	Żólkiew	Kulików
Dorozów	Sambor	Sambor
Doznamorycz	Tarnopol	Tarnopol
Drabimanka	Rzeszów	Rzeszów
Draganowa	Krosno	Dukla
Draganówka	Tarnopol	Tarnopol
Drahasymów	Śniatyn	Śniatyn
Droginia	Myślenice	Myślenice
Drohiczówka	Zaleszczyki	Uścieczko

Town	Main District	Subdistrict
Drohobycz	Drohobycz	Drohobycz
Drohobyczka	Przemyśl	Dubiecko
Drohojów	Przemyśl	Sosnica
Drohomirczany	Bohordczany	Lysiec
Drohomyśl	Jaworów	Wielkie Oczy
Drohowycze	Bóbrka	Brzozdowiec
Drohowyże	Żydaczów	Rozdól
Drozdowice	Gródek	Gródek
Drozdowice	Przemyśl	Niżankowice
Drwinia	Bochnia	Bochnia
Dryszczów	Brzeżany	Brzeżany
Dryszczów	Podhajce	Zawałów
Duba	Dolina	Rożniatów
Dubaniowice	Rudki	Rudki
Dubas	Kolbuszówa	Kolbuszów
Dubie	Brody	Brody
Dubie	Chrzanów	Trzebina
Dubie	Złoczów	Olesko
Dubiecko	Przemyśl	Dubiecko
Dubienko	Buczacz	Monasterzyska
Dubkowce	Skałat	Touste
Dubkowice	Jarosław	Radymno
Dublany	Lemberg	Zniesienie
Dublany	Sambor	Sambor
Dubowce	Tarnopol	Tarnopol
Dubowica	Kalusz	Wojnilów
Dubrawka	Żydaczów	Żurawno
Dubryniów	Rohatyń	Rohatyń
Dubszara	Dolina	Rożniatów
Dubszcze	Brzeżany	Kozowa
Dudyn	Brody	Podkamień
Dudynice	Sanok	Nowtanice

Town	Main District	Subdistrict
Dukla	Krosno	Dukla
Dulcza Mała	Mielec	Radomyśl Wiel.
Dulczówka	Pilzno	Pilzno
Duliby	Bóbrka	Strzeliska Nowe
Duliby	Buczacz	Jazłowice
Duliby	Stryj	Stryj
Dulowa	Chrzanów	Chrzanów
Dunajowce	Przemyślany	Dunajowce
Duninów	Zaleszczyki	Gródek
Duńkowice	Jarosław	Radymno
Duńkowiczki	Przemyśl	Przemyśl
Dupliska	Zaleszczyki	Zaleszczyki
Durdy	Mielec	Mielec
Dusanów	Przemyślany	Przemyślany
Dusowce	Przemyśl	Sosnica
Duszatyn	Sanok	Bukowsko
Dwerniaczek	Lisko	Lutowiska
Dwernik	Lisko	Lutowiska
Dworce	Brzeżany	Narajów
Dworce	Żółkiew	Gross Mosty
Dwory	Biała	Oświęcim
Dybków	Jarosław	Sienawa
Dyczków	Tarnopol	Tarnopol
Dydiatycze	Mościska	Sądowa Wisznia
Dydnia	Brzozów	Brzozów
Dylągówa	Brzozów	Dynów
Dylągówka	Rzeszów	Tyczyn
Dyniska	Rawa Ruska	Uhnów
Dynów	Brzozów	Dynów
Dytiatyn	Rohatyń	Bursztyn
Dzial	Nowy Targ	Nowy Targ
Dzianisz	Nowy Targ	Nowy Targ

Town	Main District	Subdistrict
Dzibułki	Żólkiew	Kulików
Dzieduszyce Małe	Żydaczów	Żurawno
Dzieduszyce Wielkie	Stryj	Stryj
Dziedziłów	Kam. Strumiłowa	Busk
Dziekanowice	Wieliczka	Klasno
Dzierdziówka	Tarnobrzeg	Rozwadów
Dzierzaniny	Brzesko	Czchów
Dziewięcirez	Rawa Ruska	Rawa Ruska
Dziewiętniki	Bóbrka	Strzeliska Nowe
Dziewin	Bochnia	Bochnia
Dziezki	Rohatyń	Rohatyń
Dzików	Cieszanów	Oleszyce
Dzików	Tarnobrzeg	Tarnobrzeg
Dzikowice	Rzeszów	Głogów
Dzikowiec	Kolbuszowa	Kolbuszowa
Dziurdziów	Lisko	Lisko
Dżurków	Brzesko	Czchów
Dżurków	Kołomea	Gwozdziec
Dżurów	Śniatyn	Zabłotów
Dżuryn	Czortków	Czortków
Dżwiniacz	Zaleszczyki	Zaleszczyki
Dżwiniacz Dolny	Lisko	Ustrzyki Dolne
Dżwiniaczka	Borszczów	Mielnica
Dżwinogród	Bóbrka	Mikalajów
Dżwinogród	Borszczów	Mielnica
Dżwinogród	Buczacz	Buczacz
Dzwonowa	Pilzno	Brzostek
Ebenau	Gródek	Gródek
Einsiedel	Lemberg	Szczerzec
Einsingen	Rawa Ruska	Rawa Ruska
Eleonorówka	Skałat	Grzymałów
Engelsberg	Dolina	Dolina

Town	Main District	Subdistrict
Engelsbrunn	Bircza	Dobromil
Ernsdorf	Bóbrka	Bóbrka
Facimiech	Wadowice	Zator
Falejówka	Sanok	Sanok
Falisz	Stryj	Stryj
Faliszowice	Brzesko	Czchów
Faliszówka	Krosno	Dukla
Falkenberg	Bircza	Dobromil
Falkenstein	Lemberg	Szczerzec
Falkowa	Grybów	Bobowa
Falkowa	Nowy Sącz	Nowy Sącz
Falkowice	Wieliczka	Klasno
Faściszowa	Brzesko	Czchów
Fehlbach	Cieszanów	Lubaczów
Feliksówka	Kam. Strumiłowa	Kam. Strumiłowa
Feliksówka	Kam. Strumiłowa	Witków Nowy
Felizienthal	Stryj	Skole
Felsendorf	Cieszanów	Lubaczów
Felsztyn	Staremiasto	Felszytn
Filipkowce	Borszczów	Mielnica
Filipowice	Brzesko	Czchów
Filipowice	Chrzanów	Chrzanów
Firlejów	Przemyślany	Przemyślany
Fitków	Nadwórna	Nadwórna
Florynka	Grybów	Grybów
Fojna	Żólkiew	Żólkiew
Folwarki	Buczacz	Monasterzyska
Folwarki	Złoczów	Złoczów
Folwarki Małe	Brody	Brody
Folwarki Wielki	Brody	Brody
Folwarki Żydaczowskie	Żydaczów	Żydaczów

Town	Main District	Subdistrict
Fox	Pilzno	Dębica
Fraga	Rohatyń	Rohatyń
Fredropol	Przemyśl	Niżankowice
Freifield	Cieszanów	Cieszanów
Fron	Nowy Targ	Nowy Targ
Frycowa	Nowy Sącz	Łabowa
Frydrychowice	Wadowice	Andrychów
Frysztak	Jasło	Frysztak
Frywald	Chrzanów	Trzebina
Furmany	Tarnobrzeg	Tarnobrzeg
Futoma	Rzeszów	Błazowa
Futory	Cieszanów	Oleszyce
Gabon	Nowy Sącz	Stary Sącz
Gabryelin	Tarnobrzeg	Tarnobrzeg
Gać	Łańcut	Przewórsk
Gaj	Nowy Sącz	Nowy Sącz
Gaj	Wieliczka	Podgórze
Gaje	Lemberg	Winniki
Gaje Ditkowieckie	Brody	Brody
Gaje Niżne	Drohobycz	Drohobycz
Gaje Smoleńskie	Brody	Brody
Gaje Starobrodzkie	Brody	Brody
Gaje Wyżne	Drohobycz	Drohobycz
Gałówka	Staremiasto	Staremiasto
Gałyszów	Gorlice	Gorlice
Ganczary	Lemberg	Winniki
Garbek	Tarnów	Tuchów
Gasówka	Jasło	Jasło
Gassendorf Hurucko	Drohobycz	Drohobycz
Gawłów Nowy	Bochnia	Bochnia
Gawłów Stary	Bochnia	Bochnia
Gawłówek	Bochnia	Bochnia

Town	Main District	Subdistrict
Gawluszowice	Mielec	Mielec
Gawrzyłowa	Pilzno	Dębica
Gbiska Tropie	Rzeszów	Strzyżów
Gdeszyce	Mościska	Hussaków
Gdeszyce	Przemyśl	Niżankowice
Gdów	Wieliczka	Klasno
Gebiczyna	Pilzno	Pilzno
Gelsendorf	Stryj	Stryj
Germakówka	Borszczów	Mielnica
Gerynia	Dolina	Bolechów
Gesiówka	Bohordczany	Bohordczany
Giedlarowa	Łańcut	Leżajsk
Gieraltowice	Wadowice	Zator
Gieraltowiczki	Wadowice	Zator
Gierczyce	Bochnia	Wiśnicz Nowy
Gierowa	Nowy Sącz	Nowy Sącz
Gillershof	Łańcut	Leżajsk
Gilowice	Żywiec	Zabłocie
Głęboczek	Borszczów	Borszczów
Głęboka	Borhodczany	Sołotwina
Głęboka	Sambor	Sambor
Głębokie	Sanok	Rymanów
Głębowice	Wadowice	Zator
Głęmieniec	Biała	Lipnik
Glichów	Wieliczka	Klasno
Gliczarów	Nowy Targ	Nowy Targ
Glinianka	Nisko	Ulanów
Gliniany	Przemyślany	Gliniany
Gliniczek	Jasło	Jasło
Glinik	Nowy Sącz	Nowy Sącz
Glinik	Ropczyce	Wielopole
Glinik Charzawski	Rzeszów	Strzyżów

Town	Main District	Subdistrict
Glinik Maryampolski	Gorlice	Gorlice
Glinna	Brzeżany	Kozłów
Glinna	Lemberg	Nawarya
Glinne	Lisko	Lisko
Glinne	Sambor	Sambor
Glinnik Dolny	Jasło	Frysztak
Glinnik Górny	Jasło	Frysztak
Glinnik Niemiecki	Jasło	Jasło
Glinnik Polski	Jasło	Jasło
Glinnik Średni	Jasło	Frysztak
Glińsko	Żółkiew	Żółkiew
Gliny Małe	Mielec	Radomyśl Wiel.
Gliny Wielkie	Mielec	Radomyśl Wiel.
Glisne	Limanowa	Mszana dolna
Głogoczów	Myślenice	Myślenice
Glogów	Rzeszów	Głogów
Głogówiec	Łańcut	Przeworsk
Głojsce	Krosno	Dukla
Głów	Tarnów	Zabno
Głowienka	Krosno	Dukla
Głuchów	Łańcut	Łańcut
Głuchów	Sokal	Krystynopol
Głuchowice	Lemberg	Szczerzec
Głuchowice	Lemberg	Winniki
Głuszków	Horodenka	Horodenka
Gniewczyna	Łańcut	Przeworsk
Gniłowody	Podhajce	Podhajce
Gnojnica	Jaworów	Krakówiec
Gnojnica	Ropczyce	Ropczyce
Gnojnik	Brzesko	Brzesko
Goczałkowice	Tarnobrzeg	Rozwadów
Godowe	Rzeszów	Strzyżów

Town	Main District	Subdistrict
Godusza	Limanowa	Limanowa
Gody	Kołomea	Kołomea
Godziska Nowa	Biała	Lipnik
Godziska Stara	Biała	Lipnik
Godziska Wilkowska	Biała	Lipnik
Gogolów I	Jasło	Frysztak
Gogolów II	Jasło	Frysztak
Gołąbkowice	Nowy Sącz	Nowy Sącz
Golce	Nisko	Ulanów
Golcowa	Brzozów	Jasienica
Goleszów	Mielec	Radomyśl Wiel.
Gołkowice	Wieliczka	Klasno
Gołogórki	Złoczów	Gologory
Gołogóry	Złoczów	Gologory
Gołonka	Tarnów	Tuchów
Gołouchowice	Wadowice	Zator
Gontowa	Brody	Zalocze
Góra Motyczna	Pilzno	Dębica
Góra Ropczycka	Ropczyce	Sędziszów
Górajec	Cieszanów	Cieszanów
Górajowice	Jasło	Jasło
Górka	Brzesko	Szczurowa
Górka	Chrzanów	Chrzanów
Górki	Brzozów	Brzozów
Górki	Mielec	Radomyśl Wiel.
Gorlice	Gorlice	Gorlice
Gorliczyna	Łańcut	Przeworsk
Górnawieś	Myślenice	Myślenice
Górno	Kolbuszowa	Sokołów
Gorowa	Nowy Sącz	Nowy Sącz
Goruszów	Dąbrowa	Dąbrowa
Góry	Limanowa	Limanowa

Town	Main District	Subdistrict
Góry Luszowskie	Chrzanów	Chrzanów
Gorzanka	Lisko	Baligród
Gorzejowa	Pilzno	Dębica
Gorzejowa	Pilzno	Pilzno
Gorzeń Dolny	Wadowice	Wadowice
Gorzeń Górny	Wadowice	Wadowice
Gorzków	Bochnia	Wiśnicz Nowy
Gorzków	Wieliczka	Klasno
Gorzów	Chrzanów	Chrzanów
Gorzyce	Dąbrowa	Dąbrowa
Gorzyce	Łańcut	Przeworsk
Gorzyce	Tarnobrzeg	Tarnobrzeg
Gosprzydowa	Brzesko	Brzesko
Gostwica	Nowy Sącz	Stary Sącz
Gotkowice Niemieckie	Nowy Sącz	Stary Sącz
Gotkowice Polskie	Nowy Sącz	Stary Sącz
Grab	Krosno	Dukla
Grabanina	Krosno	Dukla
Grabicz	Tłumacz	Ottynia
Grabie	Wieliczka	Klasno
Grabieuznanskie	Bochnia	Wiśnicz Nowy
Grabina	Bochnia	Wiśnicz Nowy
Grabiny	Pilzno	Dębica
Grabkowce	Złoczów	Zborów
Grabnia	Nisko	Rudnik
Grabno	Brzesko	Wojnicz
Graboszyce	Wadowice	Zator
Grabów	Dolina	Dolina
Grabowa	Kam. Strumiłowa	Busk
Grabowa	Nowy Sącz	Nowy Sącz
Grabowce	Stryj	Skole

Town	Main District	Subdistrict
Grabowce	Stryj	Stryj
Grabowice	Bohordczany	Bohordczany
Grabowice	Przemyśl	Sosnica
Grabowice	Tarnopol	Tarnopol
Grabówka	Brzozów	Brzozów
Grabówka	Kalusz	Kalusz
Grabownica	Bircza	Nowemiasto
Grabownica	Brzozów	Brzozów
Grabowski	Wieliczka	Klasno
Grajów	Wieliczka	Klasno
Grąziowa	Bircza	Rybotycze
Grąziowa	Staremiasto	Staremiasto
Grebelki	Kam. Strumiłowa	Kam. Strumiłowa
Grębów	Tarnobrzeg	Rozwadów
Grobla	Bochnia	Bochnia
Grobla Jankowiecka	Tarnopol	Tarnopol
Groble	Nisko	Rudnik
Grochowie	Mielec	Mielec
Gródek	Gródek	Gródek
Gródek	Grybów	Grybów
Gródek	Nowy Sącz	Nowy Sącz
Gródek	Zaleszczyki	Gródek
Grodkowice	Bochnia	Bochnia
Grodowice	Staremiasto	Felszytn
Grodzisko	Bircza	Nowemiasto
Grodzisko	Jasło	Frysztak
Grodzisko	Łańcut	Leżajsk
Grodzisko	Wadowice	Zator
Grodzisko Dolne	Łańcut	Leżajsk
Grodzisko Górne	Łańcut	Leżajsk
Grójec	Biała	Oświęcim
Grójec	Chrzanów	Trzebina

Town	Main District	Subdistrict
Gromiec	Chrzanów	Chrzanów
Gromnik	Tarnów	Tuchów
Grondy	Brzesko	Brzesko
Grondy	Dąbrowa	Dąbrowa
Gronków	Nowy Targ	Nowy Targ
Gross Mosty	Żólkiew	Gross-Mosty
Grudna Dolna	Pilzno	Brzostek
Grudna Górna	Pilzno	Brzostek
Grudna Kępska	Jasło	Jasło
Grudza	Tarnobrzeg	Radomyśl
Gruszka	Tłumacz	Tłumacz
Gruszki	Wieliczka	Klasno
Gruszów	Limanowa	Limanowa
Gruszów	Wieliczka	Klasno
Gruszów Mały	Dąbrowa	Dąbrowa
Gruszów Wielki	Dąbrowa	Dąbrowa
Gruszowiec	Limanowa	Mszana dolna
Grybów	Grybów	Grybów
Grywałd	Nowy Targ	Krościenko
Grzęda	Kam. Strumiłowa	Chołojów
Grzęda	Lemberg	Zniesienie
Grzegorzowka	Rzeszow	Tyczyn
Grzekhynia	Myślenice	Maków
Grzeska	Łańcut	Przeworsk
Grzybów	Mielec	Radomyśl Wiel.
Grzybowice	Lemberg	Zniesienie
Grzymałów	Skałat	Grzymałów
Grzymałówka	Brody	Szczurowice
Guminska	Pilzno	Dębica
Guminska	Tarnów	Tarnów
Gura	Sokal	Bełż
Gusztyn	Borszczów	Skała

Town	Main District	Subdistrict
Gusztynek	Borszczów	Skała
Gutynka	Żydaczów	Żurawno
Guzowa	Tarnów	Tarnów
Gwizdów	Łańcut	Żolynia
Gwoździanka	Rzeszów	Niebylec
Gwoździec	Brzesko	Wojnicz
Gwoździec	Kolbuszowa	Ranizów
Gwoździec	Kołomea	Gwoździec
Gwoździec Nowy	Kołomea	Gwoździec
Gwoździec Stary	Kołomea	Gwoździec
Gwoźnica Dolna	Brzozów	Jasienica
Gwoźnica Dolna	Rzeszów	Niebylec
Gwoźnica Górna	Brzozów	Jasienica
Gwoźnica Górna	Rzeszów	Niebylec
Habkowce	Lisko	Baligród
Hacaki	Tarnobrzeg	Baranów
Haczów	Brzozów	Jasienica
Hadle Kańczudzkie	Łańcut	Kańczuga
Hadle Szklarskie	Rzeszów	Tyczyn
Hadykówka	Kolbuszowa	Kolbuszowa
Hadynkowce	Husiatyn	Kopyczyńce
Haiworonka	Podhajce	Złotniki
Hałbów	Krosno	Dukla
Halcnów	Biała	Lipnik
Halicz	Podhajce	Podhajce
Halicz	Stanisławów	Halicz
Haliczanów	Gródek	Gródek
Haller	Wadowice	Zator
Halowice	Sokal	Warez
Haluszczynce	Skałat	Skałat
Haluszowa	Nowy Targ	Nowy Targ
Hamulec	Lemberg	Zniesienie

Town	Main District	Subdistrict
Hanaczów	Przemyślany	Gliniany
Hanaczówka	Przemyślany	Gliniany
Hanczarów	Horodenka	Obertyn
Hanczowa	Gorlice	Gorlice
Handzlówka	Łańcut	Łańcut
Haniowce	Rohatyń	Bursztyn
Hańkowce	Śniatyn	Zabłotów
Hańkowice	Mościska	Hussaków
Hankówka	Jasło	Jasło
Hanmowce	Stanisławów	Jezupol
Hanowce	Żydaczów	Żydaczów
Hanunin	Kam. Strumiłowa	Radziechów
Harasymów	Horodenka	Obertyn
Harbutowice	Wadowice	Kalwarya
Harbuzów	Złoczów	Zborów
Harklowa	Nowy Targ	Nowy Targ
Harmięże	Biała	Oświęcim
Harta	Brzozów	Dynów
Hartfield	Gródek	Gródek
Haszcze	Trembowla	Trembowla
Hatki	Podhajce	Złotniki
Hawlowice Dolne	Jarosław	Pruchnik
Hawlowice Górne	Jarosław	Pruchnik
Hawrylak	Horodenka	Obertyn
Hawryłówka	Nadwórna	Nadwórna
Hecznarowice	Biała	Kęty
Heinrichsdorf	Kam. Strumiłowa	Witków Nowy
Helenków	Brzeżany	Kozowa
Hemia	Dolina	Dolina
Herbutów	Rohatyń	Bursztyn
Hermanów	Lemberg	Jaryczów
Hermanowa	Rzeszów	Tyczyn

Town	Main District	Subdistrict
Hermanowice	Przemyśl	Przemyśl
Hińkowce	Zaleszczyki	Uścieczko
Hinowiec	Brzeżany	Brzeżany
Hladki	Tarnopol	Tarnopol
Hlebówka	Borhodczany	Sołotwina
Hleszczawa	Trembowla	Trembowla
Hlibów	Skałat	Grzymałów
Hłomcza	Bircza	Bircza
Hłuboczek Wielki	Tarnopol	Tarnopol
Hłudno	Brzozów	Dynów
Hnatkowice	Przemyśl	Sosnica
Hnidawa	Brody	Zalocze
Hnizdyesów	Żydaczów	Żydaczów
Hoczew	Lisko	Lisko
Hodów	Złoczów	Pomorzany
Hodowice	Lemberg	Nawarya
Hodwisznia	Rudki	Rudki
Hodynie	Mościska	Mościska
Hoffnungsau	Dolina	Dolina
Hohenbach	Mielec	Radomyśl Wiel.
Hohołów	Sokal	Krystynopol
Holbocze	Podhajce	Podhajce
Hołdowice	Bóbrka	Strzeliska Nowe
Hołdówka	Rudki	Komarno
Hołe Rawskie	Rawa Ruska	Rawa Ruska
Holeszów	Bóbrka	Chodorów
Holholuka	Stryj	Stryj
Holihrady	Zaleszczyki	Zaleszczyki
Hołobutów	Stryj	Stryj
Hołodówka	Mościska	Sądowa Wisznia
Hołodówska	Cieszanów	Lubaczów
Hołosko Małe	Lemberg	Zniesienie

Town	Main District	Subdistrict
Hołosko Wielkie	Lemberg	Zniesienie
Hołowczynce	Zaleszczyki	Tłuste
Hołowecko	Staremiasto	Staremiasto
Hołowy	Kossów	Żabie
Hołozkowice	Brody	Brody
Hołsków	Nadwórna	Lanczyn
Hołubica	Brody	Podkamień
Hołubice	Złoczów	Olesko
Hołuczków	Sanok	Tyrawa woloska
Hołwiecko	Stryj	Skole
Hołyn	Kalusz	Kalusz
Honiatycze	Rudki	Komarno
Honoratatówka	Rohatyń	Rohatyń
Horbacze	Rudki	Komarno
Horbków	Sokal	Tartaków
Hordynia	Sambor	Sambor
Horochowlina	Bohordczany	Bohordczany
Horod	Kossów	Kossów
Horodek	Lisko	Baligród
Horodelec	Sokal	Tartaków
Horodenka	Horodenka	Horodenka
Horodlowice	Sokal	Sokal
Horodnica	Horodenka	Horodenka
Horodnica	Husiatyn	Husiatyn
Horodnica	Skałat	Skałat
Horodyłów	Złoczów	Złoczów
Horodysławice	Bóbrka	Mikalajów
Horodyszcze	Brzeżany	Kozłów
Horodyszcze	Sambor	Sambor
Horodyszcze	Tarnopol	Tarnopol
Horodyszcze Bazy	Sokal	Krystynopol
Horodyszcze Krol.	Bóbrka	Chodorów

The Galitzianers

Town	Main District	Subdistrict
Horodyszcze Warezskie	Sokal	Warez
Horodzów	Rawa Ruska	Magierów
Horoszowa	Borszczów	Mielnica
Horożanka	Podhajce	Zawałów
Horożanna Małe	Rudki	Komarno
Horożanna Wielka	Rudki	Komarno
Horpin	Kam. Strumiłowa	Kam. Strumiłowa
Horyhlady	Tłumacz	Niźniów
Horynice	Cieszanów	Cieszanów
Horysławice	Mościska	Hussaków
Hostów	Tłumacz	Ottynia
Hoszany	Rudki	Rudki
Hoszów	Dolina	Bolechów
Hoszów	Lisko	Ustrzyki Dolne
Hoszowczyk	Lisko	Ustrzyki Dolne
Hów	Żydaczów	Rozdól
Howilów Wielki	Husiatyn	Chorostków
Howiłów Mały	Husiatyn	Chorostków
Hranki	Bóbrka	Brzozdowiec
Hrebenne	Rawa Ruska	Rawa Ruska
Hrebenne	Żółkiew	Kulików
Hrebenów	Stryj	Skole
Hrehorów	Buczacz	Monasterzyska
Hrehorów	Rohatyń	Rohatyń
Hroszówka	Bircza	Bircza
Hrusiatycze	Bóbrka	Strzeliska Nowe
Hruszatyce	Mościska	Hussaków
Hruszatyce	Przemyśl	Niżankowice
Hruszów	Drohobycz	Drohobycz
Hruszów	Jaworów	Wielkie Oczy
Hruszowice	Jarosław	Radymno

Town	Main District	Subdistrict
Hrycówka	Trembowla	Janów
Hrycowola	Brody	Szczurowice
Hryniawa	Kossów	Żabie
Hryniów	Bóbrka	Bóbrka
Hryniowce	Tłumacz	Tłumacz
Hrynkowce	Husiatyn	Probużna
Huba	Nowy Targ	Nowy Targ
Hubenice	Dąbrowa	Dąbrowa
Hubice	Bircza	Dobromil
Hubice	Bircza	Dobromil
Hubice	Drohobycz	Drohobycz
Hubin	Buczacz	Potok
Hubinek	Rawa Ruska	Uhnów
Hucisko	Bóbrka	Bóbrka
Hucisko	Brzeżany	Brzeżany
Hucisko	Rzeszów	Głogów
Hucisko	Wieliczka	Klasno
Hucisko	Żólkiew	Żólkiew
Hucisko ad Niwiska	Kolbuszowa	Kolbuszowa
Hucisko ad Przewrotne	Kolbuszowa	Ranizów
Hucisko Brodzkie	Brody	Podkamień
Hucisko Jawornickie	Rzeszów	Tyczyn
Hucisko Łodygowskie	Biała	Lipnik
Hucisko Oleskie	Złoczów	Olesko
Hucisko Żywieckie	Żywiec	Zabłocie
Huczko	Bircza	Dobromil
Hujcze	Rawa Ruska	Rawa Ruska
Hukalowce	Złoczów	Zborów
Huki	Jaworów	Krakówiec
Hulcze	Sokal	Warez

Town	Main District	Subdistrict
Hulicze	Podhajce	Zawałów
Hulskie	Lisko	Lutowiska
Humenów	Kalusz	Kalusz
Humienice	Lemberg	Szczerzec
Humienice	Sambor	Sambor
Humniska	Brzozów	Brzozów
Humniska	Kam. Strumiłowa	Busk
Humniska	Trembowla	Trembowla
Hureczko	Przemyśl	Przemyśl
Hurko	Przemyśl	Przemyśl
Hurnie	Stryj	Stryj
Husiatyn	Husiatyn	Husiatyn
Hussaków	Mościska	Hussaków
Hussów	Łańcut	Łańcut
Huta	Bóbrka	Bóbrka
Huta	Brzozów	Dynów
Huta	Ropczyce	Ropczyce
Huta Brzuska	Bircza	Bircza
Huta Deręgowska	Nisko	Ulanów
Huta Gogolowska	Jasło	Frysztak
Huta Komorowska	Kolbuszowa	Majdan
Huta Krasnianska	Skałat	Touste
Huta Krzysztalowa	Cieszanów	Lubaczów
Huta Lubycka	Rawa Ruska	Lubycza
Huta Nowa	Buczacz	Monasterzyska
Huta Pieniacka	Brody	Podkamień
Huta Polańska	Krosno	Dukla
Huta Połoniecka	Kam. Strumiłowa	Busk
Huta Roźaniecka	Cieszanów	Narol
Huta Stara	Buczacz	Monasterzyska
Huta Stara	Cieszanów	Lipsko
Huta Stara	Kam. Strumiłowa	Radziechów

Town	Main District	Subdistrict
Huta Szklana	Kam. Strumiłowa	Radziechów
Huta Zielona	Rawa Ruska	Rawa Ruska
Hutar	Stryj	Skole
Hutka Obedynska	Rawa Ruska	Rawa Ruska
Huwniki	Bircza	Rybotycze
Huzele	Lisko	Lisko
Huziejów Nowy	Dolina	Bolechów
Huziejów Stary	Dolina	Bolechów
Hwozd	Borhodczany	Sołotwina
Hybie	Brzesko	Wojnicz
Hyki et Dębiaki	Mielec	Mielec
Hyrniówka	Bohordczany	Bohordczany
Hyrowa	Krosno	Dukla
Hyżne	Rzeszów	Tyczyn
Ilińce	Śniatyn	Zabłotów
Ilkowice	Sokal	Sokal
Ilkowice	Tarnów	Zabno
Inwald	Wadowice	Andrychów
Isaków	Horodenka	Obertyn
Isep	Brzesko	Wojnicz
Isep	Żywiec	Zabłocie
Iskan	Bircza	Bircza
Iskrzynia	Krosno	Korczyna
Ispas	Kołomea	Jabłonów
Isypowce	Tarnopol	Tarnopol
Iszerków	Podhajce	Złotniki
Iwaczów	Złoczów	Zborów
Iwaczów Dolny	Tarnopol	Tarnopol
Iwaczów Górny	Tarnopol	Tarnopol
Iwańce	Borszczów	Mielnica
Iwanie	Zaleszczyki	Uścieczko
Iwanikówka	Bohordczany	Lysiec

Town	Main District	Subdistrict
Iwanków	Borszczów	Skała
Iwankówka	Husiatyn	Chorostków
Iwanowce	Kołomea	Peczeniżyn
Iwanowce	Żydaczów	Żydaczów
Iwanówka	Skałat	Skałat
Iwkowa	Brzesko	Czchów
Iwkowska	Brzesko	Czchów
Iwla	Krosno	Dukla
Iwonicz	Krosno	Dukla
Izabelin	Buczacz	Monasterzyska
Izbiska	Mielec	Radomyśl Wiel.
Izby	Grybów	Grybów
Izdebki	Brzozów	Dynów
Izdebnik	Wadowice	Kalwarya
Izlickie	Rudki	Komarno
Izydorówka	Żydaczów	Żurawno
Jabłonica	Jasło	Jasło
Jabłonica	Kossów	Żabie
Jabłonica	Nadwórna	Delatyn
Jabłonica Polska	Brzozów	Jasienica
Jabłonica Ruska	Bircza	Bircza
Jabłonka	Borhodczany	Sołotwina
Jabłonka	Borhodczany	Sołotwina
Jabłonka	Brzozów	Brzozów
Jabłonki	Lisko	Baligród
Jabłonów	Husiatyn	Kopyczyńce
Jabłonów	Kołomea	Jabłonów
Jabłonów	Rohatyń	Bursztyn
Jabłonówka	Kam. Strumiłowa	Busk
Jabłonówka	Podhajce	Zawałów
Jachówka	Myślenice	Maków
Jackowce	Złoczów	Jezierna

Town	Main District	Subdistrict
Jackówka	Tłumacz	Tłumacz
Jacmanice	Przemyśl	Przemyśl
Jacmierz	Sanok	Rymanów
Jadachy	Tarnobrzeg	Tarnobrzeg
Jadamwola	Limanowa	Limanowa
Jadowniki	Brzesko	Brzesko
Jagieła	Łańcut	Przewórsk
Jagielnica	Czortków	Jagielnica
Jagielnica Stara	Czortków	Jagielnica
Jagodnik	Kolbuszowa	Kolbuszowa
Jagunia	Kam. Strumiłowa	Kam. Strumiłowa
Jahłusz	Rohatyń	Rohatyń
Jajkowce	Żydaczów	Żurawno
Jakimczyce	Rudki	Komarno
Jakimów	Kam. Strumiłowa	Busk
Jaktorów	Przemyślany	Gliniany
Jakubów	Dolina	Dolina
Jakubówka	Horodenka	Obertyn
Jala	Nisko	Rudnik
Jałowe	Lisko	Ustrzyki Dolne
Jamda	Nisko	Rudnik
Jamelna	Gródek	Janów
Jamelnica	Stryj	Skole
Jamna	Grybów	Bobowa
Jamna	Nadwórna	Delatyn
Jamna Dolna	Bircza	Rybotycze
Jamna Górna	Bircza	Rybotycze
Jamne	Kam. Strumiłowa	Kam. Strumiłowa
Jamnica	Stanisławów	Stanisławów
Jamnica	Tarnobrzeg	Rozwadów
Jamy	Mielec	Radomyśl Wiel.
Janczowa	Nowy Sącz	Nowy Sącz

Town	Main District	Subdistrict
Janczyn	Przemyślany	Przemyślany
Janikowice	Dąbrowa	Dąbrowa
Jankowce	Lisko	Lisko
Jankowce	Tarnopol	Tarnopol
Jankowice	Chrzanów	Chrzanów
Jankowice	Jarosław	Jarosław
Jankówka	Wieliczka	Klasno
Janów	Gródek	Janów
Janów	Sambor	Sambor
Janów	Trembowla	Janów
Janowice	Biała	Lipnik
Janowice	Limanowa	Limanowa
Janowice	Tarnów	Tarnów
Janowice	Wieliczka	Klasno
Janówka	Buczacz	Buczacz
Janówka	Tarnobrzeg	Tarnobrzeg
Janówka	Tarnopol	Tarnopol
Januszkowice	Pilzno	Brzostek
Januszowa	Nowy Sącz	Nowy Sącz
Jarczowce	Złoczów	Zborów
Jarhorów	Buczacz	Monasterzyska
Jarosin	Nisko	Ulanów
Jarosław	Jarosław	Jarosław
Jarosławice	Złoczów	Zborów
Jaroszowice	Wadowice	Wadowice
Jaroszówka	Wieliczka	Klasno
Jaroszyce	Stryj	Stryj
Jaryczów	Lemberg	Jaryczów
Jaryczów Nowy	Lemberg	Jaryczów
Jaryczów Stary	Lemberg	Jaryczów
Jarymówka	Jasło	Jasło
Jasiel	Sanok	Bukowsko

Town	Main District	Subdistrict
Jasień	Brzesko	Brzesko
Jasień	Kalusz	Kalusz
Jasień	Lisko	Ustrzyki Dolne
Jasienica	Brzozów	Jasienica
Jasienica	Myślenice	Myślenice
Jasienica Solna	Drohobycz	Drohobycz
Jasienica Sufczyńska	Bircza	Bircza
Jasienna	Nowy Sącz	Nowy Sącz
Jasienów Górny	Kossów	Żabie
Jasienów Polny	Horodenka	Horodenka
Jasienowice	Dolina	Rożniatów
Jasienówka	Dolina	Rożniatów
Jasionka	Gorlice	Gorlice
Jasionka	Krosno	Dukla
Jasionka	Rzeszów	Głogów
Jasionów	Brody	Sokołówka
Jasionów	Brzozów	Dynów
Jasionów	Złoczów	Olesko
Jasionówa	Brzozów	Brzozów
Jaskowice	Wadowice	Zator
Jaslany	Mielec	Mielec
Jasliska	Sanok	Rymanów
Jasło	Jasło	Jasło
Jasna	Limanowa	Limanowa
Jaśniska	Gródek	Janów
Jaśniszcze	Brody	Podkamień
Jastew	Brzesko	Brzesko
Jastkowice	Tarnobrzeg	Rozwadów
Jastrebia	Wadowice	Kalwarya
Jastrzałka Nowa	Tarnów	Zabno
Jastrzębia	Grybów	Bobowa
Jastrzębia	Limanowa	Limanowa

Town	Main District	Subdistrict
Jastrzębiec	Łańcut	Leżajsk
Jastrzębiec	Stanisławów	Jezupol
Jastrzębków	Lemberg	Szczerzec
Jastrzębnik	Nowy Sącz	Krynica
Jaszczew	Krosno	Dukla
Jaszczurowa	Jasło	Frysztak
Jaszczurowa	Ropczyce	Wielopole
Jaszczurowa	Wadowice	Wadowice
Jaszkowa	Grybów	Grybów
Jasztrebica	Sokal	Krystynopol
Jatwięgi	Bóbrka	Strzeliska Nowe
Jatwięgi	Mościska	Mościska
Jatwięgi	Rudki	Rudki
Jawcze	Rohatyń	Rohatyń
Jawczyce	Wieliczka	Klasno
Jawiszowice	Biała	Oświęcim
Jaworec	Lisko	Baligród
Jaworki	Nowy Sącz	Szczawnica
Jawornik	Myślenice	Myślenice
Jawornik	Tarnów	Zabno
Jawornik Górny	Sanok	Bukowsko
Jawornik Niebyłecki	Rzeszów	Niebylec
Jawornik Polski	Rzeszów	Tyczyn
Jawornik Ruski	Bircza	Bircza
Jaworów	Dolina	Dolina
Jaworów	Jaworów	Jaworów
Jaworów	Kossów	Kossów
Jaworów	Mościska	Mościska
Jaworówka	Kalusz	Kalusz
Jaworsko	Brzesko	Wojnicz
Jaworze	Krosno	Dukla
Jaworze	Pilzno	Pilzno

Town	Main District	Subdistrict
Jaworzna	Limanowa	Limanowa
Jaworzno	Chrzanów	Chrzanów
Jazienica Polska	Kam. Strumiłowa	Kam. Strumiłowa
Jazienica Ruska	Kam. Strumiłowa	Kam. Strumiłowa
Jazłowczyk	Brody	Brody
Jazłowice	Buczacz	Jazłowice
Jazów Nowy	Jaworów	Jaworów
Jazów Stary	Jaworów	Jaworów
Jazowa	Jasło	Frysztak
Jazowa	Ropczyce	Wielopole
Jazowsko	Nowy Sącz	Łącko
Jedlicze	Krosno	Dukla
Jędruszków	Sanok	Nowtanice
Jelechowice	Złoczów	Złoczów
Jeleń	Chrzanów	Chrzanów
Jeleńkowate	Stryj	Skole
Jeleśnia	Żywiec	Zabłocie
Jelna	Nisko	Rudnik
Jelna	Nowy Sącz	Nowy Sącz
Jeriorko	Tarnobrzeg	Tarnobrzeg
Jesionowce	Złoczów	Złoczów
Jeszczyna	Żywiec	Zabłocie
Jezierna	Złoczów	Jezierna
Jezierzanka	Borszczów	Borszczów
Jezierzany	Borszczów	Borszczów
Jezierzany	Buczacz	Barysz
Jezierzany	Rohatyń	Bursztyn
Jezierzany	Tłumacz	Tłumacz
Jezierzenka	Złoczów	Zborów
Jeżów	Grybów	Bobowa
Jeżów	Nisko	Rudnik
Jezupol	Stanisławów	Jezupol

Town	Main District	Subdistrict
Jodłowa	Pilzno	Jodłowa
Jodłówka	Bochnia	Bochnia
Jodłówka	Jarosław	Pruchnik
Jodłówka	Tarnów	Tarnów
Jodłownik	Limanowa	Limanowa
Jokówka	Tarnów	Tarnów
Joniny	Tarnów	Ryglice
Jordanów	Myślenice	Jordanów
Jordanówka	Mościska	Hussaków
Jósefówka	Sokal	Sokal
Josefsberg	Drohobycz	Drohobycz
Josefsdorf	Mielec	Mielec
Józefów	Kam. Strumiłowa	Radziechów
Józefówka	Rawa Ruska	Uhnów
Józefówka	Tarnopol	Tarnopol
Judaszówka	Nisko	Rudnik
Jugowiec	Wieliczka	Podgórze
Julatycze	Żydaczów	Żurawno
Junaszków	Rohatyń	Bursztyn
Juraszowa	Nowy Sącz	Stary Sącz
Jurczyce	Myślenice	Myślenice
Jureczkowa	Bircza	Rybotycze
Juriampol	Zaleszczyki	Korolówka
Jurków	Brzesko	Czchów
Jurków	Limanowa	Limanowa
Jurowce	Sanok	Sanok
Juseptycze	Żydaczów	Żydaczów
Juśkowice	Złoczów	Olesko
Just	Nowy Sącz	Nowy Sącz
Justyniówka	Podhajce	Podhajce
Juszczyn	Myślenice	Maków
Juszkowce	Bóbrka	Strzeliska Nowe

Town	Main District	Subdistrict
Kabarowce	Złoczów	Zborów
Kaczanówka	Skałat	Skałat
Kaczorowy	Jasło	Jasło
Kaczyna	Wadowice	Wadowice
Kadeza	Nowy Sącz	Łącko
Kadłubiska	Brody	Sokołówka
Kadłubiska	Złoczów	Olesko
Kadłubliska	Cieszanów	Narol
Kadobna	Kalusz	Kalusz
Kadowa	Grybów	Grybów
Kajmów	Tarnobrzeg	Tarnobrzeg
Kałahorówka	Skałat	Touste
Kalembina	Jasło	Frysztak
Kalembina	Ropczyce	Wielopole
Kalinów	Sambor	Sambor
Kalinowszczyzna	Czortków	Czortków
Kalna	Biała	Lipnik
Kalna	Dolina	Bolechów
Kalne	Brzeżany	Kozowa
Kalne	Stryj	Skole
Kalne	Złoczów	Pomorzany
Kalnica	Lisko	Baligród
Kaltwasser	Lemberg	Zniesienie
Kalusz	Kalusz	Kalusz
Kalwarya	Wadowice	Kalwarya
Kalwarya	Wadowice	Kalwarya
Kamesznica	Żywiec	Zabłocie
Kamień	Kalusz	Kalusz
Kamień	Nisko	Rudnik
Kamienica	Limanowa	Limanowa
Kamienna	Grybów	Grybów
Kamienna	Nadwórna	Nadwórna

Town	Main District	Subdistrict
Kamienna Góra	Podhajce	Zawałów
Kamienna Góra	Rawa Ruska	Magierów
Kamienne	Sanok	Bukowsko
Kamienobród	Gródek	Gródek
Kamienopol	Lemberg	Zniesienie
Kamionka	Dolina	Bolechów
Kamionka	Nowy Sącz	Łabowa
Kamionka	Ropczyce	Ropczyce
Kamionka	Sanok	Rymanów
Kamionka Mała	Limanowa	Limanowa
Kamionka Strumiłowa	Kam. Strumiłowa	Kam. Strumiłowa
Kamionka Wielka	Grybów	Grybów
Kamionka Wołoska	Rawa Ruska	Rawa Ruska
Kamionki	Lisko	Baligród
Kamionki	Skałat	Skałat
Kamionki Małe	Kołomea	Kołomea
Kamionki Wielkie	Kołomea	Kołomea
Kamionna	Bochnia	Wiśnicz Nowy
Kamionna	Bochnia	Wiśnicz Nowy
Kamyk	Bochnia	Wiśnicz Nowy
Kanafosty	Rudki	Rudki
Kańczuga	Łańcut	Kańczuga
Kańczuga Kobiernice	Biała	Kęty
Kanina	Limanowa	Limanowa
Kaniów Dankowski	Biała	Oświęcim
Kaniów Stary	Biała	Oświęcim
Kanna	Dąbrowa	Dąbrowa
Kapelanka	Wieliczka	Podgórze
Kaplince	Brzeżany	Kozowa
Kaptury	Trembowla	Trembowla
Kapuścińce	Zaleszczyki	Tłuste

Town	Main District	Subdistrict
Karaczynów	Gródek	Janów
Karanie	Kam. Strumiłowa	Chołojów
Karaszyńce	Husiatyn	Chorostków
Karemków	Rudki	Rudki
Karezmiska	Tarnobrzeg	Rozwadów
Karlików	Sanok	Bukowsko
Karłów	Śniatyn	Śniatyn
Karlsdorf	Stryj	Skole
Karniowice	Chrzanów	Chrzanów
Karolówka	Zaleszczyki	Tłuste
Karów	Rawa Ruska	Uhnów
Karwodna	Tarnów	Tuchów
Kasina Mała	Limanowa	Mszana dolna
Kasina Wielka	Limanowa	Mszana dolna
Kasna Dolna	Grybów	Bobowa
Kasna Górna	Grybów	Bobowa
Kasperowce	Zaleszczyki	Zaleszczyki
Kaszyce	Przemyśl	Sosnica
Kąt. Pozekalec	Skałat	Touste
Kątarzynice	Rudki	Komarno
Kąty	Brzesko	Czchów
Kąty	Chrzanów	Chrzanów
Kąty	Nisko	Ulanów
Kąty	Złoczów	Olesko
Katyna	Bircza	Dobromil
Kawczykat	Stryj	Stryj
Kawec	Wieliczka	Klasno
Kawęczyn	Mielec	Radomyśl Wiel.
Kawęczyn	Pilzno	Dębica
Kawęczyn	Ropczyce	Sędziszów
Kawęczyn	Tarnobrzeg	Rozwadów
Kawsko	Stryj	Stryj

Town	Main District	Subdistrict
Kazimirowska	Złoczów	Zborów
Kęblów	Mielec	Mielec
Kędzierzawce	Kam. Strumiłowa	Busk
Kędzierzynka	Wieliczka	Klasno
Keiklów	Mielec	Radomyśl Wiel.
Kępa	Kam. Strumiłowa	Stajanów
Kępanów	Bochnia	Wiśnicz Nowy
Kęparze Czycka	Tarnobrzeg	Rozwadów
Kępie	Tarnobrzeg	Rozwadów
Kęty	Biała	Kęty
Kiczna	Nowy Sącz	Łącko
Kidałowice	Jarosław	Jarosław
Kielanowice	Tarnów	Ryglice
Kielanówka	Rzeszów	Rzeszów
Kielczawa Kolonice	Lisko	Baligród
Kielnacowa	Rzeszów	Tyczyn
Kierlikówka	Bochnia	Wiśnicz Nowy
Kiernica	Gródek	Gródek
Kije	Kam. Strumiłowa	Chołojów
Kijowce	Żydaczów	Rozdól
Kilichów	Śniatyn	Zabłotów
Kimirz	Przemyślany	Przemyślany
Kipiaczka	Tarnopol	Tarnopol
Kipszna	Grybów	Bobowa
Kisielówka	Limanowa	Limanowa
Kisielówka	Tarnopol	Tarnopol
Kiskora	Tarnów	Tarnów
Klapówka	Rzeszów	Głogów
Klasno	Wieliczka	Klasno
Klasno	Wieliczka	Klasno
Klay	Bochnia	Bochnia
Klecie	Pilzno	Brzostek

Town	Main District	Subdistrict
Klęcza Dolna	Wadowice	Wadowice
Klęcza Górna	Wadowice	Wadowice
Klęcza Srednia	Wadowice	Wadowice
Klęczany	Gorlice	Gorlice
Klęczany	Nowy Sącz	Nowy Sącz
Klęczany	Ropczyce	Sędziszów
Klęczany	Wieliczka	Klasno
Kleindorf	Jaworów	Jaworów
Klekotów	Brody	Brody
Kleparów	Lemberg	Zniesienie
Kleszczowna	Przemyślany	Przemyślany
Klikowa	Tarnów	Tarnów
Klikuszowa	Nowy Targ	Nowy Targ
Klimkówka	Gorlice	Gorlice
Klimkówka	Nowy Sącz	Nowy Sącz
Klimkówka	Sanok	Rymanów
Kliniec	Stryj	Skole
Kliszów	Mielec	Mielec
Kłodne	Limanowa	Limanowa
Kłodnica	Stryj	Stryj
Kłodno	Żółkiew	Kulików
Kłodowa	Pilzno	Jodłowa
Kłodzienko	Żółkiew	Kulików
Kłokowice	Przemyśl	Niżankowice
Kłonice	Jaworów	Wielkie Oczy
Kłonów	Tarnobrzeg	Rozwadów
Kłubowce	Tłumacz	Tyśmienica
Kluczów Mały	Kołomea	Peczeniżyn
Kluczów Wielki	Kołomea	Peczeniżyn
Klusów	Sokal	Krystynopol
Kluszkowce	Nowy Targ	Nowy Targ
Kluwince	Husiatyn	Chorostków

Town	Main District	Subdistrict
Klyżów	Nisko	Ulanów
Knapy	Mielec	Mielec
Kniaźdwór	Kołomea	Peczeniżyn
Kniaże	Śniatyn	Śniatyn
Kniaże	Złoczów	Złoczów
Kniaziołuka	Dolina	Dolina
Kniażowskie	Dolina	Rożniatów
Kniaźpol	Bircza	Dobromil
Kniażyce	Przemyśl	Niżankowice
Kniesioło	Bóbrka	Strzeliska Nowe
Knihinin	Stanisławów	Stanisławów
Knihinin Colonie	Stanisławów	Stanisławów
Knihynice	Rudki	Rudki
Knihynicze	Rohatyń	Rohatyń
Knurów	Nowy Targ	Nowy Targ
Kobacki	Kossów	Kuty
Kobielnik	Wieliczka	Klasno
Kobienrzyn	Wieliczka	Podgórze
Kobierzyn	Tarnów	Zabno
Kobło Stare	Staremiasto	Staremiasto
Kobylanka	Gorlice	Gorlice
Kobylany	Krosno	Dukla
Kobyłczyna	Limanowa	Limanowa
Kobyle	Bochnia	Wiśnicz Nowy
Kobyle	Jasło	Frysztak
Kobyle	Nowy Sącz	Nowy Sącz
Kobylec	Bochnia	Wiśnicz Nowy
Kobylec	Kołomea	Gwozdźiec
Kobylnica Ruska	Cieszanów	Lubaczów
Kobylnica Wołoska	Cieszanów	Lubaczów
Kobylowłoki	Trembowla	Janów
Kochanówka	Jaworów	Krakówiec

Town	Main District	Subdistrict
Kochany	Tarnobrzeg	Rozwadów
Kochawina	Żydaczów	Żydaczów
Kocierz ad Moszczanica	Żywiec	Zabłocie
Kocierz ad Rychwald	Żywiec	Zabłocie
Kocierzyn	Mościska	Sądowa Wisznia
Kociubińce	Husiatyn	Kopyczyńce
Kociubińczyki	Husiatyn	Husiatyn
Kocmierzów	Tarnobrzeg	Tarnobrzeg
Kocoń	Żywiec	Zabłocie
Kocurów	Bóbrka	Mikalajów
Kojszówka	Myślenice	Maków
Kokoszyńce	Skałat	Touste
Kokotkowce	Tarnopol	Tarnopol
Kokotów	Wieliczka	Klasno
Kokuszka	Nowy Sącz	Piwniczna
Kolaczyce	Pilzno	Brzostek
Kolanki	Horodenka	Czernelica
Kolanów	Bochnia	Bochnia
Kolbuszowa	Kolbuszowa	Kolbuszowa
Kolbuszowa Dolna	Kolbuszowa	Kolbuszowa
Kolbuszowa Górna	Kolbuszowa	Kolbuszowa
Kołdziejów	Stanisławów	Halicz
Koledziany	Czortków	Czortków
Koleśniki	Kam. Strumiłowa	Radziechów
Kolin	Rohatyń	Rohatyń
Kolińce	Tłumacz	Tłumacz
Kolko	Bochnia	Bochnia
Kolkówka Strzyzewski	Gorlice	Rzepienik
Koło	Rohatyń	Rohatyń
Koło	Tarnobrzeg	Baranów

Town	Main District	Subdistrict
Koło Tynieckie	Wieliczka	Podgórze
Kołodrobka	Zaleszczyki	Korolówka
Kołodziejówka	Skałat	Skałat
Kołodziejówka	Stanisławów	Stanisławów
Kołohury	Bóbrka	Bóbrka
Kołomea	Kołomea	Kołomea
Kołowa Wola	Tarnobrzeg	Rozwadów
Kołpice	Drohobycz	Drohobycz
Kołtów	Złoczów	Sassów
Komańcza	Sanok	Bukowsko
Komarno	Rudki	Komarno
Komarów	Sokal	Tartaków
Komarów	Stanisławów	Halicz
Komarów	Stryj	Stryj
Komarowice	Bircza	Nowemiasto
Komarówka	Brzeżany	Kozowa
Komarówka	Tłumacz	Uście Zielone
Kombornia	Krosno	Dukla
Komorniki	Wieliczka	Klasno
Komorów	Kolbuszowa	Majdan
Komorów	Tarnów	Zabno
Komorowice	Biała	Lipnik
Komorówka	Brody	Leszniów
Konary	Tarnów	Zabno
Konary	Wieliczka	Podgórze
Kończyce	Nisko	Rudnik
Kończyska	Brzesko	Czchów
Kondratów	Złoczów	Gologory
Koniaczów	Jarosław	Jarosław
Konice	Ropczyce	Wielopole
Koniczkowa	Rzeszów	Niebylec
Konieczna	Gorlice	Gorlice

Town	Main District	Subdistrict
Konigsau	Drohobycz	Drohobycz
Konigsberg	Nisko	Rudnik
Konina	Limanowa	Mszana dolna
Koniów	Sambor	Sambor
Koniuchów	Stryj	Stryj
Koniuchy	Brzeżany	Kozowa
Koniusza	Przemyśl	Niżankowice
Koniuszki	Przemyśl	Niżankowice
Koniuszki	Rohatyń	Rohatyń
Koniuszki Królewskie	Rudki	Komarno
Koniuszki Nanowskie	Mościska	Hussaków
Koniuszki Siemianów	Rudki	Rudki
Koniuszki Tuligłowskie	Rudki	Komarno
Koniuszków	Brody	Brody
Koniuszowa	Grybów	Grybów
Konkolniki	Rohatyń	Bursztyn
Konkulówka	Rzeszów	Błazowa
Konopkówka	Tarnopol	Mikulińce
Konotopy	Sokal	Sokal
Końskie	Brzozów	Brzozów
Konstancja	Borszczów	Borszczów
Konstantynówka	Tarnopol	Tarnopol
Konstantynówka	Tłumacz	Ottynia
Konty	Brody	Sokołówka
Konty	Krosno	Żmigród
Kopacze Księże	Brzesko	Szczurowa
Kopaczyńce	Horodenka	Czernelica
Kopaliny	Bochnia	Wiśnicz Nowy
Kopaliny	Brzesko	Brzesko
Kopan	Przemyślany	Świrz
Kopaniny	Brzesko	Szczurowa

Town	Main District	Subdistrict
Kopanka	Kalusz	Kalusz
Kopanka	Wieliczka	Podgórze
Kopcie	Kolbuszowa	Majdan
Kopcie	Rzeszów	Głogów
Kopyczyńce	Husiatyn	Kopyczyńce
Kopytne	Bircza	Rybotycze
Kopytów	Sokal	Tartaków
Kopytowa	Krosno	Dukla
Kopytówka	Wadowice	Zator
Korabina	Kolbuszowa	Ranizów
Korabniki	Wieliczka	Podgórze
Korbielów	Żywiec	Zabłocie
Korczmin	Rawa Ruska	Uhnów
Korczów	Rawa Ruska	Uhnów
Korczówka	Żydaczów	Żurawno
Korczyn	Sokal	Krystynopol
Korczyn	Stryj	Skole
Korczyna	Gorlice	Gorlice
Korczyna	Krosno	Korczyna
Kordówka	Kołomea	Kołomea
Korków	Sokal	Warez
Kornałowice	Sambor	Sambor
Kornatka	Wieliczka	Klasno
Kornclówka	Żydaczów	Żydaczów
Korniaktów	Łańcut	Żolynia
Kornice	Mościska	Mościska
Kornicz	Kołomea	Kołomea
Kornie	Rawa Ruska	Lubycza
Korniów	Horodenka	Czernelica
Korolówka	Tłumacz	Tłumacz
Korolówka	Zaleszczyki	Korolówka
Koropiec	Buczacz	Potok

Town	Main District	Subdistrict
Koropuz	Rudki	Komarno
Korościatyn	Buczacz	Monasterzyska
Korostów	Stryj	Skole
Korostowice	Rohatyń	Bursztyn
Korsów	Brody	Leszniów
Korszów	Kołomea	Kołomea
Korszyłów	Złoczów	Zborów
Korzelice	Przemyślany	Przemyślany
Korzelów	Żólkiew	Kulików
Korzenica	Jarosław	Radymno
Korzeniec	Bircza	Bircza
Korzenna	Grybów	Grybów
Korzowa	Podhajce	Zawałów
Korzuchów	Jasło	Frysztak
Korzuchów	Ropczyce	Wielopole
Kościaszyn	Sokal	Warez
Kościejów	Lemberg	Zniesienie
Kościelec	Chrzanów	Chrzanów
Kościelisko	Nowy Targ	Nowy Targ
Kościelniki	Buczacz	Potok
Kościelniki	Rudki	Rudki
Kościelniki	Zaleszczyki	Gródek
Kosina	Łańcut	Przewórsk
Kosmacz	Borhodczany	Sołotwina
Kosmacz	Kossów	Pistyn
Kośmierzyn	Buczacz	Potok
Kosowa	Wadowice	Zator
Kosowice	Gródek	Gródek
Kosowy	Kolbuszowa	Kolbuszowa
Kossocice	Wieliczka	Klasno
Kossów	Czortków	Budzanów
Kossów	Kossów	Kossów

Town	Main District	Subdistrict
Kossów Stary	Kossów	Kossów
Kostarowce	Sanok	Sanok
Kostenjów	Przemyślany	Przemyślany
Kostrza	Limanowa	Limanowa
Kostrze	Wieliczka	Podgórze
Koszarawa	Żywiec	Zabłocie
Koszary	Limanowa	Limanowa
Kosztowa	Brzozów	Dynów
Koszyce Małe	Tarnów	Tarnów
Koszyce Wielkie	Tarnów	Tarnów
Koszyłowce	Czortków	Jagielnica
Kotań	Krosno	Dukla
Kotiatycze	Kalusz	Kalusz
Kotoryny	Żydaczów	Żurawno
Kotów	Bircza	Bircza
Kotów	Brzeżany	Brzeżany
Kotów	Nowy Sącz	Łabowa
Kotowania	Sambor	Sambor
Kotówka	Husiatyn	Kopyczyńce
Kotuzów	Podhajce	Podhajce
Kowalówka	Buczacz	Monasterzyska
Kowalówka	Kołomea	Jabłonów
Kowalowy	Jasło	Jasło
Kowalowy Dolne	Tarnów	Ryglice
Kowalowy Górne	Tarnów	Ryglice
Kowenice	Sambor	Sambor
Kozaczówka	Borszczów	Mielnica
Kozaczyzna	Borszczów	Borszczów
Kozakowa Góra	Złoczów	Złoczów
Kozara	Rohatyń	Bursztyn
Koziarnia	Nisko	Rudnik
Koziary	Tarnobrzeg	Rozwadów

Town	Main District	Subdistrict
Kozice	Lemberg	Zniesienie
Koziekie	Bircza	Rybotycze
Kozielniki	Lemberg	Winniki
Kozina	Stanisławów	Halicz
Kozina mit Bilka	Skałat	Touste
Koziowa	Stryj	Skole
Kozipice	Wadowice	Wadowice
Kozłów	Brzeżany	Kozłów
Kozłów	Dąbrowa	Dąbrowa
Kozłów	Kam. Strumiłowa	Busk
Kozłówek	Jasło	Frysztak
Kożmice Małe	Wieliczka	Klasno
Kożmice Wielkie	Wieliczka	Klasno
Kozodrza	Ropczyce	Ropczyce
Kozowa	Brzeżany	Kozowa
Kozówka	Brzeżany	Kozowa
Kozówka	Tarnopol	Mikulińce
Kożuszne ad Wysocz	Sanok	Bukowsko
Kozy	Biała	Lipnik
Krajna	Bircza	Rybotycze
Krajowice	Jasło	Jasło
Kraków	Kraków	Kraków
Krakowice	Borhodczany	Solotwina
Krakówiec	Jaworów	Krakówiec
Krakuszowice	Wieliczka	Klasno
Kramarzówka	Jarosław	Pruchnik
Kranszów	Nowy Targ	Nowy Targ
Kranzberg	Sambor	Sambor
Krasice	Przemyśl	Krzywcza
Krasiczyn	Przemyśl	Krzywcza
Krasiczyn	Żólkiew	Kulików
Krasiejów	Buczacz	Monasterzyska

Town	Main District	Subdistrict
Krasiełówka	Tłumacz	Ottynia
Krasna	Brzeżany	Kozłów
Krasna	Kalusz	Kalusz
Krasna	Krosno	Korczyna
Krasna	Nadwórna	Nadwórna
Krasne	Limanowa	Limanowa
Krasne	Rzeszów	Rzeszów
Krasne	Skałat	Touste
Krasne Potockie	Nowy Sącz	Nowy Sącz
Krasno	Jarosław	Sienawa
Krasnoila	Kossów	Żabie
Krasnopuszcza	Przemyślany	Dunajowce
Krasnosielce	Złoczów	Pomorzany
Krasnosielce	Złoczów	Złoczów
Krasów	Lemberg	Szczerzec
Krasówka	Tarnopol	Tarnopol
Krawce	Tarnobrzeg	Rozwadów
Krechów	Żólkiew	Żólkiew
Krechów	Żydaczów	Żurawno
Krechowce	Stanisławów	Stanisławów
Krechowice	Dolina	Rożniatów
Krecilów	Skałat	Touste
Kreców	Bircza	Bircza
Krempna	Krosno	Dukla
Kreszów	Żywiec	Zabłocie
Krogulce	Husiatyn	Kopyczyńce
Królik Polski	Sanok	Rymanów
Królik Wołoski	Sanok	Rymanów
Krolówka	Bochnia	Wiśnicz Nowy
Kropielniki	Rudki	Rudki
Kropiwinik Nowy	Drohobycz	Borysław
Kropiwinik Stary	Drohobycz	Borysław

Town	Main District	Subdistrict
Kropiwiszcze	Kołomea	Kołomea
Kropiwna	Złoczów	Gologory
Kropiwnik	Kalusz	Kalusz
Kropwinik	Bircza	Dobromil
Krościenko	Lisko	Ustrzyki Dolne
Krościenko	Nowy Targ	Krościenko
Krościenko Niżne	Krosno	Korczyna
Krościenko Wyżne	Krosno	Korczyna
Krosienice	Przemyśl	Przemyśl
Krośna	Limanowa	Limanowa
Krośnica	Nowy Targ	Nowy Targ
Krosno	Krosno	Dukla
Krotoszyn	Lemberg	Nawarya
Krowica Lasowa	Cieszanów	Lubaczów
Krowica Sama	Cieszanów	Lubaczów
Krowice	Tarnopol	Tarnopol
Krowinka	Trembowla	Trembowla
Krowniki	Przemyśl	Przemyśl
Kruhel	Przemyśl	Przemyśl
Kruhel Pawłosiowski	Jarosław	Jarosław
Kruki	Biała	Oświęcim
Krukienice	Mościska	Mościska
Krulin	Mościska	Sądowa Wisznia
Krupsko	Żydaczów	Rozdól
Kruszelnica	Stryj	Skole
Krużlowa Niżna	Grybów	Grybów
Krużlowa Polska	Grybów	Grybów
Krużlowa Ruska	Grybów	Grybów
Krużlowa Wyżna	Grybów	Grybów
Krużyki	Sambor	Sambor
Kryczka	Borhodczany	Sołotwina
Kryg	Gorlice	Gorlice

Town	Main District	Subdistrict
Kryłos	Stanisławów	Halicz
Krynica	Drohobycz	Drohobycz
Krynica	Nowy Sącz	Krynica
Krysowice	Mościska	Mościska
Krystynopol	Sokal	Krystynopol
Krywa	Gorlice	Gorlice
Krywe	Lisko	Baligród
Krywe bei Tworylne	Lisko	Lutowiska
Krywka	Lisko	Lutowiska
Kryzywołuka	Czortków	Jagielnica
Krzadka	Tarnobrzeg	Tarnobrzeg
Krzęcin	Wadowice	Zator
Krzeczkowa	Przemyśl	Przemyśl
Krzeczów	Bochnia	Bochnia
Krzeczów	Myślenice	Jordanów
Krzeczowice	Łańcut	Kańczuga
Krzemienica	Łańcut	Łańcut
Krzemienica	Mielec	Mielec
Krzesławice	Wieliczka	Klasno
Krzeszowice	Chrzanów	Trzebina
Krzewica	Rawa Ruska	Uhnów
Krzezoniów	Myślenice	Myślenice
Krzyszkowice	Myślenice	Myślenice
Krzyszkowice	Wieliczka	Klasno
Krzywa Rzeka	Wieliczka	Klasno
Krzywaczka	Myślenice	Myślenice
Krzywcza	Przemyśl	Krzywcza
Krzywcze	Borszczów	Mielnica
Krzywcze Dolne	Borszczów	Mielnica
Krzywcze Górne	Borszczów	Mielnica
Krzywczyce	Lemberg	Zniesienie
Krzywe	Bircza	Rybotycze

Town	Main District	Subdistrict
Krzywe	Brzeżany	Kozowa
Krzywe	Brzozów	Brzozów
Krzywe	Cieszanów	Cieszanów
Krzywe	Kam. Strumiłowa	Radziechów
Krzywe	Skałat	Skałat
Krzywenkie	Husiatyn	Probużna
Krzywice	Borhodczany	Sołotwina
Krzywice	Borhodczany	Sołotwina
Krzywice	Przemyślany	Gliniany
Krzywiecka Wola	Przemyśl	Krzywcza
Krzywki	Tarnopol	Mikulińce
Krzyworównia	Kossów	Żabie
Krzywotuly Nowe	Tłumacz	Ottynia
Krzywotuly Stare	Tłumacz	Ottynia
Krzywulanka	Kam. Strumiłowa	Kam. Strumiłowa
Krzyż	Tarnów	Tarnów
Krzyżanowice	Bochnia	Bochnia
Krzyżowa	Żywiec	Zabłocie
Krzyżówka	Nowy Sącz	Łabowa
Książnice	Bochnia	Bochnia
Księczy Most	Mościska	Sądowa Wisznia
Księże Kolano	Tarnobrzeg	Rozwadów
Księżnice	Mielec	Radomyśl Wiel.
Kuczwice	Lisko	Baligród
Kudobińce	Złoczów	Zborów
Kudryńce Dolne	Borszczów	Mielnica
Kudryńce Górne	Borszczów	Mielnica
Kudynowce	Złoczów	Zborów
Kuhajów	Lemberg	Nawarya
Kujdance	Kołomea	Kołomea
Kujdanów	Buczacz	Buczacz
Kukizów	Lemberg	Jaryczów

Town	Main District	Subdistrict
Kuków	Żywiec	Zabłocie
Kułaczkowce	Kołomea	Gwozdźiec
Kułaczyn	Śniatyn	Śniatyn
Kułakowce	Zaleszczyki	Gródek
Kulaszne	Sanok	Bukowsko
Kulawa	Żólkiew	Żólkiew
Kulczyce	Sambor	Sambor
Kulerzów	Wieliczka	Podgórze
Kuliczków	Sokal	Bełż
Kulików	Kam. Strumiłowa	Radziechów
Kulików	Żólkiew	Kulików
Kulmatycze	Mościska	Sądowa Wisznia
Kulparków	Lemberg	Zniesienie
Kulyska	Tłumacz	Niźniów
Kunaszów	Rohatyń	Bursztyn
Kunice	Wieliczka	Klasno
Kunicze	Rohatyń	Bursztyn
Kunin	Żólkiew	Żólkiew
Kunina	Nowy Sącz	Łabowa
Kunisowce	Horodenka	Czernelica
Kunkowa	Gorlice	Gorlice
Kunkowce	Przemyśl	Przemyśl
Kunowa	Jasło	Jasło
Kupcze	Kam. Strumiłowa	Busk
Kupczynce	Tarnopol	Tarnopol
Kupiatycze	Przemyśl	Niżankowice
Kupiczwola	Żólkiew	Gross-Mosty
Kupienin	Dąbrowa	Dąbrowa
Kupna	Przemyśl	Krzywcza
Kupno	Kolbuszowa	Kolbuszowa
Kupno	Rzeszów	Głogów
Kupnowice Nowy	Rudki	Rudki

Town	Main District	Subdistrict
Kupnowice Stary	Rudki	Rudki
Kurdwanówka	Buczacz	Buczacz
Kurmanice	Przemyśl	Niżankowice
Kurniki	Jaworów	Jaworów
Kurniki Szlacheckie	Tarnopol	Tarnopol
Kuropatniki	Brzeżany	Brzeżany
Kuropatniki	Rohatyń	Bursztyn
Kurów	Bochnia	Wiśnicz Nowy
Kurów	Nowy Sącz	Nowy Sącz
Kurów	Żywiec	Zabłocie
Kurowce	Tarnopol	Tarnopol
Kurowice	Przemyślany	Gliniany
Kurwanów Dolny	Wieliczka	Podgórze
Kurwanów Górny	Wieliczka	Podgórze
Kuryłówka	Łańcut	Leżajsk
Kurypów	Stanisławów	Halicz
Kurzany	Brzeżany	Brzeżany
Kurzyna Mała	Nisko	Ulanów
Kurzyna Wielka	Nisko	Ulanów
Kustyn	Brody	Szczurowice
Kutce	Rohatyń	Rohatyń
Kutenberg	Jaworów	Jaworów
Kutkowce	Tarnopol	Tarnopol
Kuty	Kossów	Kuty
Kuty Stare	Kossów	Kuty
Kutyly	Nisko	Ulanów
Kutyszcze	Brody	Podkamień
Kuywa	Ropczyce	Sędziszów
Kuzie	Dąbrowa	Dąbrowa
Kuźmina	Bircza	Bircza
Kwaczała	Chrzanów	Chrzanów
Kwapinka	Wieliczka	Klasno

Town	Main District	Subdistrict
Kwaszenina	Bircza	Dobromil
Kwiatoń	Gorlice	Gorlice
Kwiatonowice	Gorlice	Gorlice
Kwików	Brzesko	Szczurowa
Łabacz	Brody	Sokołówka
Łabajka	Rzeszów	Głogów
Łabowa	Nowy Sącz	Łabowa
Łabowice	Nowy Sącz	Łabowa
Lachawa	Bircza	Bircza
Lachowce	Bohordczany	Bohordczany
Lachowice	Żywiec	Zabłocie
Lachowice Podróżne	Żydaczów	Żurawno
Lachowice Zarzeczne	Żydaczów	Żurawno
Lacka Wola	Mościska	Mościska
Lackie Małe	Złoczów	Złoczów
Lackie Wielkie	Złoczów	Złoczów
Łącko	Bircza	Dobromil
Łącko	Nowy Sącz	Łącko
Łaczany	Wadowice	Zator
Łaczki	Jasło	Frysztak
Łaczki	Lisko	Lisko
Łaczki	Nowy Sącz	Łącko
Łaczki	Ropczyce	Ropczyce
Ładyczyn	Tarnopol	Mikulińce
Ładzin	Sanok	Rymanów
Ladzkie	Tłumacz	Tyśmienica
Ladzkie	Tłumacz	Uście Zielone
Laeniowa	Brzesko	Czchów
Łagiewniki	Wieliczka	Podgórze
Łahodów	Brody	Brody
Łahodów	Przemyślany	Gliniany
Łąka	Sambor	Sambor

Town	Main District	Subdistrict
Ląkta Dolna	Bochnia	Wiśnicz Nowy
Ląkta Górna	Bochnia	Wiśnicz Nowy
Lalin	Sanok	Sanok
Lamna	Bochnia	Wiśnicz Nowy
Lanckrona	Wadowice	Kalwarya
Łańcut	Łańcut	Łańcut
Łańczówka	Kam. Strumiłowa	Busk
Łanczyn	Nadwórna	Lanczyn
Landestreu	Kalusz	Kalusz
Lanowce	Borszczów	Borszczów
Lanowice	Sambor	Sambor
Łany	Lemberg	Szczerzec
Łany Niemieckie	Kam. Strumiłowa	Kam. Strumiłowa
Łany Polskie	Kam. Strumiłowa	Kam. Strumiłowa
Łany Sokołówskie	Stryj	Stryj
Łapajówka	Jarosław	Jarosław
Łapajówka	Kam. Strumiłowa	Kam. Strumiłowa
Łapanów	Bochnia	Wiśnicz Nowy
Łapczyca	Bochnia	Bochnia
Łapiszów	Tarnobrzeg	Rozwadów
Łapszyn	Bóbrka	Chodorów
Łapszyn	Brzeżany	Brzeżany
Las	Żywiec	Zabłocie
Lasek	Nowy Targ	Nowy Targ
Laski	Jasło	Jasło
Laski	Nisko	Nisko
Laskowa	Limanowa	Limanowa
Laskowa	Wadowice	Zator
Laskowce	Czortków	Budzanów
Laskówka Delastowska	Dąbrowa	Szczucin
Lasocice	Limanowa	Limanowa

Town	Main District	Subdistrict
Lasosina	Limanowa	Limanowa
Lastówki	Drohobycz	Borysław
Laszczyny	Łańcut	Żolynia
Laszki	Jarosław	Radymno
Laszki	Jaworów	Jaworów
Laszki Dolne	Bóbrka	Brzozdowiec
Laszki Górne	Bóbrka	Brzozdowiec
Laszki Gościńcowe	Mościska	Mościska
Laszki Król.	Przemyślany	Gliniany
Laszki Murowane	Lemberg	Zniesienie
Laszki Murowane	Staremiasto	Starasól
Laszki Zawiązane	Rudki	Rudki
Laszków	Brody	Szczurowice
Latacz	Zaleszczyki	Uścieczko
Łatkowce	Borszczów	Mielnica
Łatoszyn	Pilzno	Dębica
Ławoczne	Stryj	Skole
Ławrów	Staremiasto	Staremiasto
Ławryków	Rawa Ruska	Magierów
Ławrykowce	Złoczów	Zborów
Łazany	Wieliczka	Klasno
Łazarówka	Buczacz	Monasterzyska
Łazek	Tarnobrzeg	Radomyśl
Łazy	Biała	Oświęcim
Łazy	Bochnia	Wiśnicz Nowy
Łazy	Jarosław	Radymno
Łazy	Nowy Sącz	Łącko
Łazy Biegonickie	Nowy Sącz	Stary Sącz
Łazy Dębowieckie	Jasło	Jasło
Łdziany	Kalusz	Kalusz
Lecka	Rzeszów	Tyczyn
Lecówka	Dolina	Rożniatów

Town	Main District	Subdistrict
Lednica Górna	Wieliczka	Klasno
Lednica Niemicka	Wieliczka	Klasno
Łęg	Nowy Sącz	Łabowa
Łęgów	Żółkiew	Gross-Mosty
Łęka	Nowy Sącz	Nowy Sącz
Łęka Siedl.	Tarnów	Zabno
Łęka Szczucińka	Dąbrowa	Szczucin
Łęka Żabiecka	Dąbrowa	Szczucin
Łękawica	Tarnów	Tarnów
Łękawica	Wadowice	Wadowice
Łękawica	Żywiec	Zabłocie
Łękawka	Tarnów	Tuchów
Łęki	Biała	Kęty
Łęki	Brzesko	Brzesko
Łęki	Jasło	Frysztak
Łęki	Krosno	Dukla
Łęki	Nowy Sącz	Nowy Sącz
Łęki Dolne	Pilzno	Pilzno
Łęki Górne	Pilzno	Pilzno
Leksandrowa	Bochnia	Wiśnicz Nowy
Lelechówka	Gródek	Janów
Leluchów	Nowy Sącz	Muszyna
Lemberg	Lemberg	Lemberg
Lencze Górne	Wadowice	Kalwarya
Lenina Mała	Staremiasto	Staremiasto
Lenina Wielka	Staremiasto	Staremiasto
Lepina	Żółkiew	Żółkiew
Lepnica	Pilzno	Dębica
Lesieczniki	Zaleszczyki	Zaleszczyki
Lesienice	Lemberg	Winniki
Lesna	Żywiec	Zabłocie
Leśnica	Nowy Targ	Nowy Targ

Town	Main District	Subdistrict
Leśnica	Wadowice	Kalwarya
Leśniki	Brzeżany	Brzeżany
Leśniowice	Gródek	Janów
Leśniowice	Lemberg	Nawarya
Leśniówka	Krosno	Dukla
Leszczańce	Buczacz	Buczacz
Leszczatów	Sokal	Tartaków
Leszczawa Dolna	Bircza	Bircza
Leszczawa Górna	Bircza	Bircza
Leszczawka	Bircza	Bircza
Leszcze	Ropczyce	Ropczyce
Leszczków	Sokal	Warez
Leszczowate	Lisko	Ustrzyki Dolne
Leszczyn	Bóbrka	Strzeliska Nowe
Leszczyna	Bochnia	Wiśnicz Nowy
Leszczyny	Bircza	Rybotycze
Leszczyny	Gorlice	Gorlice
Leszkowice	Bochnia	Bochnia
Leszniów	Brody	Leszniów
Letnia	Drohobycz	Drohobycz
Lętowe	Limanowa	Mszana dolna
Lętowica	Brzesko	Wojnicz
Łętowina	Nisko	Rudnik
Łętownia	Myślenice	Jordanów
Łętownia	Przemyśl	Przemyśl
Łętownia	Rzeszów	Strzyżów
Lewniowa	Brzesko	Brzesko
Leżachów	Jarosław	Sienawa
Leżajsk	Łańcut	Leżajsk
Leżanówka	Skałat	Grzymałów
Lężany	Krosno	Dukla
Lężawa	Zaleszczyki	Zaleszczyki

Town	Main District	Subdistrict
Lgota	Chrzanów	Trzebina
Lgota	Wadowice	Zator
Libertów	Wieliczka	Podgórze
Libiąż Mały	Chrzanów	Chrzanów
Libiąż Wielki	Chrzanów	Chrzanów
Libochowa	Stryj	Skole
Librantowa	Nowy Sącz	Nowy Sącz
Libuchowa	Staremiasto	Chyrów
Libusza	Gorlice	Gorlice
Lichwin	Tarnów	Tuchów
Liczkowce	Husiatyn	Husiatyn
Limanowa	Limanowa	Limanowa
Lindenfeld	Lemberg	Szczerzec
Lipa	Bircza	Bircza
Lipa	Dolina	Bolechów
Lipiatyn	Brzeżany	Brzeżany
Lipica Górna	Rohatyń	Rohatyń
Lipice	Drohobycz	Drohobycz
Lipie	Limanowa	Limanowa
Lipie	Nowy Sącz	Nowy Sącz
Lipie	Rzeszów	Głogów
Lipinki	Gorlice	Gorlice
Lipiny	Dąbrowa	Dąbrowa
Lipiny	Pilzno	Pilzno
Liplas	Wieliczka	Klasno
Lipna	Gorlice	Gorlice
Lipnia Dolna	Bochnia	Wiśnicz Nowy
Lipnia Górna	Bochnia	Wiśnicz Nowy
Lipnica	Kolbuszowa	Raniżów
Lipnica	Rzeszów	Głogów
Lipnica Dolna	Pilzno	Jodłowa
Lipnica Dolna	Rohatyń	Bursztyn

Town	Main District	Subdistrict
Lipnica Górna	Jasło	Jasło
Lipnica Murowana	Bochnia	Wiśnicz Nowy
Lipnica Wielka	Nowy Sącz	Nowy Sącz
Lipnik	Biała	Lipnik
Lipnik	Wieliczka	Klasno
Lipniki	Mościska	Mościska
Lipowa	Wadowice	Zator
Lipowa	Żywiec	Zabłocie
Lipowce	Limanowa	Limanowa
Lipowce	Przemyślany	Gliniany
Lipowce	Złoczów	Gologory
Lipowica	Krosno	Dukla
Lipowice	Cieszanów	Lubaczów
Lipowice	Dolina	Dolina
Lipowice	Sanok	Rymanów
Lipowiec	Drohobycz	Drohobycz
Lipsko	Cieszanów	Lipsko
Lisia Góra	Tarnów	Tarnów
Lisiatycze	Stryj	Stryj
Lisiejamy	Cieszanów	Lubaczów
Liski	Kołomea	Kołomea
Liski	Sokal	Warez
Lisko	Kam. Strumiłowa	Busk
Lisko	Lisko	Lisko
Liskowate	Bircza	Dobromil
Lisów	Jasło	Jasło
Lisowce	Zaleszczyki	Tłuste
Lisowice	Dolina	Bolechów
Liszna	Lisko	Baligród
Liszna	Sanok	Sanok
Lisznia	Drohobycz	Drohobycz
Litewska	Rudki	Komarno

Town	Main District	Subdistrict
Litowisko	Brody	Podkamień
Litwina	Podhajce	Podhajce
Litynia	Drohobycz	Drohobycz
Liwcze	Sokal	Warez
Łobozew	Lisko	Ustrzyki Dolne
Łodygowice	Biała	Lipnik
Łodyna	Lisko	Ustrzyki Dolne
Łodzina	Bircza	Bircza
Łodzinka Dolna	Bircza	Rybotycze
Łodzinka Górna	Bircza	Bircza
Łojowa	Nadwórna	Delatyn
Lokutki	Tłumacz	Tłumacz
Lolin	Dolina	Dolina
Łomna	Bircza	Rybotycze
Łomnica	Nowy Sącz	Piwniczna
Łonie	Przemyślany	Gliniany
Łonie	Złoczów	Gologory
Łoniowy	Brzesko	Brzesko
Łopianka	Dolina	Dolina
Łopienka	Lisko	Baligród
Łopoń	Brzesko	Wojnicz
Łopuchowa	Ropczyce	Ropczyce
Łopuszanka	Bircza	Dobromil
Łopuszanka Chomina	Staremiasto	Staremiasto
Łopuszany	Złoczów	Zborów
Łopuszka Mała	Łańcut	Kańczuga
Łopuszka Wielka	Łańcut	Kańczuga
Łopuszna	Nowy Targ	Nowy Targ
Łopuszna	Rohatyń	Rohatyń
Łopuszna	Sambor	Sambor
Łopusznica	Bircza	Dobromil
Łosiacz	Borszczów	Skała

Town	Main District	Subdistrict
Łosie	Gorlice	Gorlice
Łosie	Nowy Sącz	Łabowa
Lososina Dolna	Nowy Sącz	Nowy Sącz
Lostówka	Limanowa	Mszana dolna
Loszniów	Trembowla	Trembowla
Lotatniki	Stryj	Stryj
Łowce	Jarosław	Radymno
Łowcza	Cieszanów	Cieszanów
Łowczów	Tarnów	Tuchów
Łowczowek	Tarnów	Tuchów
Łowczyce	Rudki	Komarno
Łowczyce	Żydaczów	Żurawno
Łowisko	Nisko	Rudnik
Łozina	Gródek	Janów
Łozowa	Tarnopol	Tarnopol
Łozówka	Trembowla	Trembowla
Luasz	Dąbrowa	Szczucin
Lubaczów	Cieszanów	Lubaczów
Lubanowa	Tarnów	Tuchów
Lubatowa	Krosno	Dukla
Lubatówka	Krosno	Dukla
Lubcza	Pilzno	Pilzno
Lubcza	Tarnów	Tarnów
Lubella	Żólkiew	Żólkiew
Lubenia	Rzeszów	Tyczyn
Lubeszka	Bóbrka	Strzeliska Nowe
Lubiana	Lemberg	Szczerzec
Lubianka	Lemberg	Szczerzec
Lubień	Myślenice	Jordanów
Lubień Mały	Gródek	Gródek
Lubień Wielki	Gródek	Gródek
Lubieńce	Stryj	Stryj

Town	Main District	Subdistrict
Lubienie	Jaworów	Krakówiec
Lubinka	Tarnów	Tarnów
Lubkowce	Śniatyn	Zabłotów
Lubla	Jasło	Frysztak
Lublica	Jasło	Frysztak
Lublinec Nowy	Cieszanów	Cieszanów
Lublinec Stary	Cieszanów	Cieszanów
Łubne	Lisko	Baligród
Łubno	Brzozów	Dynów
Lubomierz	Bochnia	Wiśnicz Nowy
Lubomierz	Limanowa	Mszana dolna
Łubów	Sokal	Warez
Lubsza	Rohatyń	Rohatyń
Lubsza	Żydaczów	Żurawno
Lubycza	Rawa Ruska	Lubycza
Lubycza Kniazie	Rawa Ruska	Lubycza
Lubzina	Ropczyce	Ropczyce
Luczany	Bóbrka	Strzeliska Nowe
Lucze	Kołomea	Jabłonów
Łuczka	Tarnopol	Mikulińce
Łuczki	Kołomea	Jabłonów
Lucznikowice	Biała	Oświęcim
Luczyce	Przemyśl	Przemyśl
Luczyńce	Rohatyń	Rohatyń
Ludwikówka	Dolina	Dolina
Ludwikówka	Rohatyń	Bursztyn
Ludwikówka	Tarnopol	Mikulińce
Ludwinów	Wieliczka	Podgórze
Ludzimierz	Nowy Targ	Nowy Targ
Ług	Gorlice	Gorlice
Łuh	Lisko	Baligród
Łuh	Nadwórna	Delatyn

Town	Main District	Subdistrict
Łuhy	Dolina	Rożniatów
Łuka	Horodenka	Obertyn
Łuka	Kalusz	Wojniłów
Łuka	Tłumacz	Uście Zielone
Łuka	Złoczów	Złoczów
Łuka Mała	Skałat	Tarnoruda
Łukanowice	Brzesko	Wojnicz
Łukawica	Cieszanów	Lipsko
Łukawica	Limanowa	Limanowa
Łukawica	Lisko	Lisko
Łukawica Niżna	Stryj	Stryj
Łukawica Wyżna	Stryj	Stryj
Łukawice	Brody	Podkamień
Łukawice	Cieszanów	Lubaczów
Łukowa	Nisko	Rudnik
Łukowa	Tarnów	Zabno
Łukowe	Lisko	Lisko
Łukówka	Brzesko	Czchów
Łupków	Lisko	Wola Michowa
Lupuszna	Bóbrka	Bóbrka
Lusina	Wieliczka	Podgórze
Lusławice	Brzesko	Czchów
Lusławiczki	Brzesko	Czchów
Luszowice	Chrzanów	Chrzanów
Luszowice	Dąbrowa	Dąbrowa
Lutcza	Brzozów	Jasienica
Lutera	Rzeszów	Strzyżów
Lutków	Jarosław	Radymno
Lutków	Mościska	Hussaków
Lutoryż	Rzeszów	Tyczyn
Lutowiska	Lisko	Lutowiska
Lutowiska	Sambor	Sambor

Town	Main District	Subdistrict
Lużek Górny	Staremiasto	Staremiasto
Lużki	Dolina	Bolechów
Lużna	Gorlice	Gorlice
Lyczana	Nowy Sącz	Nowy Sącz
Lyczanka	Nowy Sącz	Nowy Sącz
Łysa	Podhajce	Podhajce
Łysa Góra	Brzesko	Wojnicz
Łysa Góra	Krosno	Dukla
Łysaków	Mielec	Radomyśl Wiel.
Łysakowek	Mielec	Radomyśl Wiel.
Łysiec	Bohordczany	Lysiec
Łysiec Stary	Bohordczany	Lysiec
Łysina	Żywiec	Zabłocie
Łysków	Żydaczów	Żurawno
Łysokanie	Bochnia	Bochnia
Łyszanka	Wieliczka	Klasno
Machlinice	Stryj	Stryj
Machnów	Rawa Ruska	Uhnów
Machnowek	Sokal	Bełż
Machnówka	Krosno	Dukla
Machów	Tarnobrzeg	Tarnobrzeg
Machowa	Pilzno	Pilzno
Maciejowa	Nowy Sącz	Łabowa
Macoszyn	Żólkiew	Żólkiew
Mądrzelówka	Podhajce	Podhajce
Madziarki	Sokal	Krystynopol
Magdalówka	Tarnopol	Tarnopol
Magierów	Rawa Ruska	Magierów
Majdan	Drohobycz	Borysław
Majdan	Gródek	Janów
Majdan	Husiatyn	Kopyczyńce
Majdan	Kalusz	Kalusz

Town	Main District	Subdistrict
Majdan	Kolbuszowa	Majdan
Majdan	Złoczów	Sassów
Majdan	Żólkiew	Żólkiew
Majdan Gołogórski	Złoczów	Gologory
Majdan Górny	Nadwórna	Nadwórna
Majdan Jarosinki	Nisko	Ulanów
Majdan Lipowiecki	Przemyślany	Gliniany
Majdan Nowy	Kam. Strumiłowa	Radziechów
Majdan Pieniacki	Brody	Podkamień
Majdan Sienawski	Jarosław	Sienawa
Majdan Stary	Kam. Strumiłowa	Radziechów
Majdan Zbytniowski	Tarnobrzeg	Rozwadów
Majkowice	Bochnia	Bochnia
Majnicz	Sambor	Sambor
Majscowa	Jasło	Jasło
Maków	Myślenice	Maków
Makowa Kolonia	Bircza	Rybotycze
Makowa Nat.	Bircza	Rybotycze
Makowica	Limanowa	Limanowa
Maksymówka	Dolina	Dolina
Makuniów	Mościska	Sądowa Wisznia
Makwiska	Krosno	Dukla
Makwisko	Jarosław	Jarosław
Mała Niedźwiada	Ropczyce	Ropczyce
Mała Wieś	Nowy Sącz	Nowy Sącz
Mała Wieś	Wieliczka	Klasno
Małastów	Gorlice	Gorlice
Małaszowce	Tarnopol	Tarnopol
Maława	Bircza	Bircza
Maława	Rzeszów	Rzeszów
Maławka	Rzeszów	Niebylec
Malce	Biała	Kęty

Town	Main District	Subdistrict
Malczkowice	Lemberg	Nawarya
Malczyce	Gródek	Janów
Malechów	Lemberg	Zniesienie
Malechów	Żydaczów	Rozdól
Malejowa	Myślenice	Jordanów
Maleniska	Brody	Podkamień
Malhowice	Przemyśl	Niżankowice
Malinie	Mielec	Mielec
Malinówka	Brzozów	Jasienica
Malinowska	Lemberg	Nawarya
Małkowice	Gródek	Gródek
Małkowice	Przemyśl	Przemyśl
Malonowy	Podhajce	Podhajce
Maloszowice	Lemberg	Nawarya
Małów	Trembowla	Trembowla
Małpa	Rudki	Komarno
Małyrówka	Rzeszów	Tyczyn
Manajów	Złoczów	Zborów
Manaster Derczycki	Drohobycz	Drohobycz
Manaster Liszniański	Drohobycz	Drohobycz
Manasterce	Żydaczów	Żurawno
Manasterczany	Borhodczany	Sołotwina
Manasterek	Kam. Strumiłowa	Radziechów
Manasterek	Rawa Ruska	Magierów
Manasterek	Zaleszczyki	Korolówka
Manastersko	Kossów	Kossów
Manasterz	Lancut	Kanczuga
Manasterz	Jarosław	Sienawa
Manasterzec	Lisko	Lisko
Manasterzec	Sambor	Sambor
Manasterzec	Stryj	Stryj
Manastyrek	Brody	Stanisławczyk

Town	Main District	Subdistrict
Maniawa	Borhodczany	Sołotwina
Maniów	Dąbrowa	Szczucin
Maniów	Lisko	Wola Michowa
Maniowy	Nowy Targ	Nowy Targ
Marcinkowice	Brzesko	Radlów
Marcinkowice	Nowy Sącz	Nowy Sącz
Marcówka	Wadowice	Wadowice
Marcyporęba	Wadowice	Zator
Marjanka	Tarnopol	Tarnopol
Marjnka	Żydaczów	Żurawno
Marki	Tarnobrzeg	Baranów
Markopol	Brody	Podkamień
Markowa	Borhodczany	Sołotwina
Markowa	Kołomea	Peczeniżyn
Markowa	Łańcut	Łańcut
Markowa	Podhajce	Zawałów
Markowce	Sanok	Sanok
Markowce	Tłumacz	Tyśmienica
Markowizna	Kolbuszowa	Sokołów
Markuszowa	Limanowa	Limanowa
Marnszyna	Nowy Targ	Nowy Targ
Marszowice	Wieliczka	Klasno
Martynów Nowy	Rohatyń	Bursztyn
Martynów Stary	Rohatyń	Bursztyn
Maruszowa	Jasło	Frysztak
Maryampol	Stanisławów	Maryampol
Maszkienice	Brzesko	Brzesko
Maszkowice	Nowy Sącz	Łącko
Matejowce	Kołomea	Kołomea
Mateuszówka	Buczacz	Buczacz
Maxymowice	Sambor	Sambor
Maziarnia	Kam. Strumiłowa	Busk

Town	Main District	Subdistrict
Maziarnia	Nisko	Nisko
Mazurówka	Skałat	Grzymałów
Mazurówka	Żydaczów	Żurawno
Mazury	Kolbuszowa	Sokołów
Mchawa	Lisko	Baligród
Mechowiec	Kolbuszowa	Kolbuszowa
Męcina Mała	Gorlice	Gorlice
Męcina Wielka	Gorlice	Gorlice
Męcinka	Krosno	Dukla
Medenice	Drohobycz	Drohobycz
Medewa	Brzeżany	Kozowa
Mędrzechów	Dąbrowa	Dąbrowa
Meducha	Rohatyń	Bursztyn
Medwedowce	Buczacz	Buczacz
Medyka	Przemyśl	Przemyśl
Medyń	Zbaraz	Zbaraz
Medynia	Kalusz	Wojniłów
Medynia	Rzeszów	Głogów
Medynia Głogówska	Łańcut	Łańcut
Medynia Łańcucka	Łańcut	Łańcut
Mełna	Rohatyń	Rohatyń
Melsztyn	Brzesko	Czchów
Mertawa	Borszczów	Borszczów
Meszna	Biała	Lipnik
Meszna Opacka	Tarnów	Tuchów
Meszna Szlachecka	Tarnów	Tuchów
Meteniów	Złoczów	Zborów
Mętków Mały	Chrzanów	Chrzanów
Mętków Wielki	Chrzanów	Chrzanów
Mianowice	Sokal	Warez
Michalcze	Horodenka	Horodenka
Michalczowa	Nowy Sącz	Nowy Sącz

Town	Main District	Subdistrict
Michalewica	Mościska	Sądowa Wisznia
Michalewice	Rudki	Rudki
Michałków	Borszczów	Mielnica
Michałków	Kołomea	Kołomea
Michałowice	Drohobycz	Drohobycz
Michałówka	Borszczów	Mielnica
Michałówka	Podhajce	Podhajce
Michałówka	Rawa Ruska	Uhnów
Michowa	Bircza	Dobromil
Mickinia	Chrzanów	Trzebina
Miechocin	Tarnobrzeg	Tarnobrzeg
Międzybrody	Stryj	Skole
Międzybrodzie	Sanok	Sanok
Międzybrodzie	Żywiec	Zabłocie
Międzybrodzie Kob.	Biała	Kęty
Międzybrodzie Lipnickie	Biała	Lipnik
Międzyczerwone	Nowy Targ	Nowy Targ
Międzygorze	Tłumacz	Uście Zielone
Międzyhorce	Rohatyń	Bursztyn
Międzyrzyce	Żydaczów	Żydaczów
Miejsce	Krosno	Dukla
Miejsce	Wadowice	Zator
Miękisz Nowy	Jarosław	Radymno
Miękisz Stary	Jarosław	Radymno
Mielec	Mielec	Mielec
Mielnica	Borszczów	Mielnica
Mielnicz	Żydaczów	Żurawno
Mielnów	Przemyśl	Krzywcza
Mielnów	Przemyśl	Przemyśl
Mierów	Kam. Strumiłowa	Chołojów
Mierzasichle	Nowy Targ	Nowy Targ

Town	Main District	Subdistrict
Mierzeń	Wieliczka	Klasno
Mierzwica	Żólkiew	Żólkiew
Mieszyszczów	Brzeżany	Brzeżany
Miętniów	Wieliczka	Klasno
Mikałajów	Bóbrka	Mikalajów
Mikałajów	Brody	Szczurowice
Mikałajów	Żydaczów	Rozdól
Mikałajówice	Tarnów	Zabno
Mikłaszów	Lemberg	Winniki
Mikłuszowice	Bochnia	Bochnia
Mików	Sanok	Bukowsko
Mikulice	Łańcut	Kańczuga
Mikuliczyn	Nadwórna	Delatyn
Mikulińce	Śniatyn	Śniatyn
Mikulińce	Tarnopol	Mikulińce
Mikuszowice	Biała	Lipnik
Milatycze	Lemberg	Nawarya
Milatyń	Gródek	Gródek
Milatyń	Mościska	Sądowa Wisznia
Milatyń Nowy	Kam. Strumiłowa	Busk
Milatyń Stary	Kam. Strumiłowa	Busk
Milcza	Sanok	Rymanów
Milczyce	Mościska	Sądowa Wisznia
Milik	Nowy Sącz	Muszyna
Milków	Cieszanów	Oleszyce
Miłkowa	Nowy Sącz	Nowy Sącz
Milno	Brody	Zalocze
Miłocin	Rzeszów	Rzeszów
Miłowanie	Tłumacz	Tyśmienica
Milowce	Zaleszczyki	Tłuste
Milówka	Brzesko	Wojnicz
Milówka	Żywiec	Zabłocie

Town	Main District	Subdistrict
Mirocin	Łańcut	Przeworsk
Mirów	Chrzanów	Trzebina
Mistkowice	Sambor	Sambor
Mistyce	Mościska	Sądowa Wisznia
Mizerna	Nowy Targ	Nowy Targ
Mizuń Nowy	Dolina	Dolina
Mizuń Stary	Dolina	Dolina
Młodochów	Mielec	Mielec
Młodów	Cieszanów	Lubaczów
Młodów	Nowy Sącz	Piwniczna
Młodowice	Przemyśl	Niżankowice
Młodzatyń	Kołomea	Peczeniżyn
Młoszowa	Chrzanów	Trzebina
Młyńczyska	Limanowa	Limanowa
Młyniska	Trembowla	Janów
Młyniska	Żydaczów	Żurawno
Młynne	Limanowa	Limanowa
Młynowce	Złoczów	Zborów
Młynówka	Borszczów	Mielnica
Młyny	Jaworów	Krakówiec
Mochnaczka Niżna	Grybów	Grybów
Mochnaczka Wyżna	Grybów	Grybów
Mockowice	Przemyśl	Przemyśl
Moczary	Lisko	Ustrzyki Dolne
Moczerady	Mościska	Hussaków
Moderówka	Krosno	Dukla
Modrycz	Drohobycz	Drohobycz
Mogielnica	Trembowla	Trembowla
Mogilany	Wieliczka	Podgórze
Mogilno	Grybów	Grybów
Mohylany	Żółkiew	Kulików
Mokra Strona	Łańcut	Przeworsk

Town	Main District	Subdistrict
Mokra Wieś	Nowy Sącz	Stary Sącz
Mokre	Sanok	Bukowsko
Mokrotyn	Żólkiew	Żólkiew
Mokrotyn Kolonia	Żólkiew	Żólkiew
Mokrzany	Sambor	Sambor
Mokrzany Małe	Mościska	Sądowa Wisznia
Mokrzany Wielkie	Mościska	Sądowa Wisznia
Mokrzec	Pilzno	Pilzno
Mokrzyska	Brzesko	Brzesko
Mokrzyszów	Tarnobrzeg	Tarnobrzeg
Molczanówka	Skałat	Skałat
Mołdycz	Jarosław	Sienawa
Mołodylów	Nadwórna	Lanczyn
Mołodyńcze	Bóbrka	Chodorów
Mołoszkowice	Jaworów	Jaworów
Mołotków	Borhodczany	Sołotwina
Mołotów	Bóbrka	Chodorów
Monasterzec	Rudki	Komarno
Monasterzyska	Buczacz	Monasterzyska
Moniłowska	Złoczów	Zborów
Monowice	Biała	Oświęcim
Moosberg	Jaworów	Jaworów
Morańce	Jaworów	Krakówiec
Morawsko	Jarosław	Jarosław
Mordarka	Limanowa	Limanowa
Morszyn	Stryj	Stryj
Morwczyna	Nowy Targ	Nowy Targ
Mościska	Kalusz	Kalusz
Mościska	Mościska	Mościska
Moskale	Tarnobrzeg	Rozwadów
Moskalówka	Kossów	Kossów
Mostki	Lemberg	Nawarya

Town	Main District	Subdistrict
Mostki	Nisko	Ulanów
Mostki	Nowy Sącz	Stary Sącz
Mosty	Rudki	Komarno
Mosty Małe	Rawa Ruska	Lubycza
Moszczanica	Cieszanów	Cieszanów
Moszczanica	Żywiec	Zabłocie
Moszczaniec	Sanok	Bukowsko
Moszczenica	Bochnia	Bochnia
Moszczenica	Gorlice	Gorlice
Moszczenica niżna	Nowy Sącz	Stary Sącz
Moszczenica wyżna	Nowy Sącz	Stary Sącz
Moszków	Sokal	Warez
Moszkowce	Kalusz	Wojnilów
Motycze Poduchowne	Tarnobrzeg	Rozwadów
Motycze Szlacheckie	Tarnobrzeg	Rozwadów
Mraźnica	Drohobycz	Borysław
Mrowla	Rzeszów	Rzeszów
Mrozowice	Sambor	Sambor
Mrzygłód	Sanok	Sanok
Mszalnica	Grybów	Grybów
Mszana	Gródek	Janów
Mszana	Krosno	Dukla
Mszana	Złoczów	Zborów
Mszana Dolna	Limanowa	Mszana dolna
Mszana Górna	Limanowa	Mszana dolna
Mszanice	Husiatyn	Chorostków
Mszanice	Staremiasto	Staremiasto
Mszanice	Tarnopol	Tarnopol
Mszanka	Gorlice	Gorlice
Mucharz	Wadowice	Wadowice
Muchawka	Czortków	Jagielnica

Town	Main District	Subdistrict
Muhlbach	Bóbrka	Bóbrka
Mukanie	Kam. Strumiłowa	Radziechów
Mulne	Żywiec	Zabłocie
Munina	Jarosław	Jarosław
Musikowe	Tarnobrzeg	Rozwadów
Muszkarów	Zaleszczyki	Korolówka
Muszkatówka	Borszczów	Borszczów
Muszyłowice	Jaworów	Jaworów
Muszyłowice Czarn.	Jaworów	Jaworów
Muszyłowice Narodowe	Jaworów	Jaworów
Muszyna	Nowy Sącz	Muszyna
Muszynka	Nowy Sącz	Krynica
Mutulin	Złoczów	Gologory
Muzylów	Podhajce	Podhajce
Myców	Sokal	Bełż
Myczków	Lisko	Baligród
Myczkowce	Lisko	Lisko
Mykietyńce	Kossów	Pistyn
Mykietyńce	Stanisławów	Stanisławów
Mymoń	Sanok	Rymanów
Myscowa	Krosno	Dukla
Myślachowice	Chrzanów	Trzebina
Myślatycze	Mościska	Mościska
Myślec	Nowy Sącz	Stary Sącz
Myślenice	Myślenice	Myślenice
Myślów	Kalusz	Kalusz
Mysłowa	Skałat	Podwołoczyska
Myszków	Zaleszczyki	Korolówka
Myszkowce	Husiatyn	Kopyczyńce
Myszkowice	Tarnopol	Mikulińce
Myszyn	Kołomea	Jabłonów

Town	Main District	Subdistrict
Mytarka	Krosno	Żmigród
Naciszowa	Nowy Sącz	Nowy Sącz
Nadbrzeże	Tarnobrzeg	Tarnobrzeg
Nadiatycze	Żydaczów	Rozdól
Nadolany	Sanok	Nowtanice
Nadole	Krosno	Dukla
Nadorożna	Tłumacz	Tłumacz
Nadorożniów	Brzeżany	Brzeżany
Nadwórna	Nadwórna	Nadwórna
Nadyby	Sambor	Sambor
Nadycze	Żólkiew	Kulików
Nadziejów	Dolina	Dolina
Nagawczyna	Pilzno	Dębica
Nagnajów	Tarnobrzeg	Baranów
Nagórzanka	Buczacz	Buczacz
Nagórzanka	Czortków	Jagielnica
Nagórzany	Lemberg	Nawarya
Nagórzany	Sanok	Nowtanice
Nagórzany	Zaleszczyki	Uścieczko
Nahaczów	Jaworów	Jaworów
Nahorce	Żólkiew	Kulików
Nahorce Małe	Kam. Strumiłowa	Kam. Strumiłowa
Nahujowice	Drohobycz	Drohobycz
Nakło	Przemyśl	Sosnica
Nakwasza	Brody	Podkamień
Nalepy	Nisko	Ulanów
Nałuże	Trembowla	Strusów
Nanczułka Mała	Staremiasto	Staremiasto
Nanczułka Wielka	Staremiasto	Staremiasto
Nanowa	Lisko	Ustrzyki Dolne
Napowce	Przemyśl	Przemyśl
Naprawa	Myślenice	Jordanów

Town	Main District	Subdistrict
Naradna	Sokal	Krystynopol
Narajów	Brzeżany	Narajów
Narol	Cieszanów	Narol
Nart Nowy	Kolbuszowa	Ranizów
Nart Stary	Kolbuszowa	Ranizów
Nasiężna	Lisko	Lutowiska
Nastasów	Tarnopol	Mikulińce
Nastaszczyn	Rohatyń	Bursztyn
Naszasowice	Nowy Sącz	Stary Sącz
Nawarya	Lemberg	Nawarya
Nawojówka	Nowy Sącz	Nowy Sącz
Nawsie	Ropczyce	Wielopole
Nawsie Brzosteckie	Pilzno	Brzostek
Nawsie Kolaczyckie	Pilzno	Brzostek
Nazawirów	Nadwórna	Nadwórna
Nazurna	Kołomea	Gwozdźiec
Nehrybka	Przemyśl	Przemyśl
Nesów	Podhajce	Zawałów
Nesterowce	Złoczów	Jezierna
Neu-Kalusz	Kalusz	Kalusz
Neudorf	Drohobycz	Drohobycz
Neudorf	Nadwórna	Lanczyn
Neudorf	Sambor	Sambor
Neuhof	Gródek	Gródek
Niagryn	Dolina	Dolina
Nidek	Wadowice	Andrychów
Niebieszczany	Sanok	Bukowsko
Niebocko	Brzozów	Brzozów
Niebylec	Rzeszów	Niebylec
Niebyłów	Kalusz	Kalusz
Niecew	Nowy Sącz	Nowy Sącz
Niechobrz	Rzeszów	Rzeszów

Town	Main District	Subdistrict
Nieciecza	Tarnów	Zabno
Nieczajna	Dąbrowa	Dąbrowa
Niedary	Bochnia	Bochnia
Niedomice	Tarnów	Zabno
Niedzieliska	Chrzanów	Chrzanów
Niedzielisko	Brzesko	Szczurowa
Niedzielna	Staremiasto	Staremiasto
Niedźiwedź	Limanowa	Mszana dolna
Niedźwiedza	Brzesko	Wojnicz
Niedźwiedza	Drohobycz	Drohobycz
Niegłowice	Jasło	Jasło
Niegoszowice	Chrzanów	Trzebina
Niegowce	Kalusz	Wojnilów
Niegowie	Wieliczka	Klasno
Nieledwia	Żywiec	Zabłocie
Nielepice	Chrzanów	Trzebina
Nielipkowice	Jarosław	Sienawa
Niemerów	Rawa Ruska	Niemerów
Niemiacz	Brody	Podkamień
Niemiłów	Kam. Strumiłowa	Radziechów
Niemstów	Cieszanów	Cieszanów
Niemszyn	Rohatyń	Bursztyn
Niemszyn	Stanisławów	Halicz
Nienadowa	Przemyśl	Dubiecko
Nienadówka	Kolbuszowa	Sokołów
Nienaszów	Krosno	Dukla
Nienowice	Jarosław	Radymno
Niepla	Jasło	Jasło
Niepołomice	Bochnia	Bochnia
Nieporaz	Chrzanów	Chrzanów
Nieprześnia	Bochnia	Wiśnicz Nowy
Niesłuchów	Kam. Strumiłowa	Busk

Town	Main District	Subdistrict
Niestanice	Kam. Strumiłowa	Chołojów
Nieszkowice	Bochnia	Wiśnicz Nowy
Niewdzieliska	Przemyślany	Świrz
Niewiarów	Wieliczka	Klasno
Niewistki	Brzozów	Dynów
Niewoczyn	Bohordczany	Bohordczany
Niewodna	Jasło	Frysztak
Niewodna	Ropczyce	Wielopole
Niezdów	Wieliczka	Klasno
Nieznajowa	Gorlice	Gorlice
Nieznanów	Kam. Strumiłowa	Chołojów
Nieznanowice	Wieliczka	Klasno
Nieżuchów	Stryj	Stryj
Nieżwiska	Horodenka	Obertyn
Niklowice	Mościska	Sądowa Wisznia
Nikonkowice	Lemberg	Szczerzec
Nikowice	Rudki	Rudki
Niniów Dolny	Dolina	Bolechów
Niniów Górny	Dolina	Bolechów
Nisko	Nisko	Nisko
Niskołyzy	Buczacz	Monasterzyska
Niwa	Nowy Targ	Nowy Targ
Niwice	Kam. Strumiłowa	Radziechów
Niwiska	Kolbuszowa	Kolbuszowa
Niwka	Brzesko	Radlów
Niwra	Borszczów	Mielnica
Niżankowice	Przemyśl	Niżankowice
Niżankowice	Przemyśl	Niżankowice
Niżatycze	Łańcut	Kańczuga
Niżbork Nowy	Husiatyn	Kopyczyńce
Niżbork Stary	Husiatyn	Kopyczyńce
Niżna Łąka	Krosno	Dukla

Town	Main District	Subdistrict
Niżniów	Tłumacz	Niżniów
Nizowa	Wieliczka	Klasno
Nizyce	Mościska	Hussaków
Nizynice	Przemyśl	Niżankowice
Nockowa	Ropczyce	Sędziszów
Nosata	Sokal	Krystynopol
Nosowce	Tarnopol	Tarnopol
Nosówka	Rzeszów	Rzeszów
Nowa Góra	Chrzanów	Trzebina
Nowa Grobla	Jarosław	Radymno
Nowa Lodyna	Kam. Strumiłowa	Kam. Strumiłowa
Nowa Wieś	Biała	Kęty
Nowa Wieś	Bircza	Bircza
Nowa Wieś	Brzesko	Brzesko
Nowa Wieś	Kolbuszowa	Kolbuszowa
Nowa Wieś	Nowy Sącz	Łabowa
Nowa Wieś	Rudki	Komarno
Nowa Wieś	Rzeszów	Czudec
Nowa Wieś	Rzeszów	Głogów
Nowa Wieś	Wieliczka	Klasno
Nowe Dwory	Wadowice	Zator
Nowe Miasto	Bircza	Nowemiasto
Nowe Siolo	Cieszanów	Cieszanów
Nowe Siolo	Żólkiew	Kulików
Nowemiasto	Bircza	Nowemiasto
Nowica	Gorlice	Gorlice
Nowica	Kalusz	Kalusz
Nowiny	Cieszanów	Cieszanów
Nowiny	Tarnobrzeg	Radomyśl
Nowodworze	Tarnów	Tarnów
Nowojowa Góra	Chrzanów	Chrzanów
Nowościólki	Jaworów	Jaworów

Town	Main District	Subdistrict
Nowosielce	Bircza	Rybotycze
Nowosielce	Bóbrka	Chodorów
Nowosielce	Łańcut	Przewórsk
Nowosielce Gniewosz	Sanok	Sanok
Nowosielec	Nisko	Rudnik
Nowosielica	Dolina	Dolina
Nowosielica	Mościska	Sądowa Wisznia
Nowosielica	Śniatyn	Zabłotów
Nowosiołka	Borszczów	Mielnica
Nowosiołka	Buczacz	Potok
Nowosiołka	Lemberg	Szczerzec
Nowosiołka	Podhajce	Podhajce
Nowosiołka	Przemyślany	Dunajowce
Nowosiołka	Tłumacz	Uście Zielone
Nowosiołka Grzym.	Skałat	Touste
Nowosiołka Jazłowiecka	Buczacz	Jazłowice
Nowosiołka Skalacka	Skałat	Skałat
Nowosiołki	Bircza	Rybotycze
Nowosiołki	Kam. Strumiłowa	Busk
Nowosiołki	Lisko	Baligród
Nowosiołki	Mościska	Hussaków
Nowosiołki	Przemyśl	Przemyśl
Nowosiołki	Złoczów	Gologory
Nowosiołki Gościnne	Rudki	Rudki
Nowosiołki Kostk	Zaleszczyki	Korolówka
Nowosiołki Oparskie	Rudki	Komarno
Nowosioło	Żydaczów	Żydaczów
Nowostawce	Buczacz	Buczacz
Nowoszny	Rohatyń	Bursztyn
Nowoszyce	Sambor	Sambor

Town	Main District	Subdistrict
Nowoszyn	Dolina	Dolina
Nowotanice	Sanok	Nowtanice
Nowsiołki Kardyn.	Rawa Ruska	Uhnów
Nowsiołki Przednie	Rawa Ruska	Uhnów
Nowy Babilon	Dolina	Bolechów
Nowy Dwór	Sokal	Krystynopol
Nowy Sącz	Nowy Sącz	Nowy Sącz
Nowy Targ	Nowy Targ	Nowy Targ
Nowy Tyczyn	Trembowla	Strusów
Nozdrzec	Brzozów	Dynów
Nuśmice	Sokal	Warez
Nyrków	Zaleszczyki	Uścieczko
Obarzance	Tarnopol	Tarnopol
Obarzym	Brzozów	Dynów
Obelnica	Rohatyń	Bursztyn
Obersdorf	Lisko	Ustrzyki Dolne
Obertyn	Horodenka	Obertyn
Obidowa	Nowy Targ	Nowy Targ
Obidza	Nowy Sącz	Szczawnica
Obladów	Kam. Strumiłowa	Radziechów
Obłażnica	Żydaczów	Żurawno
Obłazy	Nowy Sącz	Piwniczna
Obodówka	Zbaraz	Zbaraz
Obojna	Tarnobrzeg	Rozwadów
Obroszyn	Gródek	Gródek
Obrotów	Kam. Strumiłowa	Witków Nowy
Obydów	Kam. Strumiłowa	Kam. Strumiłowa
Ochmanów	Wieliczka	Klasno
Ochmanów	Wieliczka	Klasno
Ochodza	Wadowice	Zator
Ochojno	Wieliczka	Klasno
Ochotnica	Nowy Targ	Krościenko

Town	Main District	Subdistrict
Ocice	Tarnobrzeg	Tarnobrzeg
Ocieka	Ropczyce	Ropczyce
Oczków	Żywiec	Zabłocie
Odaje ad Słobódka	Tłumacz	Tyśmienica
Odment	Dąbrowa	Szczucin
Odrowąż	Nowy Targ	Nowy Targ
Odrzechowa	Sanok	Rymanów
Odrzykoń	Krosno	Dukla
Okleśna	Chrzanów	Trzebina
Okniany	Tłumacz	Tłumacz
Okno	Horodenka	Horodenka
Okno	Skałat	Grzymałów
Okocim	Brzesko	Brzesko
Okoń	Kam. Strumiłowa	Kam. Strumiłowa
Okonin	Ropczyce	Ropczyce
Okopy	Borszczów	Mielnica
Okopy	Rawa Ruska	Magierów
Okrajnik	Żywiec	Zabłocie
Olchawa	Bochnia	Wiśnicz Nowy
Olchowa	Lisko	Lisko
Olchowa	Ropczyce	Sędziszów
Olchowa Lwibrat	Lisko	Lutowiska
Olchowce	Sanok	Sanok
Olchowczyk	Husiatyn	Husiatyn
Olchowice	Bóbrka	Bóbrka
Olchowice	Borszczów	Mielnica
Olchowice	Brzeżany	Brzeżany
Olchowice	Horodenka	Czernelica
Olchowice	Krosno	Dukla
Olchówka	Dolina	Rożniatów
Olejów	Złoczów	Zborów
Olejowa Korniów	Horodenka	Czernelica

Town	Main District	Subdistrict
Olejowa Korolówka	Horodenka	Czernelica
Oleksice Nowe	Stryj	Stryj
Oleksice Stare	Stryj	Stryj
Oleksińce	Zaleszczyki	Tłuste
Olendry	Trembowla	Strusów
Olesin	Brzeżany	Kozowa
Olesko	Złoczów	Olesko
Oleśnica	Dąbrowa	Dąbrowa
Oleśno	Dąbrowa	Dąbrowa
Olesza	Buczacz	Monasterzyska
Olesza	Tłumacz	Tłumacz
Oleszków	Śniatyn	Zabłotów
Oleszów	Tłumacz	Niźniów
Oleszyce	Cieszanów	Oleszyce
Oleszyce Stare	Cieszanów	Oleszyce
Olpiny	Jasło	Olpiny
Olsawica	Sanok	Bukowsko
Olszanica	Lisko	Lisko
Olszanica	Tłumacz	Tyśmienica
Olszanica	Złoczów	Gologory
Olszanik	Sambor	Sambor
Olszanka	Nowy Sącz	Stary Sącz
Olszanka	Rawa Ruska	Rawa Ruska
Olszany	Przemyśl	Przemyśl
Olszowa	Brzesko	Czchów
Olszowice	Wieliczka	Klasno
Olszówka	Limanowa	Mszana dolna
Olszyny	Brzesko	Wojnicz
Olszyny	Chrzanów	Chrzanów
Onyszkowce	Bóbrka	Strzeliska Nowe
Opacie	Jasło	Jasło
Opacionka	Pilzno	Brzostek

Town	Main District	Subdistrict
Opaka	Cieszanów	Lubaczów
Opaka	Drohobycz	Drohobycz
Opaki	Złoczów	Sassów
Opaleniska	Łańcut	Leżajsk
Oparówka	Jasło	Frysztak
Opary	Drohobycz	Drohobycz
Opatkowice	Wieliczka	Podgórze
Oplucko	Kam. Strumiłowa	Radziechów
Oporzec	Stryj	Skole
Oprynowce	Stanisławów	Stanisławów
Opulsko	Sokal	Sokal
Orawa	Stryj	Skole
Orawczyk	Stryj	Skole
Orchowice	Mościska	Sądowa Wisznia
Ordów	Kam. Strumiłowa	Witków Nowy
Orelce	Śniatyn	Śniatyn
Orelec	Lisko	Lisko
Orliska	Tarnobrzeg	Rozwadów
Orów	Drohobycz	Drohobycz
Ortynice	Sambor	Sambor
Oryszkowce	Husiatyn	Kopyczyńce
Orzechów	Tarnobrzeg	Radomyśl
Orzechowce	Skałat	Skałat
Orzechowczyk	Brody	Podkamień
Orzechowice	Przemyśl	Przemyśl
Orzechówka	Brzozów	Jasienica
Oserdów	Sokal	Bełż
Osieczany	Myślenice	Myślenice
Osiek	Biała	Kęty
Osielec	Myślenice	Maków
Oskrzesińce	Kołomea	Kołomea
Oskrzesińce	Rohatyń	Rohatyń

Town	Main District	Subdistrict
Osławy Biale	Nadwórna	Delatyn
Osławy Czarne	Nadwórna	Delatyn
Osmolna	Złoczów	Złoczów
Osobnica	Jasło	Jasło
Osowce	Buczacz	Buczacz
Ostalce	Tarnopol	Mikulińce
Ostapie	Skałat	Grzymałów
Ostapkowce	Kołomea	Gwozdźiec
Ostaszowce	Złoczów	Jezierna
Ostobusz	Rawa Ruska	Uhnów
Ostra	Buczacz	Potok
Ostre	Żywiec	Zabłocie
Ostropole	Chrzanów	Chrzanów
Ostrów	Bóbrka	Brzozdowiec
Ostrów	Jarosław	Radymno
Ostrów	Kam. Strumiłowa	Busk
Ostrów	Łańcut	Kańczuga
Ostrów	Lemberg	Szczerzec
Ostrów	Przemyśl	Przemyśl
Ostrów	Rohatyń	Rohatyń
Ostrów	Ropczyce	Ropczyce
Ostrów	Rudki	Rudki
Ostrów	Sokal	Krystynopol
Ostrów	Stanisławów	Halicz
Ostrów	Tarnopol	Tarnopol
Ostrów	Tarnów	Zabno
Ostrów Królewski	Bochnia	Bochnia
Ostrów Pohorecki	Rudki	Komarno
Ostrów Szlachecki	Bochnia	Bochnia
Ostrowczyk	Trembowla	Strusów
Ostrowczyk Polny	Złoczów	Białykamień
Ostrówek	Mielec	Radomyśl Wiel.

Town	Main District	Subdistrict
Ostrówek	Tarnobrzeg	Tarnobrzeg
Ostrowice	Cieszanów	Lubaczów
Ostrowice	Kołomea	Gwozdźiec
Ostrowsko	Nowy Targ	Nowy Targ
Ostrowy Baranowskie	Kolbuszowa	Majdan
Ostrowy Ruszowskie	Kolbuszowa	Majdan
Ostrożce	Mościska	Mościska
Ostrusza	Grybów	Bobowa
Ostrynia	Tłumacz	Niźniów
Ostrznica	Chrzanów	Trzebina
Oświęcim	Biała	Oświęcim
Oszanica	Jaworów	Jaworów
Otalez	Mielec	Radomyśl Wiel.
Otfinów	Dąbrowa	Dąbrowa
Ottenhausen	Gródek	Janów
Ottynia	Tłumacz	Ottynia
Ottyniowice	Bóbrka	Chodorów
Owieczka	Limanowa	Limanowa
Ożanna	Łańcut	Leżajsk
Ożańsko	Jarosław	Jarosław
Ożarowce	Złoczów	Złoczów
Ożenna	Krosno	Dukla
Ozimina	Sambor	Sambor
Ożomla	Jaworów	Jaworów
Ożydów	Brody	Sokołówka
Ożydów	Złoczów	Olesko
Packowice	Mościska	Hussaków
Packowice	Przemyśl	Niżankowice
Pacław	Bircza	Dobromil
Pacyków	Dolina	Dolina
Paczek Gorzycki	Tarnobrzeg	Tarnobrzeg

Town	Main District	Subdistrict
Paczołtowice	Chrzanów	Trzebina
Padew	Mielec	Mielec
Padew Narodowa	Mielec	Mielec
Pagorzyna	Gorlice	Gorlice
Pajówka	Skałat	Grzymałów
Pakość	Mościska	Mościska
Pakoszówka	Sanok	Sanok
Palcza	Wadowice	Kalwarya
Palen	Tarnobrzeg	Rozwadów
Paleśnica	Brzesko	Czchów
Palikrowy	Brody	Podkamień
Palszowice	Wadowice	Zator
Panasówka	Brody	Załoźce
Panasówka	Skałat	Skałat
Paniczna	Stanisławów	Stanisławów
Paniowce	Borszczów	Mielnica
Paniszczów	Lisko	Lutowiska
Pankowce	Brody	Podkamień
Panowice	Podhajce	Zawałów
Pantalicha	Trembowla	Strusów
Pantalowice	Łańcut	Kańczuga
Papiernia	Trembowla	Janów
Papnortno	Bircza	Dobromil
Parchacz	Sokal	Krystynopol
Parkosz	Pilzno	Pilzno
Partyń	Tarnów	Zabno
Partynia	Mielec	Radomyśl Wiel.
Parypsy	Rawa Ruska	Niemerów
Paryszeże	Nadwórna	Nadwórna
Pasicka	Dąbrowa	Dąbrowa
Pasicki Zubrzyckie	Lemberg	Winniki
Pasieczna	Nadwórna	Nadwórna

Town	Main District	Subdistrict
Pasierbice	Bochnia	Wiśnicz Nowy
Paszczyna	Ropczyce	Ropczyce
Paszkówka	Wadowice	Zator
Paszowa	Lisko	Lisko
Paszyn	Nowy Sącz	Nowy Sącz
Pauszówka	Czortków	Jagielnica
Pawełcza	Stanisławów	Stanisławów
Pawęzów	Tarnów	Zabno
Pawlikowice	Wieliczka	Klasno
Pawłokoma	Brzozów	Dynów
Pawłosiów	Jarosław	Jarosław
Pawłów	Dąbrowa	Dąbrowa
Pawłów	Kam. Strumiłowa	Chołojów
Paździmirz	Sokal	Krystynopol
Peczenia	Przemyślany	Gliniany
Peczeniżyn	Kołomea	Peczeniżyn
Peim	Myślenice	Myślenice
Pełkinie	Jarosław	Jarosław
Pełnatycze	Jarosław	Jarosław
Peratyń	Kam. Strumiłowa	Radziechów
Perechrestne	Kossów	Żabie
Perekosy	Kalusz	Wojniłów
Peremiłów	Husiatyn	Chorostków
Perenówka	Rohatyń	Rohatyń
Perepelniki	Złoczów	Zborów
Pererów	Kołomea	Kołomea
Perespa	Sokal	Tartaków
Peretoki	Sokal	Sokal
Perla	Brzesko	Brzesko
Perłowce	Stanisławów	Halicz
Persenkówka	Lemberg	Zniesienie
Perwiatycze	Sokal	Tartaków

Town	Main District	Subdistrict
Petlikowce	Buczacz	Buczacz
Petlikowce Nowe	Buczacz	Buczacz
Petlikowce Stare	Buczacz	Buczacz
Pętna	Gorlice	Gorlice
Petranka	Kalusz	Kalusz
Petryków	Tarnopol	Tarnopol
Petryków	Tłumacz	Uście Zielone
Pewel	Żywiec	Zabłocie
Pewel Mała	Żywiec	Zabłocie
Pewel Wielka	Żywiec	Zabłocie
Pewlka	Żywiec	Zabłocie
Piadyki	Kołomea	Kołomea
Pianowice	Sambor	Sambor
Piaseczna	Żydaczów	Rozdól
Piaski	Brody	Leszniów
Piaski	Brzesko	Czchów
Piaski	Lemberg	Szczerzec
Piaski	Mościska	Sądowa Wisznia
Piaski	Rudki	Komarno
Piaski	Wieliczka	Podgórze
Piątkowa	Bircza	Bircza
Piątkowa	Nowy Sącz	Nowy Sącz
Piątkowa	Rzeszów	Błazowa
Piątkowice	Mielec	Radomyśl Wiel.
Piechoty	Mielec	Mielec
Pieczarna	Zaleszczyki	Zaleszczyki
Pieczychwosty	Żólkiew	Kulików
Pieczygory	Sokal	Warez
Piekiełko	Limanowa	Limanowa
Pielawa	Buczacz	Buczacz
Pielnia	Sanok	Nowtanice
Pień	Mielec	Radomyśl Wiel.

Town	Main District	Subdistrict
Pieniaki	Brody	Podkamień
Pieniążkowice	Nowy Targ	Nowy Targ
Pierszyce	Dąbrowa	Dąbrowa
Pierzchów	Wieliczka	Klasno
Pierzchowice	Wieliczka	Klasno
Pietbuce	Bircza	Dobromil
Pietniczany	Bóbrka	Bóbrka
Pietniczany	Stryj	Stryj
Pietrusza Wola	Jasło	Frysztak
Pietrycze	Złoczów	Białykamień
Pietrzejowa	Ropczyce	Ropczyce
Pietrzykowice	Żywiec	Zabłocie
Pikarówka	Rzeszów	Czudec
Pikorowice	Jarosław	Sienawa
Pikulice	Przemyśl	Przemyśl
Pikułowice	Lemberg	Jaryczów
Piła	Chrzanów	Chrzanów
Piłatkowce	Borszczów	Borszczów
Pilichów	Tarnobrzeg	Rozwadów
Pilipy	Kołomea	Kołomea
Piły	Żółkiew	Żółkiew
Pilznionek	Pilzno	Pilzno
Pilzno	Pilzno	Pilzno
Piniany	Sambor	Sambor
Piotrkowice	Tarnów	Tuchów
Piotrów	Horodenka	Obertyn
Piotrówka	Krosno	Dukla
Pisarowce	Sanok	Sanok
Pisary	Chrzanów	Trzebina
Pisarzowa	Limanowa	Limanowa
Pisarzowice	Biała	Kęty
Pistyn	Kossów	Pistyn

Town	Main District	Subdistrict
Piszczatynce	Borszczów	Borszczów
Pitrycz	Stanisławów	Halicz
Piwniczna	Nowy Sącz	Piwniczna
Piwoda	Jarosław	Sienawa
Piwowszczyzna	Sokal	Belż
Piżany	Żydaczów	Żydaczów
Płaszów	Wieliczka	Podgórze
Płaucza Mała	Brzeżany	Kozłów
Płaucza Wielka	Brzeżany	Kozłów
Pławie	Stryj	Skole
Pławna	Grybów	Bobowa
Pławo	Mielec	Radomyśl Wiel.
Pławy	Biała	Oświęcim
Płaza	Chrzanów	Chrzanów
Płazów	Cieszanów	Narol
Płazówka	Kolbuszowa	Majdan
Plebanówka	Trembowla	Trembowla
Pleników	Przemyślany	Dunajowce
Pleskowce	Tarnopol	Tarnopol
Pleśna	Tarnów	Tarnów
Pleśniany	Złoczów	Zborów
Pleśniany	Złoczów	Złoczów
Pleśników	Złoczów	Gologory
Pleszowice	Mościska	Hussaków
Pleszowice	Przemyśl	Przemyśl
Pletenice	Przemyślany	Przemyślany
Plichów	Brzeżany	Brzeżany
Płoki	Chrzanów	Chrzanów
Płonne	Sanok	Bukowsko
Płoskie	Staremiasto	Staremiasto
Płotycz	Tarnopol	Tarnopol
Płotycza	Brzeżany	Kozowa

Town	Main District	Subdistrict
Płowe	Kam. Strumiłowa	Witków Nowy
Płowie	Sanok	Sanok
Płozówka	Rzeszów	Głogów
Płuchów	Złoczów	Złoczów
Pluty	Mielec	Mielec
Pniatyn	Przemyślany	Przemyślany
Pnikut	Mościska	Mościska
Pniów	Nadwórna	Nadwórna
Pniów	Tarnobrzeg	Radomyśl
Pobereże	Stanisławów	Jezupol
Pobidno	Sanok	Sanok
Pobiedz	Wadowice	Zator
Pobitno	Rzeszów	Rzeszów
Pobocz	Złoczów	Sassów
Pobreczyn	Limanowa	Limanowa
Pobuk	Stryj	Skole
Pobuzany	Kam. Strumiłowa	Busk
Pochówka	Bohordczany	Bohordczany
Poczajowice	Drohobycz	Drohobycz
Poczapińce	Tarnopol	Tarnopol
Podberesec	Lemberg	Winniki
Podbereż	Dolina	Bolechów
Podbereżce	Brody	Załoźce
Podbereżec	Brody	Brody
Podborce	Lemberg	Winniki
Podborze	Dąbrowa	Dąbrowa
Podborze	Mielec	Radomyśl Wiel.
Podborze	Wieliczka	Klasno
Podbrzezie	Brzesko	Czchów
Podbuz	Drohobycz	Drohobycz
Podbuże	Rohatyń	Rohatyń
Podciemne	Lemberg	Nawarya

Town	Main District	Subdistrict
Podczerwone	Nowy Targ	Nowy Targ
Podegrodzie	Nowy Sącz	Stary Sącz
Podemszczyzna	Cieszanów	Cieszanów
Podfilipie	Borszczów	Skała
Podgać	Mościska	Mościska
Podgórzany	Trembowla	Trembowla
Podgórze	Wieliczka	Podgórze
Podgórze	Wieliczka	Podgórze
Podgrodzie	Pilzno	Dębica
Podgrodzie	Rohatyń	Rohatyń
Podgrodzie	Stanisławów	Halicz
Podhajce	Podhajce	Podhajce
Podhajczyki	Kołomea	Gwozdźiec
Podhajczyki	Przemyślany	Gliniany
Podhajczyki	Rudki	Rudki
Podhajczyki	Trembowla	Janów
Podhajczyki	Złoczów	Zborów
Podhorce	Bóbrka	Brzozdowiec
Podhorce	Rudki	Komarno
Podhorce	Stryj	Stryj
Podhorce	Stryj	Stryj
Podhorki	Kalusz	Kalusz
Podhorodce	Stryj	Skole
Podhorodyszcze	Bóbrka	Mikalajów
Podhybie	Wadowice	Kalwarya
Podjarków	Bóbrka	Mikalajów
Podkamień	Brody	Podkamień
Podkamień	Rohatyń	Rohatyń
Podkościele	Dąbrowa	Dąbrowa
Podlankowina	Przemyśl	Dubiecko
Podlesie	Buczacz	Buczacz
Podlesie	Skałat	Grzymałów

Town	Main District	Subdistrict
Podlesie	Złoczów	Olesko
Podlesie Dębowe	Tarnów	Zabno
Podleszany	Mielec	Mielec
Podłęże	Bochnia	Bochnia
Podłęże	Tarnobrzeg	Tarnobrzeg
Podlipce	Złoczów	Złoczów
Podlipie	Dąbrowa	Dąbrowa
Podliski	Bóbrka	Chodorów
Podliski	Mościska	Sądowa Wisznia
Podliski Małe	Lemberg	Jaryczów
Podliski Wielkie	Lemberg	Jaryczów
Podłopień	Limanowa	Limanowa
Podluby Wielki	Jaworów	Jaworów
Podłuby Małe	Jaworów	Jaworów
Podmajerz	Nowy Sącz	Stary Sącz
Podmanasterek	Sambor	Sambor
Podmanastereż	Bóbrka	Bóbrka
Podmichale	Kalusz	Kalusz
Podmichałowce	Rohatyń	Rohatyń
Podmoszce	Przemyśl	Niżankowice
Podniebyłe	Krosno	Dukla
Podniestrzany	Bóbrka	Brzozdowiec
Podobin	Limanowa	Mszana dolna
Podolany	Wadowice	Kalwarya
Podolany	Wieliczka	Klasno
Podolce	Rudki	Komarno
Podole	Mielec	Radomyśl Wiel.
Podole	Nowy Sącz	Nowy Sącz
Podolsze	Wadowice	Zator
Podpieczary	Tłumacz	Tyśmienica
Podrudne	Kam. Strumiłowa	Dobrotwor
Podrzyce	Nowy Sącz	Nowy Sącz

Town	Main District	Subdistrict
Podsadki	Lemberg	Nawarya
Podsmykowce	Tarnopol	Tarnopol
Podsosnów	Bóbrka	Mikalajów
Podstolice	Wieliczka	Klasno
Podsuchy	Dolina	Rożniatów
Podszumlańce	Rohatyń	Bursztyn
Podubce	Rawa Ruska	Uhnów
Podusilna	Przemyślany	Przemyślany
Podusów	Przemyślany	Przemyślany
Podwale	Brzesko	Radlów
Podwerbce	Horodenka	Obertyn
Podwinie	Rohatyń	Rohatyń
Podwołoczyska	Skałat	Podwołoczyska
Podwysoka	Śniatyn	Śniatyn
Podwysokie	Brzeżany	Brzeżany
Podwysokie	Rudki	Komarno
Podzamcze	Kam. Strumiłowa	Kam. Strumiłowa
Podzamczek	Buczacz	Buczacz
Podziacz	Przemyśl	Przemyśl
Podzwierzynice	Łańcut	Łańcut
Podzwierzynice	Rudki	Komarno
Pogórska Wola	Tarnów	Tarnów
Pogorzałka	Nisko	Nisko
Pogorzany	Limanowa	Limanowa
Pogorzeliska	Rawa Ruska	Magierów
Pogorzyce	Chrzanów	Chrzanów
Pogwizdów	Bochnia	Wiśnicz Nowy
Pogwizdów	Kolbuszowa	Ranizów
Pogwizdów	Łańcut	Łańcut
Pogwizdów	Rzeszów	Głogów
Pohar	Stryj	Skole
Poherbce	Złoczów	Zborów

Town	Main District	Subdistrict
Pohonia	Tłumacz	Tyśmienica
Pohorylec	Dolina	Rożniatów
Pohorylec	Przemyślany	Gliniany
Pojawce	Brzesko	Szczurowa
Pojło	Kalusz	Kalusz
Pokrepiwna	Brzeżany	Kozłów
Pokrowce	Żydaczów	Żydaczów
Polana	Bircza	Dobromil
Polana	Lemberg	Szczerzec
Polana	Lisko	Lutowiska
Polana	Staremiasto	Chyrów
Polańczyk	Lisko	Baligród
Polanica	Dolina	Bolechów
Polanka	Krosno	Dukla
Polanka	Lemberg	Nawarya
Polanka	Myślenice	Myślenice
Polanka	Wadowice	Zator
Polanka Wielka	Biała	Oświęcim
Polanki	Kossów	Żabie
Polanki	Lisko	Baligród
Polany	Grybów	Grybów
Polany	Krosno	Dukla
Polany	Żółkiew	Żółkiew
Polany Surowiczne	Sanok	Rymanów
Poleśniki	Buczacz	Buczacz
Polna	Grybów	Grybów
Połom Mały	Brzesko	Czchów
Połomeja	Pilzno	Pilzno
Połonice	Przemyślany	Gliniany
Połoniczna	Kam. Strumiłowa	Chołojów
Połowce	Czortków	Jagielnica
Połowe	Kam. Strumiłowa	Kam. Strumiłowa

Town	Main District	Subdistrict
Połrzecki	Limanowa	Mszana dolna
Połtew	Przemyślany	Gliniany
Poluchów Mały	Przemyślany	Przemyślany
Poluchów Wielki	Przemyślany	Gliniany
Polupanówka	Skałat	Skałat
Połwieś	Wadowice	Zator
Pomianowa	Brzesko	Brzesko
Pomonieta	Rohatyń	Rohatyń
Pomorce	Buczacz	Jazłowice
Pomorzany	Złoczów	Pomorzany
Ponice	Myślenice	Jordanów
Ponikew	Wadowice	Wadowice
Ponikowica Mała	Brody	Brody
Ponikwa	Brody	Brody
Ponikwa Wielka	Złoczów	Olesko
Popardowa	Nowy Sącz	Łabowa
Popędzyna	Bochnia	Bochnia
Popielany	Lemberg	Szczerzec
Popiele	Drohobycz	Drohobycz
Popielniki	Śniatyn	Zabłotów
Popławniki	Rohatyń	Bursztyn
Popowce	Brody	Podkamień
Popowce	Zaleszczyki	Tłuste
Popowice	Mościska	Hussaków
Popowice	Nowy Sącz	Stary Sącz
Popowice	Przemyśl	Przemyśl
Popowice	Tarnobrzeg	Radomyśl
Poraba	Brzozów	Dynów
Porąbka	Biała	Kęty
Porąbka	Limanowa	Limanowa
Porąbka Mała	Brzesko	Czchów
Porąbka Uszewska	Brzesko	Brzesko

Town	Main District	Subdistrict
Poraj	Krosno	Dukla
Poraż	Lisko	Lisko
Porchowa	Buczacz	Barysz
Poręba	Myślenice	Myślenice
Poręba Wielka	Biała	Oświęcim
Poręba Wielka	Limanowa	Mszana dolna
Poręba Wolna	Tarnów	Tarnów
Poręba Żegoty	Chrzanów	Chrzanów
Poręby	Ropczyce	Ropczyce
Poręby	Sanok	Rymanów
Poręby Dębskie	Tarnobrzeg	Tarnobrzeg
Poręby Dymarskie	Kolbuszowa	Kolbuszowa
Poręby Furmanskie	Tarnobrzeg	Tarnobrzeg
Poręby Kupińskie	Kolbuszowa	Kolbuszowa
Poręby Kupińskie	Rzeszów	Głogów
Poremba	Bochnia	Wiśnicz Nowy
Pornczyn	Brzeżany	Narajów
Porohy	Borhodczany	Sołotwina
Porohy	Borhodczany	Sołotwina
Poronin	Nowy Targ	Nowy Targ
Porszna	Lemberg	Nawarya
Poruby	Jaworów	Jaworów
Porudenko	Jaworów	Jaworów
Porudno	Jaworów	Jaworów
Porzecze Grunt	Rudki	Komarno
Porzecze Nadwórne	Rudki	Komarno
Porzycze Janowskie	Gródek	Janów
Porzycze Lubieńkie	Gródek	Gródek
Posada Chyrowska	Staremiasto	Chyrów
Posada Dolna	Sanok	Rymanów
Posada Felsztyńska	Staremiasto	Felszytn
Posada Górna	Sanok	Rymanów

Town	Main District	Subdistrict
Posada Jacmierska	Sanok	Rymanów
Posada Jasliska	Sanok	Rymanów
Posada Liska	Lisko	Lisko
Posada Nowomiejska	Bircza	Nowemiasto
Posada Olchowska	Sanok	Sanok
Posada Rybotycka	Bircza	Rybotycze
Posada Sanocka	Sanok	Sanok
Posada Zarszyńska	Sanok	Rymanów
Posadowa	Grybów	Grybów
Posagowa	Nowy Sącz	Nowy Sącz
Posiecz	Bohordczany	Lysiec
Postołów	Lisko	Lisko
Postołówka	Husiatyn	Chorostków
Posuchów	Brzeżany	Brzeżany
Poswierz	Rohatyń	Bursztyn
Potakówka	Jasło	Jasło
Potoczany	Przemyślany	Dunajowce
Potoczek	Śniatyn	Śniatyn
Potoczyska	Horodenka	Horodenka
Potok	Brzeżany	Brzeżany
Potok	Buczacz	Potok
Potok	Krosno	Dukla
Potok	Rawa Ruska	Lubycza
Potok	Rohatyń	Rohatyń
Potok Czarny	Nadwórna	Delatyn
Potok Wielki	Staremiasto	Staremiasto
Potom	Bochnia	Wiśnicz Nowy
Potorzyca	Sokal	Sokal
Potutory	Brzeżany	Brzeżany
Potylicz	Rawa Ruska	Rawa Ruska
Potylicze	Tłumacz	Tłumacz
Powerchów	Rudki	Komarno

Town	Main District	Subdistrict
Powitno	Gródek	Janów
Powrożnik	Nowy Sącz	Muszyna
Poznachowice Dolne	Wieliczka	Klasno
Poznachowice Górne	Wieliczka	Klasno
Poznanka Gniła	Skałat	Skałat
Poznanka Hetmańska	Skałat	Grzymałów
Pozowice	Wadowice	Zator
Pralkowce	Przemyśl	Przemyśl
Prehinsko	Dolina	Rożniatów
Prelukie	Sanok	Bukowsko
Prinzenthal	Staremiasto	Chyrów
Probabin	Horodenka	Horodenka
Probużna	Husiatyn	Probużna
Prochowce	Przemyśl	Przemyśl
Procisne	Lisko	Lutowiska
Prokocim	Wieliczka	Podgórze
Prokurowa	Kossów	Pistyn
Proniatyn	Tarnopol	Tarnopol
Proszowa	Tarnopol	Mikulińce
Proszowki	Bochnia	Bochnia
Protesy	Żydaczów	Żurawno
Prowala	Żólkiew	Żólkiew
Pruchnik	Jarosław	Pruchnik
Prunka	Grybów	Grybów
Prusie	Rawa Ruska	Rawa Ruska
Prusinów	Sokal	Bełz
Prusy	Lemberg	Zniesienie
Prusy	Sambor	Sambor
Prybyń	Przemyślany	Świrz
Prysowce	Złoczów	Zborów
Przebieczany	Wieliczka	Klasno
Przecieszyn	Biała	Oświęcim

Town	Main District	Subdistrict
Przeciszów	Wadowice	Zator
Przecław	Mielec	Radomyśl Wiel.
Przeczyca	Pilzno	Jodłowa
Przedbórz	Kolbuszowa	Kolbuszowa
Przedbórze	Jaworów	Krakówiec
Przedmeście Strzyz.	Rzeszów	Strzyżów
Przedmieście	Buczacz	Jazłowice
Przedmieście	Łańcut	Łańcut
Przedmieście	Przemyśl	Dubiecko
Przedmieście	Rawa Ruska	Niemerów
Przedmieście	Ropczyce	Sędziszów
Przedmieście Czudeckie	Rzeszów	Czudec
Przedmieście Dynowskie	Brzozów	Dynów
Przedrzymichy Małe	Żółkiew	Kulików
Przedrzymichy Wielkie	Żółkiew	Kulików
Przędzel	Nisko	Rudnik
Przędzielnica	Bircza	Dobromil
Przegnojów	Przemyślany	Gliniany
Przegonina	Gorlice	Gorlice
Przekopana	Przemyśl	Przemyśl
Przemiwółki	Żółkiew	Kulików
Przemoziec	Buczacz	Jazłowice
Przemyśl	Przemyśl	Przemyśl
Przemyślany	Przemyślany	Przemyślany
Przemyślów	Sokal	Bełż
Przeniczniki	Tłumacz	Tyśmienica
Przenosza	Limanowa	Limanowa
Przerośl	Nadwórna	Nadwórna
Przestanie	Żółkiew	Gross-Mosty

Town	Main District	Subdistrict
Przewłoczna	Brody	Toporów
Przewodów	Sokal	Bełż
Przewołka	Buczacz	Buczacz
Przewórsk	Łańcut	Przewórsk
Przewóz	Tarnobrzeg	Baranów
Przewóz	Wieliczka	Podgórze
Przewoziec	Kalusz	Wojnilów
Przewrotne	Kolbuszowa	Ranizów
Przewrotne	Rzeszów	Głogów
Przyborów	Brzesko	Brzesko
Przyborów	Żywiec	Zabłocie
Przybówka	Jasło	Frysztak
Przybrodz	Wadowice	Zator
Przybyłów	Grybów	Bobowa
Przybyłów	Tłumacz	Chocimirz
Przybysławice	Brzesko	Radlów
Przybyszów	Sanok	Bukowsko
Przybyszówka	Rzeszów	Rzeszów
Przychojce	Łańcut	Leżajsk
Przycorów	Pilzno	Dębica
Przydonica	Nowy Sącz	Nowy Sącz
Przykop	Mielec	Mielec
Przyłbice	Jaworów	Jaworów
Przylek	Mielec	Mielec
Przyleków	Żywiec	Zabłocie
Przyłkowice	Wadowice	Kalwarya
Przysicki	Jasło	Jasło
Przysietnica	Brzozów	Brzozów
Przysietnica	Nowy Sącz	Piwniczna
Przyslup	Gorlice	Gorlice
Przyslup	Lisko	Baligród
Przysłup	Kalusz	Kalusz

Town	Main District	Subdistrict
Przyszów Kameralny	Nisko	Nisko
Przyszów Szlachecki	Nisko	Nisko
Przyszów Szlachecki	Tarnobrzeg	Rozwadów
Przyszowa	Limanowa	Limanowa
Psary	Chrzanów	Trzebina
Psary	Rohatyń	Rohatyń
Pstrągowa	Ropczyce	Wielopole
Pstrążne	Gorlice	Gorlice
Pstręgówka	Jasło	Frysztak
Ptaszkowa	Grybów	Grybów
Ptaszniki	Kam. Strumiłowa	Dobrotwor
Ptonus	Tarnobrzeg	Rozwadów
Pukaczów	Kam. Strumiłowa	Radziechów
Pukarowce	Stanisławów	Halicz
Pukienicze	Stryj	Stryj
Puklaki	Borszczów	Skała
Puków	Rohatyń	Rohatyń
Pułanki	Jasło	Frysztak
Puławy	Sanok	Rymanów
Pustawola	Jasło	Jasło
Pustomyty	Lemberg	Nawarya
Pustynia	Pilzno	Dębica
Putiatycze	Gródek	Gródek
Putiatycze	Mościska	Sądowa Wisznia
Putiatynce	Rohatyń	Rohatyń
Putków	Ropczyce	Ropczyce
Puźniki	Buczacz	Barysz
Puźniki	Tłumacz	Chocimirz
Pychowice	Wieliczka	Podgórze
Pyszkowce	Buczacz	Jazłowice
Pysznica	Nisko	Ulanów
Pyzówka	Nowy Targ	Nowy Targ

Town	Main District	Subdistrict
Raba Niżna	Limanowa	Mszana dolna
Raba Wyżna	Myślenice	Jordanów
Rabczyce	Drohobycz	Drohobycz
Rabe	Lisko	Ustrzyki Dolne
Rabka	Myślenice	Jordanów
Rąbkowa	Nowy Sącz	Nowy Sącz
Raby	Lisko	Baligród
Rachin	Dolina	Dolina
Raciborsko	Wieliczka	Klasno
Raciborzany	Limanowa	Limanowa
Raciechowice	Wieliczka	Klasno
Racławice	Gorlice	Gorlice
Racławice	Nisko	Nisko
Racławoka	Rzeszów	Rzeszów
Raczyna	Jarosław	Pruchnik
Radajowice	Nowy Sącz	Nowy Sącz
Radawa	Jarosław	Sienawa
Radcza	Bohordczany	Lysiec
Radelicz	Drohobycz	Drohobycz
Radenice	Mościska	Mościska
Radlna	Tarnów	Tarnów
Radłów	Brzesko	Radlów
Radłówice	Sambor	Sambor
Radochońce	Mościska	Hussaków
Radocza	Wadowice	Wadowice
Radoczyna	Gorlice	Gorlice
Radomyśl	Tarnobrzeg	Radomyśl
Radomyśl Wielkie	Mielec	Radomyśl Wiel.
Radoszcz	Dąbrowa	Dąbrowa
Radoszyce	Sanok	Bukowsko
Radruz	Rawa Ruska	Niemerów
Radwan	Dąbrowa	Dąbrowa

Town	Main District	Subdistrict
Radwańce	Sokal	Krystynopol
Radwanowice	Chrzanów	Trzebina
Radymno	Jarosław	Radymno
Radymno	Jarosław	Radymno
Radzichów	Żywiec	Zabłocie
Radziechów	Kam. Strumiłowa	Radziechów
Radziejowa	Lisko	Baligród
Radziszów	Myślenice	Myślenice
Rajsko	Biała	Oświęcim
Rajsko	Brzesko	Szczurowa
Rajsko	Lisko	Baligród
Rajsko	Wieliczka	Klasno
Rajtarowice	Mościska	Hussaków
Rakobuty	Kam. Strumiłowa	Busk
Raków	Dolina	Dolina
Rakowa	Sambor	Sambor
Rakowa	Sanok	Tyrawa woloska
Rakowężyk	Kołomea	Peczeniżyn
Rakowice	Horodenka	Czernelica
Rakowice	Lemberg	Szczerzec
Rakowice	Podhajce	Złotniki
Rakszawa	Łańcut	Żolynia
Raniowice	Drohobycz	Drohobycz
Ranisów	Rzeszów	Głogów
Ranizów	Kolbuszowa	Ranizów
Raniżów Kolonie	Rzeszów	Głogów
Raniżowska Wola	Kolbuszowa	Ranizów
Raszków	Horodenka	Horodenka
Rasztowce	Skałat	Touste
Ratawica	Sanok	Bukowsko
Ratnawy	Brzesko	Wojnicz
Ratulów	Nowy Targ	Nowy Targ

Town	Main District	Subdistrict
Ratyszcze	Brody	Zołożce
Rawa Ruska	Rawa Ruska	Rawa Ruska
Ray	Brzeżany	Brzeżany
Raybrot	Bochnia	Wiśnicz Nowy
Raycza	Żywiec	Zabłocie
Rażniów	Brody	Sokołówka
Rdzawa	Bochnia	Wiśnicz Nowy
Rdzawka	Myślenice	Jordanów
Rdziostów	Nowy Sącz	Nowy Sącz
Rechtberg	Jaworów	Krakówiec
Reczpol	Przemyśl	Krzywcza
Regetów Niżny	Gorlice	Gorlice
Regetów Wyżny	Gorlice	Gorlice
Regulice	Chrzanów	Chrzanów
Rehberg	Mościska	Mościska
Rehfeld	Bóbrka	Bóbrka
Reichau	Cieszanów	Lubaczów
Reichenbach	Lemberg	Szczerzec
Reichsheim	Mielec	Mielec
Rekszyn	Przemyślany	Dunajowce
Remenów	Lemberg	Jaryczów
Reniów	Brody	Zołożce
Repechów	Bóbrka	Strzeliska Nowe
Repużyńce	Horodenka	Czernelica
Reszniate	Dolina	Rożniatów
Rochynie	Kołomea	Gwozdźiec
Rocmirowa	Nowy Sącz	Nowy Sącz
Roczyny	Wadowice	Andrychów
Rodatycze	Gródek	Gródek
Rodze	Wadowice	Zator
Rogi	Krosno	Dukla
Rogi	Nowy Sącz	Stary Sącz

Town	Main District	Subdistrict
Rogoźnica	Rzeszów	Głogów
Rogoźnik	Nowy Targ	Nowy Targ
Rogoźno	Łańcut	Przeworsk
Roguźno	Jaworów	Jaworów
Roguźno	Sambor	Sambor
Roguźno	Żydaczów	Żydaczów
Rohaczyn	Brzeżany	Narajów
Rohatyń	Rohatyń	Rohatyń
Rojatyń	Sokal	Sokal
Rojówka	Nowy Sącz	Nowy Sącz
Rokieciny	Myślenice	Jordanów
Rokietnica	Jarosław	Pruchnik
Rokitno	Gródek	Janów
Roków	Wadowice	Wadowice
Rokówkat	Husiatyn	Chorostków
Rokszyce	Przemyśl	Przemyśl
Rolikówka	Sokal	Sokal
Rolów	Drohobycz	Drohobycz
Romanów	Bóbrka	Mikalajów
Romanówka	Brody	Szczurowice
Romanówka	Kam. Strumiłowa	Stajanów
Romanówka	Rudki	Komarno
Romanówka	Tarnopol	Tarnopol
Romanówka	Trembowla	Janów
Romaszówka	Czortków	Budzanów
Ropa	Gorlice	Gorlice
Ropczyce	Ropczyce	Ropczyce
Ropea Polska	Gorlice	Gorlice
Ropianka	Krosno	Dukla
Ropica Ruska	Gorlice	Gorlice
Ropienka	Lisko	Lisko
Ropki	Gorlice	Gorlice

Town	Main District	Subdistrict
Ropki	Nisko	Rudnik
Rosechy	Staremiasto	Chyrów
Rosenberg	Lemberg	Szczerzec
Rosochacz	Czortków	Ulaszkowce
Rosochate	Lisko	Lutowiska
Rosochowaciec	Podhajce	Złotniki
Rosochowaciec	Skałat	Skałat
Rosolin	Lisko	Lutowiska
Rostoka	Bircza	Bircza
Rostoki Dolne	Lisko	Baligród
Roszniów	Tłumacz	Uście Zielone
Rottenhan	Gródek	Janów
Równe	Krosno	Dukla
Równia	Kalusz	Kalusz
Równia	Lisko	Ustrzyki Dolne
Rozalin	Tarnobrzeg	Tarnobrzeg
Rozalówka	Sokal	Sokal
Rożanka	Jasło	Frysztak
Rożanka	Ropczyce	Wielopole
Rożanka	Żółkiew	Gross-Mosty
Rożanka Niżna	Stryj	Skole
Rożanka Wyżna	Stryj	Skole
Rożanówka	Zaleszczyki	Tłuste
Rozbórz	Łańcut	Przeworsk
Rozbórz Długi	Jarosław	Pruchnik
Rozbórz Okragły	Jarosław	Pruchnik
Rozdół	Żydaczów	Rozdól
Rożdżałów	Sokal	Tartaków
Rozdziałowice	Rudki	Rudki
Rozdziele	Bochnia	Wiśnicz Nowy
Rozdziele	Gorlice	Gorlice
Rozdziele	Nowy Sącz	Nowy Sącz

Town	Main District	Subdistrict
Rozembark	Gorlice	Gorlice
Rozeń Mały	Kossów	Kuty
Rozeń Wielki	Kossów	Kuty
Rozenburg	Bircza	Dobromil
Rozhadów	Złoczów	Pomorzany
Rozhurcze	Stryj	Stryj
Rozkochów	Chrzanów	Chrzanów
Rozkowice	Nowy Sącz	Nowy Sącz
Rożniatów	Dolina	Rożniatów
Rożniatów	Jarosław	Jarosław
Rożniaty	Mielec	Mielec
Rożnów	Śniatyn	Zabłotów
Rożnowa	Wieliczka	Klasno
Rozpucie	Bircza	Bircza
Rozsochacz	Kołomea	Gwozdźiec
Rozstajne	Krosno	Dukla
Roztocki	Jasło	Jasło
Roztoczki	Dolina	Bolechów
Roztoka	Brzesko	Wojnicz
Roztoka	Limanowa	Limanowa
Roztoka	Nowy Sącz	Nowy Sącz
Roztoka Mała	Nowy Sącz	Łabowa
Roztoka Wielka	Nowy Sącz	Łabowa
Roztoka Zyterska	Nowy Sącz	Piwniczna
Roztoki	Kossów	Kuty
Rożubowice	Przemyśl	Przemyśl
Rozulna	Borhodczany	Sołotwina
Rozwadów	Tarnobrzeg	Rozwadów
Rozwadów	Tarnobrzeg	Rozwadów
Rozwadów	Żydaczów	Rozdól
Rozważ	Złoczów	Białykamień
Rozwienica	Jarosław	Jarosław

Town	Main District	Subdistrict
Rozworzany	Przemyślany	Gliniany
Rożyska	Skałat	Tarnoruda
Ruchniszcze	Kołomea	Gwozdźiec
Ruda	Bóbrka	Brzozdowiec
Ruda	Brzesko	Radłów
Ruda	Nisko	Rudnik
Ruda	Rawa Ruska	Magierów
Ruda	Rohatyń	Rohatyń
Ruda	Ropczyce	Sędziszów
Ruda	Żydaczów	Żydaczów
Ruda Justkowska	Tarnobrzeg	Rozwadów
Ruda Kameralna	Brzesko	Czchów
Ruda Kochanowska	Jaworów	Krakówiec
Ruda Kołtowska	Złoczów	Sassów
Ruda Krakowiecka	Jaworów	Krakówiec
Ruda Krechowska	Żółkiew	Żółkiew
Ruda Lasowa	Rawa Ruska	Magierów
Ruda Rożaniecka	Cieszanów	Narol
Ruda Sielecka	Kam. Strumiłowa	Kam. Strumiłowa
Ruda Zazamcze	Dąbrowa	Dąbrowa
Rudance	Lemberg	Jaryczów
Rudawa	Chrzanów	Trzebina
Rudawka	Bircza	Bircza
Rudawka	Lisko	Ustrzyki Dolne
Rudawka Jaśliska	Sanok	Rymanów
Rudawka Rymanowska	Sanok	Rymanów
Rudec	Brody	Sokołówka
Rudenka	Lisko	Lisko
Rudenko Lackie	Brody	Szczurowice
Rudenko Ruskie	Brody	Szczurowice
Rudka	Brzesko	Wojnicz

Town	Main District	Subdistrict
Rudka	Cieszanów	Narol
Rudka	Jarosław	Pruchnik
Rudka	Tarnów	Zabno
Rudki	Rudki	Rudki
Rudna	Tarnów	Zabno
Rudna Mała	Rzeszów	Głogów
Rudna Wielka	Rzeszów	Głogów
Rudnik	Myślenice	Myślenice
Rudnik	Nisko	Rudnik
Rudnik	Wieliczka	Klasno
Rudniki	Mościska	Mościska
Rudniki	Podhajce	Podhajce
Rudniki	Śniatyn	Zabłotów
Rudniki	Żydaczów	Rozdół
Rudno	Chrzanów	Trzebina
Rudno	Lemberg	Zniesienie
Rudolowice	Jarosław	Jarosław
Rudy Rysie	Brzesko	Szczurowa
Rukomysz	Buczacz	Buczacz
Rumno	Rudki	Komarno
Rumosz	Sokal	Sokal
Rungury	Kołomea	Peczeniżyn
Rupniów	Limanowa	Limanowa
Rusianówka	Tarnopol	Tarnopol
Rusiłów	Buczacz	Potok
Rusiłów	Kam. Strumiłowa	Busk
Rusin	Sokal	Warez
Rusinów	Kolbuszowa	Majdan
Rusinówska Wola	Kolbuszowa	Majdan
Ruska Wieś	Przemyśl	Dubiecko
Ruska Wieś	Rzeszów	Rzeszów
Ruskie	Lisko	Lutowiska

Town	Main District	Subdistrict
Russów	Śniatyn	Śniatyn
Rustweczko	Mościska	Hussaków
Ruszelczyce	Przemyśl	Krzywcza
Ruzdwiany	Rohatyń	Bursztyn
Ruzdwiany	Stanisławów	Halicz
Ruzdwiany	Trembowla	Strusów
Rybaki	Wieliczka	Podgórze
Rybarzowice	Biała	Lipnik
Rybe Nowe	Limanowa	Limanowa
Rybe Stare	Limanowa	Limanowa
Rybień	Nowy Sącz	Łabowa
Rybitwy	Wieliczka	Podgórze
Rybne	Lisko	Baligród
Rybnik	Drohobycz	Borysław
Rybniki	Brzeżany	Brzeżany
Rybno	Kossów	Kuty
Rybno	Stanisławów	Stanisławów
Rybotycze	Bircza	Rybotycze
Rybów	Złoczów	Złoczów
Rycerka Dolna	Żywiec	Zabłocie
Rycerka Górna	Żywiec	Zabłocie
Rychcice	Drohobycz	Drohobycz
Rychwald	Gorlice	Gorlice
Rychwald	Tarnów	Tuchów
Rychwald	Żywiec	Zabłocie
Rychwaldek	Żywiec	Zabłocie
Ryczka	Kossów	Kossów
Ryczów	Wadowice	Zator
Ryczychów	Rudki	Komarno
Rydoduby	Czortków	Czortków
Rydzów	Mielec	Radomyśl Wiel.
Ryglice	Tarnów	Ryglice

Town	Main District	Subdistrict
Ryhów	Stryj	Skole
Ryje	Limanowa	Limanowa
Rylowa	Brzesko	Szczurowa
Rymanów	Sanok	Rymanów
Rymizowce	Złoczów	Złoczów
Rypianka	Kalusz	Kalusz
Rypne	Dolina	Rożniatów
Ryszkowa Wola	Jarosław	Jarosław
Ryszyce	Wieliczka	Klasno
Rytro	Nowy Sącz	Piwniczna
Rząchowa	Brzesko	Szczurowa
Rząka	Wieliczka	Klasno
Rzatkowice	Mościska	Mościska
Rzeczyca Długa	Tarnobrzeg	Rozwadów
Rzeczyca Okragla	Tarnobrzeg	Rozwadów
Rzędzianowice	Mielec	Mielec
Rzędzin	Tarnów	Tarnów
Rzędzińska Wola	Tarnów	Tarnów
Rzegocin	Ropczyce	Wielopole
Rzegocina	Bochnia	Wiśnicz Nowy
Rzeki	Limanowa	Limanowa
Rzeklińce	Żólkiew	Gross-Mosty
Rzemień	Mielec	Mielec
Rzepedź	Sanok	Bukowsko
Rzepienik Strżyż.	Gorlice	Rzepienik Strzyz.
Rzepiennik Biskupi	Gorlice	Rzepienik Strzyz.
Rzepińce	Buczacz	Jazłowice
Rzeplin	Jarosław	Pruchnik
Rzepnik	Jasło	Frysztak
Rzepnik	Krosno	Korczyna
Rzepniów	Kam. Strumiłowa	Busk
Rzęsna Polska	Lemberg	Zniesienie

Town	Main District	Subdistrict
Rzęsna Ruska	Lemberg	Zniesienie
Rzeszotary	Wieliczka	Klasno
Rzeszów	Rzeszów	Rzeszów
Rzeszyca	Rawa Ruska	Uhnów
Rzezawa	Bochnia	Bochnia
Rzochów	Mielec	Mielec
Rzozów	Wieliczka	Podgórze
Rzuchów	Łańcut	Leżajsk
Rzuchowa	Tarnów	Tarnów
Rzyczki	Rawa Ruska	Rawa Ruska
Rzyki	Wadowice	Andrychów
Sabinówka	Kam. Strumiłowa	Stajanów
Sadek	Limanowa	Limanowa
Sadki	Zaleszczyki	Uścieczko
Sadkowa	Jasło	Jasło
Sadkowa Góra	Mielec	Radomyśl Wiel.
Sadkowice	Mościska	Hussaków
Sądowa Wisznia	Mościska	Sądowa Wiśnia
Sadzawa	Bohordczany	Bohordczany
Sadzawki	Skałat	Grzymałów
Sakowczyk	Lisko	Baligród
Salamonowa Górka	Dolina	Bolechów
Salasze	Rawa Ruska	Uhnów
Salmopol	Biała	Lipnik
Salówka	Czortków	Jagielnica
Sambor	Sambor	Sambor
Samborek	Wieliczka	Podgórze
Samborówka	Tarnopol	Tarnopol
Samocice	Dąbrowa	Dąbrowa
Samołuskowce	Husiatyn	Husiatyn
Sanka Północna	Chrzanów	Trzebina
Sanka Południowa	Chrzanów	Trzebina

Town	Main District	Subdistrict
Sanniki	Mościska	Sądowa Wisznia
Sanoczany	Przemyśl	Niżankowice
Sanok	Sanok	Sanok
Sanoka	Tarnów	Zabno
Sapahów	Stanisławów	Halicz
Sapieżanka	Kam. Strumiłowa	Kam. Strumiłowa
Sapohów	Borszczów	Mielnica
Sapowa	Buczacz	Buczacz
Saranczuki	Brzeżany	Brzeżany
Sarnki	Bóbrka	Bóbrka
Sarnki Dolne	Rohatyń	Bursztyn
Sarnki Górne	Rohatyń	Bursztyn
Sarnki Średnie	Rohatyń	Bursztyn
Sarny	Jaworów	Krakówiec
Sarny	Mościska	Mościska
Sarysz	Limanowa	Limanowa
Sarzyna	Nisko	Rudnik
Sąsiadowice	Sambor	Sambor
Saska	Rudki	Komarno
Saska Kameralna	Drohobycz	Drohobycz
Sassów	Złoczów	Sassów
Sawa	Wieliczka	Klasno
Sawaluski	Buczacz	Monasterzyska
Sawczyn	Sokal	Sokal
Schodnica	Drohobycz	Borysław
Schönanger	Mielec	Radomyśl Wiel.
Schönthal	Gródek	Janów
Scianka	Złoczów	Gologory
Ścianka	Buczacz	Potok
Sędziszów	Ropczyce	Sędziszów
Sędziszowa	Grybów	Bobowa
Sękowa	Gorlice	Gorlice

Town	Main District	Subdistrict
Sękowa Wola	Sanok	Nowtanice
Semenów z Zieleńcem	Trembowla	Trembowla
Semenówka	Horodenka	Czernelica
Semerówka	Jaworów	Jaworów
Seneczów	Dolina	Dolina
Sępnica	Ropczyce	Ropczyce
Serafince	Horodenka	Horodenka
Serdyca	Lemberg	Szczerzec
Seredce	Brody	Załoźce
Seredne	Kalusz	Wojnilów
Seredne	Podhajce	Zawałów
Serednica	Lisko	Ustrzyki Dolne
Serednie Małe	Lisko	Lutowiska
Serednie Wielkie	Lisko	Lisko
Seredyńce	Tarnopol	Tarnopol
Serwiry	Złoczów	Jezierna
Siarczana Góra	Wieliczka	Podgórze
Siary	Gorlice	Gorlice
Sichów	Lemberg	Zniesienie
Sidorów	Husiatyn	Husiatyn
Sidzina	Myślenice	Jordanów
Sidzina	Wieliczka	Podgórze
Siebieczów	Sokal	Bełż
Siechów	Stryj	Stryj
Siechowce	Tarnów	Tarnów
Sieciechów	Lemberg	Jaryczów
Siedlanka	Kolbuszowa	Kolbuszowa
Siedlanka	Łańcut	Kańczuga
Siedlanka	Łańcut	Leżajsk
Siedlce	Nowy Sącz	Nowy Sącz
Siedlec	Bochnia	Bochnia

Town	Main District	Subdistrict
Siedlec	Chrzanów	Trzebina
Siedlec	Tarnów	Zabno
Siedliska	Bóbrka	Mikalajów
Siedliska	Brzozów	Dynów
Siedliska	Grybów	Bobowa
Siedliska	Jasło	Jasło
Siedliska	Jaworów	Jaworów
Siedliska	Krosno	Dukla
Siedliska	Lemberg	Nawarya
Siedliska	Przemyśl	Przemyśl
Siedliska	Rawa Ruska	Rawa Ruska
Siedliska	Rzeszów	Tyczyn
Siedliska	Stanisławów	Halicz
Siedliska	Tarnów	Tuchów
Siedliszczany	Tarnobrzeg	Baranów
Siegenthal	Lisko	Ustrzyki Dolne
Siekierczyce	Sambor	Sambor
Siekierczyn	Horodenka	Obertyn
Siekierczyna	Grybów	Bobowa
Siekierzyńce	Husiatyn	Husiatyn
Sieklerczyna	Limanowa	Limanowa
Sieklówka Dolna	Jasło	Frysztak
Sieklówka Górna	Jasło	Frysztak
Sielce	Stanisławów	Jezupol
Sielec	Kam. Strumiłowa	Kam. Strumiłowa
Sielec	Przemyśl	Przemyśl
Sielec	Ropczyce	Sędziszów
Sielec	Sambor	Sambor
Sielec	Sokal	Krystynopol
Sielec	Tarnobrzeg	Tarnobrzeg
Sielnica	Przemyśl	Dubiecko
Siemakowce	Horodenka	Horodenka

Town	Main District	Subdistrict
Siemakowce	Kołomea	Gwoździec
Siemiakowce	Czortków	Czortków
Siemianówka	Lemberg	Szczerzec
Siemiechów	Tarnów	Tuchów
Siemień	Żywiec	Zabłocie
Siemiginów	Stryj	Stryj
Siemikowce	Rohatyń	Bursztyn
Siemuszowa	Sanok	Sanok
Sieniawa	Jarosław	Sienawa
Sieniawa	Myślenice	Jordanów
Sieniawa	Sanok	Rymanów
Sieniawka	Cieszanów	Lubaczów
Sienikowice	Podhajce	Złotniki
Sieńków	Kam. Strumiłowa	Radziechów
Sienna	Nowy Sącz	Nowy Sącz
Sienna	Żywiec	Zabłocie
Siennów	Łańcut	Kańczuga
Siepietnica	Jasło	Jasło
Sierakosce	Przemyśl	Niżankowice
Sieraków	Wieliczka	Klasno
Siercza	Wieliczka	Klasno
Siersza	Chrzanów	Chrzanów
Sietesz	Łańcut	Kańczuga
Sietnica	Gorlice	Rzepienik Strzyzewski
Signiówka	Lemberg	Zniesienie
Sikorzyce	Dąbrowa	Dąbrowa
Sikorzynice	Wieliczka	Klasno
Sińków	Zaleszczyki	Korolówka
Siołko	Kalusz	Wojnilów
Siołko	Podhajce	Podhajce
Siołkowa	Grybów	Grybów

Town	Main District	Subdistrict
Siwka Kałuska	Kalusz	Kalusz
Siwka Wojniłowska	Kalusz	Wojnilów
Skała	Borszczów	Skała
Skałat	Skałat	Skałat
Skalnik	Krosno	Dukla
Skawa	Myślenice	Jordanów
Skawce	Wadowice	Wadowice
Skawica	Myślenice	Maków
Skawina	Wieliczka	Podgórze
Skawinki	Wadowice	Kalwarya
Skidzin	Biała	Oświęcim
Skład Solny	Przemyśl	Sosnica
Składziste	Nowy Sącz	Łabowa
Skole	Stryj	Skole
Skolin	Jaworów	Wielkie Oczy
Skołyszyn	Jasło	Jasło
Skomielna Biała	Myślenice	Jordanów
Skomielna Czarna	Myślenice	Jordanów
Skomierzyn	Tarnobrzeg	Rozwadów
Skomorochy	Buczacz	Potok
Skomorochy	Sokal	Sokal
Skomorochy	Tarnopol	Mikulińce
Skomorochy Nowe	Rohatyń	Bursztyn
Skomorochy Stare	Rohatyń	Bursztyn
Skomorosze	Czortków	Budzanów
Skopańce	Tarnobrzeg	Baranów
Skopów	Przemyśl	Krzywcza
Skopówka	Nadwórna	Lanczyn
Skorodne	Lisko	Lutowiska
Skorodyńce	Czortków	Czortków
Skotniki	Wieliczka	Podgórze
Skowiatyń	Zaleszczyki	Korolówka

Town	Main District	Subdistrict
Skretka	Nowy Sącz	Nowy Sącz
Skrudzina	Nowy Sącz	Stary Sącz
Skrzydlna	Limanowa	Limanowa
Skrzynka	Dąbrowa	Szczucin
Skrzynka	Wieliczka	Klasno
Skrzypne	Nowy Targ	Nowy Targ
Skrzyszów	Ropczyce	Ropczyce
Skurowa	Pilzno	Jodłowa
Skwarzawa	Złoczów	Białykamień
Skwarzawa Nowa	Żółkiew	Żółkiew
Skwarzawa Stara	Żółkiew	Żółkiew
Skwirtne	Gorlice	Gorlice
Skyrsów	Tarnów	Tarnów
Słabasz	Mościska	Sądowa Wisznia
Sławencin	Jasło	Jasło
Sławentyn	Podhajce	Zawałów
Sławki	Gródek	Janów
Sławna	Złoczów	Zborów
Sławna	Złoczów	Złoczów
Śleszowice	Wadowice	Wadowice
Ślęzaki	Tarnobrzeg	Baranów
Śliwki	Kalusz	Kalusz
Śliwnica	Przemyśl	Dubiecko
Śliwnica	Przemyśl	Krzywcza
Śliwnica	Staremiasto	Chyrów
Słoboda	Jarosław	Pruchnik
Słoboda Bolechowska	Dolina	Bolechów
Słoboda Dolińska	Dolina	Dolina
Słoboda Niebyłowska	Kalusz	Kalusz
Słoboda Równiańska	Kalusz	Kalusz
Słoboda Rungurska	Kołomea	Peczeniżyn
Słoboda Złota	Brzeżany	Kozowa

Town	Main District	Subdistrict
Słobódka	Brzeżany	Kozłów
Słobódka	Kalusz	Wojnilów
Słobódka	Kossów	Kuty
Słobódka	Stanisławów	Halicz
Słobódka	Zaleszczyki	Tłuste
Słobódka ad Odaje	Tłumacz	Tłumacz
Słobódka ad Tłumacz	Tłumacz	Tłumacz
Słobódka Bolszowiecka	Rohatyń	Bursztyn
Słobódka Bukacz.	Rohatyń	Bursztyn
Słobódka Dolna	Buczacz	Monasterzyska
Słobódka Dżuryńska	Czortków	Czortków
Słobódka Górna	Buczacz	Monasterzyska
Słobódka Janowska	Trembowla	Janów
Słobódka Konkelnicka	Rohatyń	Bursztyn
Słobódka Leśna	Kołomea	Kołomea
Słobódka Muszkat	Borszczów	Borszczów
Słobódka Polna	Kołomea	Gwozdźiec
Słobódka Strusowska	Trembowla	Strusów
Słobódka Turylecka	Borszczów	Skała
Słocina	Rzeszów	Tyczyn
Słomianka	Mościska	Sądowa Wisznia
Słomiróg	Wieliczka	Klasno
Słomka	Bochnia	Bochnia
Słomka	Limanowa	Mszana Dolna
Słona	Brzesko	Czchów
Słone	Zaleszczyki	Uścieczko
Słonne	Myślenice	Jordanów
Słońsko	Drohobycz	Drohobycz
Słopnice Królewskie	Limanowa	Limanowa
Słopnice Szlacheckie	Limanowa	Limanowa

Town	Main District	Subdistrict
Słotwina	Brzesko	Brzesko
Słotwina	Żywiec	Zabłocie
Słotwiny	Nowy Sącz	Krynica
Słowikowa	Nowy Sącz	Nowy Sącz
Słowita	Przemyślany	Gliniany
Słupice	Dąbrowa	Szczucin
Słupie	Limanowa	Limanowa
Słupki	Tarnopol	Tarnopol
Smarzów	Brody	Szczurowice
Smarzowa	Pilzno	Dębica
Smęgorzów	Dąbrowa	Dąbrowa
Smereczna	Staremiasto	Chyrów
Smereczne	Krosno	Dukla
Smerek	Lisko	Baligród
Smereków	Żólkiew	Żólkiew
Smerekowiec	Gorlice	Gorlice
Śmichów	Żydaczów	Żurawno
Śmietana	Brzesko	Radłów
Śmigno	Tarnów	Zabno
Smodna	Kossów	Kossów
Smolanka	Tarnopol	Mikulińce
Smolarzyny	Łańcut	Żolynia
Smolice	Wadowice	Zator
Smolin	Rawa Ruska	Niemerów
Smolnica	Lisko	Ustrzyki Dolne
Smolnik	Lisko	Lutowiska
Smolnik	Lisko	Wola Michowa
Smolno	Brody	Brody
Smolno	Drohobycz	Drohobycz
Smorze Dolne	Stryj	Skole
Smorze Górne	Stryj	Skole
Smorze Kolonia	Stryj	Skole

Town	Main District	Subdistrict
Smykan	Limanowa	Limanowa
Smyków Mały	Dąbrowa	Dąbrowa
Smyków Wielki	Dąbrowa	Dąbrowa
Smykowce	Tarnopol	Tarnopol
Śniatyn	Śniatyn	Śniatyn
Śniatynka	Drohobycz	Drohobycz
Śnietnica	Grybów	Grybów
Snowicz	Złoczów	Złoczów
Snówidów	Buczacz	Potok
Sobin	Kam. Strumiłowa	Radziechów
Sobjecin	Jarosław	Jarosław
Sobniów	Jasło	Jasło
Sobolów	Bochnia	Wiśnicz Nowy
Sobolówka	Złoczów	Białykamień
Soboniewice	Wieliczka	Klasno
Sobotów	Stanisławów	Halicz
Sobów	Tarnobrzeg	Tarnobrzeg
Sochnia	Limanowa	Limanowa
Sochy	Tarnobrzeg	Rozwadów
Sojkowa	Nisko	Rudnik
Sokal	Sokal	Sokal
Sokloszów	Jarosław	Radymno
Sokół	Gorlice	Gorlice
Sokole	Kam. Strumiłowa	Kam. Strumiłowa
Sokole	Lisko	Ustrzyki Dolne
Sokole	Mościska	Mościska
Sokolki	Brzesko	Szczurowa
Sokolniki	Lemberg	Nawarya
Sokolniki	Podhajce	Złotniki
Sokolniki	Tarnobrzeg	Tarnobrzeg
Sokołoska Wulka	Kolbuszowa	Sokołów
Sokołów	Buczacz	Potok

Town	Main District	Subdistrict
Sokołów	Kam. Strumiłowa	Busk
Sokołów	Kolbuszowa	Sokołów
Sokołów	Podhajce	Złotniki
Sokołów	Stryj	Stryj
Sokołówa Wola	Lisko	Ustrzyki Dolne
Sokołówka	Bóbrka	Bóbrka
Sokołówka	Brody	Sokołówka
Sokołówka	Kossów	Kossów
Sokulec	Buczacz	Potok
Sólca	Przemyśl	Niżankowice
Solce	Drohobycz	Drohobycz
Solina	Lisko	Ustrzyki Dolne
Solinka	Lisko	Wola Michowa
Solinka	Lisko	Wola Michowa
Solonice	Rohatyń	Rohatyń
Solonka	Rzeszów	Tyczyn
Solonka Mała	Lemberg	Nawarya
Solonka Wielka	Lemberg	Nawarya
Sołotwina	Borhodczany	Sołotwina
Solowa	Przemyślany	Gliniany
Sonina	Łańcut	Łańcut
Soposzyn	Żólkiew	Żólkiew
Sopotnia Mała	Żywiec	Zabłocie
Sopotnia Wielka	Żywiec	Zabłocie
Sopotnik	Bircza	Dobromil
Sopów	Kołomea	Kołomea
Soput	Stryj	Skole
Sorocko	Skałat	Skałat
Soroka	Skałat	Touste
Soroki	Buczacz	Buczacz
Soroki	Horodenka	Horodenka
Sośńica	Przemyśl	Sosnica

Town	Main District	Subdistrict
Sosnice	Ropczyce	Wielopole
Sosnów	Podhajce	Złotniki
Sosnowice	Wadowice	Zator
Sosolówka	Czortków	Ulaszkowce
Sowina	Pilzno	Brzostek
Sowliny	Limanowa	Limanowa
Sozań	Staremiasto	Staremiasto
Spas	Dolina	Rożniatów
Spas	Kam. Strumiłowa	Kam. Strumiłowa
Spas	Staremiasto	Staremiasto
Spasków	Sokal	Tartaków
Sporysz	Żywiec	Zabłocie
Spytkowice	Myślenice	Jordanów
Spytkowice	Wadowice	Zator
Średni	Kalusz	Kalusz
Średnia	Przemyśl	Krzywcza
Średnia Wieś	Lisko	Lisko
Środopolce	Kam. Strumiłowa	Radziechów
Srogów Dolny	Sanok	Sanok
Srogów Górny	Sanok	Sanok
Sroki Lwowskie	Lemberg	Zniesienie
Sroki Szcz.	Lemberg	Szczerzec
Srołmienice	Rudki	Rudki
Sromowce Niżne	Nowy Targ	Nowy Targ
Sromowce Wyżne	Nowy Targ	Nowy Targ
St. Johannesberg	Limanowa	Limanowa
St. Stanisław	Stanisławów	Halicz
Stadło	Nowy Sącz	Stary Sącz
Stadniki	Wieliczka	Klasno
Staje	Rawa Ruska	Uhnów
Stałe	Tarnobrzeg	Tarnobrzeg
Staniątki	Wieliczka	Klasno

Town	Main District	Subdistrict
Stanila	Drohobycz	Drohobycz
Stanimirz	Przemyślany	Gliniany
Stanin	Kam. Strumiłowa	Radziechów
Stanisław Dolny	Wadowice	Kalwarya
Stanisław Górny	Wadowice	Kalwarya
Stanisławczyk	Brody	Stanisławczyk
Stanisławczyk	Przemyśl	Przemyśl
Stanisławice	Bochnia	Bochnia
Stanisławów	Stanisławów	Stanisławów
Stanislówka	Żółkiew	Gross-Mosty
Staniszewskie	Kolbuszowa	Ranizów
Stańków	Stryj	Stryj
Stańkowa	Lisko	Lisko
Stańkowa	Nowy Sącz	Nowy Sącz
Stańkowa	Żydaczów	Żurawno
Stańkowce	Bóbrka	Brzozdowiec
Stańkowce	Dolina	Bolechów
Stany	Nisko	Nisko
Stara Wieś	Brzozów	Brzozów
Stara Wieś	Drohobycz	Drohobycz
Stara Wieś	Grybów	Grybów
Stara Wieś	Limanowa	Limanowa
Stararopa	Staremiasto	Starasól
Starasól	Staremiasto	Starasól
Starawieś Dolna	Biała	Kęty
Starawieś Górna	Biała	Kęty
Stare Stawy	Biała	Oświęcim
Starebystre	Nowy Targ	Nowy Targ
Staremiasto	Łańcut	Leżajsk
Staremiasto	Podhajce	Podhajce
Staremiasto	Staremiasto	Staremiasto
Staresioło	Bóbrka	Bóbrka

Town	Main District	Subdistrict
Staresioło	Cieszanów	Oleszyce
Starogród	Sokal	Warez
Staromiejszczyzna	Skałat	Podwołoczyska
Staromieście	Rzeszów	Rzeszów
Staroniwa	Rzeszów	Rzeszów
Starunia	Borhodczany	Sołotwina
Stary Sącz	Nowy Sącz	Stary Sącz
Stary Skałat	Skałat	Skałat
Starzawa	Bircza	Dobromil
Starzawa	Mościska	Mościska
Starzyska	Jaworów	Jaworów
Stasiowa Wola	Rohatyń	Bursztyn
Stasiówka	Pilzno	Dębica
Staszkówka	Gorlice	Rzepienik Strzyzewski
Stawczany	Gródek	Gródek
Stawiska	Grybow	Grybow
Stawki Kraśnieńskie	Skałat	Touste
Stawkowice	Wieliczka	Klasno
Stawsko	Stryj	Skole
Stebne	Kossów	Żabie
Stebnik	Bohordczany	Lysiec
Stebnik	Drohobycz	Drohobycz
Stebnik	Lisko	Ustrzyki Dolne
Stechnikowce	Tarnopol	Tarnopol
Stecowa	Śniatyn	Śniatyn
Stefkowa	Lisko	Ustrzyki Dolne
Steinau	Nisko	Rudnik
Steinfeld	Lisko	Ustrzyki Dolne
Steniatyn	Sokal	Sokal
Stepina z Chytrówka	Jasło	Frysztak
Sterkowiec	Brzesko	Brzesko

Town	Main District	Subdistrict
Stężnica	Lisko	Baligród
Stobierna	Pilzno	Dębica
Stochynia	Staremiasto	Felszytn
Stodółki	Gródek	Gródek
Stojance	Mościska	Mościska
Stojanów	Kam. Strumiłowa	Stajanów
Stoki	Bóbrka	Bóbrka
Stołowa	Pilzno	Pilzno
Stołpin	Brody	Toporów
Stopczatów	Kołomea	Jabłonów
Strachocina	Sanok	Sanok
Straconka	Biała	Lipnik
Stradcz	Gródek	Janów
Stradomka	Bochnia	Wiśnicz Nowy
Straszęcin	Pilzno	Dębica
Straszewice	Staremiasto	Staremiasto
Stratyń Wieś	Rohatyń	Rohatyń
Strażów	Łańcut	Łańcut
Strażydle	Rzeszów	Baligród
Stregocice	Pilzno	Pilzno
Streptów	Kam. Strumiłowa	Kam. Strumiłowa
Strojców	Dąbrowa	Dąbrowa
Stroniatyn	Lemberg	Jaryczów
Stronie	Limanowa	Limanowa
Stronie	Wadowice	Kalwarya
Stroniowice	Mościska	Hussaków
Stronna	Gródek	Janów
Stronowice	Przemyśl	Niżankowice
Strosówka	Czortków	Czortków
Stróża	Limanowa	Limanowa
Stróża	Myślenice	Myślenice
Stróże	Brzesko	Czchów

Town	Main District	Subdistrict
Stróże	Nisko	Rudnik
Stróże Małe	Sanok	Sanok
Stróże Niżne	Grybów	Grybów
Stróże Wielkie	Sanok	Sanok
Stróże Wyżne	Grybów	Grybów
Stróżna	Grybów	Bobowa
Stróżówka	Gorlice	Gorlice
Strubowiska Kalnica	Lisko	Baligród
Struga	Nowy Sącz	Nowy Sącz
Strumiany	Wieliczka	Klasno
Strupków	Nadwórna	Lanczyn
Strusów	Trembowla	Strusów
Strusówka	Trembowla	Strusów
Strutyń	Złoczów	Złoczów
Strutyń Niżny	Dolina	Rożniatów
Strutyń Wyżny	Dolina	Rożniatów
Strwiążyk	Lisko	Ustrzyki Dolne
Stryhańce	Przemyślany	Dunajowce
Stryhańce	Stryj	Stryj
Stryhańce	Tłumacz	Uście Zielone
Stryhanka	Kam. Strumiłowa	Dobrotwór
Stryj	Stryj	Stryj
Strymba	Nadwórna	Nadwórna
Stryszawa	Żywiec	Zabłocie
Stryszów	Wadowice	Kalwarya
Stryszowa	Wieliczka	Klasno
Strzałki Lany	Bóbrka	Bóbrka
Strzałków	Stryj	Stryj
Strzałkowce	Borszczów	Borszczów
Strzałkowice	Sambor	Sambor
Strzelbice	Staremiasto	Staremiasto
Strzelczyska	Mościska	Mościska

Town	Main District	Subdistrict
Strzelec Małe	Brzesko	Szczurowa
Strzelec Wielkie	Brzesko	Szczurowa
Strzeliska Nowe	Bóbrka	Strzeliska Nowe
Strzeliska Stare	Bóbrka	Strzeliska Nowe
Strzemien	Żółkiew	Gross-Mosty
Strzemilcze	Brody	Szczurowice
Strzeszyce	Limanowa	Limanowa
Strzeszyn	Gorlice	Gorlice
Strzylawka	Grybów	Grybów
Strzylcze	Horodenka	Horodenka
Strzyżów	Rzeszów	Strzyżów
Stubienko	Przemyśl	Sosnica
Stubno	Przemyśl	Sosnica
Studenne	Lisko	Baligród
Studzianka	Kalusz	Kalusz
Studziany	Łańcut	Przeworsk
Studzienne	Nisko	Ulanów
Stulsko	Żydaczów	Rozdól
Stupnica	Sambor	Sambor
Stuposiany	Lisko	Lutowiska
Styberówka	Brody	Podkamień
Styków	Rzeszów	Głogów
Stynawa Niżna	Stryj	Skole
Stynawa Wyżna	Stryj	Skole
Sucha	Żywiec	Zabłocie
Sucha Struga	Nowy Sącz	Piwniczna
Suchawola	Cieszanów	Oleszyce
Suchodół	Bóbrka	Bóbrka
Suchodół	Dolina	Dolina
Suchodół	Husiatyn	Husiatyn
Suchodół	Krosno	Dukla
Suchodoły	Brody	Brody

Town	Main District	Subdistrict
Suchoraba	Wieliczka	Klasno
Suchorów	Bóbrka	Chodorów
Suchorzów	Tarnobrzeg	Baranów
Suchostaw	Husiatyn	Kopyczyńce
Suchowola	Brody	Brody
Suchowola	Gródek	Janów
Suchy Grunt	Dąbrowa	Szczucin
Suczyca Rykowa	Staremiasto	Staremiasto
Sudkowice	Rudki	Rudki
Sufczyn	Brzesko	Wojnicz
Sufczyna	Bircza	Bircza
Sukmanie	Brzesko	Wojnicz
Sukowate	Lisko	Baligród
Sulichów	Tarnobrzeg	Rozwadów
Sulimów	Sokal	Warez
Sulimów	Żólkiew	Kulików
Sulistrowa	Krosno	Dukla
Sułków	Wieliczka	Klasno
Sułkowice	Myślenice	Myślenice
Sułkowice	Wadowice	Andrychów
Sułkowszczyzna	Mościska	Mościska
Sułów	Wieliczka	Klasno
Sułuków	Dolina	Dolina
Supranówka	Skałat	Skałat
Surmaczówka	Jarosław	Pruchnik
Surochów	Jarosław	Jarosław
Surowa	Mielec	Radomyśl Wiel.
Surowica	Sanok	Bukowsko
Surowki	Wieliczka	Klasno
Susułów	Rudki	Komarno
Suszczyn	Tarnopol	Mikulińce
Suszno	Kam. Strumiłowa	Witków Nowy

Town	Main District	Subdistrict
Suszyca Mała	Staremiasto	Chyrów
Suszyca Wielka	Staremiasto	Chyrów
Swaryczów	Dolina	Rożniatów
Swarzów	Dąbrowa	Dąbrowa
Swerzowa Polska	Krosno	Dukla
Świątkowa Mała	Krosno	Żmigród
Świątkowa Wielka	Krosno	Żmigród
Świątniki Dolne	Wieliczka	Klasno
Świątniki Górne	Wieliczka	Podgórze
Świątoniowa	Łańcut	Przeworsk
Świdnica	Jaworów	Wielkie Oczy
Świdnik	Limanowa	Limanowa
Świdnik	Nowy Sącz	Nowy Sącz
Świdowa	Czortków	Jagielnica
Świdówka	Wieliczka	Klasno
Świdrówka	Dąbrowa	Szczucin
Świebodna	Jarosław	Pruchnik
Świebodzin	Dąbrowa	Dąbrowa
Świebodzin	Tarnów	Tarnów
Święcany	Jasło	Jasło
Świerczów	Kolbuszowa	Kolbuszowa
Świerdzków	Tarnów	Tarnów
Świerkla	Nowy Sącz	Stary Sącz
Świerzkowce	Zaleszczyki	Uścieczko
Świerzowa	Krosno	Dukla
Święte	Przemyśl	Sosnica
Świlcza	Rzeszów	Rzeszów
Świniarsko	Nowy Sącz	Nowy Sącz
Świnna Poreba	Wadowice	Wadowice
Świnna Sól	Żywiec	Zabłocie
Świrż	Przemyślany	Świrż
Świstelniki	Rohatyń	Bursztyn

Town	Main District	Subdistrict
Świtarzów	Sokal	Sokal
Swoszowa	Jasło	Olpiny
Swoszowice	Wieliczka	Podgórze
Sygneczów	Wieliczka	Klasno
Synowódzko	Stryj	Skole
Synowódzko Dolne	Stryj	Skole
Synowódzko Niżne	Stryj	Skole
Synowódzko Wyżne	Stryj	Skole
Szade	Sambor	Sambor
Szaflary	Nowy Targ	Nowy Targ
Szafranów	Mielec	Radomyśl Wiel.
Szalowa	Gorlice	Gorlice
Szare	Żywiec	Zabłocie
Szarów	Wieliczka	Klasno
Szarpance	Sokal	Tartaków
Szarwark	Dąbrowa	Dąbrowa
Szczakowa	Chrzanów	Chrzanów
Szczawa	Limanowa	Limanowa
Szczawne	Sanok	Bukowsko
Szczawnica	Nowy Sącz	Szczawnica
Szczawnica Niżna	Nowy Sącz	Szczawnica
Szczawnica Wyżna	Nowy Sącz	Szczawnica
Szczawnik	Nowy Sącz	Muszyna
Szczepańcowa	Krosno	Korczyna
Szczepanów	Brzesko	Brzesko
Szczepanów	Podhajce	Podhajce
Szczepanowice	Tarnów	Tarnów
Szczepiatyń	Rawa Ruska	Uhnów
Szczepłoty	Jaworów	Wielkie Oczy
Szczerbanówka	Lisko	Wola Michowa
Szczereż	Nowy Sącz	Łącko
Szczerzec	Lemberg	Szczerzec

Town	Main District	Subdistrict
Szczerzyce	Rawa Ruska	Niemerów
Szczucin	Dąbrowa	Szczucin
Szczurowa	Brzesko	Szczurowa
Szczurowice	Brody	Szczurowice
Szczutków	Cieszanów	Lubaczów
Szczyglów	Wieliczka	Klasno
Szczyrk	Biała	Lipnik
Szczyrzyce	Limanowa	Limanowa
Szczytna	Jarosław	Jarosław
Szczytniki	Wieliczka	Klasno
Szebnic	Jasło	Jasło
Szechynie	Przemyśl	Przemyśl
Szeczygelówka	Kam. Strumiłowa	Stajanów
Szeparowce	Kołomea	Peczeniżyn
Szeptyce	Rudki	Rudki
Szerszeniowce	Zaleszczyki	Tłuste
Szertowce	Zaleszczyki	Gródek
Szerzyny	Jasło	Olpiny
Szeszerowice	Mościska	Sądowa Wisznia
Szeszory	Kossów	Pistyn
Szklary	Rzeszów	Tyczyn
Szklary	Sanok	Rymanów
Szkło	Jaworów	Jaworów
Szkodna	Ropczyce	Ropczyce
Szlachtowa	Nowy Sącz	Szczawnica
Szlacińce	Tarnopol	Tarnopol
Szlembarg	Nowy Targ	Nowy Targ
Szmańkowce	Czortków	Czortków
Szmańkowczyki	Czortków	Czortków
Szmitków	Sokal	Warez
Sznyrów	Brody	Brody
Szołomyja	Bóbrka	Mikalajów

Town	Main District	Subdistrict
Szówsko	Jarosław	Jarosław
Szpiklosy	Złoczów	Złoczów
Szufnarowa	Jasło	Frysztak
Szufnarowa	Ropczyce	Wielopole
Szulhanówka	Czortków	Jagielnica
Szumina	Staremiasto	Starasól
Szumlan	Jaworów	Jaworów
Szumlany	Podhajce	Zawałów
Szumlany Małe	Brzeżany	Brzeżany
Szuparka	Zaleszczyki	Korolówka
Szutromińce	Zaleszczyki	Uścieczko
Szwajkowce	Czortków	Czortków
Szwedy	Tarnobrzeg	Rozwadów
Szwejków	Podhajce	Podhajce
Szwiniarów	Bochnia	Bochnia
Szybalin	Brzeżany	Brzeżany
Szychtory	Sokal	Warez
Szydłowce	Husiatyn	Husiatyn
Szydłowiec	Mielec	Mielec
Szyk	Limanowa	Limanowa
Szymanowice	Nowy Sącz	Stary Sącz
Szymbark	Gorlice	Gorlice
Szynwald	Tarnów	Tarnów
Szyperki	Nisko	Ulanów
Szypowce	Zaleszczyki	Tłuste
Szyszkowce	Brody	Podkamień
Szyszkowce	Zaleszczyki	Korolówka
Tabaszowa	Nowy Sącz	Nowy Sącz
Tadanie	Kam. Strumiłowa	Kam. Strumiłowa
Tamanowice	Mościska	Hussaków
Taniawa	Dolina	Bolechów
Tapin	Przemyśl	Sosnica

Town	Main District	Subdistrict
Targanica	Wadowice	Andrychów
Targoszyna	Wieliczka	Klasno
Targowica	Horodenka	Horodenka
Targowica	Tłumacz	Ottynia
Targowiska	Krosno	Dukla
Targowisko	Bochnia	Bochnia
Targowisko	Tarnów	Zabno
Tarnawa	Bircza	Dobromil
Tarnawa	Bochnia	Wiśnicz Nowy
Tarnawa	Żywiec	Zabłocie
Tarnawa Dolna	Lisko	Lisko
Tarnawa Górna	Lisko	Lisko
Tarnawce	Przemyśl	Przemyśl
Tarnawica Polna	Tłumacz	Tłumacz
Tarnawka	Bircza	Bircza
Tarnawka	Borszczów	Borszczów
Tarnawka	Łańcut	Kańczuga
Tarnawka	Sanok	Rymanów
Tarnawka	Staremiasto	Starasól
Tarnawka	Stryj	Skole
Tarnawka	Żydaczów	Żurawno
Tarnobrzeg	Tarnobrzeg	Tarnobrzeg
Tarnogóra	Nisko	Rudnik
Tarnopol	Tarnopol	Tarnopol
Tarnoruda	Skałat	Tarnoruda
Tarnoszyn	Rawa Ruska	Uhnów
Tarnów	Tarnów	Tarnów
Tarnowica Leśna	Nadwórna	Nadwórna
Tarnowica Zielona	Nadwórna	Nadwórna
Tarnowice	Jasło	Jasło
Tarnowice	Tarnów	Tarnów
Tarnowska Wola	Tarnobrzeg	Tarnobrzeg

Town	Main District	Subdistrict
Tartaków	Sokal	Tartaków
Tartaków	Sokal	Tartaków
Tartakowice	Sokal	Tartaków
Tartarów	Nadwórna	Delatyn
Taszezówka	Skałat	Tarnoruda
Taszyce	Wieliczka	Klasno
Tatarsko	Stryj	Stryj
Tatary	Sambor	Sambor
Tatarynów	Rudki	Komarno
Tatowce	Kołomea	Gwozdźiec
Taurów	Brzeżany	Kozłów
Tęczynek	Chrzanów	Chrzanów
Tęgoborze	Nowy Sącz	Nowy Sącz
Tęhlów	Rawa Ruska	Uhnów
Tejsarów	Żydaczów	Żydaczów
Teklówka	Zaleszczyki	Uścieczko
Tekucze	Kołomea	Jabłonów
Telacze	Podhajce	Podhajce
Teleśnica Oszwar.	Lisko	Ustrzyki Dolne
Teleśnica Sanna	Lisko	Ustrzyki Dolne
Temerowce	Stanisławów	Hałicz
Temeszów	Brzozów	Brzozów
Tenczyn	Myślenice	Jordanów
Tenetniki	Rohatyń	Bursztyn
Teodorówka	Krosno	Dukla
Teodorshof	Żółkiew	Żółkiew
Teofipolka	Brzeżany	Kozowa
Teresia	Kam. Strumiłowa	Chołojów
Tereskuła	Kossów	Żabie
Teresówka	Dolina	Dolina
Terka	Lisko	Baligród
Terlo	Staremiasto	Chyrów

Town	Main District	Subdistrict
Terszaków	Rudki	Komarno
Terszów	Staremiasto	Staremiasto
Tetewczyce	Kam. Strumiłowa	Stajanów
Tetylkowce	Brody	Podkamień
Tiapeze	Dolina	Bolechów
Tiutków	Trembowla	Strusów
Tłuczan Dolna	Wadowice	Zator
Tłuczan Górna	Wadowice	Zator
Tłumacz	Tłumacz	Tłumacz
Tłumaczyk	Kołomea	Peczeniżyn
Tłuste	Zaleszczyki	Tłuste
Tłustenkie	Husiatyn	Probużna
Tobolów	Kam. Strumiłowa	Witków Nowy
Tokarnia	Sanok	Bukowsko
Toki	Krosno	Dukla
Tołszczów	Lemberg	Nawarya
Tomaszkowice	Wieliczka	Klasno
Tomaszowce	Kalusz	Wojnilów
Tomice	Wadowice	Wadowice
Tonie	Dąbrowa	Dąbrowa
Topolnica	Staremiasto	Staremiasto
Topolsko	Kalusz	Kalusz
Toporów	Brody	Toporów
Toporów	Mielec	Mielec
Toporówce	Horodenka	Horodenka
Toporzysko	Myślenice	Jordanów
Torczynowice	Sambor	Sambor
Torhanowice	Sambor	Sambor
Torhów	Złoczów	Pomorzany
Torkarnia	Myślenice	Jordanów
Torki	Przemyśl	Przemyśl
Torki	Sokal	Tartaków

Town	Main District	Subdistrict
Toroszówka	Krosno	Dukla
Torskie	Zaleszczyki	Uścieczko
Touste	Skałat	Touste
Toustogłowy	Złoczów	Zborów
Toustoług	Tarnopol	Tarnopol
Toutobaby	Podhajce	Zawałów
Towarnia	Sambor	Sambor
Trąbki	Wieliczka	Klasno
Tracz	Kołomea	Kołomea
Trawniki	Bochnia	Bochnia
Trawotłoki	Złoczów	Zborów
Trędowacz	Złoczów	Gologory
Trembowla	Trembowla	Trembowla
Trepeza	Sanok	Sanok
Tresna	Żywiec	Zabłocie
Trofanówka	Kołomea	Gwozdźiec
Trójca	Bircza	Rybotycze
Trójca	Borszczów	Skała
Trójca	Brody	Toporów
Trójca	Śniatyn	Zabłotów
Trójczyce	Przemyśl	Sosnica
Tropie	Nowy Sącz	Nowy Sącz
Trościaniec	Brzeżany	Brzeżany
Trościaniec	Dolina	Dolina
Trościaniec	Jaworów	Jaworów
Trościaniec	Śniatyn	Zabłotów
Trościaniec	Tłumacz	Uście Zielone
Trościaniec	Żydaczów	Rozdól
Trościaniec Mały	Złoczów	Złoczów
Trościaniec Wielkie	Brody	Zołożce
Trubczyn	Borszczów	Mielnica
Truchanów	Stryj	Skole

Town	Main District	Subdistrict
Truskawice	Drohobycz	Drohobycz
Truszowice	Bircza	Dobromil
Trybuchowce	Bóbrka	Strzeliska Nowe
Trybuchowce	Buczacz	Jazłowice
Trybuchowce	Husiatyn	Husiatyn
Tryńcza	Łańcut	Przeworsk
Trynitatis	Bochnia	Bochnia
Trzciana	Krosno	Dukla
Trzciana	Mielec	Radomyśl Wiel.
Trzciana	Rzeszów	Rzeszów
Trzcianice	Bircza	Rybotycze
Trzcienice	Mościska	Mościska
Trzcinica	Jasło	Jasło
Trzebienczyce	Wadowice	Zator
Trzebina	Chrzanów	Trzebina
Trzebinia	Żywiec	Zabłocie
Trzebionka	Chrzanów	Trzebina
Trzebos	Kolbuszowa	Sokołów
Trzebownisko	Rzeszów	Głogów
Trzebunia	Myślenice	Myślenice
Trzebuska	Kolbuszowa	Sokołów
Trzeiana	Bochnia	Wiśnicz Nowy
Trzemeśnia	Myślenice	Myślenice
Trzemeśnia	Tarnów	Tarnów
Trześń	Kolbuszowa	Kolbuszowa
Trześń	Tarnobrzeg	Tarnobrzeg
Trześnia	Mielec	Mielec
Trześniów	Brzozów	Brzozów
Trzęsówka	Kolbuszowa	Kolbuszowa
Trzetrzewina	Nowy Sącz	Nowy Sącz
Tuchla	Jarosław	Radymno
Tuchla	Stryj	Skole

Town	Main District	Subdistrict
Tucholka	Stryj	Skole
Tuchów	Tarnów	Tuchów
Tuczapy	Jaworów	Jaworów
Tuczapy	Śniatyn	Zabłotów
Tuczepy	Jarosław	Jarosław
Tuczna	Przemyślany	Świrż
Tudiów	Kossów	Kuty
Tudorkowice	Sokal	Warez
Tudorów	Husiatyn	Kopyczyńce
Tuława	Śniatyn	Śniatyn
Tuligłowy	Jarosław	Pruchnik
Tuligłowy	Mościska	Sądowa Wisznia
Tuligłowy	Rudki	Komarno
Tułkowice	Jasło	Frysztak
Tułkowice	Mościska	Hussaków
Tułuków	Śniatyn	Zabłotów
Tumierz	Stanisławów	Maryampol
Turady	Żydaczów	Żydaczów
Turbia	Tarnobrzeg	Rozwadów
Turka	Kam. Strumiłowa	Kam. Strumiłowa
Turka	Kołomea	Gwozdźec
Turka	Turka	Turka
Turkocin	Przemyślany	Gliniany
Turkowa	Tłumacz	Tyśmienica
Turówka	Skałat	Tarnoruda
Tursko	Grybów	Bobowa
Turylcze	Borszczów	Skała
Turynka	Żólkiew	Żólkiew
Turza	Gorlice	Rzepienik Strzyzewski
Turza	Kolbuszowa	Sokołów
Turza Gnila	Dolina	Dolina

Town	Main District	Subdistrict
Turza Wielka	Dolina	Dolina
Turzanowce	Bóbrka	Brzozdowiec
Turzansk	Sanok	Bukowsko
Turze	Brody	Toporów
Turze	Staremiasto	Staremiasto
Turzepole	Brzozów	Brzozów
Tustań	Stanisławów	Halicz
Tustanowice	Drohobycz	Borysław
Tuszków	Sokal	Bełż
Tuszów	Mielec	Mielec
Tuszów Narodowy	Mielec	Mielec
Tuszyma	Ropczyce	Ropczyce
Tutkowice	Ropczyce	Wielopole
Tużłów	Kalusz	Kalusz
Twierdza	Jasło	Frysztak
Twierdza	Mościska	Mościska
Tworkowa	Brzesko	Czchów
Tworylne	Lisko	Baligród
Tycha	Staremiasto	Staremiasto
Tyczyn	Rzeszów	Tyczyn
Tylawa	Krosno	Dukla
Tylicz	Nowy Sącz	Krynica
Tylka	Nowy Targ	Krościenko
Tylmanowa	Nowy Sącz	Łącko
Tymbark	Limanowa	Limanowa
Tymowa Wesolów	Brzesko	Czchów
Tyniatyska	Rawa Ruska	Lubycza
Tynice	Wieliczka	Podgórze
Tyniowice	Jarosław	Pruchnik
Tynów	Drohobycz	Drohobycz
Tyrawa Solna	Sanok	Sanok
Tyrawa Wołoska	Sanok	Tyrawa woloska

Town	Main District	Subdistrict
Tyskowa	Lisko	Baligród
Tyśmienica	Tłumacz	Tyśmienica
Tysowica	Staremiasto	Staremiasto
Tysowjec	Stryj	Skole
Tyszawice	Przemyśl	Przemyśl
Tyszkowce	Horodenka	Horodenka
Tyszkowice	Mościska	Hussaków
Tyszownica	Stryj	Skole
Tyszyca	Sokal	Krystynopol
Tywonia	Jarosław	Jarosław
Ubieszyn	Łańcut	Przeworsk
Ubinie	Kam. Strumiłowa	Busk
Ubrzeż	Bochnia	Wiśnicz Nowy
Udnów	Żólkiew	Kulików
Ugartsberg	Drohobycz	Drohobycz
Ugartsthal	Kalusz	Kalusz
Uhełna	Stryj	Stryj
Uherce	Lisko	Lisko
Uherce Niezabitowskie	Gródek	Gródek
Uherce Wieniawskie	Rudki	Rudki
Uherce Zapłatyńskie	Sambor	Sambor
Uhersko	Stryj	Stryj
Uhnów	Rawa Ruska	Uhnów
Uhorce	Złoczów	Pomorzany
Uhorniki	Tłumacz	Ottynia
Uhryń	Czortków	Czortków
Uhryń Dolny	Stanisławów	Stanisławów
Uhryniów Górny	Stanisławów	Stanisławów
Uhryńkowce	Zaleszczyki	Uścieczko
Uhrynów	Podhajce	Podhajce
Uhrynów	Sokal	Warez

Town	Main District	Subdistrict
Uhrynów Średni	Kalusz	Kalusz
Uhrynów Stary	Kalusz	Kalusz
Ujanowice	Limanowa	Limanowa
Ujazd	Bochnia	Wiśnicz Nowy
Ujazd	Brzesko	Czchów
Ujazd	Pilzno	Jodłowa
Ujazd	Rohatyń	Rohatyń
Ujezna	Łańcut	Przewórsk
Ujkowice	Przemyśl	Przemyśl
Ujsol	Żywiec	Zabłocie
Uka Wielka	Tarnopol	Mikulińce
Ulanica	Brzozów	Dynów
Ulanów	Nisko	Ulanów
Ułaszkowce	Czortków	Ulaszkowce
Ulazów	Cieszanów	Cieszanów
Ulicko Seredkiewicz	Rawa Ruska	Magierów
Ulicko Zarębane	Rawa Ruska	Magierów
Ulryn	Nowy Sącz	Łabowa
Ulucz	Bircza	Bircza
Ulwówek	Sokal	Sokal
Ulyczno	Drohobycz	Drohobycz
Umieszcz	Jasło	Jasło
Uniatycze	Drohobycz	Drohobycz
Uniów	Przemyślany	Gliniany
Uniszowa	Tarnów	Ryglice
Uniż	Horodenka	Czernelica
Unterbergen	Lemberg	Winniki
Unterwalden	Przemyślany	Gliniany
Urlów	Złoczów	Zborów
Urman	Brzeżany	Brzeżany
Uroż	Sambor	Sambor
Urycz	Stryj	Skole

Town	Main District	Subdistrict
Urzejowice	Łańcut	Przewórsk
Uście	Żydaczów	Rozdól
Uście Biskupie	Borszczów	Mielnica
Uście nad Prutem	Śniatyn	Śniatyn
Uście Ruskie	Gorlice	Gorlice
Uście Solne	Bochnia	Bochnia
Uście Zielone	Tłumacz	Uście Zielone
Uścieczko	Zaleszczyki	Uścieczko
Uścierzyki	Kossów	Żabie
Ustrobna	Krosno	Dukla
Ustrzyki Dolne	Lisko	Ustrzyki Dolne
Ustrzyki Górne	Lisko	Lutowiska
Ustyanowa	Lisko	Ustrzyki Dolne
Uszew	Brzesko	Brzesko
Uszkowice	Przemyślany	Przemyślany
Usznia	Złoczów	Sassów
Uszwica	Bochnia	Wiśnicz Nowy
Uthowek	Rawa Ruska	Uhnów
Utoropy	Kossów	Pistyn
Uwin	Brody	Szczurowice
Uwisla	Husiatyn	Chorostków
Uwsie	Podhajce	Podhajce
Uzin	Stanisławów	Jezupol
Vorderberg	Gródek	Gródek
Wacowice	Drohobycz	Drohobycz
Wadowice	Wadowice	Wadowice
Wadowice Dolne	Mielec	Radomyśl Wiel.
Wadowice Górne	Mielec	Radomyśl Wiel.
Waksmund	Nowy Targ	Nowy Targ
Wał Ruda	Brzesko	Radłów
Walawa	Przemyśl	Przemyśl
Walddorf	Gródek	Janów

Town	Main District	Subdistrict
Walki	Tarnów	Tarnów
Wałowa Góra	Limanowa	Limanowa
Wałówka	Sokal	Sokal
Wampierzów	Mielec	Radomyśl Wiel.
Waniów	Sokal	Bełż
Waniowice	Sambor	Sambor
Wańkowa	Lisko	Lisko
Wańkowice	Rudki	Rudki
Wapienne	Gorlice	Gorlice
Wara	Brzozów	Dynów
Warez	Sokal	Warez
Warwaryńce	Trembowla	Strusów
Warys	Brzesko	Brzesko
Warys	Brzesko	Radłów
Wasiuczyn	Rohatyń	Rohatyń
Wasyłków	Husiatyn	Probużna
Wasylkowce	Husiatyn	Husiatyn
Wasylów Wielkie	Rawa Ruska	Uhnów
Waszyce	Jasło	Jasło
Wawrzka	Grybów	Grybów
Wawrzkowa	Kam. Strumiłowa	Busk
Węcina	Limanowa	Limanowa
Węgerka	Jarosław	Pruchnik
Węglarzyska	Lemberg	Nawarya
Węgliska	Łańcut	Łańcut
Węgliska	Rzeszów	Głogów
Węglówka	Krosno	Korczyna
Węglówka	Wieliczka	Klasno
Węgrzyce Wielkie	Wieliczka	Klasno
Weinbergen	Lemberg	Winniki
Weisenberg	Gródek	Janów
Wełdzirz	Dolina	Dolina

Town	Main District	Subdistrict
Weleśnica	Nadwórna	Nadwórna
Wełykie	Bircza	Dobromil
Werbiąż Niżny	Kołomea	Kołomea
Werbiąż Wyżny	Kołomea	Kołomea
Werbie	Rudki	Komarno
Werchrata	Rawa Ruska	Rawa Ruska
Weremien	Lisko	Lisko
Wereszyce	Gródek	Janów
Werhobuz	Złoczów	Sassów
Wertelka	Brody	Zołożce
Weryń	Żydaczów	Rozdól
Werynia	Kolbuszowa	Kolbuszowa
Werynia	Rzeszów	Głogów
Wesoła	Brzozów	Dynów
Wetlina	Lisko	Baligród
Wiątowice	Wieliczka	Klasno
Wiątrowice	Nowy Sącz	Nowy Sącz
Wiązowa	Żólkiew	Żólkiew
Wiązownica	Jarosław	Pruchnik
Wiciów	Staremiasto	Staremiasto
Wicza	Sanok	Rymanów
Widacz	Jasło	Frysztak
Widaczów	Łańcut	Przeworsk
Widełka	Kolbuszowa	Kolbuszowa
Widełka	Rzeszów	Głogów
Widynów	Śniatyn	Śniatyn
Wieciorka	Myślenice	Myślenice
Wieckowice	Brzesko	Wojnicz
Wieckowice	Mościska	Hussaków
Wieczerza	Myślenice	Jordanów
Wieczorki	Żólkiew	Gross-Mosty
Wieleśniów	Buczacz	Barysz

Town	Main District	Subdistrict
Wielha	Jarosław	Radymno
Wieliczka	Wieliczka	Klasno
Wielkawieś	Brzesko	Wojnicz
Wielkie Drogi	Wadowice	Zator
Wielkie Oczy	Jaworów	Wielkie Oczy
Wielkopole	Gródek	Janów
Wielogłowy	Nowy Sącz	Nowy Sącz
Wielopole	Dąbrówa	Dąbrowa
Wielopole	Nówy Sącz	Nówy Sącz
Wielopole	Ropczyce	Wielopole
Wielopole	Sanok	Sanok
Wielowieś	Tarnobrzeg	Tarnobrzeg
Wielunice	Przemyśl	Niżankowice
Wieniawa	Lemberg	Nawarya
Wienice	Bochnia	Wiśnicznówy
Wieprz	Wadówice	Andrychów
Wieprz ad Żywiec	Żywiec	Zabłocie
Wieprzce	Myślenice	Maków
Wiercany	Ropczyce	Sędziszów
Wierchomla Mała	Nówy Sącz	Piwniczna
Wierchomla Wielka	Nówy Sącz	Piwniczna
Wierczany	Stryj	Stryj
Wieruszyce	Bochnia	Wiśnicznówy
Wierzawice	Łańcut	Leżajsk
Wierzbanówa	Wieliczka	Klasno
Wierzbiałyn	Buczacz	Barysz
Wierzbiany	Jaworów	Jaworów
Wierzbiaz	Sokal	Bełż
Wierzbica	Bóbrka	Chodorów
Wierzbica	Rawa Ruska	Uhnów
Wierzblany	Kam. Strumiłowa	Busk
Wierzblany	Żólkiew	Kulików

Town	Main District	Subdistrict
Wierzbna	Jarosław	Jarosław
Wierzbolowce	Rohatyń	Rohatyń
Wierzbów	Brzeżany	Narajów
Wierzbów	Podhajce	Podhajce
Wierzbowce	Horodenka	Horodenka
Wierzbowce	Kossów	Kossów
Wierzbowczyk	Brody	Podkamień
Wierzbowiec	Czortków	Budzanów
Wierzbówka	Borszczów	Skała
Wierzchniakowce	Borszczów	Borszczów
Wierzchosławice	Tarnów	Zabno
Wierzchowce	Husiatyn	Chorostków
Wierznica	Nowy Sącz	Łącko
Wiesenberg	Żólkiew	Kulików
Wietrzno	Krosno	Dukla
Wieza	Wieliczka	Klasno
Wiktorów	Stanisławów	Halicz
Wiktorówka	Brzeżany	Kozowa
Wilamowice	Biała	Kęty
Wilcza	Przemyśl	Przemyśl
Wilcza Góra	Jaworów	Wielkie Oczy
Wilcza Wola	Kolbuszowa	Ranizów
Wilczkowice	Biała	Oświęcim
Wilczyce	Limanowa	Limanowa
Wilczyska	Grybów	Bobowa
Wildenthal	Kolbuszowa	Ranizów
Wildenthal	Rzeszów	Głogów
Wilkonosza	Nowy Sącz	Nowy Sącz
Wilkowice	Biała	Lipnik
Wilkowisko	Limanowa	Limanowa
Wilsznia	Krosno	Dukla
Wincentówka	Kam. Strumiłowa	Chołojów

Town	Main District	Subdistrict
Winiary	Wieliczka	Klasno
Winiatyńce	Zaleszczyki	Korolówka
Winniczki	Lemberg	Winniki
Winniki	Lemberg	Winniki
Winniki	Sambor	Sambor
Winograd	Tłumacz	Ottynia
Winogród	Kołomea	Gwozdźiec
Wirchne	Gorlice	Gorlice
Wisłoboki	Lemberg	Jaryczów
Wisłoczek	Sanok	Rymanów
Wisłok Wielki	Sanok	Bukowsko
Wiśnicz	Bochnia	Wiśnicz Nowy
Wiśnicz Mały	Bochnia	Wiśnicz Nowy
Wiśnicz Nowy	Bochnia	Wiśnicz Nowy
Wiśnicz Stary	Bochnia	Wiśnicz Nowy
Wiśniowa	Jasło	Frysztak
Wiśniowa	Ropczyce	Sędziszów
Wiśniowa	Ropczyce	Wielopole
Wiśniowa	Wieliczka	Klasno
Wiśniowczyk	Podhajce	Złotniki
Wiśniowczyk	Przemyślany	Dunajowce
Wiśniowczyk	Złoczów	Gologory
Wistowa	Kalusz	Kalusz
Wistowice	Rudki	Rudki
Wiszenka	Jaworów	Jaworów
Wiszenka	Mościska	Sądowa Wisznia
Wiszniów	Rohatyń	Bursztyn
Witanowice	Wadowice	Wadowice
Witków	Sokal	Bełż
Witków Nowy	Kam. Strumiłowa	Witków Nowy
Witków stary	Kam. Strumiłowa	Witków Nowy
Witkowice	Biała	Kęty

Town	Main District	Subdistrict
Witkowice	Ropczyce	Ropczyce
Witkowice	Tarnobrzeg	Radomyśl
Witkówka	Nowy Sącz	Nowy Sącz
Witów	Limanowa	Mszana dolna
Witów	Nowy Targ	Nowy Targ
Witowice Dolne	Nowy Sącz	Nowy Sącz
Witowice Górne	Nowy Sącz	Nowy Sącz
Witryłów	Brzozów	Brzozów
Wituszyńce	Przemyśl	Przemyśl
Witwica	Dolina	Bolechów
Władypol	Mościska	Hussaków
Władypole	Sokal	Bełż
Włonowice	Nowy Sącz	Nowy Sącz
Włosań	Wieliczka	Podgórze
Włosienica	Biała	Oświęcim
Włostówka	Limanowa	Limanowa
Woczuchy	Mościska	Sądowa Wisznia
Wodna	Chrzanów	Chrzanów
Wodniki	Bóbrka	Bóbrka
Wodniki	Sokal	Warez
Wodniki	Stanisławów	Maryampol
Wodniki	Stanisławów	Stanisławów
Wojaczówka	Jasło	Frysztak
Wojakowa	Brzesko	Czchów
Wojciechowice	Przemyślany	Przemyślany
Wojcina	Dąbrowa	Szczucin
Wojków	Mielec	Mielec
Wojkowa	Nowy Sącz	Muszyna
Wojkowice	Mościska	Sądowa Wisznia
Wojkówka	Bircza	Rybotycze
Wojkówka	Jasło	Frysztak
Wojkówka	Krosno	Korczyna

Town	Main District	Subdistrict
Wojnarowa	Grybów	Bobowa
Wojnicz	Brzesko	Wojnicz
Wojnilów	Kalusz	Wojnilów
Wojsław	Mielec	Mielec
Wojsławice	Sokal	Sokal
Wojtkowa	Bircza	Rybotycze
Wojtostwo	Bochnia	Bochnia
Wojtowa	Gorlice	Gorlice
Wojutycze	Sambor	Sambor
Wokowice	Brzesko	Brzesko
Wola	Brzozów	Dynów
Wola	Pilzno	Dębica
Wola Antoniowska	Tarnobrzeg	Radomyśl
Wola Baraniecka	Mościska	Hussaków
Wola Batorska	Bochnia	Bochnia
Wola Blazowska	Sambor	Sambor
Wola Blizsza	Łańcut	Łańcut
Wola Brzosterka	Pilzno	Brzostek
Wola Buchowska	Jarosław	Pruchnik
Wola Chlipelska	Rudki	Rudki
Wola Chorzelowska	Mielec	Mielec
Wola Cicha	Rzeszów	Głogów
Wola Czerwona	Jarosław	Pruchnik
Wola Dalsza	Łańcut	Łańcut
Wola Dębińska	Brzesko	Brzesko
Wola Dębowiecka	Jasło	Jasło
Wola Dobrostańska	Gródek	Janów
Wola Dolholucka	Stryj	Stryj
Wola Drwińska	Bochnia	Bochnia
Wola Duchacka	Wieliczka	Podgórze
Wola Filipowska	Chrzanów	Chrzanów
Wola Gnojnicka	Jaworów	Krakówiec

Town	Main District	Subdistrict
Wola Gołego	Tarnobrzeg	Baranów
Wola Gorzańska	Lisko	Baligród
Wola Jakubowa	Drohobycz	Drohobycz
Wola Jasienicka	Brzozów	Jasienica
Wola Koblańska	Staremiasto	Staremiasto
Wola Komborska	Krosno	Dukla
Wola Korzeniecka	Bircza	Bircza
Wola Kosnowa	Nowy Sącz	Łącko
Wola Kręcowska	Sanok	Tyrawa woloska
Wola Krogulecka	Nowy Sącz	Piwniczna
Wola Kurowska	Nowy Sącz	Nowy Sącz
Wola Lubecka	Pilzno	Pilzno
Wola Luźniańska	Gorlice	Gorlice
Wola Mała	Żydaczów	Rozdól
Wola Matyaszowa	Lisko	Baligród
Wola Mazowiecka	Tarnopol	Mikulińce
Wola Michowa	Lisko	Wola Michowa
Wola Mielecka	Mielec	Mielec
Wola Mieszkowska	Bochnia	Wiśnicz Nowy
Wola Niżnia	Sanok	Rymanów
Wola Ostregowska	Tarnów	Tarnów
Wola Otalezka	Mielec	Radomyśl Wiel.
Wola Pelkińska	Jarosław	Jarosław
Wola Piotrowa	Sanok	Bukowsko
Wola Piskulina	Nowy Sącz	Łącko
Wola Pławska	Mielec	Radomyśl Wiel.
Wola Podłażanska	Wieliczka	Klasno
Wola Postołów	Lisko	Lisko
Wola Przemykowska	Brzesko	Szczurowa
Wola Radłowska	Brzesko	Radłów
Wola Radziszowska	Myślenice	Myślenice
Wola Rafałowska	Rzeszów	Tyczyn

Town	Main District	Subdistrict
Wola Rajnowa	Sambor	Sambor
Wola Romanowa	Lisko	Ustrzyki Dolne
Wola Rzeszycka	Tarnobrzeg	Radomyśl
Wola Skrzydlańska	Limanowa	Limanowa
Wola Starzyska	Jaworów	Jaworów
Wola Stróżka	Brzesko	Czchów
Wola Szeżucińska	Dąbrowa	Szczucin
Wola Wadowska	Mielec	Radomyśl Wiel.
Wola Węgierska	Jarosław	Pruchnik
Wola Wielka	Cieszanów	Lipsko
Wola Wielka	Żydaczów	Rozdól
Wola Wieruszycka	Bochnia	Wiśnicz Nowy
Wola Wysocka	Żólkiew	Żólkiew
Wola Wyżnia	Sanok	Rymanów
Wola Zabierzowska	Bochnia	Bochnia
Wola Zaderewacka	Dolina	Bolechów
Wola Zakrzowska	Brzesko	Wojnicz
Wola Zaleska	Jarosław	Radymno
Wola Zarczycka	Nisko	Rudnik
Wola Zdaków	Mielec	Mielec
Wola Zerekowska	Pilzno	Dębica
Wola Zglobieńska	Rzeszów	Czudec
Wola Zoltaniecka	Żólkiew	Kulików
Wolanka	Drohobycz	Borystaw
Wolczatycze	Bóbrka	Chodorów
Wolczków	Stanisławów	Maryampol
Wolczkowce	Śniatyn	Zabłotów
Wolczuchy	Gródek	Gródek
Wolczyniec	Stanisławów	Stanisławów
Wolczyszczowice	Mościska	Sądowa Wisznia
Woldzimierce	Żydaczów	Żurawno
Wolerbowce	Złoczów	Zborów

Town	Main District	Subdistrict
Wolica	Bochnia	Wiśnicz Nowy
Wolica	Brzeżany	Brzeżany
Wolica	Jasło	Jasło
Wolica	Lemberg	Nawarya
Wolica	Limanowa	Limanowa
Wolica	Lisko	Ustrzyki Dolne
Wolica	Pilzno	Dębica
Wolica	Podhajce	Podhajce
Wolica	Sanok	Bukowsko
Wolica	Skałat	Touste
Wolica	Stryj	Stryj
Wolica	Trembowla	Trembowla
Wolica	Żólkiew	Gross-Mosty
Wolica Baryłowa	Kam. Strumiłowa	Radziechów
Wolica Derewlanska	Kam. Strumiłowa	Busk
Wolica Hnizdyczowska	Żydaczów	Żydaczów
Wolica Komarowa	Sokal	Tartaków
Wolica Lugowa	Ropczyce	Sędziszów
Wolica Piaskowa	Ropczyce	Sędziszów
Wolina	Nisko	Rudnik
Wolka Gradzka	Dąbrowa	Dąbrowa
Wolkiew	Lemberg	Nawarya
Wołków	Lemberg	Nawarya
Wołków	Przemyślany	Przemyślany
Wołków	Przemyślany	Przemyślany
Wołkowce	Borszczów	Mielnica
Wołkowce ad Perejmy	Borszczów	Borszczów
Wołkowce ad Borszczów	Borszczów	Borszczów

Town	Main District	Subdistrict
Wołkowyja	Lisko	Baligród
Wołochy	Brody	Brody
Wołodzia	Brzozów	Dynów
Wołopcza	Sambor	Sambor
Wołosate	Lisko	Lutowiska
Wołosianka	Stryj	Skole
Wołoska Wieś	Dolina	Bolechów
Wołosów	Nadwórna	Nadwórna
Wołosówka	Złoczów	Zborów
Wołostków	Mościska	Sądowa Wisznia
Wołoszczyzna	Podhajce	Podhajce
Wołoszynowa	Staremiasto	Starasól
Wołoszyny	Tarnobrzeg	Rozwadów
Wołowa	Kołomea	Kołomea
Wołowe Laszki	Bóbrka	Bóbrka
Wołowice	Gorlice	Gorlice
Wołowszczyzna	Bóbrka	Bóbrka
Wołśniów	Żydaczów	Rozdól
Wołświń	Sokal	Krystynopol
Wołtuszowa	Sanok	Rymanów
Worobiówka	Tarnopol	Tarnopol
Worochta	Nadwórna	Delatyn
Worochta	Sokal	Bełż
Worochta	Sokal	Bełż
Worona	Tłumacz	Ottynia
Woroniaki	Złoczów	Złoczów
Woronów	Rawa Ruska	Uhnów
Worwolińce	Zaleszczyki	Tłuste
Woszczeńce	Rudki	Rudki
Wownia	Stryj	Stryj
Wożilów	Buczacz	Potok
Woźniczna	Tarnów	Tarnów

Town	Main District	Subdistrict
Woźniki	Wadowice	Zator
Wróblaczyn	Rawa Ruska	Niemerów
Wróblik Królewski	Krosno	Dukla
Wróblik Szlachecki	Sanok	Rymanów
Wróblowa	Jasło	Jasło
Wróblowice	Drohobycz	Drohobycz
Wróblowice	Tarnów	Tuchów
Wróblowice	Wieliczka	Podgórze
Wróblówka	Nowy Targ	Nowy Targ
Wrocanka	Jasło	Jasło
Wrocanka	Krosno	Dukla
Wroców	Gródek	Janów
Wrzasowice	Wieliczka	Podgórze
Wrzawy	Tarnobrzeg	Rozwadów
Wrzepia	Bochnia	Bochnia
Wujskie	Sanok	Sanok
Wulka	Brzeżany	Brzeżany
Wulka	Lemberg	Zniesienie
Wulka	Sanok	Rymanów
Wulka	Sokal	Sokal
Wulka beim Walde	Łańcut	Łańcut
Wulka Bielinska	Nisko	Ulanów
Wulka Dulecka	Mielec	Radomyśl Wiel.
Wulka Grodziska	Łańcut	Leżajsk
Wulka Horyniecka	Cieszanów	Cieszanów
Wulka Kuninska	Żólkiew	Żólkiew
Wulka Laneuska	Nisko	Ulanów
Wulka Letowska	Nisko	Rudnik
Wulka Malkowa	Łańcut	Przeworsk
Wulka Mazowiecka	Rawa Ruska	Rawa Ruska
Wulka Mędrzechowska	Dąbrowa	Dąbrowa

Town	Main District	Subdistrict
Wulka Niedźwiedzka	Łańcut	Leżajsk
Wulka Ogryzkowa	Łańcut	Przewórsk
Wulka pod Lasem	Rzeszów	Głogów
Wulka Rosnowska	Jaworów	Krakówiec
Wulka Suszanska	Kam. Strumiłowa	Radziechów
Wulka Turebska	Tarnobrzeg	Rozwadów
Wulka Zapałowska	Cieszanów	Oleszyce
Wulka Zmijowska	Jaworów	Wielkie Oczy
Wybranówka	Bóbrka	Bóbrka
Wybranówka	Trembowla	Janów
Wybudów	Brzeżany	Kozowa
Wychwatyńce	Skałat	Touste
Wyczółki	Buczacz	Monasterzyska
Wydma	Brzozów	Brzozów
Wydra	Sokal	Krystynopol
Wydreń	Lisko	Lutowiska
Wydrze	Łańcut	Żolynia
Wydrze	Tarnobrzeg	Rozwadów
Wygiełzów	Chrzanów	Chrzanów
Wyglanowice	Nowy Sącz	Nowy Sącz
Wygnanka	Czortków	Czortków
Wygoda	Borszczów	Mielnica
Wykoty	Sambor	Sambor
Wylewa	Jarosław	Pruchnik
Wyłkowyja	Rzeszów	Rzeszów
Wyłów	Mielec	Radomyśl Wiel.
Wymsłówka	Brzeżany	Kozłów
Wypyski	Przemyślany	Przemyślany
Wyrów	Kam. Strumiłowa	Kam. Strumiłowa
Wyrzne	Rzeszów	Czudec
Wyskitna	Grybów	Grybów
Wysocko	Brody	Brody

Town	Main District	Subdistrict
Wysocko	Jarosław	Radymno
Wysocko	Złoczów	Olesko
Wysoczany	Sanok	Bukowsko
Wysoka	Jasło	Frysztak
Wysoka	Łańcut	Łańcut
Wysoka	Myślenice	Jordanów
Wysoka	Rzeszów	Głogów
Wysoka	Wadowice	Kalwarya
Wysokie	Limanowa	Limanowa
Wyspa	Rohatyń	Rohatyń
Wysuczka	Borszczów	Borszczów
Wyszatyce	Przemyśl	Przemyśl
Wyszowa	Gorlice	Gorlice
Wyszowadka	Krosno	Dukla
Wytrzyszczka	Brzesko	Czchów
Wywczanka	Stanisławów	Halicz
Wyzków	Dolina	Dolina
Wyżlów	Sokal	Bełż
Wyżlów	Stryj	Skole
Wyżniany	Przemyślany	Gliniany
Wyżyce	Bochnia	Bochnia
Wzary	Wieliczka	Klasno
Wzdów	Brzozów	Brzozów
Zabawa	Brzesko	Radłów
Zabawa	Kam. Strumiłowa	Witków Nowy
Zabawa	Wieliczka	Klasno
Żabcze Murowane	Sokal	Bełż
Zabełcze	Nowy Sącz	Nowy Sącz
Żabie	Kossów	Żabie
Zabierzów	Bochnia	Bochnia
Zabierzów	Rzeszów	Rzeszów
Żabińce	Husiatyn	Probużna

Town	Main District	Subdistrict
Zabledna	Tarnów	Tuchów
Zabłocie	Wieliczka	Klasno
Zabłocie	Żywiec	Zabłocie
Zabłotce	Brody	Sokołówka
Zabłotce	Jarosław	Radymno
Zabłotce	Przemyśl	Niżankowice
Zabłotce	Sanok	Sanok
Zabłotów	Śniatyn	Zabłotów
Zabłotowce	Żydaczów	Żurawno
Zabłotówka	Czortków	Ulaszkowce
Żabnica	Żywiec	Zabłocie
Żabno	Tarnobrzeg	Radomyśl
Żabno	Tarnów	Zabno
Żabojki	Tarnopol	Tarnopol
Żabokruki	Bóbrka	Strzeliska Nowe
Żabokruki	Horodenka	Obertyn
Zaborów	Brzesko	Szczurowa
Zaborów	Rzeszów	Czudec
Zaborze	Biała	Oświęcim
Zaborze	Rawa Ruska	Rawa Ruska
Zabratów	Rzeszów	Tyczyn
Zabrnie	Dąbrowa	Szczucin
Zabrnie	Tarnobrzeg	Rozwadów
Zabrodzie	Lisko	Lisko
Zabrzez	Nowy Sącz	Łącko
Zabrzydowice	Wadowice	Kalwarya
Zaburze	Sokal	Sokal
Zabutyń	Sanok	Sanok
Zachwiejów	Mielec	Mielec
Zaczarnice	Tarnów	Tarnów
Zaczernie	Rzeszów	Rzeszów
Zadąbrowie	Przemyśl	Sosnica

Town	Main District	Subdistrict
Zadarów	Buczacz	Monasterzyska
Zaderewacz	Dolina	Bolechów
Zadubrowce	Śniatyn	Zabłotów
Zaduszniki	Mielec	Mielec
Zadwórze	Lisko	Ustrzyki Dolne
Zadwórze	Przemyślany	Gliniany
Zadziele	Żywiec	Zabłocie
Zadziszówka	Skałat	Podwołoczyska
Zagoczyce	Ropczyce	Sędziszów
Zagoreczko	Bóbrka	Chodorów
Zagórnik	Wadowice	Andrychów
Zagorów	Limanowa	Limanowa
Zagórz	Sanok	Sanok
Zagórzany	Gorlice	Gorlice
Zagórzany	Wieliczka	Klasno
Zagórze	Brody	Zołożce
Zagórze	Chrzanów	Chrzanów
Zagórze	Kalusz	Kalusz
Zagórze	Łańcut	Kańczuga
Zagórze	Lemberg	Nawarya
Zagórze	Nowy Sącz	Nowy Sącz
Zagórze	Pilzno	Jodłowa
Zagórze	Rudki	Rudki
Zagórze	Wieliczka	Klasno
Zagórze Knihynickie	Rohatyń	Rohatyń
Zagórze Konkolnickie	Rohatyń	Bursztyn
Zagórzyn	Nowy Sącz	Łącko
Zagrobela	Tarnopol	Tarnopol
Zagródki	Lemberg	Szczerzec
Zagrody	Mościska	Sądowa Wisznia
Zagwóźdź	Stanisławów	Stanisławów

Town	Main District	Subdistrict
Zahajce	Podhajce	Podhajce
Zahajpol	Kołomea	Gwozdźiec
Zahelmno	Wadowice	Kalwarya
Zahoczewie	Lisko	Baligród
Zahorce	Złoczów	Olesko
Zakliczyn	Brzesko	Czchów
Zakliczyn	Wieliczka	Klasno
Zakomarze	Złoczów	Olesko
Zakopane	Nowy Targ	Nowy Targ
Zakościele	Mościska	Mościska
Zakowice Nowe	Tarnów	Zabno
Zakowice stare	Tarnów	Zabno
Zakrzewie	Tłumacz	Ottynia
Zakrzów	Brzesko	Wojnicz
Zakrzów	Tarnobrzeg	Tarnobrzeg
Zakrzów	Wadowice	Kalwarya
Zakrzów	Wieliczka	Klasno
Zakrzówek	Wieliczka	Podgórze
Zalanów	Rohatyń	Rohatyń
Zalas	Chrzanów	Chrzanów
Zalasowa	Tarnów	Ryglice
Zalawie	Gorlice	Gorlice
Zalcze	Jasło	Jasło
Zalęna	Wadowice	Kalwarya
Zaleśce	Bóbrka	Brzozdowiec
Zalesiany	Wieliczka	Klasno
Zalesie	Buczacz	Barysz
Zalesie	Czortków	Czortków
Zalesie	Gródek	Janów
Zalesie	Łańcut	Żolynia
Zalesie	Limanowa	Limanowa
Zalesie	Nisko	Rudnik

Town	Main District	Subdistrict
Zalesie	Rzeszów	Tyczyn
Zalesie	Złoczów	Złoczów
Zalesie Antoniowskie	Tarnobrzeg	Radomyśl
Zalesie Biskupie	Borszczów	Mielnica
Zalesie Gorzyckie	Tarnobrzeg	Tarnobrzeg
Zaleszany	Tarnobrzeg	Rozwadów
Zaleszczyki	Zaleszczyki	Zaleszczyki
Zaleszczyki Małe	Buczacz	Jazłowice
Zaleszczyki Stare	Zaleszczyki	Zaleszczyki
Zalęże	Rzeszów	Rzeszów
Zalipie	Rohatyń	Rohatyń
Załokieć	Drohobycz	Drohobycz
Załoźce	Brody	Załoźce
Załubińcze	Nowy Sącz	Nowy Sącz
Załucze	Borszczów	Skała
Załucze nad Prutem	Kołomea	Kołomea
Załucze nad Czer.	Śniatyn	Śniatyn
Załuczne	Nowy Targ	Nowy Targ
Załukiew	Stanisławów	Halicz
Załuż	Sanok	Sanok
Załuże	Cieszanów	Lubaczów
Załuże	Dąbrowa	Szczucin
Załuże	Gródek	Janów
Załuże	Jaworów	Jaworów
Załuże	Rohatyń	Rohatyń
Zamarstynów	Lemberg	Zniesienie
Zameczek	Żółkiew	Żółkiew
Zamek	Rawa Ruska	Magierów
Zamiechów	Jarosław	Radymno
Zamieście	Limanowa	Limanowa
Zamłynowe	Lisko	Ustrzyki Dolne
Zamojsce	Jarosław	Radymno

Town	Main District	Subdistrict
Zamoście	Brzesko	Wojnicz
Zamoście	Przemyślany	Gliniany
Zamowa	Rzeszów	Strzyżów
Zamulińce	Kołomea	Gwozdźiec
Zany	Stanisławów	Maryampol
Zapałów	Cieszanów	Oleszyce
Zapole	Ropczyce	Ropczyce
Zapolednik	Tarnobrzeg	Rozwadów
Zapytów	Lemberg	Jaryczów
Zarajsko	Sambor	Sambor
Zarawce	Rawa Ruska	Lubycza
Zarębki	Kolbuszowa	Kolbuszowa
Zarki	Chrzanów	Chrzanów
Żarków	Złoczów	Olesko
Żarnowiec	Krosno	Dukla
Żarnówka	Myślenice	Maków
Żarównie	Mielec	Mielec
Żarszyn	Sanok	Rymanów
Zarubińce	Skałat	Grzymałów
Zarudec	Lemberg	Zniesienie
Zarudka	Złoczów	Zborów
Zarudzie	Tarnopol	Tarnopol
Zarudzie	Złoczów	Zborów
Zarwanica	Podhajce	Złotniki
Zarwanica	Złoczów	Złoczów
Żary	Chrzanów	Trzebina
Zaryte	Myślenice	Jordanów
Zarzecze	Mościska	Sądowa Wisznia
Zarzecze	Żywiec	Zabłocie
Zarzekowice	Tarnobrzeg	Tarnobrzeg
Zarzyce	Nisko	Ulanów
Zarzyce	Rzeszów	Czudec

Town	Main District	Subdistrict
Zarzyce Małe	Wadowice	Kalwarya
Zarzyce Wielkie	Wadowice	Kalwarya
Zarzycze	Jarosław	Jarosław
Zarzycze	Nadwórna	Delatyn
Zarzycze	Nowy Sącz	Łącko
Zasadne	Limanowa	Mszana Dolna
Zasań	Wieliczka	Klasno
Zaścianka	Tarnopol	Tarnopol
Zaścinocze	Trembowla	Trembowla
Zaskale	Nowy Targ	Nowy Targ
Zasław	Sanok	Sanok
Zastawce	Podhajce	Podhajce
Zastawce	Podhajce	Zawałów
Zastawie	Rawa Ruska	Uhnów
Zastawie	Tarnopol	Mikulińce
Zasulince	Zaleszczyki	Korolówka
Zaszków	Lemberg	Zniesienie
Zaszków	Złoczów	Gologory
Zaszkowice	Gródek	Gródek
Zatawie	Trembowla	Janów
Zatoka	Bochnia	Bochnia
Zator	Wadowice	Zator
Zaturzyn	Podhajce	Zawałów
Zatwarnica	Lisko	Lutowiska
Zawada	Bochnia	Wiśnicz Nowy
Zawada	Limanowa	Limanowa
Zawada	Myślenice	Myślenice
Zawada	Nowy Sącz	Nowy Sącz
Zawada	Pilzno	Dębica
Zawada	Tarnów	Tarnów
Zawada Lanekorońska	Brzesko	Wojnicz

Town	Main District	Subdistrict
Zawada Uszewska	Brzesko	Brzesko
Zawadka	Kalusz	Kalusz
Zawadka	Limanowa	Limanowa
Zawadka	Lisko	Lisko
Zawadka	Myślenice	Myślenice
Zawadka	Nowy Sącz	Nowy Sącz
Zawadka	Wadowice	Wadowice
Zawadka ad Osiek	Jasło	Frysztak
Zawadka ad Buk	Sanok	Bukowsko
Zawadka Rymanów	Sanok	Rymanów
Zawadów	Jaworów	Jaworów
Zawadów	Lemberg	Zniesienie
Zawadów	Mościska	Mościska
Zawadów	Mościska	Sądowa Wisznia
Zawadów	Stryj	Stryj
Zawadówka	Podhajce	Zawałów
Zawale	Borszczów	Mielnica
Zawale	Śniatyn	Śniatyn
Zawałów	Podhajce	Zawałów
Zawatka	Ropczyce	Wielopole
Zawidcże	Brody	Szczurowice
Zawidowice	Gródek	Gródek
Zawierzbie	Dąbrowa	Dąbrowa
Zawisznia	Sokal	Sokal
Zawodzie	Brzesko	Wojnicz
Zawodzie	Tarnów	Tarnów
Zawoj	Kalusz	Kalusz
Zawoj	Lisko	Baligród
Zawoja	Myślenice	Maków
Zawoje	Sanok	Rymanów
Zawośnia	Sokal	Krystynopol
Zawóz	Lisko	Baligród

Town	Main District	Subdistrict
Zazameże	Dąbrowa	Dąbrowa
Zazdrość	Trembowla	Strusów
Zazule	Złoczów	Złoczów
Zbadyń	Jaworów	Jaworów
Zbaraż	Zbaraz	Zbaraz
Zbek	Nowy Sącz	Nowy Sącz
Żbik	Chrzanów	Trzebina
Żbikowice	Nowy Sącz	Nowy Sącz
Zbłudza	Limanowa	Limanowa
Zboiska	Krosno	Dukla
Zboiska	Lemberg	Zniesienie
Zboiska	Sanok	Bukowsko
Zboiska	Sokal	Tartaków
Zbora	Kalusz	Kalusz
Zborczyce	Wieliczka	Klasno
Zborów	Złoczów	Zborów
Zborowek	Wieliczka	Klasno
Zborowice	Grybów	Bobowa
Zbrzyż	Borszczów	Skała
Zbydniów	Bochnia	Wiśnicz nowy
Zbydniów	Tarnobrzeg	Rozwadów
Zbydniowice	Wieliczka	Podgórze
Zbyszyce	Nowy Sącz	Nowy Sącz
Zbytkowska Góra	Tarnów	Tarnów
Zdarzec	Brzesko	Radłów
Zdonia	Brzesko	Czchów
Zdroheć	Brzesko	Radłów
Zdzianna	Staremiasto	Staremiasto
Ździary	Nisko	Ulanów
Ździary	Ropczyce	Ropczyce
Żebranówka	Śniatyn	Zabłotów
Żędowice	Przemyślany	Przemyślany

Town	Main District	Subdistrict
Żegartowice	Wieliczka	Klasno
Żegestów	Nowy Sącz	Muszyna
Żeglce	Krosno	Dukla
Żełdec	Żółkiew	Żółkiew
Żelechów Mały	Kam. Strumiłowa	Kam. Strumiłowa
Żelechów Wielki	Kam. Strumiłowa	Kam. Strumiłowa
Żeleźnikowa	Nowy Sącz	Piwniczna
Żembrzyce	Wadowice	Wadowice
Żeniów	Przemyślany	Gliniany
Żeraków	Pilzno	Dębica
Żerdenka	Lisko	Baligród
Żerebki Krolewskie	Skałat	Skałat
Żerebki Szlacheckie	Skałat	Skałat
Żerków	Brzesko	Brzesko
Żernica Niżna	Lisko	Baligród
Żernica Wyżna	Lisko	Baligród
Żerosławice	Wieliczka	Klasno
Zgłobice	Tarnów	Tarnów
Zgłobień	Rzeszów	Czudec
Zieleńce	Borszczów	Borszczów
Zielensko	Sanok	Bukowsko
Zielona	Borszczów	Mielnica
Zielona	Buczacz	Buczacz
Zielona	Husiatyn	Husiatyn
Zielona	Kam. Strumiłowa	Radziechów
Zielona	Skałat	Grzymałów
Zielonka	Kolbuszowa	Sokołów
Zielów	Lemberg	Zniesienie
Ziempniów	Mielec	Radomyśl Wiel.
Zimna Woda	Jasło	Jasło
Zimna Woda	Lemberg	Zniesienie
Zimno Wódka	Grybów	Bobowa

Town	Main District	Subdistrict
Zimno Wódka	Lemberg	Zniesienie
Ziniatyn	Sokal	Bełż
Złockie	Nowy Sącz	Muszyna
Złoczów	Złoczów	Złoczów
Złoczówka	Brzeżany	Kozowa
Złota	Brzesko	Czchów
Złotkowice	Mościska	Hussaków
Złotne	Nowy Sącz	Łabowa
Złotniki	Mielec	Mielec
Złotniki	Podhajce	Złotniki
Złucisko	Nisko	Rudnik
Zmiąca	Limanowa	Limanowa
Zmiennica	Brzozów	Brzozów
Żmigród	Krosno	Zmigród
Żmigród Nowy	Krosno	Zmigród
Żmigród Stary	Krosno	Zmigród
Żmijowiska	Jaworów	Wielkie Oczy
Zmysłówka	Łańcut	Żolynia
Zmysłówka	Sanok	Rymanów
Znamirowice	Nowy Sącz	Nowy Sącz
Zneżyce	Sokal	Tartaków
Żnibrody	Buczacz	Jazłowice
Zniesienie	Lemberg	Zniesienie
Zniesienie	Lemberg	Zniesienie
Zohatyń	Bircza	Bircza
Zolczów	Rohatyń	Rohatyń
Zolibory	Rohatyń	Bursztyn
Żólkiew	Żólkiew	Żólkiew
Żołków	Jasło	Jasło
Żołnówka	Brzeżany	Brzeżany
Żołobek	Lisko	Ustrzyki Dolne
Zołtańce	Żólkiew	Kulików

Town	Main District	Subdistrict
Żołynia	Łańcut	Żołynia
Żornska	Lemberg	Zniesienie
Zręcin	Krosno	Dukla
Zręczyce	Wieliczka	Klasno
Zródła	Chrzanów	Chrzanów
Zrotowice	Mościska	Hussaków
Zrotowice	Przemyśl	Niżankowice
Zrzyce	Jasło	Jasło
Zubarmosty	Żółkiew	Gross-Mosty
Zubków	Sokal	Tartaków
Zubów	Trembowla	Strusów
Zubów	Złoczów	Gologory
Zubracze	Lisko	Wola Michowa
Zubrzec	Buczacz	Barysz
Zubrzyk	Nowy Sącz	Muszyna
Zubsuche	Nowy Targ	Nowy Targ
Zuchorzyce	Lemberg	Jaryczów
Żuklin	Łańcut	Kańczuga
Żukocin	Kołomea	Kołomea
Żuków	Brzeżany	Brzeżany
Żuków	Cieszanów	Cieszanów
Żuków	Kołomea	Kołomea
Żukowce	Złoczów	Zborów
Żulice	Złoczów	Białykamień
Żulin	Stryj	Stryj
Żupanie	Stryj	Skole
Żupawa	Tarnobrzeg	Tarnobrzeg
Żuraki	Borhodczany	Sołotwina
Żuratyn	Kam. Strumiłowa	Busk
Żurawica	Przemyśl	Przemyśl
Żurawiczki	Jarosław	Jarosław
Żurawienko	Rohatyń	Bursztyn

Town	Main District	Subdistrict
Żurawin	Lisko	Lutowiska
Żurawińce	Buczacz	Buczacz
Żurawków	Żydaczów	Żydaczów
Żurawniki	Lemberg	Jaryczów
Żurawno	Żydaczów	Żurawno
Żurów	Rohatyń	Rohatyń
Żurowa	Jasło	Olpiny
Żuszyce	Gródek	Janów
Żużel	Sokal	Bełż
Zwertów	Żólkiew	Kulików
Zwiahel	Borszczów	Borszczów
Zwiary	Tarnów	Tarnów
Zwieczyca	Rzeszów	Rzeszów
Zwiernik	Pilzno	Pilzno
Zwierzeń	Lisko	Lisko
Zwierzyce	Ropczyce	Sędziszów
Zwiniacz	Czortków	Budzanów
Zwór	Sambor	Sambor
Zwyżeń	Brody	Podkamień
Żydaczów	Żydaczów	Żydaczów
Żydatycze	Lemberg	Zniesienie
Żydnia	Gorlice	Gorlice
Żydowskie	Krosno	Dukla
Żygodowice	Wadowice	Zator
Zyndranowa	Krosno	Dukla
Żyrawa	Bóbrka	Chodorów
Żyrawa	Żydaczów	Żurawno
Żyrawka	Lemberg	Nawarya
Żyrawka	Zaleszczyki	Zaleszczyki
Żyrnów	Rzeszów	Strzyżów
Żywaczów	Horodenka	Obertyn
Żywiec	Żywiec	Zabłocie

Town	Main District	Subdistrict
Żywiec Stary	Żywiec	Zabłocie
Żyznomierz	Buczacz	Buczacz

References & Bibliography

Arad, Yitzhak, Shmuel Krakowski and Shmuel Spector, eds. *The Einsatzgruppen reports: Selections from the Dispatches of the Nazi Death Squads' Campaign Against the Jews, July 1941–January 1943.* New York: Holocaust Library, 1989.

Austria, Government of. *Justiz Ministerium. Fuhrung Der Geburts-, Ehe- und Sterbematrikeln Fur Die Israeliten in Galicien.* Vienna, 1877.

Bałaban, Majer. *Dzieje Żydów w Galicji i Rzeczypospolitej Krakowskiej, 1772–1868* (History of the Jews of Galicia and Kraków Republic, 1772–1868). Lwów, 1914.

———. *Historja Żydów w Krakowie i na Kazimierzu, 1304–1868* (History of the Jews of Kraków and Kazimierz, 1304–1868), vols. 1 and 2. Lwów, 1936, (reprinted in the 1990s in Yiddish).

Beider, Alexander. *A Dictionary of Jewish Surnames from Galicia.* Bergenfield, NJ: Avotaynu, Inc., 2004.

Boak, A.E.R., Albert Hyma & Preston Slosson. *The Growth of European Civilization.* New York, F.S. Crofts & Co., 1938.

Bonar, Andrew A., and Robert Murray M'Cheyne. *Narrative of a Mission of Inquiry to the Jews from the Church of Scotland in 1839.* Philadelphia: Presbyterian Board of Publication, 1839.

Bronstein, Sz. *Ludność żydowska w Polsce w okresie międzywojennym* (Jewish population in Poland during the interwar period). Wrocław: Studium Statystyczne, 1963.

Brook-Shepherd, Gordon. *The Austrians: A Thousand-Year Odyssey.* New York: Carroll & Graf, 1996. (ISBN: 0-7867-0520-5

Buzek, J. *Rozsiedlenie ludnosci Galicji według wyznania i języka* (Migration of the population of Galicia by denomination and language). Lwów, 1909.

Chorzempa, Rosemary A. *Korzenie Polskie: Polish Roots.* Baltimore: Genealogical Publishing Company, 1993.

Cohen, Chester G. *Shtetl Finder,* second edition. Bowie, Md.: Heritage Books, 1989.

Crankshaw, Edward. *The Fall of the House of Hapsburg.* London: Papermac, a division of Pan Macmillan Publishers, ltd., 1992 edition.

Dydyński, Krzysztof. *Poland.* Victoria, Australia: Lonely Plant Publications, 1996 edition.

Dabrowska, Danuta, Abraham Wein and Aharon Weiss, eds., *Pinkas Hakehillot: Poland, vol. II, Eastern Galicia,* Jerusalem: Yad Vashem, 1976.

Encyclopedia Judaica, "Galicia." Jerusalem, 1972.

Eidelberg, Shlomo. *Jewish Life in Austria in the XVth Century: As Reflected in the Legal Writings of Rabbi Israel Isserlein and His Contemporaries.* Philadelphia: Dropsie College for Hebrew and Cognate Learning, 1962.

Eisenbach, Arthur. *The Emancipation of the Jews in Poland, 1780-1870* Oxford: Basil Blackwell, 1991.

Frazin, Judith. *A Translation Guide to 19th Century Polish-Language Civil-Registration Documents.* Self published. 1025 Antique Lane, Northbrook, IL 60062.

Fuks, Marian, Zygmunt Hoffman, Maurycy Horn and Jerzy Tomaszewski. *Polish Jewry: History and Culture.* Warsaw: Interpress, 1982.

Gilbert, Martin. *The Boys: The Story of 732 Young Concentration Camp Survivors.* New York: Henry Holt, 1997.

Griffiths, Clare, Editor. *Insight Guide: Poland.* Maspeth, NY: Langenscheidt Publishers, 2001. (insight@apaguide.demon.co.uk)

Gruber, Ruth Ellen. *Upon the Doorposts of Thy House: Jewish Life in East-Central Europe, Yesterday and Today.* New York: John Wiley and Sons, 1994.

Gruinski, S. *Materialy do kwestii żydowskiej w Galicji* (Material about the Jewish question in Galicia).

Guzik, Estelle. *Genealogical Resources in the New York Metropolitan Area,* Revised Edition. New York: Jewish Genealogical Society, 2003. (ISBN: 0-9621863-1-7) To order, contact info@jgsny.org.

Hall, Walter Phelps & William Stearns Davis. *The Course of Europe Since Waterloo.* New York: D. Appleton-Century Company, 1947 edition.

Hoshen, Sarah Harel, Editor. Beth Hatefutsoth, The Nahum Goldmann Museum of the Diaspora. *Treaures of Jewish Galicia:*

Judaisca fromo the Museum of Ethnography and Crafts in L'vov, Ukraine. Tel Aviv: Israel, 1996.

Hauser, L. *Monografia miasta Przemyśla* (Monograph of the town of Przemyśl). wyd. II. Przemyśl, 1991.

Henisch, Meir. "Galician Jews in Vienna" in *The Jews of Austria: Essays on their Life, History and Destruction,* edited by Joseph Fraenkel. London: Valentine, Mitchell & Co., 1967.

Heshel, Rabbi J. "The History of Hassidism in Austria" in *The Jews of Austria: Essays on Their Life, History and Destruction,* 2nd ed. Edited by Josef Fraenkel. London: Vallentine Mitchell, 1970.

Honey, Michael. "Jewish Family Names in Tarnobrzeg Demonstrated by Propinacja and Konsygnacya Listings" *The Galitzianer,* vol. 2, Winter 1994/5.

Jewish Encyclopedia, "Galicia." New York: Funk & Wagnalls, 1925.

Hupchick, Dennis P. & Harold E. Cox. *The Palgrave Concise Historical Atlas of Eastern Europe, revised.* New York: Palgrave, 2001. (ISBN: 0-312-23985-8 paperback)

Kagan, Joram. *Poland's Jewish Heritage.* New York: Hippocrene Books, 1992. (ISBN: 0-87052-991-9)

Kaganoff, Benzion C. *A Dictionary of Jewish Names and their History.* New York: Schocken Books, 1977. (ISBN: 0-8052-0643-4 paperback)

Kramarz, W. *Ludność Przemyśla w latach 1521–1921* (Population of Przemyśl for the years 1521–1921). Przemyśl, 1930.

Krochmal, Anna. "Izraelickie Gminy Wyznaniowe" in *Akta Wyznaniowe w Zasobie Archiwiwum Państwowego w Przemyślu.* Przemysl: 1993. Translation into English by Jerzy Gorzyca.

Kugelmass, Jack and Jonathan Boyarin, *From A Ruined Garden: The Memorial Books of Polish Jewry.* New York: Schocken Books, 1983.

Kurzweil, Arthur. *From Generation to Generation,* paperback ed. San Francisco: Jossey-Bass, 2004

Lenius, Brian J. *Genealogical Gazetteer of Galicia.* Box 18, Group 4 R.R. #1, Anola, Manitoba, Canada R0E 0A0, 1993.

Levine, Hillel. *Economic Origins of Antisemitism: Poland and Its Jews in the Early Modern Period.* New Haven: Yale University Press, 1991.

Lewin, Isaac. *The Jewish Community in Poland: Historical Essays.* New York: Philosophical Library, 1985.

Lukowki, Jerzy and Hubert Zawadski, *A Concise History of Poland.* Cambridge: Cambridge University Press, 2001. (ISBN: 0-521-55917-0 paperback)

Magosci, Paul Robert. *Historical Atlas of East Central Europe.* Toronto: University of Toronto Press, 1993.

Mahler, Raphael. *History of Modern Jewry, 1780-1815.* New York: Schocken Books, 1971.

McCagg, William O., Jr. *History of Habsburg Jew, 1670-1918.* Bloomington: Indiana University Press, 1983.

Menczer, Arie. *Sefer Przemyśl.* Israel: Irgun Yotzei Przemyśl, 1964.

Mendelsohn, Ezra. *The Jews of East Central Europe Between the World Wars.* Bloomington: Indiana University Press, 1983.

Metzler, Wilhelm. *"Die Heimat und Ihre Geschichte: Galizien, Land und Leute* (The Home and their history: Galicia, country and people)" *Galizien German Descendants* 10 April 1997 (translated by John Forkheim and Eva Rowley).

Najnowsze dzieje Żydów w Polsce (Modern history of the Jews of Poland), pod. red. J. Tomaszewskiego, Warsaw: 1993.

Niezabitowska, Małgorzata & Tomasz Tomaszewski. *Remnants: The Last Jews of Poland.* New York: Friendly Press, Inc., 1986. Translated from the Polish by William Brand & Hanna Dobosiewicz. (ISBN: 0-914919-05-9)

Opalski, Magdalena. *The Jewish Tavern Keeper and His Tavern in 19ᵗʰ Century Polish Literature.* Jerusalem: The Zalman Shazar Center, Center for Research on History and Culture of Polish Jews, 1986. (P.O. Box 4179, 91141 Jerusalem, Israel)

Patai, Raphael. *The Vanished Worlds of Jewry.* New York: Macmillian, 1980. (ISBN: 0-02-595120-3)

Pogonowski, Iwo Cyprian. *A Historical Atlas..* New York: Hippocrene Books, 1987.

Rubinowitz, Harry M. *Hasidsim: The Movement and Its Masters.* Northvale, NJ: Jason Aronson, Inc., 1988. (ISBN: 0-87668-998-5)

Sack, Sallyann Amdur and Israel Genealogical Society. *A Guide to Jewish Genealogical Resources in Israel..* Teaneck, N.J.: Avotaynu, 1993.

———& Gary Mokotoff. *Where Once We Walked,* revised edition. Bergenfield, New Jersey: Avotaynu, Inc., 2001.

———& Gary Mokotoff, Editors. *Avotaynu Guide to Jewish Genealogy.* Bergenfield, NJ: Avotaynu, Inc., 2004.

Salamander, Rachel. *The Jewish World of Yesterday: 1860-1938.* New York: Rizzoli, 1990.

Salter, M. & G. McLachlan. *Poland: The Rough Guide.* London: Rough Guides, Ltd., 1996. (ISBN: 1-85828-168-7)

Sanders, Ronald. *Shores of Refuge: A Hundred Years of Jewish Emigration.* New York: Henry Holt, 1987.

Schevill, F. *History of Europe: From the Reformation to the Present Day.* New York: Harcourt, Brace, 1930.

Schipera, I., A. Tartakowera and A. Haftki. *Żydzi w Małopolsce* (Jews in the Małopolska). *Studia z dziejow osadnictwa i zycia spoleczna, gospodarcza, oswiatowa i kulturalna.* Warsaw b.d.w.

Schmidl, Erwin A. *Jews in the Habsburg Armed Forces.* Eisenstadt, Germany: Osterreichisches Judische Museum, 1989. Includes an English translation of the German text.

Schorr, M. *Żydzi w Przemyślu do Konca XVIII w.* (Jews in Przemyśl to the end of the 18th century). Reprinted in Jerusalem from the original publication, 1991.

Schwartz, Rosaline and Susan Milamed, *A Guide to YIVO's Landsmanshaftn Archive.* New York: YIVO Institute for Jewish Research, 1986.

Silvain, Gérard & Henri Minczeles. *Yiddishland.* Corte Madera, CA: Gingko Press, Inc., 1999. English edition edited by Donna Wiemann. (ISBN: 1-58423-018-5)

Subtelny, Orest. *Ukraine: A History..* Toronto: Toronto University Press, 1988. (ISBN: 0-8020-5808-6)

Yad Vashem. *Black of Localities Whose Jewish Population Was Exterminated by the Nazis.* Jerusalem: Yad Vashem, 1965.

Volovici, H., Medykowski, W., Assouline, H., & Lukin, B. *Polish Sources at the Central Archives for the History of the Jewish People.* Bergenfield, NJ: Avotaynu Foundation, 2004.

Wein, Abraham and Aharon Weiss, eds. *Pinkas Hakehillot,* vol. III, Western Galicia & Silesia. Jerusalem: Yad Vashem, 1984.

Weiner, Miriam. *Jewish Roots in Poland: Pages from the Past and Archival Inventories.* Secaucus, N.J.: Miriam Weiner Routes to Roots Foundation, and New York: YIVO Institute for Jewish Research, 1997.

_ *Jewish Roots in Ukraine and Moldova: Pages from the Past and Archival Inventories.* Secaucus, NJ: Miriam Weiner Routes to Roots Foundation, Inc. and New York: YIVO Institute for Jewish Research (out of print).

Weinryb, Bernard Dov. The Jews of Poland: A Social and Economic History of the Jewish Community from 1100-1800.. Philadelphia: Jewish Publication Society, 1973.

Wierzbieniec, W. *Przemyska izraelicka gmina wyznaniowa w okresie autonomii Galicji* (Jewish community in Przemyśl during the autonomy of Galicia), vols. 6 ad 7. Przemyśl: Przemyskie Zapiski Historyczne, 1990.

Wunder, Rabbi Meir. *Meorei Galicia* (Encyclopedia of Galician rabbis and scholars) vols. 1-5, Jerusalem: Institute for Commemoration of Galician Jewry, 1978–1995.

PHOTO & ILLUSTRATION CREDITS

Introduction:

Map 1:   Partitions of Poland, 1772, 1793, 1795.
           *History of Europe: From the Reformation to the Present
           Day.* Harcourt, Brace & Co., 1925

Chapter 1:

Map 2:   Galicia. Attribution unknown.

Photo 1:   Postcard of Kraków street scene.
           Private collection of author.

Photo 2:   Place na Bramie in Przemyśl.
           Private collection of David Semmel.

Photo 3:   Market scene at Old Synagogue, Przemyśl.
           Private collection of Blossom Glasser.

Photo 4:   Market scene, Stryj market.
           Miriam Weiner Archives.

Photo 5:   Fragment of Łancut synagogue ceiling.
           Photo taken by Leon Gold.

Photo 6:   Kahal of Strzyz w, 1931.
           From the Jewish History Research Center, Rzeszów.

Photo 7:   The Temple in Przemyśl.
           Private collection of David Semmel.

Photo 8:   Tarnopol street scene.
           Private collection of author

Printed in the United States
54806LVS00002B/112-183